THE
MONEY
BAZAARS

Also by Martin Mayer

Martin Mayer

THE MONEY BAZAARS

UNDERSTANDING THE BANKING
REVOLUTION AROUND US

A Truman Talley Book

E. P. DUTTON, INC.   NEW YORK

For Jerry Dunne,
who in so many ways
keeps the faith.

Parts of this book have been published in somewhat different form in various magazines: Sections of Chapter 2, 5, 6, and 10 in *Fortune,* of Chapters 3 and 4 in *Institutional Investor,* of Chapter 11 in *Financier.* Some of Chapter 9 is adapted from the Introduction to *The Report of the President's Commission on Housing,* which was written by the author, who was a commissioner. The book as a whole is based on an unpublished study of the structure of banking prepared by the author for the Twentieth Century Fund.

Published in the United States by Truman Talley Books •
E. P. Dutton, Inc., 2 Park Avenue, New York, N.Y. 10016

Library of Congress Cataloging in Publication Data

Mayer, Martin, 1928–
The money bazaars.
"A Truman Talley book."
1. Banks and banking—United States. 2. Finance—
United States. I. Title.
HG2491.M36   1984   332.1′0973   83-20595
ISBN: 0-525-24221-X

Published simultaneously in Canada by Fitzhenry & Whiteside Limited,
Toronto

10 9 8 7 6 5 4 3 2 1

First Edition

CONTENTS

I

The Twilight of the Banks

1

THE BANK IS DEAD...

A few years ago," said Tom Storrs, a professor turned entrepreneur who runs North Carolina National Bank in Charlotte (and Tampa—he has wormed his way across the Florida state line through a loophole in the banking regulations), "you could describe the banking industry as a group of institutions with defined characteristics. In the 1990s, you'll have to describe it as a group of services provided by a range of institutions."

"You're writing a book on the future of banking?" asked Willis Alexander, once a small-town Missouri banker, now the elegant executive vice-president of the American Bankers Association, his trim gray moustache sensing every change in the force and direction of every wind. "I'm not much interested in that. What I'm concerned about is the future of *bankers*."

"We're trying to make a decision about what is a bank," said Paul Volcker cheerlessly, describing the dilemmas of the Federal Reserve Board as 1982 ended. "My instinct is that there's something unique about a bank."

1

Nine years ago, I opened a book on banks and bankers with a paraphrase of Marx and Engels, equating the changes in banking in the previous fifteen years with the specter of revolution that the German socialists had believed was haunting the rulers of Europe. The central thesis of that book—that institutional and technical developments would make money and finance increasingly important factors in the United States and world economies—has worn well. What I had not foreseen was that the revolution in banking would so quickly find—perhaps create—its own particular Thermidor. For the technology that exalted the banks in the 1960s and 1970s has now cast them down. While the functions historically performed by banks continue to grow in significance, the role of bankers in performing them has already diminished and will be reduced further. The future of banking is up for grabs, and there are many grasping hands in the air.

From the point of view of the consumers of financial services, there is a great deal to be said for the changes now shaking the banks. The fact is that banks have never been much for tailoring their services to customer needs. For years, they kept "banker's hours," delayed the availability of funds, insisted that corporate borrowers keep "compensating balances," and dealt with both depositors and borrowers in a lordly, if lazy, manner. Their selling efforts were directed all but exclusively to pulling in customers for their established services, everything from toasters for depositors to nights on the town for the financial officers of the corporations; they had neither interest in nor talent for redesigning their services to meet the wishes of users. They had a monopoly; and, as monopolists will, they abused it without thinking overmuch about what they were doing.

A savings bank created the interest-bearing checking account; Wall Street underwriters brought borrowers and lenders together in the context of a commercial-paper market; mutual funds and brokerage houses pioneered the money-market fund and cash-management services for individuals; government agencies, mortgage bankers, and stockbrokers developed the secondary market in mortgage-backed securities; retail chains, credit unions, and loan companies grabbed the lion's share of consumer finance; insurers and finance companies ran away with the opportunities offered by leasing. With few exceptions, banks marched in place, happily dedicating their shiny new computers to the improvement of demand-deposit accounting.

These matters are more important than they seem. Financial flows are the bloodstream of societies organized by the division of labor, and participation in the monetary economy is the key link in the modern citizen's relations with his community. This is especially true in the United States, as Federal Reserve Board Governor Henry Wallich likes to point out, because "people themselves are intermediaries"—that is, Americans prefer to own stocks and savings balances while owing on a mortgage and a car, rather than to net out their personal financial positions. Access to credit is a significant aspect of people's status and even of their sense of self-worth.

The institutions of banking are interrelated intricately with the other institutional structures of the economy, but do not gain support from them. Financial institutions are uniquely vulnerable to disturbances because there are inherent contradictions in the three uses of money—as a medium of exchange, as a measure of value, and as a store of wealth. Achieving an equilibrium among the different kinds of financial institutions was a central political task of nineteenth-century America and an obsession of both Woodrow Wilson's New Freedom and Franklin Roosevelt's New Deal. Now this hard-won if still faulty equilibrium has been cast aside; partly because bankers and legislators don't study history, partly because, in truth, the present has become different from the past.

"A bank is a countinghouse," said George Mitchell, a scrappy, funny, profound economist nearly eighty years old, formerly a governor of the Federal Reserve Board and still a consultant to the Board because he knows more than anybody else about how banks really run, and sometimes that's useful. "The most efficient way to run a countinghouse is with a computer." This commonplace remark was intended as a palindrome: you can read it backwards. Backwards, it says that anybody with a computer can run a countinghouse, which means he can run a bank.

Conceptually, what had made a bank unique was its ability to create money. If a man or a company lends money to someone, in person or through the "mediation" of an insurance company or savings association, the result is merely to transfer the purchasing power of that money, temporarily, from one party to another. If the loan is made through the agency of a bank, however, both parties continue to have the use of the money. When a merchant starting a shoestore stocks his shelves on credit from the shoe manufacturer, the quantity of money in a society does not change: the manufacturer makes do with accounts receivable rather than cash. If the shoestore is financed by a bank loan, however, the shoe manufacturer is paid for his shoes before the public pays the store for them, and he has money to spend on other things. The deposit in the bank that funds the loan, meanwhile, is still money, which the depositor can use at any time by writing a check. This is true even if the depositor is the shoe manufacturer himself: there is a great difference between an account receivable and money in the bank. What the bank as mediator does, then, has an element of magic, and, like other magic tricks, it rests partly on illusion, on "confidence." Best not to inquire too closely, say the bankers.

Operationally, what had made a bank unique was that it could handle the storage and payment of money, an immense job requiring armies of tellers at windows and clerks with ledgers and sorters who stood before honeycombs of pigeonholes to slot checks first according to the city from which they came, then the bank on which they were drawn, then the branch in which the account was maintained, and finally the account itself. The results would then be "posted," by other armies of clerks, in the ledgers that kept the records of the individual accounts.

Commercial banks had to expect that many of their accounts would require daily posting, and nearly all would have to be opened for entries at least once a week. Banks were staffed to handle such work. Savings associations and credit unions were not banks, couldn't be banks. They were organized to hold accounts that lay dormant, month after month, with only very occasional deposits or withdrawals. The ledgers of many accounts had to be opened only once a quarter for the posting of interest earned. Essentially, the "thrift institutions" had no back office: the teller at the cage posted the account while registering the deposit or withdrawal in the customer's passbook. Automation, when it came, would ease the teller's task without disrupting, as it did at banks, an established bureaucracy of "operations."

Brokerage houses, too, updated inactive customer portfolios in quarterly statements; if the stock was held in "street name" and the dividend checks came to the broker, he might or might not tell his customer. (When the customer left money in his account, the broker kept the interest on it—indeed, brokers argued piously that they couldn't legally pay interest on money in their customers' accounts because that would be banking.) At insurance companies, the ideal policyholder was one whose account had to be updated only twice a year: once for the payment of a premium, once for the crediting of dividends.

Then came the computer. When you keep your ledgers in a computer, as a purely practical matter, you cycle through all the accounts every day. It is easier to run the entire bank customer list past the post, pausing when an entry must be made, than to hunt through the memory for just those accounts that need updating. When the computers came to the S&Ls and the savings banks, then, the first thing changed was the posting of interest, which was done every night instead of once a month or once a quarter. This produced a certain amount of advertising offering interest "from date of deposit to date of withdrawal" and "daily compounding of dividends."

To a young savings bank president in Worcester, Massachusetts, the computer presented a more interesting opportunity: a chance to sell his depositors an interest-bearing checking account. This was Ron Hasleton, an irreverent Bostonian (there are such), veteran of commercial banking with First National Bank of Boston and Citibank in New York, who had become president of the Worcester Five Cents Savings Bank in 1965 at the age of thirty-four. Four years later, he petitioned the Massachusetts Banking Department for permission to offer a "Negotiable Order of Withdrawal" service, a "NOW account"—in effect, a checking account on an interest-bearing balance. His Boston correspondent bank, State Street, had agreed to accept at the clearinghouse checks written by his depositors, just as they accepted checks written by the depositors of respondent commercial banks all over New England. Such an account was clearly illegal for federally insured banks and S&Ls because the deposit insurance laws forbade the payment of interest on any money on deposit less than thirty days. But the Massachusetts savings banks had their own insurance fund—and there was nothing in Massachusetts law about "premature withdrawal." The state banking supervisors were horrified and forbade Hasleton to do anything of the sort, so he sued, and he won.

In 1972 the customers of what Hasleton had renamed Consumer Savings were given a chance to order a fancy checkbook and to pay their bills from their savings accounts, at a price of 15¢ per check. Consumer Savings, like a bank, was creating money: some fraction of the money it loaned out was still available for use by the depositors, who had put it in the savings bank.

This was a clumsy way to create money. A check that draws funds from a bank goes quickly to another bank, increasing the money on deposit there, and each bank can expect that the inflow of funds from its peers will just about match the outflow of funds from depositors spending their money, week by week if not day by day. A check from a savings bank, however, reduces the deposits in the savings system, because the money will pass through "real" banks several times before some wage earner puts it back into a "thrift institution." But as checking accounts proliferated at the savings institutions, they would become more like banks: it was a wedge in the door. And meanwhile, the banks would have more formidable competition for deposits than they had known before.

George Mitchell saw handwriting on the wall. "The banks have to expect," he said in 1973, "that some day they won't have any money they don't directly pay for." Law and custom both changed in halting steps. First Congress authorized NOW accounts for federally insured banks and S&Ls in the northeastern quadrant. Then the regulators allowed banks elsewhere in the country to offer Automatic Transfer Services (ATS) accounts, in which checks written for sums greater than the balance in the no-interest demand-deposit account would be covered by money in interest-bearing savings accounts in the same bank. Then the courts said ATS violated the deposit insurance laws, and finally Congress wrote the Depository Institutions Deregulation and Monetary Control Act of 1980, a landmark law if ever there was one. Suddenly, for payment purposes, there were no more banks and S&Ls and credit unions—just "depository institutions," all of which would have to keep reserves against such accounts at the Federal Reserve Bank, the government agency charged with the duty of controlling the stock of money.

By then, the tide was rising so fast that even landmark laws were soon covered over. For it was not only the savings banks and associations that had acquired computers with countinghouse capabilities: the brokerage houses, the mutual-fund managers, the insurance companies, and the proprietors of credit-card services like Sears and American Express were also cycling routinely through all their accounts every day and could post entries and withdrawals conveniently *en passant.* They too could offer something almost indistinguishable from a bank's checking account, and presently they did.

For individuals, it matters whether they make their payments with cash or checks or electronic funds transfers, through home computers or on telephone touch pads or on multipurpose point-of-sale terminals (fancy customer-operated cash registers) at supermarkets and department stores; whether they borrow money through the old formal procedures in banking offices or by automatic overdrafts or on a credit-card chassis or through margin on their securities holdings or on the equity of their homes. For corporations, it matters whether they are to borrow from lending offices or in an anonymous market or from banks to which they are tied by a multiplicity of relations.

Most important of all is the question of how such changes affect the relations between financial and nonfinancial corporations, between the government and financial institutions, and thus, in the end, between the polity and the economy. The biologist-ecologist Garret Hardin has stated as his first truth the premise that in the natural world "you can never change just one thing," and the same premise holds in the artificial worlds of politics and economics. The bigger the changes, the louder the reverberations, sometimes in the most unexpected places. "We are dealing," says E. Gerald Corrigan, president of the Federal Reserve Bank of Minneapolis, "with a bread-and-butter practical issue that will determine how our economic system works over a period of time."

Revolutions matter not because they change the cast of

characters or the who-does-what-to-whom that is the stuff of traditional history, but because they change the framework of concepts within which people house their experiences. Definitions, ways of thinking about the world, are important far beyond the subject matter defined. The congruence of theory and reality will make the results of human decisions relatively predictable; divergences of theory and reality mean that actions neither implement the decisions that called them forth nor produce the results expected from them. No small part of the economic malaise of the period 1970–82 expresses the uneasiness of banking and monetary theory stuck with a reality that cannot be squeezed inside the four corners of its long-established framework. The losses are reflected in governmental incapacity, economic inefficiency, and social incomprehension. In fall 1980 Paul Volcker looked at what was coming at him and stamped out a cigar in a giant pewter ashtray marked with the legend *When you've left New York, you ain't going nowhere.* "I liked the old comfortable world, where there were specialized institutions," he said.

2

From its beginnings, banking has been infected uniquely by a mutable virus of the public interest. The Renaissance bankers were by no means tools of their princes, but they required considerable protection from the state, both as the possessors of (or trustees for) coveted hoards, and as the practitioners of a mystery that made apparent wealth grow without apparent work. In return for that protection, the Renaissance princes extorted the equivalent of large license fees from those who wished to start banks—and large loans on concessional terms when the state needed money. The notion that "sovereign risk" lending is really safe, because states cannot default on their debts—vigorously promoted in our day by David Rockefeller,

Walter Wriston of Citicorp and various of their friends—would have been more ludicrous than astonishing to the Medicis and the Fuggers. It isn't likely to make much sense to Rockefeller's and Wriston's successors, either.

Lenin placed the banks on "the commanding heights of the economy," which the state would have to seize if politicians were to be able to tell everybody what to do all the time, and the Russian constitution enshrines the mujhik's fury against those who live by the labor of others. Its stark injunction—so contrary to the tenets of the welfare state—is that "those who do not work shall not eat." All popular uprisings in bourgeois societies have been directed at least partly against banks. Outnumbered today, the farmer and the artisan and the operative have pretty much given up the war against parasite lawyers and bureaucrats and bankers, but some of the attitudes are still there, especially at the universities. When the French Socialists came to power in 1981, one of their first steps was to nationalize the 15% or so of French banking enteprise not already owned by the French state. When President Lopez Portillo of Mexico needed a scapegoat for the effects of his policy of mortgaging the nation's future to enrich its present middle classes, he expropriated his country's banks.

In most countries, banks individually and banks as part of a "banking system" have always had significant responsibilities to the state authorities and significant supervision by them. All corporations have state charters of one sort or another, because the necessary legal immortality of the corporation—its power to make contracts enforceable beyond the lifetime of its owners and officers—requires enforcement by the immortal state. But bank charters everywhere have differed from other corporate charters. While stockholders in a traditional corporation have always been able to limit their risk to the investment they made when they bought the stock, stockholders in banks were liable for decades to a call on their personal resources (usually a doubling of the par value of the stock when issued) to pay off the debts of a failing bank. In the United States, corporate charters for wholly private enterprise are granted only by the individual states—except in the case of banks, which can be chartered (and supervised) by either a state or the federal government.

In Sweden, Britain, and France, where the real ancestors of today's banks were chartered in the late seventeenth and early eighteenth centuries, a bank's responsibilities to the government were highly specific: the bank had to buy government securities and hold them among its assets. In return, the banks received the power to issue "banknotes," which served their communities as currency at a time when the government did not print its own paper money (partly because businessmen would have been reluctant to accept government paper—they had considerably more faith in the integrity of their fellow businessmen at the bank). The seeds of the French Revolution were sown when the French monarchy, a Renaissance princedom writ large, abused this system to fund itself through the operation of its bank.

In the United States the federal government chartered its first bank in 1793 to act as repository of government funds and to manage the retirement of the national debt accumulated during the Revolutionary War. This charter was permitted to lapse after twenty years, but a Second Bank of the United States was created for similar purposes after the chaos following upon the War of 1812. The successful fight against renewal of that charter was the triumph of Jacksonian populism. For a quarter of a century after Jackson's victory in 1836 over the Second Bank of the United States, the nation had not only local banks, but to a significant degree localized currencies, because banknotes from out-of-state banks could be used for purchases only at a discount, if at all.

In 1863 difficulties in financing the Civil War led to the passage of the National Bank Act, which put the federal government back into the business of chartering banks, and imposed a tax on all banknotes issued by state-chartered banks. The expectation that this tax would force the state banks to apply for national charters was frustrated by the spread and growth of checking accounts, which permitted banks to make their loans by crediting deposits to borrowers instead of by issuing banknotes to them. For half a century, nationally chartered and state-chartered banks stood side by side, reporting their condition to different masters, but otherwise identical. That the national banks were to be local in their focus was expressed by the original insistence that each carry the name "National Bank of [wherever city]," and banks did not necessarily give additional credence to out-of-state colleagues simply because both were chartered by the national Comptroller of the Currency. In fact, most banks would not accept at "par" checks drawn on other banks that were not members of the same local clearinghouse.

If customers were to have nationwide use of their deposits, then, both state banks and national banks had to enter into "correspondent" relations with larger banks in the clearinghouse cities. Among the accomplishments of the Federal Reserve Act of 1913 was the unification of a national monetary system, as the twelve regional Federal Reserve Banks established by the Act developed procedures to assure that checks would be honored everywhere at face value. To facilitate such clearings, the regional Federal Reserve Banks in 1918 established the first "FedWire" network for telegraphic communication of funds transfers.

Correspondent banking had raised legislative fears from the beginning of bank chartering because it was observably true that whenever money grew tight, the city banks could outbid the country banks for available funds. Most states, hoping to keep local savings and working balances available for local use, forbade the city banks to branch out beyond their own cities or counties; to the politicians, correspondent banking seemed a way to get around the rules. As early as the 1820s, Connecticut sought to impose a ceiling on the interest rates banks could pay for funds, in hopes of keeping capital in the towns and farming communities. But the fact was that money was needed by the farmers in the spring and the merchants in the fall. The efficiencies of moving funds around to meet seasonal needs overcame legislative frictions, and the banks bound themselves to each other in a relatively cheerful symbiosis—until the time of crisis, when developments quite extraneous to a local economy (a war in Europe, a panic on Wall Street, a railroad bankruptcy) might produce a great drain of funds from the towns to the cities.

It was generally understood that banks were chartered to meet the short-term needs of trade: lending would expand as business grew and contract as it diminished, keeping the supply of credit adjusted to community needs. "Make your discounts on as short a time as the business of your customer will permit," wrote Hugh McCulloch, the first Comptroller of the Currency, in his famous *Advice* to the banks he was chartering, "and insist upon the payment of all paper at maturity, whether you need the money or not. . . ." (Copies of this document hang on the wall in places as different as the Money Market and Bank Regulation Office of the Bank of England and the chairman's private washroom at First Tennessee Bancshares in Memphis.) Until the 1920s nationally chartered banks were not permitted to write mortgages because real property was an illiquid asset that could not quickly be sold or called when depositors needed funds.

Both state and national charters required banks to keep prudential reserves in liquid form—cash on hand, deposits in other banks, "call" loans, bankers' acceptances (essentially, short-term loans guaranteed by other banks), and the like. Under McCulloch and his nineteenth-century successors, in fact, "cash assets" at the nationally chartered banks rarely fell below 30% of total deposit and note liabilities; at state banks, cash assets were more likely to be in the 10% to 15% range, which was one of the reasons banks kept their state charters. Some part of the funds the banks would lend—usually about 10%—was expected to be the owners' capital rather than the customers' deposits, providing a cushion for repayment to the depositors in full even if some of the loans went sour.

(Perhaps because the ownership of today's banks is now

totally diffused through the stock market, modern bankers have a peculiar notion of how much of the money they have to lend is really theirs. Speaking to *Business Week* in 1981 about the Bankers Trust division that advises issuers of commercial paper, chairman Alfred Brittain III commented, "It was important to us to lend other people's money instead of just our own." But with its capitalization below 5% of its assets, more than 95% of the money Bankers Trust lends in the course of its routine business is already "other people's money.")

Just as commercial banks could not write mortgages, they could not—until World War II!—offer "savings accounts." (They were allowed to take "time deposits," presumably something different.) Savings banks and later savings-and-loan associations grew, many of them from roots in ethnic burial societies, as "mutual" co-op organizations from which members could borrow when buying a home. In the 1920s Boston department-store magnate Edward Filene made it a personal cause to organize credit unions through which some preexisting group (usually the employees of a single employer) could band together to pool their savings and lend from the pool to each other to finance the purchase of consumer durables—another kind of loan that commercial banks rarely made until the Depression proved that ordinary people, one way or another, paid their debts. With no stockholders, no paid officers, and no premises to speak of, credit unions (Filene hoped) could at the same time pay workers more interest on their savings and charge them less interest on their borrowings. Thrift institutions and credit unions could lend safely for longer terms than commercial banks because their sources of funds were more stable. Even longer-term loans could be made by insurance companies, the other major "financial intermediary" of the period before the Depression, because the inflow and outflow of money at the insurance companies was predictable actuarially.

This system did not work very well. Because lending expanded in good times and shrank in bad times, finance became a "procyclical" factor in the business cycle. Because the monetary system had a metallic base (gold and just a little silver), signs of economic trouble could produce hoarding that reduced the reserves of the banking system and its capacity to lend. The worst sufferers would be the savings institutions, which saw an increased demand for repayment by depositors or shareholders at precisely the time when the value of the assets that backed their loans was shrinking—if they could be sold at all.

In 1913 the Federal Reserve System was created to provide American banking with a flexible money supply and with a government-based "lender of last resort" that could create money on the pledge of bank assets, saving the banks from the need to call loans or sell paper when there was a demand for cash. In an ingenious compromise, Congress agreed to let state banks be members if they wished. (Nationally chartered banks had no choice.) Members were required to sterilize, at their regional Fed, some fraction of the money deposited with them in checking accounts. Nationally, the Federal Reserve could encourage or discourage lending: bluntly, by changing the reserve ratio, or subtly, by adding reserves to (or subtracting them from) the assets of the banking system. Changing the reserves in the system is quite easy for the Fed to do because every time it makes a purchase, whether of a paper clip or a Treasury bill, it pays by increasing bank reserves, and every time it sells an investment, it collects by reducing bank reserves. Each move by the Fed has a multiplier effect in the banking system; if reserves were set at 10%, each dollar added would enable the banking system to increase total loans and deposits by ten dollars.

This scheme met its first crisis with flying colors in 1914, when the European war broke out (and the New York Stock Exchange closed for eight months—think what a different time that was!), partly because the head of the New York Federal Reserve Bank was Benjamin Strong, an imaginative financier whose strength in the market was greatly enhanced by the fact that he was J. P. Morgan's son-in-law. When the big crunch came in 1930, however, the New York Fed was led less strongly. The Federal Reserve Board in Washington was dominated by the Secretary of the Treasury, Andrew Mellon, himself a banker (and a member of the Fed board, as the system was then organized), who was willing to see a perpetuation of high interest rates because he feared the loss of gold to Europe. The savings associations and the country banks dropped like flies. The money-center banks hunkered down, denying credit to borrowers who needed it desperately, and a process of deflation made the existing debt burden a weight that the nation's shrunken commerce could not carry.

The Roosevelt administration, and especially the overwhelmingly Democratic Congress that came in with it, was much more conservative than noneconomic historians believe in its approach to the nation's systems of banking and finance. It was Hoover's administration—not Roosevelt's—that launched the Reconstruction Finance Corporation, the direct intervention of government in lending to private enterprise. Roosevelt himself wished to see the banking system reorganized on a far more national basis: the small-town bankers were not only broke, but resolutely Republican; the big-city bankers, while surprising numbers of them had turned out to be at least a little crooked, were at least still in business and thus the fittest to survive. Congress was having none of it: in the House, especially, representatives wanted federally chartered local savings associations to replace the state-chartered S&Ls that had collapsed in the Depression, and they wanted deposit insurance to lure money back into the vaults of the country bankers.

Over Roosevelt's objections, the new banking legislation retained the geographical restrictions put in place in 1926 by the MacFadden Act, which forbade banks to open offices outside their home state and denied nationally chartered banks the right to open branches within a state unless the state-chartered banks had equal rights. Indeed, the aim of New Deal legislation was to *increase* the insulation between the different kinds of banks, between banks and savings institutions, between banks and other financial intermediaries. Transaction balances were to be kept separate from investable funds by a provision in the deposit insurance law prohibiting the payment of interest on funds left in the bank for less than thirty days. The thrust of the new rules throughout was to keep each financial institution on its own turf; what had got the banking system in trouble, Congress and many economists believed, was its ventures into activities not classically considered to be banking.

3

Congressman Wright Patman, an imp of a populist from West Texas who for years chaired the House Banking Committee, liked to complain that the Constitution gave the Congress the power to coin the nation's money but that Congress had "farmed it out" to the Open Market Committee of the Federal Reserve Board. Though far from the last word on the subject, this was essentially true. Depending on definitions, between 70% and 90% of the American money supply was created by the activities of the banks, which theory says are controlled by the regulations, actions, and lifted eyebrows of the Federal Reserve.

The theory, however, rests upon an essentially circular analysis, and upon definitions that have become misleading with the passage of time. The money supply is estimated by means of "aggregates" that include as "money" only the liabilities of the banking system (its "deposits") and of the central banks ("currency"). It is then tautological that the quantity of money is dictated by the actions of the central bank—in the United States, the Federal Reserve System—which controls both the issuance of currency and the creation of deposit liabilities by the banks. Moreover, the theory—and all legislation affecting banking rests on this theory—assumes an impermeable line between money and credit. For the theory to be true, then, there must be an operational difference between the piece of plastic in the card case of your wallet and the Federal Reserve Note in your billfold.

Obviously, there is no such difference, even on higher levels of abstraction and sophistication. When Lawrence Connell was National Credit Union Administrator in 1979, he tried to order the institutions he supervised to maintain a 5% "liquidity ratio"—that is, to keep in cash, overnight bank deposits, short-term Treasury bills, and the like a sum amounting to 5% of the total "deposits" in the credit union, to be certain that the institution could pay back its members on demand if there were a sudden rush for funds. Over and over again, the managers of the credit unions assured Connell that they had no liquidity concerns. They had standby credit arrangements with their local banks that would allow them to draw money to pay back more than Connell's 5% of "deposits" if the members suddenly came asking for cash. They could not understand why Connell saw such a difference between cash on hand and an established line of credit; when needed in their lives, the two were identical. In the new teller machines, there is no difference between drawing cash from an account and drawing it from a line of credit the bank adds to the account.

"If a depository institution wasn't sure it could borrow funds, it would behave very differently," said former Fed governor George Mitchell. Paul Volcker reports that even the nation's largest banks refuse to listen when Federal Reserve examiners criticize their low ratios of cash and quick assets: "They say their liquidity is in the market; it never occurs to them that the market might question their solvency."

"The basic fallacy the banking system is still living under," says Gerald Corrigan of the Minneapolis Fed, "is that everyone can go to London. But you can't *all* go to London."

Because money is defined as a "commodity," like corn, the theory holds that by dictating how much of it is produced the government can control the effective quantity. But money is not a commodity like corn, which is consumed and disappears (or even a commodity like gold, much of which vanishes every year into industrial and costume jewelry use through the reverse alchemy of the electroplaters). Money is never consumed. It circulates. Its effective quantity is a function not only of the measured aggregates, but of the speed of circulation. When credit substitutes for money, when communications technology and data processing make it possible for firms to do business with much smaller cash balances, when transactions are bartered outside the monetary economy, the result appears in the published figures as an increase in the speed of circulation—the "velocity" of money.

Thus the information about what is happening to the money supply and to the economy corrects itself automatically to fit the theory: if money is tight and the economy is expanding, "velocity" is increasing; if money is loose and the economy is contracting, "velocity" is diminishing. After a while, all but the professors get a little tired of this self-justifying analysis, and the leaders of the central banks begin asking new questions about the nature of money in a modern industrial society. They don't have answers. "I don't know what money is today," said Richard Pratt, the black-haired, bulldog chairman of the Federal Home Loan Bank Board who had to keep the savings and loan industry out of the tar pits in 1982. "And I don't think anybody at the Fed does, either. The problems we have defining a bank are in a way a reflection of the problems we have defining money."

The theory of government intervention in the private economy through manipulation of the money supply rested on an unspoken assumption that only banks could create meaningful amounts of credit. The Federal Reserve as the central bank— the bankers' bank—would then have great leverage. A minor change in the "monetary base" the Fed controls would constrict (or stimulate) lending throughout the economy. But if nonbanks can create credit that easily substitutes for money, accelerating the velocity of money as measured—or reduce such credit as business slows down, reducing the velocity of money—the leverage of the Fed is greatly diminished.

And that—alas!—has happened. No one can plan monetary policy for an industrial country today without keeping in mind

(1) that there is no longer a useful line between money and credit, money being nothing more than the credit of the government (which is none too good these days, after a generation when all the world's democratic governments cheated their people by inflating their currency); in Italy, government bonds actually pay higher rates of interest than top-quality corporate debt instruments;

(2) that credit usable as money can be generated outside the banking system by the government itself almost incidentally, in the process of funding the deficit; by private business issuing negotiable commercial paper; most obviously, on the credit-card chassis; less obviously, via the Merrill Lynch checkbook that allows the customer to pay bills by drawing against his equity in his stocks or in his home;

(3) that money is whatever people who make and receive payments say it is, and thus that the nature of money is (in the fine phrase of R. S. Sayers, historian of the Bank of England), "determined by the commercial habits of businessmen."

Though the severe oscillations that have afflicted the economies since the 1960s are not to be explained by a single cause, the reduced effectiveness of the central banks must be the reason why the monetary system exacerbated rather than countered the swings induced by government policies, investment flows, commodity shortages or surpluses, and international shocks. There can be no question that the banks, the government, and the economy were all better off in the departed days when the Fed and its peers in other countries could discipline the real economy without punishing it.

4

Meanwhile, the banks themselves have become less efficient as allocators of credit to businessmen and consumers. In the days when the Fed could control the supply of lendable funds, the key job in the bank was that of the "platform officer," who decided (perhaps with help from a committee) where the bank's limited funds should be lent. A man's status among the officers of the bank was measured by the quantity of assets he "controlled"—if he was a lending officer on $200 million of loans, he was a vice-chairman; $50 million, only a vice-president. Beyond that, the profitable bank—First National Bank of Boston in the Serge Semenenko days was the shining example—was the one that found safety where others saw risk, and would finance movie-making, for example, at the higher rates the riskier customer had to pay without suffering the losses implied in the word "risk." There was a base of business with "prime" customers that paid for the marble, the tellers, the deeply carpeted offices upstairs. What lifted the bank out of the ruck was imaginative lending.

By finding new borrowers who would not only pay higher interest charges but also pay back their loans, lending officers could earn themselves promotions, better salaries, a leading voice in the operation of the bank. This is not the way things really worked in most banks because banking was a stuffy and oversocialized world, where lending officers got their jobs through family connections and made their loans because Aunt Sarah knew these people for years (you could get a loan from a bank, the old saw said, only if you didn't need the money). "I spent thirty years in commercial banking," said George Rutland, a portly, white-haired model of a banker, moved over from Crocker National Bank to be number-two at the aggressive California Federal Savings & Loan, which plans to make full use of the new commercial banking powers awarded the S&Ls in the 1982 banking legislation. "And most of the lending officers I've seen, I wouldn't hire." When Justin Watson was Deputy Comptroller of the Currency in the mid-1970s, picking up the pieces of the Real Estate Investment Trusts the banks had launched and financed, he said in a heartfelt way that "most of the bank failures I see are just plain stupidity." Still, smart or not, it was the loan officers who controlled the bank, and thus it was possible for odd fellows like Semenenko, or A. P. Giannini (Bank of America) in San Francisco, or Walter Bimson (Valley National) in Phoenix, or Mills Lane (Citizens and Southern) in Atlanta to create an institution and change the face of an industry or a community by their choice of assets for the bank.

As the sources of funds diversified—as an electronics age developed markets that enabled banks to buy money overnight as well as gather deposits for a longer haul—the role of the lending officer diminished. He became a money salesman more than a judge of applicants for credit. Top management assumed that the lending market was "efficient," that all banks lend to the same customers and charge them the same interest rates. Profitability, then, would derive from cleverness at funding the loan—buying the money a little cheaper than other banks could buy it. Loan judgment was partly by formula, partly by follow-the-leader, as banks found they could save personnel costs in the lending area domestically by taking "participations" in loans made and presumably policed by banks that had closer relations with the borrower, and internationally by joining "syndicates" that lent jointly to foreign entities with a "lead bank" doing all the work for a fee on all the loan.

Chase Manhattan carried this parsimony in lending personnel to its ultimate stage: having saved itself the costs of investigating loan applications in the Oklahoma oil patch by taking participations in loans made by the up-and-coming Penn Square Bank of Oklahoma City, Chase economized further by asking its accountants, Peat, Marwick & Mitchell, to take a look at how those loans were coming along. After all, Peat, Marwick was Penn Square's auditor, too. It came as a great surprise to Chase and to Peat, Marwick when the march of time revealed that Penn Square was crooked and that some hundreds of millions of dollars of loans in which Chase had participated were more-or-less fraudulent.

In the 1960s and 1970s high-quality borrowers found they could often get money cheaper than the interest rates charged by the banks. Between periodic tax payment dates, dividend dates, and debt-service dates, corporations acquire considerable cash they will not need for several weeks. Banks had found a way to bid for this money through the negotiable certificate of deposit, but then they had to make a spread when they lent it because banks are expensive to run—and by guaranteeing their certificates, whether or not their debtors pay them, they run a credit risk. A commercial-paper dealer, operating strictly on a wholesale basis on the upstairs floors, with no capital investment but a desk and a hand-held calculator, can bring together very inexpensively borrowers who wish to write and sell IOUs and companies that wish to purchase them. The borrowers can pay less interest for their loans, and the lenders can earn more interest on their money because the broker takes only about a fifth as much as the bank demands.

Bank CDs were safer than IOUs from nonbanks. (Until 1982 the regulators saw to it that no purchaser of a bank CD lost money if a bank went under—even under conditions as discreditable as those of U.S. National Bank in San Diego, which had been funneling depositors' cash into enterprises owned by its controlling stockholder.) Every so often there would be a shock in the corporate IOU ("commercial paper") market, as when a Penn Central collapsed, leaving the holders of its commercial paper $82 million poorer. But in an inflationary society, prudential considerations lack motive power. And with the deterioration of the foreign-loan portfolio, some major sources of funds began to doubt that the path of prudence really did lead to the doors of the bank. "The market," said Aiden Harland of the Darien Consulting Group in late 1982, when CD rates actually rose above commercial-paper rates, "perceives the big companies as better risks than the banks."

In the 1970s very large corporate loans, to the best "names," moved out of the banks and into a market where corporations issued their own short-term debt instruments for purchase by other corporations that were in a different phase in their cash-gathering cycle. In the dark days of spring 1982 the quantity of commercial paper in the market reached a total four-fifths as great as all the commercial and industrial loans of the American banking system. That total ran down (as did the loan portfolio, but more slowly) when long-term interest rates declined in the bond market and the paper issuers could pay off their short-term loans with long-term funding. But the disturbing fact remained that the banks had lost and had no way to regain much of what had been their best business.

By 1983 the larger banks, without exception, were talking about the need to cultivate a "middle market": companies with annual sales in the $50 to $100 million range, whose "names" were not well enough known in the market to permit the sale of commercial paper. But the banks were already on the way to losing much of this business, through greed and the mistaken belief that a temporary near-monopoly would last forever. Traditionally, small business loans had been written at rates a percentage point or two higher than the prime rate charged the big boys, but in August 1983 the spread had grown to more than three points, which meant that the gap between commercial-paper rates and small business loan rates was more than four percentage points. Commercial credit companies and the financing divisions of insurance companies can easily make a market inside this one for the better small borrowers, and they are already beginning to pick off the businesses the banks want and need most. But the banks have boxed themselves in between the need to compete directly with commercial-paper brokers for the giant customers and their bidding for deposit funds in deregulated accounts. To conduct profitably what middle-market business they can keep, avoiding the loan defaults that can rapidly devour earnings, the banks will have to restore to its old high status in management the analytical foot-slogging work of choosing among possible borrowers.

"A number of the larger banks," said Deputy Comptroller Robert Bench, not without amusement, "are going back and hiring some of their retirees to collect loans. They know how to do it."

5

The problem that got the most publicity in the early 1980s was a deterioration of the banks' potency on the other side of the ledger: their ability to draw and hold both consumer and corporate deposits. To a large extent, this was the result of government regulations that prohibited the payment of interest on demand deposits and restricted the interest the banks could pay for time deposits. Competition in the form of free toasters and convenience (neighborhood branches) proved ineffective against the pull of the money-market interest rates offered by money-market funds, which at their peak in late 1982 had outstanding "shares" (*not* deposits: heaven forfend—that would have been illegal) amounting to a sixth of the entire deposit base of the banks.

When the government effectively released all interest-rate restraints on banks and savings associations on December 14, 1982, the new freedom to bid for high interest rates for consumer accounts exposed banks' weaknesses not unlike those from which they suffered on the lending side. In the first preposterous weeks, the banks paid more for consumer deposits in $2,500 pieces than the "prime rate" they asked their big borrowers to pay for loans in million-dollar pieces. (In Atlanta the banks offered up to 25% on an annualized basis for the first thirty days, on accounts of up to $500,000. For anyone with half a million dollars' worth of marginable securities in a brokerage account this was a free gift of $6,000, because that was the difference between the thirty-day margin loan on $500,000 and what the banks were paying. Many brokers made these arrangements for their customers, and within a few days the banks were restricting these accounts to $25,000: they may be slow learners, but you shouldn't say they're ineducable.)

Even after the early lunacy subsided, however, the rates the banks had to pay to keep money from flowing back to the funds, added to the costs of servicing small accounts, ran considerably higher than what they could earn on short-term investments. Despite all the new machinery in the back offices and the Automated Teller Machines on the streets, agglomerating funds through thousands of small deposits is a labor-intensive activity for banks—but not for money-market mutual funds, which never meet their "depositors" face to face.

Sherman Lewis, vice-chairman of Shearson/American Express, remembered from his time with Loeb, Rhoades in the 1970s that Temp Fund, the broker's pioneer money-market fund, sold mostly to institutional investors, ran $1.5 billion with only four employees. He told a savings-and-loan convention about this, and one of the conventioneers came up sorrowfully at the end and said to him, "You are running a $1.5 billion *bank*, and you have only four people." That's an exaggeration—a money-market mutual fund is really not a bank—but a bank with $1.5 billion in assets would have at least a thousand employees. Even a consumer-oriented money-market fund like Dreyfus Liquid Assets needs only two to three employees for each $100 million under management, and its payments to The Bank of New York for account maintenance and checking services represent the cost of only another two or three. Under these circumstances, it must be cheaper for a bank to buy money from (sell CDs to) money-market funds than to gather its own interest-bearing deposits.

As a result, the banks are likely to lose their best consumer credits as they have lost their best commercial customers. In 1983 General Motors made a splash on the airwaves and stimulated the revival of auto sales by offering an 11.9% interest rate on all new cars. Banks were charging 16% and up for such loans at the time, in part to cover their costs in introducing the money-market-rate accounts newly authorized by the federal bank regulators. Despite much talk to the contrary, the lower rates of the General Motors Acceptance Corporation were not a subsidy to car buyers: they were profitable to the lender, which was acquiring its funds in the commercial-paper market at rates that ran about 9%. This was six-month money to fund a three- or four-year loan, which meant that GMAC was accepting an "interest-rate risk" (if rates rose during the time of the car loan, the finance company might find itself paying more than it was collecting from the car buyer), but there was a cushion of profit at the start.

An anonymous executive of Manufacturers Hanover growled to Julie Salomon of *The Wall Street Journal* late in 1982 that "Consumers have to realize that if we pay them X for their money, we have to charge X plus something for loans." Having realized that, however, consumers can turn their footsteps away from the bank door and cross the street to the finance company, which is buying its money cheaper, at wholesale, and thus can charge X minus something for loans. It is hard to believe that many customers were drawn by the full-page ad The Bank of New York took in *The New York Times* to celebrate its reduction of car-loan rates to 13.75% right in the middle of the auto-makers' loudly proclaimed offer of loans at 11.9% from their captive finance companies.

If a bank has to buy its funds in the market and needs a big margin to pay the overhead, there is only one out: "The only way you can maintain your margin," says George Mitchell, "is to change your risk tolerances." In the old days, banks were the most finicky lenders to consumers, setting the highest standards for "qualification" and charging the lowest rates. In the future, it seems likely that the finance companies and the brokerage houses will be able to offer the lowest rates and will soon acquire the pick of the crop of borrowers. It will be difficult for banks to adjust psychologically as well as economically to a world where their customers are the more risky and the less well-to-do.

Much the same scenario seems likely to play itself out in the home mortgage market. There was a lesson in the near-disaster in 1979–82 in the savings industry and at those banks with heavy mortgage portfolios. (The California banks were especially hard-hit; during the time of political troubles in the 1960s, Bank of America used to claim that it was really the nation's largest savings-and-loan association, and lo-and-behold, the saying came true in the early 1980s.) If banks are going to have to pay short-term money-market rates for most of their funds, they will not be able to make mortgage loans that carry fixed interest rates for periods of two and three decades—especially in a real world where homeowners can refinance their mortgages to pay less when interest rates decline, but the lenders are stuck when interest rates go up.

The only likely alternatives (we shall have occasion later to examine some plausible but less likely proposals) are general public acceptance of the "Adjustable Rate Mortgage" or the movement of home finance away from "depository institutions" and into the bond market. But the first of these asks homeowners to tie their housing costs to the roller coaster of the banks' cost of funds; they won't want to do that, and they will be right. (Before 1981 housing experts in the United States spoke respectfully of the "Canadian rollover" mortgage, with interest rates set anew at stated intervals; in 1982 the head of the Canadian end of the United Automobile Workers was explaining that whatever the Chrysler workers in the United States might do in terms of concessions to their employer, the Canadians simply couldn't afford any give-backs: they were losing their homes as it was, because of the horrendous escalation of mortgage payments.)

Late in 1983, the banks and the thrifts did find a way to increase the proportion of their mortgages written with adjustable rates: they offered them as loss leaders for the first year, sometimes at rates actually below those they were paying their depositors. A survey by the Federal Home Loan Mortgage Corporation in fall 1983 reported that "82% [of mortgage lenders] believe price (the spread between what lenders offer on ARMs and fixed-rate mortgages) is the most important factor in consumer acceptance of ARMs." The price cutting allowed a number of homebuyers who would not otherwise have "qualified" for mortgages to acquire houses. When the rates on these mortgages rise to "market," as they will after one year, many borrowers and lenders may be in trouble. Over time, the second alternative—mortgages at fixed rates, sold like bonds (which also carry fixed rates) in packages of "mortgage-backed securities"—would seem to be a more likely pattern, and a more desirable pattern, for home finance. In 1983, mortgage-backed bonds were sold in the market to a total of $83 billion, representing more than 40% of all the new money available for one-to-four family housing.

Banks and savings associations will originate mortgages to be packaged into bonds or "pass-through certificates" for sale on the market; banks and savings associations will be buyers or sellers of such paper at various times in the interest-rate cycle. But mortgage companies are likely to be more efficient at this activity, especially if they are part of a business that also does real estate brokerage and insurance (read: Sears, Shearson/American Express, Merrill Lynch, eventually others). Again, fall 1982 looked like the handwriting on the wall: home mortgages were available from mortgage companies in many parts of the country at less than 13% when nearly all the banks and savings associations were still charging more than 14%. Even when the rate-reducing factor of federal insurance is washed out of the comparison (most mortgage companies deal in FHA mortgages; most banks and S&Ls don't). The banks were pricing themselves out of the market.

Banks are by no means without resources to delay and even to exploit many of these developments. The big ones are immense institutions, quite beyond normal imagining. Bank of America and Citicorp each has liabilities adding up to nearly 10% of the U.S. national debt; Bank of America has almost 100,000 employees and Citicorp, more than 60,000. (The phone book of its employees' work numbers is thicker than that of many small cities.) Every day each of them will move a volume of money equal roughly to the annual gross national product of Belgium. Relatively modest banks, 5% to 10% the size of those behemoths, will be the dominant enterprises and employers of their home cities throughout the United States—in places like Charlotte and Memphis and Phoenix. Even in Boston, St. Louis, Dallas, and Houston, the skyline is dominated by the

31

home office buildings of the local banks. And because there are banks everywhere, the industry has political clout to match or even exceed its economic importance.

Bank holding companies can and do raise some of the funds their banks need by selling their own commercial paper. A bank holding company can (and many do) include a mortgage company and a consumer finance company among its subsidiaries. The two largest credit-card operations, Visa and MasterCard, are essentially co-ops owned if not controlled by banks. Diners Club is owned and controlled by Citicorp, which has also invented a new card called Choice, essentially a mini-mail-order bank that pays interest on customer credits in the account as well as charging interest on customer debits. Savings banks can and do write and sell life insurance; savings and loan associations can be property developers. Both banks and S&Ls can offer stockbroker services. They can buy, sell, and trade precious metals, government securities, foreign exchange, and various money-market instruments. Banks have always earned fees for providing trust and custodial services. In recent years, they have established departments that earn fees advising corporations on mergers and acquisitions. They own and operate data-processing service subsidiaries. They purchase capital equipment and lease it to customers, splitting the tax benefits. They routinely run collection services and cash-management services for corporations.

As technology makes it easier for companies that are not banks to offer banking services—and, indeed, to acquire banks or banklike savings associations for their own purposes—banks will gain increasingly the power to diversify geographically and the right to diversify into activities not previously regarded as banking. The foreign subsidiaries or parents of American banks (for dozens of American banks, as big as California's Crocker and Union, New York's Marine Midland, and Chicago's Harris Trust, are now owned by foreign banks), can carry on in foreign parts any number of investment and securities market activities from which banks are barred in the United States.

With the passage of time, banks—or, at least, bank holding companies—will be relieved of some of the rules and regulations that now keep them from entering businesses where they could employ their financial muscle and their skills. (Maybe: Paul Volcker is prepared to fight them, because "the bank is inextricable from the holding company. In the process of protecting the bank, you have to protect all the other activities.")

Anything that has to go through Congress is at the mercy of the attitudes of legislators whose strongest desire is not to get anybody mad at them—to win the extension of their powers that they gained under the Garn–St. Germain bill of fall 1982, the banks had to accept an absolute prohibition on writing insurance not related to the repayment of their loans. (They then found a way around the law by acquiring some under-$50 million state-chartered banks exempted from the prohibition, in states that permit banks to be in the insurance business.) Still, over the long run, "fairness" (that most emotive of political words), will require that the government regulate everybody or nobody. Regulating the banklike activities of the new competitors looks like work for a Don Quixote (or a King Canute) rather than for practical politicians. "When I'm asked a question by a client," said professor Harold Scott at the Harvard Law School, head of the American Law Institute task force on the banking sections of the Uniform Commercial Code, "I don't ask what the law is. I ask, 'What are people doing?'" So the banks will, in the end, get much of the freedom they want.

There is no use pretending that the changes are occurring "according to some grand strategy," said James Smith, Comptroller of the Currency for Gerald Ford. "I can't think of *any* important public law that resulted from a grand strategy." Nor can it be said with any confidence that the banks will know what to do with their freedom when they get it. Their success as mere providers of financial services will depend on their sensitivity to the needs of the users. Bankers' minds have not worked that way in the past, and they don't have much time to learn. The barbarians are inside the gates.

2

...LONG LIVE THE FINANCIAL SERVICES INSTITUTION!

I have a slogan for Sears Financial Services," said one of the few wicked bankers. " 'If you lose your shirt, we'll sell you another.' "

1

Charles Merrill came out of retirement to resume the firm of Merrill Lynch in 1940 not because he needed the money (he had got his personal fortune pretty much out of the market in 1928 and had closed his old firm, leaving $5 million capital in it to help stake his successors, in 1930), and not because he was bored (he was a man of several wives, seriatim, and of many interests), but because he felt the need to make a political statement. His was the brokerage firm that would serve the ordinary customer. His "account executives" would be on salary, rather than on the piece of the trading commission earned by the other brokers' "customer's men." Literature distributed by Merrill Lynch would give customers straight information, rather than advice to buy or sell. His firm would never charge for custodial services, would always charge the lowest commissions permitted by stock exchange regulations, and would vote against all proposals to raise the basic commission. Within a very few years, Merrill Lynch was the largest brokerage house in the country, doing more than 10% of all the trades on the New York Stock Exchange. *Fortune* described it as "The Thundering Herd of Wall Street," thereby fathering the bull that would later wander through china shops on television screens.

Much of what Merrill proposed was not workable or did not happen or was modified with the passage of time. Salaries were supplemented by "bonuses" related to the commissions on each account executive's accounts. The Merrill Lynch research department, like others, eventually began issuing buy and sell recommendations. The customer's men sold like crazy (particularly the securities for which the firm acted as underwriter, as it increasingly did, the armies of account executives making it cherishable as a distributor for a new issue). And when the Securities and Exchange Commission put a stop to fixed minimum commissions, Merrill became one of the higher-priced brokers—definitely not a discount house.

Still, people trained in the Merrill ethos had none of the old Wall Street private-club attitudes. They really believed that the best way to sell brokerage services was to find out what the customer wanted, and then hunt up a way to produce it. Among the masters of this approach was an enthusiastic and energetic but notably scrupulous salesman from the firm's Boston shop, name of Donald Regan, Harvard '40, a lieutenant-colonel in the

Marines during World War II, who was called in to clean up and manage the firm's over-the-counter stock-trading department after its reputation was sullied in a kickback scandal, and who became the youngest partner the firm ever appointed.

Regan became chairman and chief executive officer in 1971, when the winds of change were tearing through Wall Street. He had said that he wanted the firm to be "a financial department store," strong across the board in everything from commodities brokerage to government bond dealing. It was clear enough what that meant to the organization of the brokerage house, now a corporation—indeed, a holding company, with proliferating subsidiaries. But nobody had answered the question of what it might mean to the customer. Regan commissioned a study from Stanford Research Institute: what would people want and expect from a financial department store in the 1980s? And he beefed up his planning group, placing in charge of it Thomas Chrystie, a twenty-year veteran of the firm's underwriting group.

"One of the things I found on my desk when I came in 1975 was the detailed SRI proposal," Chrystie recalled. "I didn't like it. But it had gone so far I thought I owed them a trip out there." SRI was planning to take a year on the project and write a book on the opportunities that would open up in the 1980s. Chrystie told them he would give them no more than six months, that he planned to assign a Merrill Lynch man to their team full-time to monitor their progress, and that what he wanted was not an overall study but a worked-out recommendation for one or two specific new services. He flew to California on a Wednesday night in December 1975 for a Thursday meeting, and the SRI team began skimming through the lists of possible services opened up by the researchers' preliminary studies. "They came to checking and credit cards," Chrystie said some years later, "and they brushed that aside—they'd concluded those services didn't fit Merrill Lynch. I was intrigued. I said, 'Wait a minute—what if checking and cards are interesting to *us*?'"

By the end of this meeting, which took ten hours, Chrystie had set up a joint SRI–Merrill team with which he would meet monthly, and which would produce, in half a year, detailed proposals for at least one new business Merrill Lynch could enter. He was so excited that he took the red-eye back from San Francisco to make sure he saw Regan and told him about it before the weekend. A superb salesman and organizer of salesmen (later to be overmatched by what he had to sell for Ronald Reagan), Regan saw the huge potential of what Chrystie and the SRI group then labeled the "Ready Money Account." (Oddly, the term "Cash Management Account" was used from the beginning, but only inside the group: because of its specific reference to the work of corporate treasurers, the sophisticates on the team failed to see its sales strength as a description of a service for individuals.) At the third meeting of Chrystie's little SRI–Merrill group, in March 1976—at Chrystie's condominium in Jackson Hole: "We had individual meetings on ski lifts"—the team committed to what was thereafter called CMA, and Regan guaranteed whatever funds would be needed.

"It's interesting when you think about it," said Paul Stein, the reticent, carefully forceful former customer's man from the St. Paul office who became manager of the CMA project. (Among his customers had been the illustrator-artist Leroy Neiman, whose originals for some *Playboy* sporting prints— gifts of the artist in gratitude for good advice—hang in Stein's office.) "Usually a new idea meets objections, and that was certainly true of CMA—why would anyone need another Visa card or another checkbook? It took eighteen months and seventy-five people—a hundred man-years of computer programming time—and Regan never wavered."

What made CMA especially exotic as an idea for Merrill Lynch is that it was something the firm could not do by itself. "Unlike a lot of things coming into the banking realm," said John B. McCoy, president of Banc One in Columbus, Ohio, a fair young man in gold-rimmed glasses who is son of the John G. McCoy who is chairman of Banc One, "this is something where they gotta have a partner. We were in the credit-card processing business—except for Bank of America itself, the largest processor of BankAmericard in the country." Processing is not a service that sells itself, and Banc One had a staff that went around to banks to promote the idea that Columbus was the fastest, most accurate, least expensive place for turning all those flimsy slips into bills for other banks' customers and credits for the bank. "One of our marketing guys called, said, 'I've had an inquiry from the treasurer of Merrill Lynch. He wants to have lunch with our treasurer, and you, and your father.' I said, 'I don't see any reason why we need all these people.' The marketing guy called back and said, 'No. They need everybody.' So they came out and had lunch. It was like dealing with IBM—you had to sign a letter of confidentiality before you could talk. And they told us what they had in mind."

Different people saw CMA differently. For Paul Volcker—distastefully—it was "a complicated form of overdraft." For John Heimann, then Comptroller of the Currency, it was "a confirmation of the basic trend in the financial services industry, to provide the services the public wants." For Jack Ohlin, commissioner of banks for the State of Oregon, who originally forbade Merrill Lynch to offer the service in that state (a later state attorney general reversed the opinion), it was "the business of banking." For Martin Schwartz, a gray-haired big producer for Merrill Lynch at its Morristown, New Jersey office, "CMA crystallized my ability to take verbal advice and turn it into a product." In the larger focus, Deputy Comptroller of the Currency Charles Muckenfuss said of CMA that "the end result of the government monetizing its debts is that the public now wants to monetize its assets." For the Banc One and Merrill Lynch teams that labored another eighteen months to get the product ready for test marketing, it was a hell of a job.

Objectively, the Merrill Lynch Cash Management Account was a brokerage account available to those with a minimum of $20,000 in cash and securities. It was a margin account—that is, it gave the customer the right to buy stocks with only partial payment (usually 50%—the degree of margin is subject to regulation by the Federal Reserve), or to borrow against existing holdings at an interest rate from 0.75% to 2.50% over what the brokerage house has to pay for overnight money from the banks. Historically, most people had used margin powers to buy more securities, but not infrequently customers would take cash out of their brokerage accounts by margin borrowings, in which case the firm would send the customer a check.

The Cash Management Account would permit the customer to borrow against his holdings by writing his own check, or even by using a Visa card to make a purchase or to draw cash from a bank that was part of the Visa system. This would have been an attractive service at any time, but in past years probably would not have roused great enthusiasm. Only a minority of Merrill customers had margin accounts, and few of them thought of their stock and bond holdings as a cash reserve. What made CMA so brilliant and ultimately so successful was its exploitation of the new investment medium that many people did regard as a cash reserve: the money-market mutual fund. Merrill Lynch had organized such a fund—called Ready Assets—in 1974. With CMA and its separate Money Trust, the firm was in a position to blend two previously separate investment systems.

The first advantage of CMA to the brokerage customer was that money from stock and bond investments would not lie around idle. When a stock was sold, the proceeds would be invested automatically and immediately in the Money Trust. Dividends and interest coupons would not go into the money-market fund on the day they arrived, but every account would be "swept" each Monday, and whatever loose cash was in it would then go into the fund. If the customer wrote a check, or made a Visa card withdrawal, from his CMA, the money would be supplied first from whatever cash might be in the account, then (if necessary) from the redemption of Money Trust shares. Only after these cash resources had been exhausted would the broker reach into the investment portfolio and pledge securities for a loan. Checks could be written for any size, from a few dollars up to the total margin value in the brokerage account. The customer could, if he wished, pay all his bills with Merrill Lynch instead of checks on a bank account. And, of course, he would continue to earn interest on the money-market fund until the check actually cleared. Merrill Lynch, which was in the habit of paying New York customers with checks drawn on accounts in Tacoma, and California customers with checks on banks in North Carolina, understood the value of float.

For travelers, CMA provided a check that was, or seemed to be, local all over the country—for Merrill Lynch had offices in every one of the fifty states. Tom Ryan, a tall young account executive in a New Jersey Merrill Lynch office, liked to tell the story of a trip on the town in New York with friends, which culminated with dinner in a fancy restaurant that turned out not to take credit cards. The party didn't have enough cash to pay the bill, and the restaurant wasn't taking checks from New Jersey banks—but it took a Merrill Lynch check. A young Wall Street lawyer, working on a trial in Houston that went on and on and on, found that his CMA gave him an advantage over the other New Yorkers on the legal team when the firm's paychecks arrived. The others had to put them in the mail to New York for deposit and make arrangements with local colleagues to cash New York checks for their current needs. He took his check into a local Merrill Lynch office, which accepted it (not as a "deposit," of course—that would have been banking); and the local banks gave him cash advances on the Merrill Lynch Visa card.

In theory, Merrill could have operated this program by itself. Customers could have been issued checkbooks that permitted them to draw on the firm's own accounts, with the signature filed at the banks. Diners Club and Carte Blanche (and, indeed, American Express, which is a bank overseas but not in the United States) had run credit-card businesses as independent enterprises doing their own processing. But as a practical matter, the brokerage house did not wish to give its customers checks that could draw on a Merrill Lynch account and thus could not be bounced; and the costs of a card system would be much greater—and the convenience of the card much less—if the firm had to make its own arrangements to have the card honored around the country. Among the earliest decisions of Chrystie's working group was that, as John McCoy said, they needed a partner.

Chrystie's staff made a list of sixty-seven banks and service bureaus that processed credit-card paper, and SRI winnowed the list down to ten. From the ten, Chrystie chose three: Banc One, American Express itself, and Valley National in Arizona. Each was asked to bid for a job that the brokerage house thought would quickly involve the processing of tens of thousands of checks and credit-card slips every day.

Relations between Banc One and Merrill Lynch have never been entirely smooth, and there is some disagreement between them as to why Banc One won the contest. "I'd been white-water canoeing with one of their executives in an Outward Bound program, and I thought it would be fun to work with him," Chrystie says. "And they were BankAmericard processors at a time when that system was going to spend millions to advertise the change of name to Visa. We thought we'd get a free ride."

Says McCoy, "They were wildly optimistic about this thing, and they had a certain naïveté about what banking was. They gave us some volume numbers we didn't think they could ever meet: we cut their estimates by ninety percent on our own calculations. And they had some strange ideas—they wanted to give customers a one percent discount for using the card. We started talking with them in fall '76, and it took a year to put the thing together. I think we really won it by changing some of their concepts." (Interestingly, Citicorp has adopted the feature Banc One found impractical: the new "Citicorp Financial Account" being marketed by mail through Citibank's South Dakota subsidiary offers not only a choice of interest-bearing transaction accounts and a Citibank MasterCard but also "Citidollars," coupons that can be used for discounts on mail-order merchandise, travel, and long-distance phone calls through one of the new competitors of AT&T.)

The complexity of the arrangements that had to be made is most impressive. The checkbook the CMA customer receives is a Banc One checkbook, but the customer does not in fact have an account at Banc One. What he has is access to a Merrill Lynch line of credit at Banc One. The checks move through the traditional check-clearing system, and are presented to Banc One through the Federal Reserve Regional Check Processing Center, together with all the "real" Banc One checks. The "cash letter" from the RCPC shows the total amount of the presented checks, which is the amount by which Banc One's accounts at the Federal Reserve Bank of Cleveland will be debited tonight. (Actually, it's early tomorrow morning: the Feds, like the banks themselves, do their posting in the wee hours.) In the sorting process at Banc One, all the CMA checks are slotted in a single pocket and sent over to the Visa processing section.

Now the bank runs through the disc of CMA accounts, which was updated at 6:30 that morning by wire from Merrill Lynch to indicate the maximum balance—cash, Money Trust funds, and marginable securities—against which a customer can draw a check. These can be large checks, too; the record is one for $365,000 to the Internal Revenue Service. If the check exceeds that maximum balance, it should be bounced. The numbers on the valid checks are totaled, together with the numbers on Visa slips from that day, and a telephone call to New York tells Merrill Lynch how much money is needed to restore its Banc One account to its invariable overnight zero balance. Merrill Lynch then has one of its New York banks send the funds to Columbus on FedWire. The details of the day's transactions are sent separately by wire to the Merrill Lynch computer center, where all the CMA accounts are updated every night, for communication to Banc One at 6:30 the next morning. . . . The customer's CMA statement includes the identification of the party to whom the check was written because the check itself is not returned. Banc One clerks read this info and tap in the description just as fast as they can; the error rate is high but not, of course, very important.

Visa validation is more sophisticated electronically. Like the checkbook, the CMA Visa card is the property of Banc One—Visa is a banker's co-op, and only banks can have their names on the front of a Visa card. (Merrill Lynch establishes its identity on the front of the CMA card with a drawing of a bull; early in 1984 the broker acquired a charter for a bank in New Jersey, in part to take Banc One's name off the Visa card, in part to get access to an Automated Clearing House for the day when the brokerage house decides to offer home banking.) When the Visa card is presented to a bank for a cash withdrawal—or to the better-equipped vendors who accept the card for large sums, airlines and the like—an electronic message is sent (by satellite to San Mateo, California, and then by leased line to Columbus) from the Visa bank to Banc One, querying whether the customer's balance permits this charge or withdrawal. The computer responds, usually within three seconds, and the transaction proceeds.

A unique feature of the Merrill Lynch Visa card is that withdrawals—including cash withdrawals—are limited only by the size of the customer's account. A bank in Atlanta once had a man come in on three successive days to withdraw $50,000 on his Visa card: he was a dealer in antique cars, in town for a show, and he had found some things he wanted to buy. The Atlanta banker was outraged—the Visa fee for a cash withdrawal is $1.50, which is a neat, profitable bit of business when the tourist is taking $100 or $200, which the bank will recover from the Visa card issuer in two or three days, but a dead loss of some substance when the withdrawals run $50,000 in one piece. As a result, Visa rules had to be amended to give banks a percentage rather than a flat fee on large withdrawals. Very large purchases have been made on the Merrill Lynch Visa card. Among the bits of CMA folklore is the jeweler who got an okay on a $91,000 purchase by a holder of a Merrill Visa card, and as soon as the customer left the shop, he closed for the day to go to a Merrill Lynch office and open an account himself. Moreover, the card can be used for cash withdrawals abroad, if the local bank is part of the worldwide Visa system: the satellite that carries the confirmation request and the answer reaches overseas effortlessly.

As a practical matter, the Merrill Lynch Visa card is a debit card rather than a credit card: the customer's account is debited by the amount of his purchase or cash withdrawal, and he gets a statement at the end of the month telling him what has happened rather than a bill telling him what to pay. Legally, however, it is a credit card because Banc One has to put up the money before Merrill Lynch pays off. The 80,000 banking offices across the country and abroad that honor the card for very large withdrawals do so not because it is guaranteed by Merrill Lynch, but because it is guaranteed by Banc One.

From the customer's point of view, of course, the Visa debit card is far less attractive as a way to make a purchase than an American Express (or indeed a bank-issued Visa or Master) card, because he loses the use of the money immediately. As almost every CMA customer will have a credit card, the Merrill Lynch Visa is not much used in stores or for travel and entertainment. Nor do many of the checks turn up in supermarket cash registers. Several customers' men report that as much as 40% of all the CMA checks written by their clients are made out to American Express. For some customers, one disadvantage of CMA is that their broker can learn who has been receiving their checks.

CMA was a hard sell *to* the customer's men because of its heavy reliance on the Money Trust, the money-market mutual fund, which yielded no commissions. More subtly, a number of the customer's men realized that CMA would bring to fruition one of Charles Merrill's dearest hopes: that his firm would have customers loyal to the firm itself, rather than to the individual who handled their account. It is one thing for a customer's man to leave a brokerage house and take his accounts with him when what is involved is simply a stock portfolio, but when it's a full bundle of investments and services, the customer may think about it awhile.

In any event, CMA did not by any means burn up the test markets—Athens, Georgia; Columbus and Denver/Boulder—when the product was first offered in September 1977. The Colorado test was marred by a long fight with the local commissioner of banking, who withdrew a threat to challenge in court only after the minimum check size was raised to $200 for Colorado residents. The experiment moved on to California, with tests in San Diego, Escondido, and La Jolla; plans to extend the test to Eugene, Oregon were dropped after that state's banking commissioner issued a ukase absolutely forbidding checkable brokerage accounts. (In 1980, as Merrill Lynch edged toward going national, Fritz Elmendorf of the American Bankers Association noted almost wistfully opposition by the state banking commissioners in "Louisiana, Georgia, Tennessee, Utah, Oregon and now Arkansas. They're going to make a stand in Utah. If Merrill Lynch loses in two or three states, they may be discouraged enough to drop the fight. . . .")

Market research indicated that CMA would be hugely popular; test marketing gave mixed signals. Merrill Lynch cut prices—from $4 a month (including all the checks you wished to write) to $20 a year. (By early 1984 the annual fee had climbed to $50.) The newspaper ads didn't pull enough people to pay out. But the people who did come in were those Merrill wanted: the best-paid professionals, the chief executive officers. As many as half the accounts in some offices were new customers; as much as a quarter of them were people who simply walked in off the street because a friend had told them about CMA. The last of Charles Merrill's rules was dropped overboard: customers' men were paid bonuses of $100 to $150 for each CMA account they opened, and as more of the country came on line, Merrill set up contests, with trips to Puerto Rico and Hawaii for the winners.

Gradually the customers' men came around, partly because the CMA account seemed to unlock new doors in their clients' mansions. "There's an old saw in the brokerage business," said Jack Armstrong, a very large former football coach who ran the Morristown office, "that there is no new money in the stock market, just old money that moves from one broker to another. This account gave us the first time we'd seen new money in quantity." Martin Schwartz, an older man and one of the firm's largest producers, noted that when his long-standing customers opened a CMA, "They'd come running in with shopping bags full of securities, things they'd been keeping in the bank vault that I didn't even know about. And presumably I was their financial adviser."

When the project was new, Paul Stein would go around to bankers' conventions to try to calm the bankers down. "The banker looks at CMA as a banker, not as a consumer," Stein said in 1980, "and he says, 'How can I compete with *that?*' But he's not competing with *that*. These are upscale customers, average age, fifty-five. They value their banking connections. More than ninety-two percent of them have another credit card, and they don't like the idea of charging their dinner to their brokerage account, which is how they perceive it." At no time has checkwriting in the average CMA account exceeded four a month, and the checks tend to be big tickets, averaging more than $700 each in 1982. Nevertheless, the bankers were right, because once the features were sorted out, there was one aspect of the CMA account that was going to take away banking business not only valuable in itself, but crucial to the forward planning of many of the banks. CMA was a much better chassis for personal borrowing than anything the banks could offer.

As noted earlier, Americans tend to maximize both sides of their personal ledgers: they borrow to buy while building up their savings and investments. A good many people who take car loans to buy new automobiles are also the owners of securities. Banks are used to charging four and five points over the prime rate for auto loans, and there is a certain amount of nuisance paper work involved in establishing the terms of the chattel mortgage that secures the bank's property interest in the car it is financing. A Merrill Lynch CMA customer could walk into the showroom with his Visa card and simply charge the car (or write a check, if he preferred). To the extent that the car cost more than his cash resources in the Money Trust, he borrowed automatically on the security of his stockholdings. And that loan Merrill Lynch gladly made to him at margin rates, which were a point or two over the special lower-than-prime "call" rate at which brokers borrow funds. Moreover, this was excellent business for Merrill Lynch, because by the Stock Exchange rules governing margin accounts, the firm now had the power to lend out that margined stock (making additional interest for itself) to fill the delivery needs of a short seller.

In early 1983, when the banks were scrambling around to find places where they could lend profitably the money they were acquiring through their new high-interest money-market accounts, many of them circularized their higher-income credit-card customers, informing them that their credit limit had been raised (often to $15,000 or more), and the bank would be happy to help them finance their purchases as the economy recovered from the deep recession. Of the 8,000,000 or so households eligible for such treatment, however, more than 900,000 were already holders of Merrill Lynch CMAs. As the richest of the bank's consumer borrowers acquired CMAs and similar accounts, the long-term project for making lucrative loans to high-income cardholders was greatly diminished.

And Merrill Lynch was moving on, to corporate and pension trust CMAs, arrangements with companies for direct deposit of executive salaries into the individual's CMA, and a plan by which homeowners could take an open line of credit on the equity in their homes, permitting them to borrow inexpensively (at two percentage points over prime)—with maximum convenience, of course, simply by writing a check—against what had previously been the most illiquid asset in anyone's portfolio.

By fall 1983 this "Equity Access" account was available in ten states (including California, Illinois, and New York), and Merrill expected that by the end of 1984 it would be offered in twenty-nine states. Such loans cannot be made as part of a CMA, because Federal Reserve rules prohibit brokers from "arranging credit" to help customers buy stocks; and the check- and Visa-processing for this account will be done by banks other than Banc One (different banks will get the business from different states). The up-front profits for Merrill should be considerable, because the entrance fee to Equity Access is a one-time charge of 2% of the whole line of credit, regardless of how much is used. Thereafter, there is an annual maintenance fee of $35, which should more than pay for the paper work. And as Merrill's blended cost of funds will be well below prime (a broker has the use of a good deal of free money, especially customer balances and receipts on the loan of margined securities), the lending operation should be profitable on its own—provided there are few defaults.

For once, the banks moved quickly with similar programs to make the home a checkable asset, on terms similar to Merrill's. In fact, the terms offered by some banks are slightly more favorable to the borrower. But even if the banks should succeed in dominating this rather dubious business, the triumph will be bittersweet, for with their cost structures they probably can't make money at it—and much of what is borrowed in this way from brokers or banks would once upon a time have been unsecured and second mortgage loans at the highest rates the banks charge.

2

Merrill's first line of defense against imitators of the CMA was the cost of developing the service, which ran well into the tens of millions of dollars, considerably more than other brokers were likely to have available for such experiments. Still, the fact was that the contract with Banc One was nonexclusive, and as the brokerage business became increasingly capital-intensive the old-line firms were looking around for acquisition-minded partners. In August 1980 Merrill filed for a patent on CMA, from software to systems. Then the brokerage houses were bought up by rich uncles—Bache by Prudential Insurance; Paine Webber (temporarily) by INA, a Philadelphia insurance company later merged with Connecticut General into CIGNA; Shearson by American Express; Dean Witter by Sears. One by one, together with E. F. Hutton and Smith, Barney, they began to offer their own versions of CMA. Several of these brokers also bought some of their processing services from Banc One. In summer 1982 Merrill sued Dean Witter for patent infringement. The scuttlebutt of the Street was that this was cheap publicity for Merrill, but people at the brokerage house say the suit is deadly serious: if others are going to offer CMA–like acounts, Merrill Lynch wants a license fee. In December 1983, Dean Witter settled the suit, apparently paying $1 million for a license and agreeing to a trivial continuing fee.

That the suit was brought against the Sears subsidiary also cannot be an accident, for it is Sears that worries everybody in the new financial-services industry, banks and nonbanks alike. As early as 1978, Walter Wriston of Citibank was describing Sears as "the biggest bank in the country." This was taken as clever rather than descriptive, but it was intended seriously. The extent of Sears's involvement in financial services was impressive. Sears owned, and had owned for some years, the nation's second-largest property-casualty insurance company (Allstate) and the seventh-largest savings-and-loan association (also Allstate, restricted, despite its name, to California). Its credit card was the most widely distributed and used in the country, with more then 42 million cards outstanding, 26 million of them active in the average week, with $7 billion in outstanding debits at any time. The company had also dipped a toe into the mortgage-insurance and mortgage-packaging business through its acquisition of PMI, an aggressive deviser of new instruments created by Preston Martin, who had leaped from academia to commerce through a position as chairman of the Federal Home Loan Bank Board, and who would later move on to be vice-chairman of the Federal Reserve.

Clayton Banzhaf, executive vice-president for financial services, a large, ruminative man, denied vigorously in 1979 that Sears had any intention of getting into competition with the banks, or any desire to quarrel with them. Banzhaf commented on Wriston's description, "We say to Walter, 'We're *friends.*' We are not a depository institution. We can't take over the world; it's not legally possible. We refund to our credit customers in cash any overpayment or cash credits in their accounts—in the mail-order business, down to one penny. It's illegal for us to hold customers' cash. We deal with Allstate as though it were a completely separate entity—so far as we're concerned, it could be Prudential or State Farm. We pay three, four million dollars a year in insurance premiums. We borrow our own money. And we publish for God and everybody to see what we're doing.

"We are possibly the largest single user of banking services in the United States, with almost 4,000 physical locations that have the Sears, Roebuck name on them, and very few that don't need a banking facility. We have the largest number of corporate bank accounts with one name on them—3,700 accounts in 2,500 banking corporations, domestically, and possibly another 1,000 relationships globally. Every single day, we are making deposits—we have no other place to put our money. We couldn't exist without the banking system.

"We have about 1,300 lines of credit, aggregate maybe $3.5 billion—second only to General Motors. It's a unique relationship. For a couple of decades, as a matter of corporate policy, we have used bank credit all the time for a portion of our short-term working capital needs, and we are very large borrowers on balance." Sears's actual loans from the banks, however, normally run only about $300 million, which is about 5% of the company's daily financing needs—and considerably less than the $800 million or so intermediated by the banks in the form of master notes held by their trust departments. Meanwhile, Sears runs a cash balance of about $300 million at the banks and invests it at interest rates that probably compare nicely with the banks' interest charges on the borrowings. "Our internal cash flow," Banzhaf said pleasantly, "is monitored every day, regionally controlled. My people find out the cash position in each region, and they play put-and-take with it."

As the interest rates fluctuated in the late 1970s, the profitability of the Sears credit-card operation (and thus of the company itself) oscillated dramatically. In 1979 all the profit was in the insurance company. The credit corporation ran at a loss, as the cost of borrowing in the commercial-paper market exceeded the rates that could be charged customers in a number of states. While Banzhaf was denying any intention of reaching for self-funding by offering people interest-bearing balances in their credit-card accounts, others in the company were in fact registering with the SEC a special issue of $250 consumer bonds Sears could sell its customers with stuffers in the same envelopes that brought the bills.

Where Sears might have gone without the example of the CMA is an interesting question impossible to answer—if the patent-infringement suit had come to trial, we might have learned some striking things from the documents "discovered" by the lawyers, and this may be why it didn't come to trial.

It is reasonable to believe that the spread and success of CMA made the idea of acquiring a brokerage house more attractive to Sears than it otherwise might have been. Sears had pioneered in the use of electronic gadgetry for inventory control and cash registers in large stores. There was a considerable amount of computer sophistication in-house at Sears, and much confidence that what Merrill Lynch could do, Dean Witter, with Sears's help, could duplicate. Just in case, Banc One was given the bank-processing contract.

In 1982–83 Sears moved into high gear in its "Financial Network." It opened offices across the country for its predominantly California real estate brokerage house of Coldwell Banker. Allstate S&L made perhaps the biggest push in the country for the SuperNow checking accounts with uncontrolled interest rates, which came into being in January 1983. And Dean Witter created a confusing array of products and services, advertised on television and radio, in newspapers and magazines, and by stuffers in Sears credit-card envelopes. A Dean Witter check could be cashed weekends and up to nine at night in your neighborhood store. What research said was that after the big splash of ads for the banks' new money-market accounts, people wanted high yield and safety. Very well: Dean Witter would offer six-year variable-rate consumer CDs issued by banks to its order, paying about 2.5% more than Treasury bills the first three months, and "at least" 0.6% more than the 91-day Treasury bill rate each week thereafter. As bank CDs, these investments would be guaranteed by the FDIC, but under federal regulatory rules, the account holder would have to pay a penalty if he cashed them in prior to maturity. Never fear: Dean Witter itself would make a secondary market in these CDs, presumably very near par (insured floating-rate notes cannot get very far away from par in either direction). So the Dean Witter customer could reasonably expect to get his money out without penalty. By late 1983 Sears had 130 "financial service centers" in its stores, open-walled offices with a dignified counter and widely spaced desks, combining stock brokerage, real estate brokerage, mortgage lending and, really, banking.

Toward the end of 1982 all the large Wall Street brokers tried to get their version of CMA into gear, somehow. In December of that year, as a kind of Christmas present, Prudential-Bache offered a six-month free trial of the account to brokerage customers and a selected list of Prudential policyholders; Shearson/American Express, which in the first ten months had opened only 18,000 of its F(inancial)MAs, began incentive programs not unlike those Merrill Lynch had used with the customer's men. For CMA, it turned out, had positioned both the customer and the broker to take quick advantage of any lunacy that came down the pike. In 1981, when Congress authorized the crazy "All-Savers Certificates"—which permitted banks and S&Ls to offer tax-exempt one-year certificates at an interest rate 70% that of the most recent auction of one-year Treasury bills (a direct gift from the Treasury to the depositories, which the pet congressmen of the thrifts and the banks extorted from the Reagan administration as their price for approving the 1981 tax package)—the law provided for payment of a commission of up to 2% of the deposit. In a matter of days Merrill Lynch brokered $700 million of CMA money into California Federal Savings & Loan All-Savers Certificates, at a commission of 1%. (Nobody loves a hog.) Fifteen months later, Merrill brokers were fast enough to get for their customers' hundreds of millions of dollars worth of those thirty-day 25% annual rate money-market accounts of up to $500,000 idiotically offered by the Atlanta banks.

Most convincingly, the stock-market boom of 1982 had revealed the value of an immediately available pool of funds, *which the customer's man knew all about,* that could be put in the market. As of fall 1982, the average Merrill Lynch CMA was $63,000, of which $23,000 was in the Money Trust. With interest rates declining and excitement in the stock market rising, it was duck soup for the account executives to sell the customers on the idea that some of that Money Trust reserve should be invested commissionably. CMA manager Sanderson said that one-third of all the commission income Merrill Lynch took in during that astonishing last third of 1982 was from sales to customers with CMA accounts. And on those monster trading days at the New York Stock Exchange, when the Merrill Lynch volume soared over 15,000,000 shares a day, the automated features of the CMA system—the fact that the customer's man could tap out an order on a keyboard instead of writing a slip—were no small help in preventing the sort of paperwork snafus that had bollixed the brokerage houses in the euphoric booms of the late 1960s.

53

3

Banks have always been involved in stock-market purchases and sales for their trust-department customers. Indeed, they have run in-house mutual funds for corporate pension plans and for Keogh and IRA retirement programs. In the late 1960s Citibank not unreasonably sought to offer such "commingled accounts" to any customer of the bank, in open competition with the mutual funds, but the Supreme Court decided that was underwriting—distributing securities—which was prohibited by the Glass–Steagall Act of 1933. Year after year, the American Bankers Association sought congressional approval of commingled accounts as its major legislative goal in Washington; and year after year, the Securities Industries Association and the Investment Company Institute, the lobbying branches of the broker/dealers and the mutual funds, fought the bankers off.

In small towns the banker had always been a stockbroker, of sorts—that is, some of the people who bought stocks, many of the people who bought bonds, and most of the people who bought Treasury papers did so through the agency of the bank. Banks had always entered brokerage orders for their trust accounts. The trust paid the brokerage fee, probably plus an override. (Banks are in trouble with the public because historically they *have* been hogs.) The bank got various free services from the brokerage house, which was forbidden by law to split its commission. Then the SEC prohibited fixed commissions on the exchanges, and banks had an opportunity to work out arrangements with brokers that would allow the banks to handle orders from depositors—payments for or receipts from securities transactions to be debited from or credited to checking accounts automatically—with some part of the commission paid to their banks for their services. It took only seven years for the first bank to grasp this opportunity. The pioneer was Security Pacific in Los Angeles, which in February 1982 announced arrangements with Fidelity Brokerage in Boston, the captive brokerage house of a mutual-fund group, to offer order-taking services at a discount (no advice for the customers) in Security Pacific branches. "A new era of opportunity for independent-minded investors capable of making their own trading decisions," says the brochure.

Presently, Citibank in New York and Crocker National in California established similar relations with the discount-brokerage firm of Quick & Reilly, and Chemical Bank in New York established a computer link through a division of Donaldson, Lufkin, Jenrette, via which any officer in any branch could process stock orders for customers, promising confirmation of the purchase and sale in something like two minutes. Fidelity began franchising its brokerage services to smaller banks and by mid-1983 had more than 400 banks on line. SEI Corp., a specialist in computer services for banks' trust departments, expanded to offer brokerage through whatever bank employees might be assigned to the task. And a group of S&Ls (combined assets, about $20 billion) set up a captive broker in Sarasota, Florida. "Hasn't done very well," said Robert Dockson, chairman of Cal Fed, one of the group. "I think we've let it down in our advertising." Maybe.

Finally, Bank of America made arrangements to purchase (for $53 million, or roughly three times book value) the largest of the discount brokers, Charles Schwab & Co. Approval from the Federal Reserve did not come through for that transaction until January 1983, and Union Planters National Bank of Memphis actually became the first modern bank to own a brokerage house when it bought the much smaller firm of Brenner Steed & Associates in fall 1982. (Union Planters could move faster because the bank itself was making the acquisition, and needed the consent only of the Comptroller; Bank of America was buying through its holding company, which meant the more cumbersome Federal Reserve Board had to approve.) Even before the Fed gave its approval to ownership of Schwab by Bank of America, Schwab was advertising a CMA-like service, presently improved by the new money-market accounts Bank of America promoted very heavily (and very successfully—$13 *billion* of deposits were logged in those accounts in this one bank in the first month). Meanwhile, in a charming example of turnabout-is-fair-play, Banc One has asked Merrill Lynch for advice on getting into the brokerage business.

It is by no means clear that the banks understand what they are doing. Citibank, for example, offered an "Asset Network Account," later renamed "Focus." A young sales manager in a branch, selling the account to this reporter, says, "You've heard of the Merrill Lynch Cash Management Account? Well, this is the same thing, only better, because we use a discount broker, saves you money." The brochure features a sample monthly statement, a "Confidential Client Update," with a list of the client's "Asset Position," which shows Uninvested Cash, Cash Management Fund, Government Fund, Certificates of Deposit, Cash Securities Account, and Margin Securities Account. But the statement does not list the securities that are in the Asset Position and does not indicate whether the asset value is calculated at cost or market. Indeed, the "Financial Activity This Month" chronicled in the Update does not show the movement in the price of the customer's stocks, which is apparently not considered part of the "client's" financial activity. The statement, in short, is financial activity as seen through the eyes of a banker, not through the eyes of a customer.

What is offered by the banks often seems a little cheesy next to what the brokerage houses do. Security Pacific, for example, will pay interest in the brokerage account only over the first $500, and the interest is credited monthly rather than daily. In the original Citibank account, the loan facilities offered were worse than no bargain at all. What the bank pushed was an unsecured line of credit, apparently at the usual horrendous rates. "Secured Credit for General Purposes" was also available at an unspecified rate, "lower than that on unsecured credit." But money cannot be borrowed on this chassis in quantities less than $5,000.

There was also a borrowing facility for margin purchases of stock—again, without any indication of the rate the customer was charged. (With the name change to "Focus" came an improvement in the terms of the margin loan, which was made competitive with Merrill's. But Citibank would not automatically kill the loan when new money came in: customers would have to pay interest to the bank until they specifically transferred the funds. Outrageously, the bank offered this rip-off as an *advantage,* proclaiming in its ads that while Merrill ran down your money-trust balances before putting your stock in margin, Citibank allowed you to borrow while maintaining your cash position.) Only the line of unsecured credit was available at the customer's own motion, through the Merrill Lynch device of simply writing a check; the others had to be negotiated out with the client's Account Officer. And this Account Officer is far from a customer's man—he will not give advice on buying or selling securities. The bank stresses that "because our Account Officers don't work on commission, you won't be badgered by telephone calls."

In fact, none of the banks that offered brokerage services in 1982 offered what the normal stock-market investor wants more than anything else: advice on how to make money. It may be—no one has tested—that the offering of full brokerage services would violate the Glass–Steagall Act, though in today's deregulatory atmosphere the fact that trust departments have always advised on investments (indeed, hold discretionary authority to *make* investments for trusts) would probably carry more weight in the courts than it did in 1971, when Citibank was enjoined from offering a mutual fund. The cases are clearly distinguishable by a court that wishes to make distinctions. In August 1983 the Comptroller allowed a nationally-chartered Texas bank to set up a division to give advice on the market, which ought to be—but three months later still had not become—an entering wedge. The Securities Industry Association has sued to overturn the Comptroller's approval.

Certainly, there is not much money for the banks in discount brokerage. The discount brokers have taken between 5% and 10% of the stock-market business, and with the advantage of a new presence in banks they can probably raise that percentage perceptibly—perhaps even double it. But the ceiling is relatively low because the brokerage customer *likes* to be "badgered by telephone calls": it's exciting, and he can be persuaded to believe it's financially rewarding. As the television commercials indicate—"Thank you, Paine, Webber"; "You look like you just heard from Dean Witter"; "When E. F. Hutton talks, people listen"; "At Smith Barney they make money the old-fashioned way: they *earn* it"—people like the idea of supposedly professional help with their investments. Very few people are, or should be, really confident of their ability to pick winners in the stock market.

In its fall 1982 pilot program Bank of America worked its brokerage operation through self-service stations on the banking floors of half a dozen branches. Each station had a Quotron machine from which the bank's customer could pick up current bid-and-asked, locked deposit boxes where the customer could deposit the securities he was selling, and a telephone plugged permanently into a Charles Schwab switchboard, through which the customer could enter buy orders or sell orders. (In June 1983 the bank set up manned Schwab brokerage stations in five of its thousand branches.) Purchases are paid for by automatic debits to Bank of America accounts; sales are accompanied by automatic credit to the accounts. Securities safekeeping is free—indeed, not the least of the attractions of the account is the greater safety of a Bank of America/Schwab depositary, with a record of the holdings maintained by the bank, much more secure than a mere safe-deposit box.

"The brokerage business in the banks will grow," said Joseph Pinola, chairman of First Interstate Bank Corp. (formerly United California Banks) in Los Angeles, one of the nation's ten largest, and of the ten the most dependent on middle-sized deposits and middle-market loans. "But it will not grow ad infinitum. And the number of players in the game will grow ad infinitum. We have to copy what the other banks are doing—it's a product, and customers will perceive us as a less useful bank if we don't offer it. But I don't expect to make any money on it."

Chemical Bank, which was into brokerage early, agrees: "We did a market study," said vice-chairman William Carson. "And we found it wasn't profitable and wasn't worth the flak from the securities people. But . . ." And Chemical offers what may be the best of the bank brokerage services—very low rates, margin loans as low as 0.75% above broker's call rates (over $50,000; 2% above call rates for loans below $10,000), plus a monthly "Statement of Investments," listing, among other things, the customer's holdings and their market price on the last day of the month. But it's no CMA—no credit card, no checkbook offering an automatic loan against the margin value of the account.

"We're making a commitment, not to discount brokerage," says Robert Thaler of Security Pacific, "but to an affluent delivery system. We can sell gold through a discount brokerage, or insurance. . . ." But there remains the question of why the affluent customer would wish to buy such services from a bank rather than from someone with whom his relations are likely to be more personal.

The problem is inescapable: anyone with a computer can offer banking services, and some of these services fit neatly into the pattern of what a brokerage customer would like from his broker. But the brokerage services a bank can offer *as a bank* remain second-class services, which will command second-class prices and yield second-class profits. The upper-income 20% has no reason whatsoever to wish for a bank-related "management account" rather than a brokerage account; most of the people who might find such an account attractive need more help with investments than the banks will—maybe can—give them. It is probably significant that Citibank's Focus requires a gross asset position of only $10,000, as against the Merrill Lynch $20,000: Citibank is offering a service for people who can't qualify at Merrill Lynch. To say the least, that's not Citicorp's self-image.

4

A further, unexpected challenge to the banks has come from the blurring of lines on the question of who can and who cannot own a bank. It seems not to have occurred to the bankers who developed the bank holding company in the 1920s that by finding a form through which banks could own nonbank enterprises they had also made it more difficult to keep off their turf nonbank enterprises that might wish to acquire a bank. In the Bank Holding Company Acts Congress did (over a number of dead bodies of bankers) make such developments less likely by restricting the subsidiaries of such holding companies to activities "closely related to banking," a category the Federal Reserve came to define rather narrowly. In the course of drafting the 1970 Amendments to the Bank Holding Company Act, however, Congress left an opening in the law by defining a bank as an institution that "(1) accepts deposits that the depositor has a legal right to withdraw on demand, and (2) engages in the business of making commercial loans."

In an article in the *Banking Law Journal,* Bruce Golden of the Chicago law firm of McDermott, Will & Emery points out the significance of the conjunctive: *both* requirements must be met. It cannot be said that Congress did not know what it was doing, for in the absence of such a definition, S&Ls and commercial-credit companies might have been held to be banks, subjecting them to a panoply of meaningless regulation and hugely overburdening the Federal Reserve, which is charged with regulating bank holding companies. But it seems likely that Congress did not know until after the event what in fact it had done.

In 1980 the fertile imagination of Charles Bluhdorn, a Viennese immigrant stock-market speculator whose deal-making genius had created the conglomerate Gulf + Western, produced the idea that the cheapest way into a funds-management business would be the acquisition of a bank that was doing only fair. The comptroller and the FDIC were pleased to see someone who wished to buy Fidelity National Bank of Concord, California; and the Fed decided that once the commercial loan portfolio was divested from the bank, its ownership was no longer subject to regulation under the Bank Holding Company Act.

Gulf + Western put its new bank into partnership with The Associates, the conglomerate's factoring and personal finance division. Meanwhile, efforts were made to enlarge the bank by selling Individual Retirement Accounts trusteed by Fidelity National across the country, wherever The Associates had an office. Avco, Household International, and Beneficial Finance followed in G + W's footsteps, also acquiring California banks, selling off the commercial portfolio, and redirecting the money into consumer finance.

The first of the brokerage houses to acquire a bank was Shearson/American Express, which bought The Boston Company in summer 1981, shortly before its absorption by American Express. A holding company for various trust banks, Boston had already acquired letters from the Fed exempting it from regulation under the 1970 Act: Shearson simply acquired in the normal course of business, without asking the Fed's permission. What Shearson wanted was a legal fiduciary that would enable the brokerage house to handle all aspects of pension funds and the trust side of money-market funds. Soon after the acquisition, Congress passed the "All-Savers" program, which opened up a gap of four percentage points between what banks had to pay on tax-exempt certificates of deposit and what they could earn on investment paper of matched length—and Shearson gratefully recouped most of the cost of acquiring the bank in a single year. Because American Express does so much banking business—traveler's checks, foreign lending and deposit taking, data processing for bank credit cards as well as its own through its First Data Resources subsidiary—it has always been careful to avoid supervision by bank regulators, and there is probably a limit to how prominent Shearson/American Express would like to see its bank become.

Others did not feel so constrained. Early in 1983, Prudential-Bache announced an intention to purchase a bank, and followed through later in the year by buying one in Georgia. In fall 1983, E. F. Hutton gained a Delaware charter to start a bank. Dreyfus Funds followed the Gulf + Western model, acquiring the Lincoln State Bank in New Jersey and winning a charter from the Comptroller for a brand new bank in New York City. By now the Federal Reserve was deeply concerned, and when the Garn–St. Germain bill was pending in Congress, chairman Volcker asked for an amendment to redefine a bank as a deposit-taking institution with deposits insured by the FDIC. The amendment failed, but in December 1982 the Fed intervened forcefully against Dreyfus, with a formal objection to the Comptroller and the FDIC, on the grounds that the purchase of other bank CDs—which the Dreyfus bank would continue to do, after selling off the commercial-loan portfolio—would still leave the institution within the Bank Holding Company definitions. The Comptroller did not find this argument convincing (neither, in truth, did the Board of Governors of the Fed, but it was the only handle they had).

A year later, on the theory that you might as well try it, the Board voted to write its objections to the Dreyfus charter into a regulation that would, as a story in *The Wall Street Journal* put it, "broaden significantly the legal definition of a bank." The Fed does not, in fact, have the power to do this, and the means chosen open some large cans of worms. It is more than a little awkward for the Fed to define the purchase of bank CDs or bankers' acceptances as commercial loans when it wishes to drive Dreyfus and Prudential out of the banking business while defining them as something other than loans when calculating whether a bank's portfolio violates the law against lending more than 15% of capital to a single borrower. (In the normal course of events when money is tight, big-city banks sell CDs to their country correspondents in quantities far exceeding 15% of the country cousins' capital; and the Fed had deliberately excluded bankers' acceptances from the category of "loans" earlier in 1983 to enable Bank of America and some scores of others in its syndicate to roll over credits to Mexico's Pemex that would otherwise have exceeded their lending limits.) Moreover, the Fed in the Gulf + Western case had quite specifically okayed (in an unpublished but well-publicized ruling) what it is now trying to forbid. The courts give a regulator considerable leeway but usually look askance when precedents are directly overruled—especially if the regulator has asked Congress to change the law that created the precedent, and Congress has refused to do so.

One of the companies planning a chain of consumer banks across the country—Dimension Financial Corp. of Denver—has sued to void the Fed's changes in "Regulation Y." The others are mostly lying low, because the Fed's staff apparently failed to investigate what in fact these "nonbank banks" did with their customers' deposits, and in fact the new definitions did not, as the Fed thought, bring them under the Bank Holding Company umbrella. Merrill Lynch cheerfully proceeded to start a bank, under charter from the State of New Jersey in early 1984—*after* the Fed's ukase—making itself exempt from the Bank Holding Company Act by not offering demand deposits; anyone who wants a checking account from Merrill Lynch, after all, can open a CMA. . .

Howard Stein, chairman of Dreyfus, a soft-spoken, slightly aggrieved man with superb marketing instincts, said when he first got his bank charter that he did not know for sure what he was going to do with it. Obviously, it would give Dreyfus an opportunity to sell an FDIC-insured money-market account if too much money ran out of its funds to the accounts the banks began offering at the end of 1982. Ownership of a bank would also strengthen Stein's bargaining position vis-à-vis The Bank of New York in his periodic negotiations over the cost of depositary and transfer services, and it would permit Dreyfus to issue a credit card under its own name.

The first publicized use of Dreyfus's New Jersey bank, however, was a more flamboyant gesture. At a time when the automobile companies' captive financing arms were making a splash with 11.9% auto loans, the Lincoln State Bank undercut the market with an 11% rate for Chrysler and Ford products. This quickly moved the $9 million that had flowed back to the bank through the sale of the commercial-loan portfolio, and because these two auto companies were willing to provide a subsidy (apparently enough to boost the effective rate by two percentage points), the car loans were profitable.

Early in 1983, Stein told *Fortune* magazine that he planned to use his banks to compete for consumer loan business nationwide: he thought he could make money at spreads much thinner than those the banks charge. He also wanted an S&L, he said, because he thought he could make money writing mortgages at rates lower than the S&L rates. His only problem, as he saw it, was gathering the deposits to fund the loans. Among his advantages in making loans, Stein suggested, was the mailing list of investors in Dreyfus funds. In late 1983, Dreyfus Bank (formerly Lincoln State) was busily devising "products" to lure both deposits and borrowings from Dreyfus Fund holders. It is by no means clear that the Fed ruling will make any change in these plans: Stein has plenty of consumer business to absorb his deposit base and can with only minimal sacrifice restrict his investment portfolio to Treasury paper and municipal bonds, leaving him still free from the new Fed definitions. You can find some cynics who believe (I do not) that the purpose of the Fed's new ruling against the nonbank banks was to open a new market for that paper the Treasury must sell so much of during the next few years.

Yet another mutual fund operator, Fidelity—which was also a brokerage house, the supplier of discount brokerage services to hundreds of banks—bought a bank in New Hampshire in 1982, to consolidate its offering of what was probably the most complete CMA-like service on the market. Fidelity's "USA" account had certain advantages over the Merrill Lynch original (daily investment of interest and dividends rather than a weekly sweep, checks returned with the monthly statement rather than held by the broker, free transfer among a wide choice of Fidelity mutual funds, pay-by-phone services, commission discounts, and cash at Automated Teller Machines). "New features and technologies will be continuously added," the ad proclaimed, "to keep Fidelity USA the most up-to-date financial service available." It was a credible claim, and a source of some bitterness to the banks that they could not match it.

Even more disturbing to the bankers than these small-scale ventures by the brokers was the arrival in the financial services industry of several large corporations from outside. Sears has been noted, but Sears had always been there. Now J. C. Penney was to follow, first on the wholesale level, offering its data-processing services to the oil companies' credit-card subsidiaries, then with a project to grab onto one of the banks' dreams for the future: home banking. In 1983 Penney bought from First Bank Systems of Minneapolis all rights to a system based on French teletext techology (including use of the French "Smart Card" for security), which the bank had developed and offered on a test basis to two hundred North Dakota farmers. By mid-1983 Penney was beginning to install Automated Teller Machines in its stores and was exploring cooperative ventures with several of the brokers.

Another newcomer was Parker Pen, which acquired a bank in New Hampshire and was permitted to run it as a bank, without Federal Reserve objections: it was through the Parker Pen subsidiary that Charles Schwab was able to launch his Schwab One account, a less expensive version of the Merrill Lynch CMA, even before he became associated with Bank of America. A chain of California furniture stores that ran its own credit department convinced the Comptroller to permit its solicitation of insured consumer deposits as a funding source for similar loans. ("We meet all the requirements," Richard A. McMahan, president of the chain, told Merle Lincoln Wolin of

The Wall Street Journal. "People just never thought they would go to a furniture store and be provided with banking services.") At the other end of the scale, General Electric, flush with $2.4 billion from the sale of its mining subsidiary Utah International, was seen prowling the halls and rattling doorknobs, looking for a more bankerly use of its data-processing capacities and of the General Electric Credit Corporation, which already had a loan portfolio larger than that of any but the thirty largest banks. But the purchase that really raised the hackles on the bankers' spines was National Steel's acquisition of Citizens Savings & Loan of San Francisco in 1979.

This was not a matter of bailing out a troubled thrift: When National acquired Citizens Savings, it was up-and-coming and highly profitable. The price was $250 million for a $3-billion S&L, and the man who had built the business, an impatient Californian named Anthony Frank, came along to manage it. He had a special philosophy: "I want to be all the bank a middle-class Californian needs." The aim, in 1979, was to win deposits with services rather than with interest rates. Citizens Savings, for example, gave free income-tax-preparation help to 25,000 people a year and offered free estate planning for people with trust accounts as small as $20,000. Frank wrote as many mortgages as he could—the year before National Steel acquired Citizens Savings, the S&L loaned $750 million to homebuyers, on an increase of only $50 million in its deposits and certificates. The mortgages were sold almost as fast as Frank could write them, leaving him with the fees for their origination and a profitable service contract thereafter. When the interest rates turned adverse to the thrifts, Citizens Savings was hurt much less than the others and was strong enough to pick up major S&Ls in New York City and Florida—pretty much free of charge, guaranteed against loss by the Federal Savings and Loan Insurance Corporation—and to create what Frank named 1st Nationwide Savings. In 1983 Penney arranged with 1st Nationwide to open financial service centers in half a dozen of its stores.

When SuperNow, the checking account with unrestricted interest rates, appeared on the scene in January 1983, 1st Nationwide Savings went after the deposits harder than any bank because checking accounts were the part of the mix it lacked. The commercial lending powers given to S&Ls in the Garn–St. Germain bill of 1982 widened the horizons of opportunity for the kind of equity-kicker, expanded upside loan Frank liked to make. (As early as 1979, he had $130 million in construction loans for buildings where Citizens Savings, in return for lending 85% rather than the traditional 80% of the cost, would get a share of the rental income and resale profits as well as the interest on the loan.)

The banks' obvious answer to such challenges is to acquire S&Ls themselves. Banks are prohibited by law from buying stock in S&Ls, but the Bank Holding Company Acts say nothing specifically about the linkage of a bank and a thrift in common ownership. It comes down to a question of whether the Fed accepts the ownership of an S&L as an activity "closely related to banking" and a "proper incident thereto." In listing the activities automatically permissible for a bank holding company, the Fed did not include the operation of an S&L, but it was understood that a bank takeover of a troubled thrift might be okayed if the circumstances were right. There was, in any event, little opportunity. Only a few S&Ls, on or near the West Coast, were owned by stockholders rather than by depositors. State commissioners chartered and supervised such institutions (until the 1970s, federally chartered S&Ls had to be mutual companies), and they did not look kindly on takeovers by banks. And while nothing in the law forbade federally chartered S&Ls from opening offices in other states—and the Federal Home Loan Bank Board had long been willing to authorize branching by S&Ls within a state whether or not the state approved such activities for its own thrifts and banks—it was understood that the FHLBB would not permit interstate activity without the approval of the state authorities.

Such fastidiousness went overboard with the crisis in the

thrifts in 1979–82. As part of the rescue operation, the Federal Savings and Loan Insurance Corporation arranged interstate mergers routinely (one of them, of course, resulting in the creation of 1st Nationwide Savings). And the FHLBB asserted the power to approve a takeover by an out-of-state commercial bank if that was the least expensive way for FSLIC to keep an ailing S&L alive. The opportunity to do this on the largest scale came the way of chairman Richard Pratt in 1982, and he seized it.

Fidelity Savings and Loan, at $2.9 billion in assets the fifteenth largest thrift in California, had gone quite seriously under water, victim of its proprietor's habit of borrowing—even at penalizing rates—from the Federal Home Loan Bank of San Francisco to meet loan commitments he could not fund from his deposit base or in the money market. This was a rather downscale S&L in terms of its locations, depositors, and loan portfolio. Headquarters was in Oakland, and Fidelity had been rather more responsive than most to California S&L Commissioner Linda Tsao Yang's push for socially purposeful lending. She tried to save it, first as a going institution and then as a merger partner for one of the other California S&Ls. When FSLIC took it over and held an auction for possible successors to buy the place out, the best bidder was Citicorp from New York. Miss Yang forced a new auction, but Citicorp won again. In September 1982 the Federal Reserve added its *nihil obstat* to the approval of the Federal Home Loan Bank Board, and Citibank had a foothold on the West Coast.

As part of the agreement with the regulators, Citicorp promised to continue to run the new "Citicorp Savings" as an S&L, with all but exclusive emphasis on real estate lending. This was not much of a sacrifice: Citicorp's captive finance company already had 19 offices in California for consumer loans, and the 400,000 Californians who already carried Citicorp Visa cards outnumbered the 300,000 Fidelity depositors. Though there would be economies of paper work in making commercial loans to California businesses through a

California lender, the scores of Citibankers already working the territory through the bank's Loan Production Offices were generating a California loan portfolio well in the billions long before chairman Walter Wriston cast his acquisitive eye on Fidelity. What the S&L offered Citicorp was the chance to build a major deposit base on the West Coast by providing the high-quality services by which the bank, despite its awful manners, has built the largest consumer franchise in New York.

Ten weeks after Citicorp won Fidelity, Bank of America launched the nation's biggest and most expensive drive to draw consumer deposits through the new money-market accounts. It is impossible not to believe that B of A, with its long history of paying savers the least it could get away with, took this uncharacteristic step as a preemptive strike against Citibank competition on the home turf. In fact, Citibank did not then wish to get into a bidding war for deposits in either California or New York, and more or less abstained, advertising its services rather than its rates. The Citibank rates on the "MMAs" ran as much as two percentage points below those offered by Chase Manhattan in New York and Bank of America on the West Coast. This experience was apparently unsatisfactory; when rates on six-month certificates were deregulated in October 1983, Citibank and Chase held an auction in the newspapers and on broadcast media, driving up the rates on such paper in New York 1.5% above the rates elsewhere in the country. (This bonanza was not offered to the depositors of Citicorp Savings in the more placid California market.)

At the beginning, the New York bank had no great stake in rocketing Fidelity's deposits, for most of the money taken in at the teller windows would have had to be used to pay off the S&L's enormous indebtedness at the Home Loan Bank. As rates dropped in early 1983, however, Citicorp moved to buy out of the Home Loan Bank, selling $1.1 billion of consumer CDs and pumping in $600 million of the parent's funds. By mid-1983, Citicorp began moving to make the S&L a flagship for a

West Coast flotilla, announcing plans to build a Los Angeles Citicorp Center for $600 million, merging its finance company offices into the Citicorp Savings structure, securing from the Federal Reserve Board a modification of its original takeover agreement that would permit the S&L division to use all the commercial lending powers allowed such institutions by the Garn–St. Germain bill. And in November 1983, Citicorp arranged with Safeway to allow cash withdrawals at the Safeway Automated Teller Machines by Citicorp Visa card holders, thereby giving Citicorp Savings a network of ATMs without a dime of capital investment.

Shortly before Christmas 1983, Citicorp used the continuing agony of the S&Ls—and of the Federal Savings & Loan Insurance Corporation—to take two giant steps toward its long-standing goal of national banking. On successive days, the FHLBB allowed Citicorp to enter the local markets on a thrift chassis in Chicago (where the New York holding company acquired First Federal, a recently created amalgam of three failing S&Ls, which did not get stronger when linked) and in Florida, where FSLIC wanted to get out of running Biscayne Federal, which was losing $2 million a month. With deposit-taking facilities in four of the nation's six largest states—on the opposite coasts, on the Great Lakes, and on the Gulf—Citicorp would become, indeed, a national institution. Both acquisitions were approved by the Federal Reserve Board in January 1984, even though Citicorp will be assuming some $7 billion of additional deposit liabilities while actually *reducing* its capital. (To win Federal approval, Citicorp pledged to raise another $350 million of what the Fed would be willing to call "capital.") Local banks and regulators in both Illinois and Florida would much rather not have Citicorp in their midst. But the FSLIC is in much worse shape than anyone has yet admitted, and the continuing high interest rates have left many S&Ls in a condition where they are going to need substantial help; for the sake of intragovernmental comity, the Fed swallowed its concerns about Citicorp.

The Federal Reserve is not particularly unhappy with interstate expansion by bank holding companies—with Fed approval, several of the larger banks now have finance-company subsidiaries, mortgage-banking subsidiaries, leasing subsidiaries, stock-brokerage subsidiaries and the like, that spread into dozens of states. In theory they cannot take deposits except where they are licensed to do so, but in fact the Fed has looked the other way when Citicorp markets across state lines a "Financial Account" that allows people to write checks against interest-bearing balances (this is, of course, only fair: what Citi offers here is nothing more than what the money-market funds do every day). What worries the Fed is not interstate banking *per se* but interstate operation of depository institutions owned by nonfinancial national corporations, especially insurance companies and stockbrokers that operate in areas the law has forbidden to banks and their holding companies.

In mid-1983 Volcker appealed to Congress for a moratorium on nonbank acquisitions of banks and bank acquisitions of additional nonbanking financial institutions. The regulators split: Comptroller C. T. Conover imposed his own moratorium on the purchase or formation of nationally chartered banks by anybody whose basic business was something other than banking, but FDIC chairman William Isaac announced a willingness to insure the deposits of any soundly operated or projected state-chartered bank, regardless of ownership. The SEC couldn't decide whether it liked or disliked the idea of banks owning brokerage firms; the Secretary of the Treasury (the former chairman of Merrill Lynch) said, Let 'er rip. The Congress, pressured by banks and S&Ls, investment houses, insurance agents, realtors, and others, went looking desperately for a place to hide. The Fed's remarkable coup in December was not so much an effort to accomplish the announced objectives—if worst came to worst, after all, most of the organizations the Fed was trying to drive out of "banking" could acquire state-chartered S&Ls and do virtually everything they can do with bank charters—but an attempt to win more urgent Congressional consideration.

II

The Transactions Business

3

EIGHT HUNDRED BILLION DOLLARS A DAY

T here is only one real money in the world," said Samuel Newman, a compact, chubby, balding New Yorker who manages the electronics end of fund transfers for Irving Trust, "and that's balances at the Federal Reserve."

"It's very hard," said E. Gerald Corrigan, a rotund, dark-haired New Yorker of aggressive mien transplanted to Minneapolis as president of that city's Federal Reserve Bank, "to find people who really understand the plumbing of the banking system."

THE TRANSACTIONS BUSINESS

1

Q. What did the banks do when you were a boy, grampa?
A. They made float.

Americans make on the order of one hundred billion payments a year, roughly two-thirds of them in cash. The average cash payment is something like $20, and the total of cash transactions is on the order of $1,250,000,000,000. The best guess of the cost of printing, replacing, handling cash is something like two billion dollars a year. Most but not quite all of this cost is met by the government, which prints the money at the Bureau of Printing and Engraving (or coins it at the Mint). It should be noted that U.S. paper money is a liability of a Federal Reserve Bank and is printed exclusively to the order of one of the twelve district banks in the Federal Reserve System, which pay the costs of printing it, about 2.3¢ per bill. Each bill is printed with a rosette identifying which of the Federal Reserve Banks has ordered it, letters A through L. Once upon a time, this question of the provenance of a Federal Reserve Note was quite a serious matter, and the district banks were required to return to the issuing bank any bill that had wandered across district lines, to make sure that rich districts that got lots of payments didn't draw gold from the South and West. When the promise to redeem the paper in gold came off the bills, the currency became wholly national except for the letter in the rosette, and each district bank simply puts back in circulation any Federal Reserve Note that comes its way from one of its sisters.

A Federal Reserve Bank issues currency in response to orders from the banks of its district, which pay for it (at face value) in the form of debits to the reserve accounts they must keep at their local Fed. The modifying "not quite all" in the statement that the government bears the cost of the cash system expresses the fact that the Feds charge the banks for the cost of trucking this money from their vaults, which is done by privately owned armored cars chartered for this purpose.

There is also, of course, a cost for both banks and merchants (and some lunatic fringe householders) in the expense of vaults, safes, etc., to hold the bundles. But of all the ways of paying small bills, cash is by far the cheapest. The pundits who have called for a "cashless society" have a wrongheaded sense of efficiencies.

All but a few hundred million of the other 35 billion payments are in the form of pieces of paper: checks and credit-card slips. These account for about $20 trillion in transactions, and the system is much more complicated than most people think. In my book *The Bankers,* I traced a check I had written to Piccozzi's Service Station on Shelter Island, New York, through the office of the Valley National Bank on Shelter Island, to the encoding room of the Valley National Bank in East Hampton (where the amount of the check was printed in machine-readable numbers under my signature, to enable computers to process the amount), to the Valley National Bank processing center in Valley Stream, New York, to the Federal Reserve Regional Check Processing Center in Jericho, New York, to the Federal Reserve Bank of New York main building at 33 Liberty Street, to the New York Clearing House on Broad Street, to the downtown processing center of Manufacturers Hanover Trust, to the midtown branch of Manny Hanny where I had my account. Nearly two dozen people had their hands on that check, or on the sack that contained it, during the course of the forty-five hours between the moment when Jake Piccozzi gave it through the teller's window and the moment a clerk on 43rd Street and Fifth Avenue put it in the folder in which my checks were kept pending their return to me with my monthly statement.

For Jake and myself, it was as though all these people worked for nothing: we paid no charge for the checking service. But nobody works for nothing—and the machinery that processed the checks cost the banks a bundle. By 1983, according to Paul Henderson of the Federal Reserve Bank of New York, who has organized a four-year, nationwide study of payments systems, the costs of operating a noncash, paper-based payments system averaged out to about 50¢ an item, or roughly $17 billion a year. That figure is bigger than the profits of the banking system. Nothing would improve the profitability of banking more quickly, more certainly, and more substantially than a reduction in the costs of these "operations," either through doing the job more cheaply or getting the users of the system to pay for it directly. By the same token, nothing would erode the profits of the system more quickly than an increase in the average cost per item in the operations division.

Unfortunately for the banks, the practical limits of mechanization and automation in check handling seem to have been reached. IBM did develop a machine that converted people's handwritten numbers to machine-readable MICR (Magnetic Ink Character Recognition) code, but the error rate was 50%, which made it impractical (particularly because a person must be employed at each machine to find out which 50%). The reader-sorters have gone about as far as they can go, separating checks into twenty-four or even thirty separate pockets on each pass, making a microfilm record of each check as it whizzes past; and the proportion of checks the machine can't handle has dropped to less than 1%. The new laser printers, gulping paper, can report what the computers are doing at a rate of 10,000 lines per minute. Admittedly, one never knows for sure what wonders they will think of next, but further technological improvement in check processing seems very unlikely. As check volume grows—and in the early 1980s it was still rising at a rate of more than 5% a year—the costs are now likely to rise, probably faster than the numbers: some operations gurus put the number as high as 15% a year, which is probably too high. A 15% increase in the cost of processing checks would depress the earnings of the U.S. banks as a group about as much as a default on the interest payments on their loans to Argentina.

The central feature of this paper-based noncash payments system is that it is a *debit-transfer* system. What circulates is a claim on the person who wrote the check or signed the credit-card slip. The final step in the long money-transfer process, the one that closes the transaction, is the debiting of the amount of the check from the account of its author. Thus there is a time delay between the use of the instrument to make a payment and the moment when the payment is actually accomplished from the payer's point of view. Legally, however, in the absence of specific instructions to the contrary (and always, of course, subject to collection), the payment is made as of the moment when the person being paid takes the check. There are even circumstances in which payment is deemed to have been made at the moment the post office takes possession. (Every April 15 there is a television feature on the late-night news about people clustering at the main post office somewhere, to make sure their payments to IRS are postmarked before midnight.) Someone who pays by check, then, gains a real advantage: he has the use of the money for some time after he pays, the time depending on the postal service, the speed of the bill collector in processing the check through its own accounting department, and the efficiency of the banks in moving the paper. If he can pay with a check on a bank far away, he gets an additional advantage in the time necessary to deliver the piece of paper—physically deliver it—to the only place where the debit can be entered to his account. This is the banking customers' "float": they not only like it, they count on it in planning their budgets. One of the reasons it's hard to rationalize the payments system is that *everybody* worries about losing his piece of the float.

Meanwhile, of course, the bill collector is best off if he can accelerate the passage of the check back to the bank on which it is drawn. Banks have offered services to speed up such collections, sometimes for a fee, more often as part of a "relationship" in which the corporation keeps interest-free demand balances at the bank. The most common of these "cash management services" is the "lock box," to which bills are paid by customers of public utilities, tenants in apartment houses, borrowers from finance companies, etc. The lock box is a post office facility emptied after each delivery by a bank rather than by the company being paid. When the check comes in, the bank credits it to the company's account, notes the bill as paid, and passes it on to the company. Instead of waiting for their money until after they have done the accounting that shows the bill as paid, the utility gets the money before it does the accounting, enabling it to earn interest on its funds or reduce its borrowings for working capital. The first lock box—I am indebted for this information to Paul Ben-Susan of Citicorp—was arranged by RCA with Bankers Trust in New York and the First National Bank of Chicago in 1947, when interest rates were only 2%. Nobody seems to remember why.

For large-value checks, banks may offer the biggest customers something more dramatic: a courier service that presents the check at the bank on which it is drawn, overnight or even the same day. Thus a check for $1,000,000 drawn on the First National Bank of Chicago and deposited in New York's Irving Trust Co. might be hustled out to an aircraft and presented before 2:00 P.M. (the deadline in the Universal Commercial Code) in Chicago. When pushed through the teller's window in Chicago, the check becomes an "on us" instrument, processed entirely within the bank, available that same day as part of the "correspondent balance" Irving maintains at First Chicago, and available to the Irving customer only one day later, if he has enough clout.

Getting the money was only part of "cash management": the banks also offered to put it to work, in Treasury paper or commercial paper, or overnight Eurodollar deposits, or whatever medium of investment the corporate treasurer might prefer. To make such investments efficiently, the corporations had to assemble their funds, and this "cash concentration" function was something else for which a bank could earn fees. Cash concentration is especially important for retail chains, which deposit the contents of the cash register every night in local banks. To know how much money they had available for investment, such companies needed the totals available in each bank, both from the previous day's cash deposits and from the checks deposited a few days back which had just become available funds in the account. The company gives one bank in each region the assignment to sweep all those accounts every morning and invest the money as the treasurer instructed or make it available for investment by others. Nonbanks as well as banks could perform cash concentration services, and perhaps the first venture by the S&Ls onto the banks' historic turf was in this area. In 1983 at least half the cash concentration assignments were performed by data-processing companies or thrifts.

But what really makes money in the debit-transfer system is not cleverness at accelerating credit to the recipient but audacity in delaying the debit to the payer, dragging out the time he can continue to earn interest on money after he has put the check in the mail. For years, businesses with offices in various parts of the country have cheated on the payments system by using accounts in remote places to pay their bills. United Airlines, for example, routinely paid its Chicago-based employees with checks drawn on accounts in San Francisco, and its San Francisco employees with checks drawn on accounts in Chicago. Until a lawsuit made the practice embarrassing, Merrill Lynch paid its East Coast customers who had sold stock with checks drawn on accounts in Tacoma, Washington, and West Coast customers with checks drawn on accounts in Charlotte, North Carolina. (Since the lawsuit, Merrill has paid everyone with checks on San Francisco banks, which means that people on the West Coast get the use of the money fast, but people on the East Coast, where most Merrill customers live,. do not.)

In principle, this "remote disbursement" is a zero-sum game: the delay in debiting the funds against the payer's account is matched by a delay in the availability of the funds to the depositor. In fact, it is usually worse than a zero-sum game because the price of two or three days' additional use of the funds by the payer is often a delay of a week or ten days before the depositor can draw against the check.

When remote disbursement became something nice girls did not do, emphasis came to be placed on a corporation's need to know, at a fairly early hour every morning, how much money it would have available for investment that day. This was quite impossible in New York or Chicago, where the banks exchanged checks with each other at the Clearing House at 10:00 in the morning. Thereafter there were fifteen minutes or so of striking the balance ritually in the little sunken amphitheater of the Clearing House, and the sacks of checks had to be delivered physically to the banks' operations center and run through the reader-sorters—and it was going to be afternoon before the corporate customer could be told how much had been debited to his account because of checks presented that day. But if the company had its disbursement account in, say, the Syracuse rather than the New York office of Chemical Bank, the checks being paid would be delivered to Syracuse from the Regional Check Processing Center in Utica at 6:00 A.M. , and by 10:00 (maybe 9:00) the corporation could find out precisely how big a hole in its account had been made by the checks paid today. In the late 1970s the RCPCs had become the fastest-growing operation of the Federal Reserve. The value of the checks cleared through the RCPC in Charlotte was greater than the value cleared through any Federal Reserve Bank main office except New York and Chicago, and the value cleared through Utica was greater than that through Cleveland or St. Louis or San Francisco.

From the point of view of the Federal Reserve, the banks' arguments were casuistry: the real point of the new "controlled" as of the old "remote" disbursement was to get the bill payer an extra day before his checks were debited to his account. And it was true until summer 1983 that the check written on the Syracuse account was likely actually to be paid out a day later than the check on the New York account. Irwin Ross reported in *Fortune* that McKesson Corp., with disbursement accounts in nine banks scattered across the country, made $5.5 million a year in interest on money invested overnight rather than paid out, because the accounts were kept in out-of-the-way banks. But just as paranoids may have real enemies, casuists sometimes have a case: efficient cash management does require controlled disbursement. In any event, changes we shall be considering in Chapter 6 have meant that checks drawn on Syracuse banks will be charged against an account on the same day as checks drawn on New York banks. If Charlotte and Utica keep their processing volume, the banks will be entitled to a few moments' resentment about unfair accusations.

If the first characteristic of the checking system is that debits move, the second is that the items can be dishonored (in the vernacular, "bounced") by the paying bank. There are three variants of this problem, depending on geographical situation. When the bounced check is "on us"—when one depositor of the bank has paid another one with a check not backed by sufficient funds or credit—the bank can handle the matter expeditiously, notifying (and charging) the parties for an unpaid item.

When the bounced check is used to pay someone with an account in another bank in the same clearinghouse, the Uniform Commercial Code provides that the bank refusing to pay the check must return it to the bank that presented it before midnight on the day after presentation. Generally speaking, the clearinghouses accelerate this process a few hours, requiring a bank bouncing a check presented by another bank to get it back to the clearinghouse the evening of the day after it first appeared there. The clearinghouse credits the bank returning the check (which had been debited for that amount in the previous day's settlement, on the assumption that the check was good), and debits the bank that presented it (which had been credited the first time around). The check itself returns to the bank that had sought to cash it, for return to the company or individual that had sought to deposit it, who can now seek their own remedies. Thus the rule that deposits in the form of checks drawn on local banks become "good funds" on the third business day: the check is presented to the payer's bank the day after it's deposited, must be returned the day after that if it is to be dishonored, and after passing through the depositor's bank's processing machinery once again that night, will be known as NG on the third day. If it is *not* known as No Good on that third day, the depositor should be able to draw against it.

All bets are off, however, when the bounced check is drawn on an out-of-town bank (and almost two-fifths of all checks not "on us"—i.e., not written to another depositor in the same bank—*are* from out-of-town banks). For reasons by no means entirely clear, the Federal Reserve System, which is not bound by the Uniform Commercial Code, has never felt itself under any obligation to expedite the handling of dishonored checks. There is a Regulation J, which echoes the UCC, but the Fed does not enforce it. A check written on Bank of America and deposited in Wachovia in Winston-Salem, North Carolina (and there are such) will go first to the Regional Check Processing Center in Charlotte, where Wachovia gets provisional credit, the money to be made available to Wachovia, by the Fed, in two days. It is then flown to Atlanta to be agglomerated with the other checks from the Sixth District, and flown on to San Francisco, to the Federal Reserve Bank for the Twelfth District, which presents it to Bank of America.

Because the Fed does not require Bank of America to return the check the next day if it is to be dishonored, the Bank of America processing center sends it on to the branch somewhere out in the Valley where the person who wrote it has his account. Bouncing a check is often a judgment call, especially when it is drawn against uncollected funds (perhaps an out-of-town check deposited four or five days earlier), and a credit manager may wish to look at it before he gives mortal offense to what may be a good customer. This can be done in a single day when it's a branch in the same city; but in a state like California, it takes time to move the paper. Either the Fed or Wachovia could demand that B of A pay off on any item not returned by midnight of the day after its presentation, but in fact they won't. From the Fed's point of view, after all, it's Bank of America's problem: the B of A reserve account has been debited by the amount of the check, B of A is losing interest on the money, and if B of A wishes to let that condition persist a little longer, it is no skin off the back of the Federal Reserve Bank. Wachovia, meanwhile, is ahead of the game: it now has credit from the Federal Reserve Bank of Atlanta, the funds are available to the bank, but it still has not made the money available to its depositor, for the very good reason that the check may turn up bounced any day.

Presently, the branch manager in California decides that this payer does not and in the immediate future will not have good funds on deposit to cover his check to his North Carolina supplier, and returns the check NSF (Insufficient Funds) to the Bank of America processing center, which returns it to the Federal Reserve Bank of San Francisco, which returns it to the Federal Reserve Bank of Atlanta, which returns it to the Regional Check Processing Center in Charlotte, which returns it to the Wachovia National Bank in Winston-Salem, which mails it back to the depositor with a little notice to the effect that he has X dollars fewer in his account than he thought he had.

It should be noted that this process is much slower than the process by which the check got from North Carolina to California. The magentic code recognition number on the check refers to the payer's bank, not to the bank that, by receiving and endorsing the check, has started the collection processing. Endorsements must be read by people rather than by machines, and the planes that fly checks between the Feds' processing "hubs" do not carry return items, which normally go out air mail. Since 1916 the Fed has required banks to notify *someone* "by wire" when they are planning to dishonor "high-value" items (now $2,500 and above), but as the regulation does not specify *who* is to be notified, or what is meant when the words say "by wire," the regulation has not been worth much. At one point some years ago, the Board of Governors came within an ace of requiring banks that use Fed clearing services to send a notice that they were bouncing a check directly to the bank seeking to collect it, but that would complicate the Feds' own bookkeeping, and the proposal was dropped.

Roughly 100,000,000 checks bounced back through the Federal Reserve Banks in 1982, just over 1.25% of the checks processed. Boston and Minneapolis were the only districts where less than 1% of the checks bounced; in Dallas, St. Louis, and San Francisco, the rates of dishonor were more than 1.5%. The figure for the Feds argues that 175,000,000 checks bounced from bank to bank in the system—and that another 175,000,000 bounced inside individual banks as "on us" items that were processed internally. Many of these dishonored checks were simply resubmitted by the companies that received them, and about three-fifths of them cleared the second time around: they had been bounced originally only because the person who wrote them was slow or optimistic about getting the money to the bank in time to cover the check. But some nontrivial portion represented uncollectible bills—no small part of the societal cost of a system that operates through a debit-transfer payments system.

The average check written in the United States in 1982 was for about $600, a figure clearly inflated by the small number (0.6%) of checks written for large amounts ($10,000 and more). A quarter of the checks were for $16 or less. At both ends of the continuum, the use of checks to pay bills is nothing short of preposterous. The large items should move through wire transfer of funds, and the small items should be paid in cash— though admittedly there is a problem with the small checks written to be mailed in payment of small bills, because nobody wants to see cash in the mails. What keeps much of the paper flying around the country in the 1980s is the fact that the banks consider themselves beneficiaries of the inefficiencies—and, to a large extent, they are.

The most obvious and profitable break the system gives the banks is their power to deny depositors the use of funds from out-of-state checks for periods of up to ten business days.

(Indeed, one of the arguments that sold computers to the community banks was that the daily printout would enable them to distinguish between collected and uncollected funds, and to control the availabilities they gave their depositors.) Something like $3 trillion of deposited checks are delayed this way during the course of a year. For ease of calculation, assume that the average delay is five business days beyond the date when the Fed makes the money available to the bank presenting the check. On the average, with this assumption, the banks have the use of $60 billion a day of depositors' money that the depositor cannot draw. This is the banks' float on their customers, and it's not to be laughed at. At $60 billion and a 10% interest rate, the contribution to the banks from this artifice of the payments system would be $6 billion a year—two-fifths the estimated cost of operating the system.

On the other hand, the banks are entirely correct in their claim that they cannot afford to absorb the losses from returned checks. Senator Christopher Dodd of Connecticut, who has been trying to write a law that would compel banks to give earlier credit for out-of-state checks, argues scornfully that "only one-half of one percent of the checks are ultimately 'uncollectible.'" That spells disaster for the banks. On a $3 trillion volume, Dodd's figure of 0.5% would mean a loss of $15 billion a year, wiping out the profitability of the industry. Nevertheless, New York and California have passed laws limiting the banks' powers to delay availability of funds to their depositors. The regulations written by the New York Banking Department require that checks for less than $100 be given immediate credit, checks for higher sums written on banks in the same community receive credit in two business days, and checks on out-of-town banks be credited within five business days. The California law is still at this writing a general injunction to that state's banking department to *do something,* but eventually rules will be forthcoming. If nothing changes, the losses to the banks could be considerable.

But there is a relatively easy solution to this problem,

discussed under the code name "truncation." With truncation of returns, each Fed would assemble every day the data on checks bounced by the banks in its district, and pass the message on electronically through its sister Feds to the banks that are going to have to give back the credits. Coupled with a determination to live up to Regulation J and the Uniform Commercial Code rules for how soon a check must be bounced, truncation would reduce to four days the maximum time between the deposit of the check and the discovery by the bank in which it was deposited that this one isn't going to be paid. Indeed, one of the services the Federal Reserve Banks already offer subscribers to their direct-wire communications system is early warning of high-value returned checks—but the warning is given only after the item returns to the collecting bank's own district Fed. (And it is a significant service only to remote and rather innocent banks: the big-city banks will have handled high-value checks through courier services and direct presentment, without putting the paper into the Fed at all.) There is, however, no evidence that banks receiving this Fed service are quicker than others to make funds available to depositors. And, to say the least, there has been no pressure on the Fed from the banks to move toward check truncation; what pressure there is goes against it.

Part of the problem is that bouncing checks is the most profitable activity a bank performs. The most common charge for a bounced check in 1983 was probably $7, but $10 is common and some banks go much higher—Philadelphia's Girard, now a subsidiary of Mellon Bank, charges $30. Assuming 400 million bounced checks a year, charges imposed for half of them and an average penalty of $8, banks' income from this source runs $1.6 billion annually. Costs are low: the Fed makes no charge at all for its handling of return items. And some banks charge the depositors of dishonored checks as well as the issuer, which is a classic case of *chutzpah,* for the customer has never had the use of the money from the bounced check, while the bank has had two to ten days' worth of credit in that amount from the Fed.

In the end, all these ways to cheat on the chassis of the debit-transfer system will die out, victims of deregulation. Competing with each other, banks will have to offer better availability of funds; Citibank is already winning balances from New Yorkers by offering instant credit on checks deposited in a teller machine by customers who have a certain minimum on account in a range of Citibank certificates, etc. As part of their cash-management program, large corporations have already negotiated their own availability schedules with the banks, taking the lion's share of the value of accelerated availability through the use of courier services and direct presentment to the bank on which the check is drawn. Rising public consciousness of the problem, whether or not expressed in legislation, will speed up the banks' response, and will perhaps lead to truncation of all checks—that is, to the electronic capture of the information on all paper checks in their first processing pass, and the subsequent clearing, crediting, and debiting in response to electronic messages rather than the arrival of the paper. "When you move to the point where most checks are collected in twenty-four hours," says E. Gerald Corrigan, president of the Federal Reserve Bank of Minneapolis, a chunky young Irishman who was Paul Volcker's walking delegate to the committees planning the Fed's future role in the payments system, " you remove much of the incentive for the paper-based system."

Banks will lose income when they must reduce their delays in giving the depositors the use of their money, and more income when faster availability diminishes the incidence of bounced checks (most of which bounce because of uncollected funds). Meanwhile, their costs in maintaining the payments system will rise as the market compels them to pay interest on demand deposits. The obvious response is the reintroduction of charges for checking services. By themselves, these charges will reduce the number of checks written for less than $16 and speed the development of a better, credit-transfer system for the payment of bills. In Chapter 5 we shall look at how that system should work for consumers and for ordinary business transactions. First we need to know about the wholesale credit-transfer systems that already exist, and that move about seven times as much money as moves by checks, every day.

2

FedWire is a system for the electronic transfer of Fed Funds. It has been around since 1918 as the means by which the regional Federal Reserve Banks adjusted their accounts with each other. Fed Funds are nothing more nor less than the noncash reserves of the banking system: the credits "depository institutions" that offer checking accounts must keep on the books of their local Fed. Because the Fed also operates the check-clearing mechanism for the system—the concluding episode even at a nongovernmental clearinghouse is a transfer to or from its reserves at the Fed for each of the participating banks—these reserves serve functionally as the transaction balances of the banks themselves.

As early as the 1920s, a broker named George Garvin saw that the dual function of bank reserves made it possible for banks to borrow from each other by the direct transfer of reserves on the books of the Fed. His firm of Garvin, Bantel & Co. developed a sideline in the brokerage of Fed Funds, helping banks that had excess reserves in their accounts lend them to banks that needed such credits on the Fed's books to maintain the proper ratios (or, on some days, to meet payments when the checks drawn by their customers greatly exceeded the new deposits coming into the bank). Reserves could be transferred instantaneously from one bank to another by means of a telephone call to the Fed (which would promptly call back to confirm), and because of FedWire it was almost equally easy to transfer bank reserves from district to district. The beauty of a Fed Funds borrowing was that it produced immediate money—just about the only immediate money possible to the banking system. It took time to move cash. If a bank bought a CD from another bank the payment was by check, which would be presented the next morning at the clearinghouse: the payment was in "clearinghouse funds," good with a one-day lag. But if a bank borrowed Fed Funds directly from another bank, the payment was good the same day.

What limited the Fed Funds market before 1963 was the law prohibiting an insured bank from lending to any one customer a sum equal to more than 10% of its capital and surplus. For a $20 million bank, say, with $1.5 million capitalization, the maximum Fed Funds loan would be $150,000, which was scarcely worth the candle on either side of the transaction. But in 1963 Kennedy's Comptroller of the Currency, James Saxon, ruled that an overnight Fed Funds transaction was a purchase and then a resale, not a borrowing and then a repayment, and all limits were off. When interest rates soared in 1966, 1969, 1974, 1979, and 1981, banks in smaller cities and in the countryside found that by holding off on loans and building up their transaction balances at the Fed (or their deposits in correspondent banks, if they were not Fed members), they could sell their money overnight to the money-center banks at interest rates much higher than they could charge their local customers. Smaller banks rented their money out through correspondents, larger banks did their own trading from expanded "money desks" or used the services of a broker, usually Garvin, Bantel or its major rival, Mabon, Nugent.

By the 1980s there were sixty men and women at Garvin, Bantel, fully occupied with the brokerage of Fed Funds, sitting at ranks of phone consoles in the old Equitable Building just north of Wall Street, telling hundreds of banks that called in every fifteen minutes or so that as of this instant they could buy Fed Funds for, say, 9.8% ($268.50 per million dollars per night) or sell them at 9.75%. Early on, the banks were fastidious about which banks they would sell to—for whatever the Comptroller might say, a Fed Funds transaction is really an unsecured loan from one bank to another—but as time went on, the banks lengthened their lists of acceptable recipients of their money. It was part of the expertise of the Garvin, Bantel broker to know whether the bids in the market were from banks with which the individual bank on the telephone was willing to do business.

By the late 1960s the volume of Fed Funds trading had made it awkward for the Fed to do this business by hand, with telephone calls from the banks and to the banks to place the orders and secure the confirmations, and telephone operators at the Fed writing tickets to tell the bookkeepers to shift the money. The phone-call system was accident prone; the clerks were overloaded and the ledgers were confusing. As the decade passed, the larger bank began keyboarding their wire transfer information to machines at the Fed. In 1969 Fed Funds transfers were computerized, and the banks that dealt heavily in Fed Funds were given direct access to the computer—that is, they could key their sales into the Fed's books without any intervention by a Fed employee, and the confirmation to the purchaser that the transfer had been made would print out automatically in the computer room of the bank making the purchase.

By now we are in the era of "cash management," with banks offering their large corporate customers a service guaranteeing them that the balances in their accounts will never lie idle in the bank overnight, but will always be invested in interest-earning assets. As the bank still cannot legally pay interest itself on demand deposits, the device is the "repurchase agreement," by which the company uses its deposit to "buy" a Treasury security, which the bank will buy back (at a very slightly higher price: really, the interest on the secured loan) the next day. In the old days, such a "repo" would have involved the physical transfer of the security from the custody of the bank to the custody of the corporate customer, but now there are no such certificates—holdings of Treasury bills are represented by book entries at the Fed rather than by pieces of parchment. So FedWire does double duty, transferring book-entry T-bills as well as Fed Funds. In effect, the corporate customer has sold the bank Fed Funds; because in the absence of such a transaction, the corporation would have lent its money elsewhere, moving funds in a way that reduced the original bank's reserve/clearing account at the Fed.

Everything has speeded up enormously. Instead of companies collecting their bills and depositing the proceeds in the bank, the bank, for a fee, operates a "lock box" in the post office and takes the payments, notifying the company after its account has been credited. The company wants that money at work *now;* for another fee, the bank sees to it that the company has no idle balances. Banks offer "zero-balance" and "controlled-disbursement" accounts to large customers, who may write "payable through drafts" instead of checks when paying their bills; for yet another fee, the bank honors the drafts and the large customer provides the funds later, paying interest if (and only if) the bank has to carry the burden overnight. In this atmosphere, customers want to make their payments at the last possible moment—and they want to receive wire transfer of funds from the firms that owe money to them.

But it is not so easy for these payments to be made if the only address on the FedWire message is that of the bank to which the funds are being sent. Company A can notify Company B that it is instructing its bank to wire funds to Company B's bank to pay money A owes B. But B then has the problem of making sure that the bank enters the resulting credit to the right account. For wire transfer to work without an unacceptable level of foul-up in our fouled-up world, the message that moves the funds must contain the address of the ultimate recipient as well as the address of the bank. In 1973, confident of the capacity of its Xerox-built "Sigma" computer system, the New York Fed began to encourage the use of FedWire "third-party payments." The messages on FedWire began to tell the receiving bank that the sending bank was transferring the money from the account of its (named) customer to be credited to the account of (named) customer at the receiving bank. One more step remained: the banks hooked up their computers to the big customers' computers in such a way that the Hertz division of RCA, for example, could pay Ford $6 million for a thousand new cars by pushing keys on a terminal that would move that much money out of, say, the Chase Manhattan Bank, through the New York Fed, through the Chicago Fed, to its Detroit branch for credit to the National Bank of Detroit and specifically to the account of the Ford Motor Company.

All this would be untouched by human hands. Provided that $6 million was within the Hertz credit limit at Chase, the message would simply flow through (leaving an automatically generated audit trail of paper printout and magnetic blip), and the money would move—irrevocably, in a payment as final as handing over the cash.*

Once upon a time, lawyers closed a big deal by having the buyer ritually present the seller with a certified check in the amount of the purchase. In the 1980s a deal closes when the lawyer for the seller puts on the table the Telex message confirming that the buyer has made a wire transfer of funds in the requisite amount.

3

The quantities of money that move electronically every day are quite unimaginable. In 1983 about 100 million payments a year were being made through FedWire or one of the other three wire-transfer systems, and they were moving at least $150 trillion a year—a total forty times the nation's Gross National Product and almost two hundred times the federal budget. And all this is very recent: in 1974, when I wrote *The Bankers,* FedWire was still something pretty much internal, part of the

---

*Names are for illustration only; the corporations cited may use these or other banks for such transactions.

lubrication of the banking system. Real money—the stuff people and businesses use to make payments to each other—moved through by check.

FedWire is the largest and simplest of the electronic payments systems. On behalf of its customer, a bank simply transfers part of its reserve balance on the books of its local Fed to another bank, which accepts the money on behalf of its depositor. On an ordinary day, these reserves turn over about twelve times—that is, the average bank of median size and larger will pay out (and, God willing, receive) sums totaling twelve times their actual overnight reserve balances. From bank to bank, the payment is immediate: one bank's reserves at the Fed are debited and the other bank's reserves are credited.

Each district Fed has its own computer system for the maintenance of the accounts of the banks in its area. Transfers from one district to another used to be accomplished through a switching center in Culpeper, Virginia. As FRCS 80 (Federal Reserve Communications System for the 80s) phased in, the districts got into direct contact, through packet-switching nodes, with a central processor in Chicago to keep records. The payment is final, like cash—if a bank makes a mistake, sending the wrong amount or addressing the payment to the wrong bank on the other side of the transaction, it's a matter for the two banks (and maybe their lawyers) to work out between themselves. On the other hand, if the Fed makes an error, it will rewrite the ledgers for the day to appear as though the mistake had not happened. Being the government is a little like being God.

The first step in a FedWire payment is a debit by the paying bank from the account of the customer making the payment. This prior debit creates the credit that then moves to the customer receiving the payment: nothing can be bounced because if the customer has insufficient funds (or an insufficient line of credit), the sending bank never enters the order. How soon the customer receiving the payment gets word that this money is now his, to have and to hold, depends on the arrangements between that customer and the bank receiving the money on his behalf. Among the cash-management services offered by the big banks is automatic and immediate notification to the customer through a computer link. Otherwise, the receiving bank gets on the telephone at its convenience to convey the good news.

Before examining the details, pleasures, and problems of FedWire payments, it would be best to look at the competition, which comes in three varieties: CHIPS (the New York Clearing House Interbank Payments System); BankWire (a.k.a. Cash-Wire, a cooperative venture of about two hundred U.S. banks); and SWIFT (the Society for Worldwide Interbank Financial Telecommunications, a Belgian-based bank-to-bank network now hooked into about a thousand banks worldwide, and interacting with the other three transfer systems). There is also another system for the electronic transfer of funds, on a batched rather than an on-line basis, through the nation's 32 Automated Clearing Houses; we shall take a look at that one in Chapter 5.

CHIPS was the first electronic transfer system for bankers' use; it opened for business in 1970. Its purpose was to blend the enormous and rapidly growing volume of offshore dollar transactions into the daily New York clearing, without putting the New York banks to the nuisance and delay of writing checks to each other on behalf of their foreign correspondent banks. Eurodollars may be domiciled abroad, but their use inevitably takes them through the United States. The only "real" dollars are those created under the aegis of the U.S. Government, and the only lender of last resort that can create dollars in time of need is the Federal Reserve System. In theory, banks can clear their dollar-denominated transactions with each other wherever they wish (London has a small "retail" clearing that moves about $30 million a day), but U.S. banks with access to the U.S. money market and the Fed are all but required if the payments system is to operate smoothly.

CHIPS has two categories of members: "settling" banks, which will balance the books of the Clearing House at the end of the day, and "participating" banks, which are empowered to make and receive payments through the Clearing House computer but must deliver or receive the funds through a correspondent "settler." Until 1979, only the twelve New York banks that were members of the Clearing House could settle at CHIPS, which diminished somewhat the attractiveness of the out-of-town banks as correspondents for foreigners doing a dollar business that had to be cleared every night. (Charles F. Bates of the American Bankers Association, a feisty, chubby bank operations specialist in his forties, argues that CHIPS "shovels money to New York—it's a funnel that runs one way, to New York.") In 1979, responding to complaints from Chicago and San Francisco, the Clearing House turned over to the Federal Reserve Bank of New York the power to choose the banks that would be acceptable as settling members, and ten others have joined. Some, like Bank of America, have become settling members through their "Edge Act" subsidiaries (foreign trade branches: the B of A Edge Act in New York has about $6 billion in assets); others, like Continental–Illinois, have joined from their headquarters offices out-of-town.

About 125 banks are CHIPS participants. To participate, a bank must have $250 million in capital and surplus. Local capital and surplus are required: foreign branches and Edge Act subsidiaries will be admitted to the club only if they provide a "comfort letter" from their parent, pledging to pick up debits if necessary. All must have New York City offices that are linked by direct wire to the CHIPS computer. As with FedWire, the banks make payments through CHIPS to other banks, with a memo item indicating the customer who is paying and the account to which the payment should be credited. To make sure there is no mistake about that, this information may be conveyed separately from the paying bank to the receiving bank by Telex or SWIFT or BankWire. Where the bank that will ultimately receive the payment is not a CHIPS member, its correspondent in New York takes responsibility for sending the necessary "advices."

A CHIPS entry is not in itself a payment: it is a promise to pay at the moment of settlement. As in a check clearing, the end result of a day's entries is a net balance owed (if a bank's payments out for the day have exceeded its payments in) or claimed (if the payments in have exceeded the payments out). About 70,000 payments are entered every day, roughly two-fifths of them by the New York banks, one-third by foreign banks. The Clearing House processes all entries from all banks and winnows them down to twenty-two payments from or payments to the settling banks. On $300 billion of transactions, which was a large but not extraordinary day in CHIPS in 1983, the transfers at the end might total only $4 billion to $5 billion. Once upon a time, CHIPS payments, like those at a check clearing, were made to or from the Clearing House itself. The Fed in the late 1970s decided it didn't like that system, and now CHIPS tells the banks that owe how large a FedWire payment each should make directly to the banks with black ink on that day's electronic ledger.

At the moment of settlement, then, the Federal Reserve Bank of New York becomes intimately involved in the process. The money due the Clearing House from participating banks that do not settle for themselves must be wired through Fed-Wire to the settling bank that represents them. And the actual payments and receipts that the Clearing House certifies when the CHIPS computer blips its goodnight are (like FedWire payments and receipts) transfers of the reserve balances of the settling banks. Until October 1, 1981, CHIPS settled the morning after the transactions were registered, at the same time (though on a different settlements sheet) as the balance was struck in the New York check clearing. Since October 1981, CHIPS has run on a basis of same-day settlement: that is, each bank that makes a payments entry into CHIPS must be prepared to get the money to its correspondent bank or to the Fed by 6:00 that same evening.

It should be noted now—we shall study the significance of the fact a little later—that from the point of view of the banks this really is a same-day payment because the Fed measures their actual reserves against their required reserves only in the still of the night. Any addition to reserves from the CHIPS settlement is part of a bank's reserve the same night; any disbursement through the CHIPS settlement leaves the bank's reserves shorter than they would have been. From the customer's point of view, however, a CHIPS payment is tomorrow's money: there isn't much he can do about investing his newly arrived funds after six in the evening.

BankWire is a far smaller operation, tracing back to a decision in 1952 by the New York and Chicago clearinghouse banks, which decided they needed a dedicated wire system to interchange information about high-value checks en route from one to the other. The wire was operated by Western Union and was simply a specialized Telex service. In 1968 this operation was computerized, given the name BankWire, and made available to banks all around the country; more than 200 of them subscribed. With the arrival of third-party payment over Fed-Wire, BankWire assumed new importance, for the Fed did not give senders an opportunity to edit their FedWire messages to provide confirmation that money had been received at the other end. In 1975 BankWire recruited Bernhard Romberg, a computer expert and systems designer with Arthur D. Little, to run what was becoming a complicated operation, handling 20,000 messages a day, and to plan for CashWire, a more elaborate system that would be capable of managing, in effect, an electronic clearinghouse to settle that day's payments among the participating banks.

But clearinghouses can operate in the United States only with the consent and cooperation of the Federal Reserve because the final act of settlement is the transfer of funds in the banks' reserve accounts. Romberg, a large, earnest ruminative man whose slow manner and placid exterior conceal a fighting temperament, had his settlement system ready to go by 1979, but the Fed dragged its feet in giving approval to BankWire as a funds transfer system, and it was not until 1982 that CashWire was permitted to set up shop as a competitor to FedWire and

CHIPS. Even then, the value of the system was somewhat reduced by a peculiarity in the Fed's agreement. Though the 100-odd participating banks would send their FedWire payments to settle their CashWire accounts by 6:00 P.M., the settlement would not be "final"—the banks would not receive Fed notification of the change in their reserve positions—until nine o'clock the following morning. The ostensible reason was that CashWire required bookkeeping at all twelve district Feds (as against only the Federal Reserve Bank of New York for CHIPS, which *did* offer finality at 6:30 the evening of the same day), and thus could not be fully accomplished until those banks closed their own books early in the morning of the following day. The real reason, Romberg and his associates feel darkly, is that the Fed was crippling a potentially serious competitor. In January 1984, Romberg moved on to his own electronics consulting firm, and the leadership of BankWire was given to a former Wells Fargo vice-president who was less likely to become impatient with the Federal Reserve.

As a service designed for a large bankers' cooperative, BankWire offers features to make the banks' life a little easier, notably a complete daily ledger (retrievable for sixty days from the computers) of all payments activities through CashWire for each participating bank. This information can be gathered during the course of the day as well as after settlement: "What we have," says Romberg, "is a payments *management* system, not just a payments system."

The fourth of the on-line credit-transfer systems is SWIFT, the Society of Worldwide Interbank Financial Telecommunications, which started operations in 1977 on a European base, in large part to escape what were seen as discriminatory rules favoring U.S. banks on both Fedwire and CHIPS. Very much the creation of one irascible man, general manager Carl Reuterskiöld, SWIFT is a "payments *message* handling system," transferring funds only on a bank-to-bank basis through reductions or increases in correspondent accounts the member banks maintain with each other. This, of course, was the way banking was done in the old days, before the creation of international markets: banks served their domestic customers when abroad through direct relations, including mutual deposit of interbank funds, with networks of correspondents around the world. SWIFT takes the old ways and brings them up to date by exploiting the possibilities of telecommunications and the existence of the other payments systems. In 1983 almost 400,000 messages (19% originating in the United States) were sent from bank to bank each day over SWIFT operating centers in the Netherlands (for Northern Europe), Belgium (for Southern Europe), and the United States, through Burroughs processing units maintained in each country. The banks themselves have special terminals dedicated to SWIFT use, made to the SWIFT order by Burroughs and Texas Instruments.

Many of these SWIFT messages instructed a remote bank to act, in effect, as the Fed acts in FedWire, transferring money from the account of one correspondent to the account of another. How much money moves within individual banks in response to such SWIFT messages is quite undiscoverable. Other SWIFT messages are purely informational, as when a bank alerts the system to bad checks or stolen securities in circulation. Still others seek verification, confirmation or correction of payments or other information, or status reports on accounts. Perhaps the largest single group of messages, however, are instructions relating to payments orders to be made through national payments systems or in CHIPS. George Mitchell of the Federal Reserve estimates that three-quarters of all CHIPS entries originate in SWIFT wires.

Periodically, rumors report that SWIFT is seeking an *agrément* with the Fed to permit multilateral settlement among members rather than today's bilateral credits and debits. W. Robert Moore, senior vice-president of Chemical, a rangy, laconic banker of an older school who is the American vice-chairman of SWIFT, says the staff would like the settlement but the board knows better; this probably translates into an observation that the Europeans and Japanese would like to escape the Fed's veto on daylight overdrafts by foreign banks, and the New York banks have said, Forget it. "The New York banks make money," said one of their less obedient servants, "by having other banks hold deposits to handle transactions across the books of the New York banks."

All these systems were required by—and promoted the expansion of—international financial markets. As the stock market makes possible the issuance of new equity securities (in a volume that may amount to perhaps 2% of the value of the stocks traded), the wholesale electronic funds transfer systems do contribute to the extension of credit both domestically and internationally, and promote the flow of real goods through trade channels. But the numbers are ludicrously outscale to those in the real economy. By far the most important commodity in international trade is oil, which accounts for almost 15% of all international payments. For all of 1982, that meant about $250 billion—which was about as much as CHIPS moved each *day*.

Foreign-exchange trading accounts for the largest single piece of funds transfer, probably $100 billion a day. The market for currencies works through the dollar—that is, someone with Dutch guilders who wants Italian lire will probably sell guilders for dollars and then dollars for lire, which means two dollar payments for every transaction. There are separate currency markets in New York, London, Frankfurt, Paris, Zurich, Tokyo, Bahrain, Singapore, and Hong Kong, and during several hours of the day it is possible to arbitrage among them—that is, to take advantage of any difference in currency prices on different markets, buying on one and selling on another for a tiny but sure profit. Because of the extreme volatility that has characterized currency values since the arrival of floating rates in 1973—it is nothing extraordinary for the price of one currency in terms of another to move more than 1% in a single day—traders like to smooth out their positions (selling forward what they now own, buying forward what they owe) not only before they go to sleep at night, but repeatedly during the course of the day. The result is a torrent of transactions that would have been inconceivable as recently as ten years ago, and floods of payments through CHIPS, SWIFT, and FedWire.

Domestically, too, the growth of "cash management" has meant the incessant buying and selling of paper for overnight earnings. At 10%, which has been no great shakes of an interest rate in the last few years, $10 million overnight is worth $2,704. With the total FedWire costs at $5.20 to move both money and securities back and forth in a repurchase agreement, even a $100,000 overnight "repo" is worthwhile for banks. The major money-center banks turn over the entire bank every day, and purchase on a very short-term basis half or even more of the funds they lend. Outside the banking system, the availability of same-day funds transfer has promoted the growth of new instruments, up to and including futures markets on options, which can be used for hedging or gambling on the shortest time horizons. It is by no means clear that the gains in efficiency—the income-producing use of every available bit of money and credit every day—are worth the increased fragility of the system. But the bomb has been invented; we all have to live with unthinkable propositions in the economic world as we do in the military world. Somehow everyone gets used to not thinking about it.

"People ask me what I do at Morgan," said James T. Byrne, a square-shouldered, youthful vice-president in that bank's operations department. "I tell them that every day between two and four in the afternoon, I move a billion dollars a minute. They sort of change the subject."

4

SYSTEM RISKS

I would be frightened," said
John F. Lee, the brisk yet casual executive vice-president who
runs the New York Clearing House, "and I think any congressman would be terrified, if the banks were snapshot at noon.
They've paid it all out, and they haven't collected it yet."

1

What gives the industry occasional fits about FedWire is the
risk that someone will break into the system and make himself
rich beyond the dreams of avarice with a single, multimillion-
dollar misappropriation of a payments message. There are, in
fact, four known instances of swindles perpetrated through

FedWire: one by a consultant working with Security Pacific Bank; one by a clerk at Bausch & Lomb in Rochester (he got one of the numbers wrong in his firm's code, and the woman monitoring the message at Lincoln Rochester Bank kindly corrected him); one within the Atlanta Fed (the miscreant sent million-dollar deposits to accounts he had just opened in Los Angeles, at bank branches across the street from each other; by an extraordinary stroke of fate, the new-account officers at the two banks were friends, lunched together, and each told the story of a man who had just opened an account with a million-dollar wire deposit from Atlanta); and one at a money-market fund based in Virginia, where a young lady successfully got the money out to her boyfriend, who then transferred it to a Swiss bank but called attention to himself by raising hell about the $90 fee the bank had charged for the international transfer. All these were caught. Conceivably, there have been others that were not caught; the banks, Lord knows, are careless enough to invite larceny. In spring 1983, Chase permitted the withdrawal of $14.3 million from the London account of the government of Colombia, by wire messages that mixed English and Spanish and were otherwise implausible. One can envision a corporate treasury scratching its collective head while trying to explain to the auditors why that $1.5 million is not to be found in any of the company's bank accounts. There are people who think about this every day, on both sides of the law.

But there is a larger problem with FedWire, very simply stated. The total reserve balances of U.S. banks on the books of the Fed in 1983 were something less than $30 billion. (Total reserves are higher, because banks can count as part of their reserves the cash in their vaults.) To move $350 billion on FedWire in a day, which is a routine number, those reserves must turn over twelve times a day, at a nice, even rate. This can't be done. The Fed Funds transactions by which the banks bring their reserve positions up to snuff every night are by tradition unwound at the very start of the next day—7 A.M., New York time. The results of the check clearing get to the Fed around 10:30 or so, reducing some banks' reserves at the Fed while increasing others'. With more than half a trillion of Eurodollars sloshing around the West and arbitrage between the London and New York markets playing so large a part in the generation of transactions, money-market activity tends to be greatest before noon, which is 5:00 P.M. or 6:00 P.M., close-down time, in Europe. "NatWest [National Westminster Bank] tried to go to twenty-four-hour banking in London to catch all the markets," Michael Seibel of Bank of America's London branch commented, "but it's fallen to sleep. People who call at night are all on one side of the market."

Starting with three New York banks in the late 1970s (Irving, Bankers, and Chemical—which has done very well franchising its system under the name BankLink), banks have offered their large corporate customers access to FedWire through computers hooked into the banks' computers. General Motors can pay U.S. Steel, for example, by tapping out a payments message on its computer; the message runs through, say, the Chemical computer and out to FedWire for immediate delivery to, say, Mellon Bank for the account of U.S. Steel. At the moment of payment, General Motors does not have sufficient funds at Chemical to pay the bill, but it informs Chemical that "cover" will be received later in the day from, say, Citibank on behalf of National Car Rental. Chemical, which monitors payments through its computer, permits the General Motors message to go through because it's General Motors and they are good for the money. In other words, Chemical permits General Motors to take a "daylight overdraft"—a loan for a few hours during the day—to make its payment. No interest is charged on the loan. There are other customers of the bank (International Harvester, say) that might be restricted in the payments they could make: the computer would flag the message and delay it pending approval from a bank credit officer.

Chemical's problem—except that it isn't a problem, yet— is that the bank doesn't have the reserves at the Fed to cover the payment to Mellon. What with the return of purchased Fed Funds early in the morning and transactions entered for European customers and correspondents at the start of the business day, Chemical's reserve account is already in a debit position before the General Motors message comes through. The reason it isn't a problem (yet) is that the Federal Reserve Bank of New York is willing to give *Chemical* a daylight overdraft—no charge—to conduct its business in the most fluid way, with no need to set up the intricate arrangements that would be required to assure that "cover" arrives in payment from National Car Rental before the money is expended for General Motors. Until summer 1983, when a new computer system was installed at the Federal Reserve Bank of New York, the Fed didn't even know Chemical was in a debit position in its reserve account because the Fed's machinery wasn't fast enough or capacious enough to keep up with the action.

The rapid growth of third-party payment on FedWire came as a great surprise to the Fed, as did the limits of the Xerox computer system it had installed in 1973 to handle the traffic. "They thought their system had a capacity of ten messages a second," said Paul Henderson, who came to the Federal Reserve Bank of New York in 1974 from an electrical engineering background at Westinghouse, Allis Chalmers, and United Aircraft. "When I arrived, we were running about three messages a second—all the banks were clamoring to get on line to make payments on FedWire, but in fact they really weren't ready themselves. My people told me we had plenty of capacity, but it turned out all the samples they had run on the machines were misleading. We really had a capacity of about four messages a second, reached that, and couldn't go further." By 1975, then, the Fed itself was generating daylight overdrafts for its member banks by failing to get the "cover" to the paying bank on time. The only operational procedure anyone could think of was to "throttle" FedWire—to tell big banks with lots of messages to hold off for half an hour or so on the payments messages, and then put them all in at once in a batch mode to improve the efficiency of the computer. "We worked on the software," Henderson recalls, "got the machine up to five-and-a-half messages per second, but that was it."

Corporations, not surprisingly, liked the idea of free daylight overdrafts from their banks; Europeans liked the fact that they could pay their bills during their normal working hours, though their American partners in transactions didn't pay them until much later in the day. So long as U. S. bankers could get their free daylight overdrafts from the Fed, they were happy to oblige. Eventually, the head of the dinosaur in Washington became conscious that the district banks were extending credit every day in enormous amounts—that the total daylight overdrafts at their peak each day were probably greater than the total reserves of the banking system.

The Federal Reserve had two major reasons for concern. One, which was not articulated, was the corruption of the Board's monetary control efforts by this enormous extra generation of Reserve Bank credit. All the figures reported for all the "M's" are as of the close of the banking day. During the hours when business was being done, the money supply was not only much greater—but uncontrollably greater—than what the Fed was reporting. The Fed seemed to be saying that the money supply exists only when people go to sleep.

More frightening to the Fed, which is accountable to Congress, was the thought that a bank might go belly-up during a day when its reserve account was in deficit. After all, daylight overdrafts began to grow in the years when Franklin National collapsed owing the Fed $1.5 billion, and the Herstatt Bank in Germany went down with liabilities to U.S. banks in the tens of millions. "Extensive overdrafts," the Board of Governors complained in a letter to all the district bank presidents in September 1980, "are an undesirable banking practice that create financial risks borne by the System. . . . Daylight overdrafts in reserve accounts should be discouraged."

Asked how this was to be done, the members of the Board said, in effect, "We just make policy." One of the district banks—Kansas City—did get a computer into play that would keep up with the transactions of the one bank in the district that did run noticeable daylight overdrafts (United Missouri, which handled payments for DST, Inc., a major factor in mutual-fund transactions that buys money-market instruments for the funds before they wire in the money). The rest drifted, every so often making cluck-cluck sounds at their member banks to assure the Board of Governors they were paying attention.

The New York Fed moved to deny daylight overdrafts to the branches of foreign banks, and to Edge Act subsidiaries of out-of-state banks unless their parents were prepared to pledge house and home as a guarantee of the subsidiary's payments. Large overdrafts on reserve accounts by Edge Acts and foreign branches might generate losses for the Fed. "We monitor in a rather simplistic way," said Ernest Patrikis, the compact, darked-haired, moustachioed young deputy general counsel of the New York Fed, who got into the history books as the officer of the Fed who delayed signing off on the deal that released the Iranian hostages because he didn't think the terms were spelled out precisely enough. (He was right, too.) "We take their opening balance and add what's come in for them, and say that's the maximum they can pay out." In fact, the foreign branches and the Edge Act subsidiaries do feel constrained because it would be most embarrassing if a customer learned that a payments message had been refused by the Fed.

In dealing with the giant New York banks, however, the Federal Reserve Bank of New York doesn't really see the point of crusading against overdrafts: the Fed knows better than any civilian that the government won't let Chase Manhattan fail. In fact, for reasons we shall examine in Chapter 6, the Federal Reserve Bank of New York considers it unwise to stop the big banks from taking daylight overdrafts. In November 1983, New York got its new giant computers up and running, and began monitoring the big banks, and it is reported that in the following weeks several of them were called in and "counseled" about excessive use of this facility. But the New York Fed and the Board have very different views of what constitutes excessive overdrafts, and at some time in the next year or two there is likely to be a war of some substance—not the first such war, and not the last—between Washington and New York.

The CHIPS computer, of course, inevitably generates the

functional equivalent of daylight overdrafts. At any given moment of the day at CHIPS, there will always be some banks that have promised to pay out more than has yet been promised to them and some banks that stand to be receivers of gigantic funds. The debits can be extremely large. In a talk at a seminar in 1981, Seymour Rosen of Citibank said that during the preceding thirty months, every bank in the system had lived through a day when its debit to CHIPS at some point was more than double its entire capital and reserves base, and in one case the debit position had been almost *twenty times* the bank's capital and reserves before the payments to that bank began to show up on the machine and restore something closer to balance.

The worst of these debit positions in the old days (pre–1981) expressed the borrowings by foreign banks, which used the money to arbitrage the New York and London markets over the weekend. In those days CHIPS ran on "clearinghouse funds"—that is, the banks settled their accounts the morning of the business day after the day the payment was entered. The foreign banks would borrow heavily on Thursday, for delivery of the funds on Friday; then they would lend out the money from London over the weekend, returning it to New York on Monday morning.

Confidence in this system had been shaken severely in 1974, when the German regulatory authorities closed Herstatt Bank at 3:00 P.M. German time, 9:00 A.M. in New York. "June 26th," John Lee said; it is not a day he would forget. CHIPS is a "store-and-release" system: every payment is first put into a memory device, and only later released, by the payer, to the general pool, for settlement. In 1974 participants could find out what was in the pool for them, but not what was unreleased, in storage. After Herstatt, banks became reluctant to release their payments until they saw the "cover" for them already in the machine.

"The manifestation first was an unusually light day on June 28th," Lee recalls. "We were aware of Herstatt, but not of its impact. Herstatt was unknown around here, just a name in the

110

file. But our system had started to grind to a halt. Phone calls came in—what's wrong with your system?" CHIPS normally closed for entries at 4:30 P.M. "I got calls, Don't close the system. I'm a reasonable guy—when six of my chairmen call me and tell me not to close the system, I don't close the system. We kept it open Friday night, through Saturday, into Sunday."

On Monday CHIPS changed the rules temporarily, requiring that all messages put into storage be released to the settlements pool for calculation purposes—with the right to withdraw them entirely the next morning, at settlement time. The late Thomas O. Waage, then senior vice-president of the Federal Reserve Bank of New York, strolled over every morning for the meeting held in conjunction with the settlement, to be a presence and symbolize the willingness of the Fed to lend to a bank that might be tempted to pull its payments entries because somebody else had pulled the cover for them. Thomas LaBrecque, the elegant president of Chase Manhattan (one of few top executives at big banks with experience in bank operations), remembers that "we were all standing around, passing pieces of paper; all that sophisticated equipment and we were eyeball to eyeball." There were one or two hairy moments when members of what Lee obscurely calls "a family of banks" did back out of relatively small CHIPS payments, threatening to start a chain reaction, but the damage was contained.

After a few weeks, it was possible to return to the old system—payments stored and released, and after release, irrevocable—with a single change: participants were given access to the stored as well as the released documents, for information. And the accessible data base was enlarged to permit banks to find out not only the total current position of a bank that was making a payment to them, but what its position had been at comparable hours of previous days.

In the nature of things, it wasn't enough. "Herstatt was a *terrible* shock to us," Lee says. "The risk factors pre-Herstatt and post- were considerably different." There had been an almost fatal flaw in the planning for CHIPS; as Ernest Patrikis put it, "Payments systems are designed by computer people, not by bankers. The bankers learned there have to be prudential considerations." And the operations divisions of the banks had to face up to what it meant to be doing business with foreigners (a lesson their superiors in the lending offices would not learn until 1982). "We had the account of the New York branch of Bank Siderat in Iran," says James Peale of Irving Trust. "On November 3, 1979, they appeared all right—but it's overnight in New York while the rest of the world is up. Siderat was in a debit position at CHIPS, counted on making it up in Fed Funds before 10:00 A.M. They woke up in the morning and found the bank ringed with tanks."

Committees were formed and proposals floated to make the system more secure. Given the domination of the Clearing House by the New York banks, most of them involved prior authorization by the settling banks for any payments entered by the nonsettling participants. It is fair to say that such proposals encountered negative reactions outside New York—such severe negative reactions that the Bank of England launched an exploratory study of the possibilities of establishing a rival dollar clearing in London. Significantly, the committee included representatives of the American Bankers Association. "The thought was," said Leslie Lloyd of the Bank of England, who chaired the committee, "that a decent wholesale clearing here would solve some of CHIPs' enormous problems. The basic reason for coming down against it is that banks have computer systems built around current arrangements. Also, the banks in London would be shouldering a great deal of risk and exposure now taken in New York, and there was no desire to do that. You could get involved in horrible legal problems in the event of a default, with two different legal systems."

In the end, the solution to the overnight exposure problem was to accelerate settlement in CHIPS from the next morning to the same evening. Not the least of the Herstatt horror had been the realization that a failure between 7:00 A.M. and 10:00 A.M. meant the collapse of *two* days' transactions—yesterday's, to be settled at 10:00, and today's, which had begun at

7:00. Starting October 1, 1981, CHIPS moved to "same-day settlement": every CHIPS payment had to be completed by 6:00 P.M. of the day it was put into the machine.

Between 4:30 P.M., which is still closing time for transactions, and 5:00 P.M., the CHIPS computer nets down the $300 billion or so of payments owed from and receipts due to each of the participants, then makes a second sweep to allocate the debits and credits among the twenty-two settling participants. At 6:00, if all goes well, the twenty-two confirm to CHIPS on the terminal with the words "Ready to Pay." When all the confirmations are in, CHIPS sends out a general message, "Pay," and by 6:30 all the wire transfers have been made through the Federal Reserve. If all has not gone well, Lee keeps the CHIPS computer open, the Federal Reserve Bank of New York keeps the discount window open, FedWire extends its hours, and in 130 banks or so around the world, the operations staff remains at its posts, pending resolution. On one nasty Thursday in December 1982, the failure of Banco do Brasil to meet its debit to CHIPS kept its settling agent, Bankers Trust, from proclaiming a readiness to pay, and there were some hours of considerable anguish before Bankers and Citibank, with no little encouragement from the Fed, ponied up an additional $360 million for the Brazilians (maybe even more: that was the market's best guess) to bring CHIPS into balance.

In short, the move to same-day settlement did not end credit worries at CHIPS. And by ending the difference between payment in Next Day Funds on CHIPS and Same Day Funds on FedWire, the new regime increased the banks' very short credit lines to customers. For many of these customers were receiving payments on CHIPS, especially from abroad, and wanted the banks to regard that money (which the banks would not actually receive until the close of day) as acceptable cover for FedWire payments out some hours earlier. The Fed found daylight overdrafts growing despite the Board of Governors' command that such activity "be discouraged," and the banks found themselves at risk to a far greater degree than they had ever anticipated. "Of course there are credit risks involved,"

113

says John Lee with some asperity of the CHIPS operation. "That's why we have bankers here rather than clerks."

The difficulty is that in the competitive world of banking a customer may be able to find someone who *will* give him Fed-Wire out for CHIPS in if his current bank refuses the facility: this is called "relationship banking." Unless you're prepared to sacrifice some relationships—and few banks are, if only because it's an *individual's* relationship, property of someone important within the bank, and you make an enemy of him—you might as well use clerks. "The basic fallacy the banking system is still living under," says E. Gerald Corrigan of the Minneapolis Fed, "is that everybody can go to London. But you can't *all* go to London."

Adding a settlements system to BankWire was a proposal stimulated by the big banks' inability to win from CHIPS the kind of controls they thought necessary after Herstatt and by their reluctance to be completely at the mercy of Fed regulations in an area so important to their customer relations. In CashWire, each member bank sets a ceiling on the payments it is willing to receive from any other member bank, and the unwinding process to reach settlement if one of the participants has failed allocates losses pro rata among the banks expecting payments from the late departed rather than according to the more arbitrary criteria at CHIPS. And there are no foreign participants.

But the fact that payments are not "final" until the following morning means that a CashWire settlement does not convey to bank managers the same degree of comfort as a FedWire payment or a CHIPS settlement, which means, in turn, that bankers and customers making very large dollar payments prefer FedWire even though the per-transfer charge is higher. BankWire's Bernhard Romberg agrees with them: "Our market is the 80% of the traffic under $10 million. If you've got a $100 million real estate deal, you want to be paid in gold bullion. FedWire is gold bullion pushed through the door. CashWire is only a cashier's check." As operated in 1983, the BankWire system did not have the capacity to take over much traffic from

FedWire or CHIPS. Romberg claimed a possibility of 3,000 funds transfers an hour, but as a practical matter, the maximum was 10,000 a day. In fact, volume in 1983 ran only about 2,500 transactions a day, with average values a third of less of those at FedWire or CHIPS.

SWIFT has no system risk whatever because it does not commingle payments orders from many banks: if credit is extended at all, it is by one bank to another. Often enough, a transaction managed by SWIFT puts money through the other transfer systems. Thus, a payment from Britain's PYE to the Sandia Corporation in Albuquerque may well involve Barclay's in London entering a credit in CHIPS for Citibank to give Barclay's a correspondent balance at Citibank large enough to cover a payment to the Bank of New Mexico. (This is one of those cases when Citi will be expected to make a FedWire payment out in response to a CHIPS payment in; because it's Barclay's, Citi will oblige.) But SWIFT itself is involved only as a carrier of messages. Significantly, SWIFT takes responsibility for getting a message from its sender to its addressee within the time frame specified by the system: if a message comes late or has been garbled in transmission, SWIFT will pick up whatever losses a member has suffered through interest uncollected or paid unnecessarily.

Except for SWIFT, all these systems are bedeviled by sloppy work inside the banks. ("The banks," says an inside observer who does not wish to be named, "screw up their correspondent transfers something fierce.") Errors are a source of much nervousness, not to say terror: "As he's running to catch the 5:15," senior vice-president John Dorman of Chemical Bank told an ABA meeting on CHIPS shortly before the move to same-day settlement, describing the life a credit officer could expect under the new dispensation, "he's going to find a $700 million debit which is twice the legal limit of the bank. That money is coming from Chemical Bank, as soon as they find it. . . ." In the days when the banks had overnight to straighten out their CHIPS position, Dorman reported, "*fifty percent* of the values in New York City were affected by adjustments and back-valuing." That was rhetoric; few others would put the proportion that high. But it's high enough to be scary.

The move to same-day settlement improved these procedures considerably, but the problem persists. Hans Boettcher, vice-president of the New York branch of Germany's Commerzbank, notes, "Everybody has to be very cautious with all these amounts that are so similar. You add a zero or leave out a zero, 20,000,000 becomes 200,000,000." Even the addressing is a problem: a clerk in Frankfurt, Boettcher's assistant Hecko Dingler suggests, can easily make a mistake, "choosing among the Royal Bank of New Zealand, the Royal Bank of Canada, the Royal Bank of Scotland." One of the reasons CHIPS preferred to work with a small number of settling banks—only seven of the twelve original settling members did any amount of correspondent work—was that errors of that nature are best corrected when only a few cooks are responsible for the broth.

As usual, there is a compensation for the risks and the terror and the occasional long weekend's work: money. Wholesale electronic funds transfers are a source of profits for the banks. In 1983 the Fed charged 65¢ to the sender and 65¢ to the recipient of a payment on FedWire; CHIPS charged about 30¢ per entry; BankWire charged 60¢ for a CashWire message; SWIFT charged 25¢. The bank's per-message charge to a large corporate customer was typically $5 in, $5 out. (To an individual customer who wished to make a wire transfer, the charge was usually $10 at each end.) That's worth several hundred million dollars a year, with more to come. "And when you're moving that much money," a young Texas banker said gnomishly, "some of it sticks with you overnight." Bank managements have always looked upon operations as a cost center, as the price the bank had to pay to hold deposits in the form of transaction balances. Among the little tests of flexibility they will have to face in the next decade is the need to plan operations as a profit center, since operations is one of very few activities where they have a situational advantage over other providers of financial services. The real test will come in consumer banking.

5

ELECTRONICS
FOR EVERYMAN

The typical CEO of a bank doesn't know what an ACH is," said George Mitchell at the Fed.

"That's our survival—the whole electronics game," said George Haigh, the handsome white-haired CEO of Toledo Trust Co., who came to banking late, after a career in that city's industry.

"I am not impressed with the mangement of banks," said Keith Garner, a confident young man who does strategic planning for Automatic Data Processing. "I have seen too many large and profitable businesses that exist because of the stupidity of banks."

I

In August 1972, as I was starting work on *The Bankers,* I found myself in San Francisco speaking to the annual convention of the American Bar Association on quite different subjects and enjoying the company of lawyers at play. Mine is, of course, a business like meatpacking, where you use every part of the animal (including the squeal), so I started around to see what I could learn about banks in San Francisco in a brief visit. My contact at Bank of America directed me to a meeting at the Federal Reserve Bank, where the Special Committee on Paperless Entries (SCOPE) was holding a press conference to announce the results of four years of work. Twenty-odd reporters and bankers were assembled in a plain, relatively small meeting room in the old headquarters of that bank, listening while Russell Fenwick of Bank of America outlined the wonders to be worked by the new Automated Clearing House that the California banks and the Fed would launch in a few weeks.

It was going to relieve the banks of what looked like a hopeless and mounting cost burden from check processing: by 1970 the number of checks written in America had reached 20 billion a year and was rising. ACH would allow banks to transfer depositors' money to other banks and their depositors, and to receive payments to depositors from other banks, via a handful of reels of magnetic tape rather than hundreds of thousands of paper checks. It was going to save millions and millions of dollars a year in mailing costs. It was going to change the relationship of people with the big institutions— public utilities, department stores, local governments, even their own corporate employers. And it was ready to roll.

ACH would get people paid more efficiently and allow them to pay their bills more efficiently. Instead of receiving a paycheck, people would receive notice of a direct deposit into their bank account: the payments notices would be distributed to the employees' banks by the ACH in its daily delivery of tape reels. Instead of writing checks to pay the bills that came in monthly—telephone company, power company, department stores, mortgage banker, credit cards—people would "preauthorize" their bank to pay for them (ten days or so after they received the bill so they could stop payment, if necessary).

Their bank statement would contain a computer-generated memo to the effect that the bank had paid this bill for them, and while that memo had no particular standing in law (in 1983 there was still no body of legislation governing ACH payments; what court cases have arisen have been decided on the basis of National Automated Clearing House Association rules), the companies agreeing to receive payments through ACH credits signed up to respect the banks' certification that the money had been paid. Fenwick gave an example in which the bank paid somebody's electricity bill "on the first of the month."

There were a number of questions about who would be members (all banks, whether or not members of the Fed, would be eligible), how companies would sign up (by negotiation with their own bank), what would happen when a payment was to be made by someone who had his account in a bank that was not an ACH member, or just someone who had not agreed to take payments by ACH credit (the bank offering the preauthorized payment would cut a check on behalf of the person paying the bill), how the Fed would participate (it would physically operate the computer and maintain the software that directed payments to this account at that bank or that account at this bank).

I listened to all of this, dewey-eyed and all, with some of the little boy's wonder at the magnificence of the parade; but I had a problem nobody else seemed to be asking about, so finally I raised my hand. Why, I inquired, would anyone wish to preauthorize a payment to the power-and-light company on the first of every month when normally he didn't pay that bill until the tenth? Oh, said Fenwick, that had nothing to do with ACH. That was a problem between the power-and-light company and its customers; the power-and-light company would have to handle it. And I, in turn, said, "Oh," enjoying one of those moments of reportorial epiphany, when an answer to a question tells you so much more than the respondent thought he was saying. The emperor really *didn't* have any clothes. These eminent gentlemen from the California banks and the Federal Reserve had labored four years to produce a lemon.

They had cut themselves off deliberately from the interests of the end users of their service, and if the end users didn't want to buy it, in the end it wouldn't sell. Clearly, this answer had a significance beyond the question: it meant that banks, unlike almost every other form of commercial enterprise in the country, still were not accustomed to considering what the customer wanted. Remember "banker's hours."

In fairness, ACH was much harder to create than any outsider could imagine. It was all very well to make a payment, but there also had to be a system by which the receiver of the payment knew whose account had thereby been paid. Even the simplest activity—disbursing the payroll—required the creation of a considerable address file for each user, to get the deposit to the accounts of people who banked at different institutions all over the area, keeping in mind the need for the message to be acceptable to the processing machinery in each of these institutions. (If a check is "nonmachineable," you still have the check; if an electronic entry is nonmachineable, you may have nothing but a most disgruntled employee and a disgusted corporate customer.) For the worker who needed cash for part of his paycheck, there would have to be an Automated Teller Machine of some sort. (Nothing would be gained for the bank or the worker if people had to wait on line for a teller to cash their own checks following direct deposit.) That would come, but in 1972 its time was not yet—indeed, Bank of America, which had in effect created the original ACH, was bearish on the ATM and did not make widespread installations until the 1980s.

On the bill-paying side, the customer could pay directly through the ACH only to bill collectors who had accounts with participating banks and were prepared to accept ACH credits via reels of tape—unless his bank was prepared to accept the expense of preparing his checks for him. A separate address file of recipients of payments would have to be constructed for each individual because his account number at each of the corporations he was paying would have to be part of the message. Some sort of "prenotification," comparable to a SWIFT message that triggers the CHIPS payment, would be required. And, of course, there had to be a secure and certain procedure to get the precise amount of each preauthorized payment onto the tapes. Banks would have to undertake considerable expense to gear up for the service.

In the end, there wasn't much demand and there wasn't much supply. But the American Bankers Association, through its Monetary and Payments Systems Study, had endorsed the work of SCOPE even before the committee reported; a similar group came up with similar results in Atlanta; and the Federal Reserve System (at that time looking for services that would help it retain members) was eager to help. One of the necessary objectives, obviously, was the creation of intercity links that would enable the ACHs to originate, process, and deliver entries to and from each other and remote locations. In 1974 the four existing ACHs—California, New England, Atlanta, and St. Paul—formed a National Automated Clearing House Association, which developed rules for interregional exchange. These things take time: the rules were not approved by NACHA until 1976 and not adopted by the Federal Reserve (which could put them into effect) until 1978. As part of this agreement, the Feds arranged (rather grudgingly) to give each ACH a "window" in FedWire in the evening, so the contents of tape reels could be communicated electronically to other ACHs. By then ACH was off the ground, though just barely. There were thirty-two operating associations, blanketing the country, and about two-thirds of the nation's banks were members. Volume remained derisory: the ACHs in 1982 processed fewer privately originated items than the check-processing system handled in a day. The banks couldn't even sell the most likely corporate participants: at this writing, for example, the New York Telephone Co. still refuses to accept ACH payments because they don't include a copy of the payer's bill.

But ACH did acquire the most important possible customer: the U.S. Governent. In 1975 the Treasury Department decided to make as many as possible of its payments to individuals through direct deposit—salaries, Social Security, civil service and military retirement, military active duty pay (only the Air Force and the Marines went along with this: we do *not* have a monolithic Defense Department), etc. This goosed the New York banks into action, and in 1976 the New York Clearing House started the first wholly private ACH, with processing done internally rather than by the Fed. The savings to the banks from direct deposits of Treasury payments were substantial: a 1981 study indicated that it cost the banks 25¢ to handle a stiff green check deposited over the counter, 59¢ to handle such a check deposited by mail, and only 7¢ to handle a payment deposited directly as an ACH entry. With about 180,000,000 payments moving to individuals from the federal government through an ACH that year, the savings to the banks (and thrifts) ran in the neighborhood of $50 million, which was about four times what the banks paid the ACHs and the Fed for the service.

The arrival of the New York banks in the ACH network gave the system another large source of volume, via Chase Manhattan, which had made a specialty of handling the processing needs of insurance companies. Chase had developed for them a system whereby policyholders could pay their premiums through a preauthorized debit to their accounts, using the paper-check chassis. Every month, Chase would prepare well over a million paper checks (600,000 for Metropolitan Life alone), each of which would trigger a transfer from a policyholder's bank account to Chase. This system was obviously adaptable to direct debit through ACH. By 1982 about 15% of all insurance premiums were being paid by direct-debit entries initiated by the Chase Manhattan Bank; such entries accounted for roughly a fifth of all privately generated ACH items and for about two-thirds of all nongovernmental items processed by the New York ACH.

The two other significant sources of volume were direct deposit of corporate payrolls and payments of bills from financial institutions, mortgages, and consumer-credit items. At a few electronically oriented companies like IBM and Xerox, direct deposit had been accepted by three-quarters or more of the employees, and the overwhelming majority of bank employees (who get certain benefits from banking where they work) simply had their salaries deposited in their accounts. In January 1983 Chase reported a year-on-year rise from 47,000 to 136,000 a month in the number of payroll transactions handled electronically, and Valley National Bank in Phoenix, which has made ACH a high priority (and led the Arizona financial institutions into the formation of the second privately operated ACH in the country in 1982) had almost a thousand companies delivering payrolls through electronic means. But the total nationwide—including the one-third of federal employees who are paid by direct deposit—amounted to only about 5% of all payrolls. The banks had done only slightly better in persuading customers to make mortgage payments through direct debit, though this should be the most acceptable ACH operation of all. (People do want to pay their mortgages on time, and the number is the same every month: there's no need to check the bill.) Nationwide in 1983, something less than 10% of all mortgage and bank consumer-credit payments were being made electronically. ACH payments to public utilities, which was where ACH started, ran just over 1% of payments by check in 1983; payments to department stores via ACH, which was the exciting frontier in 1972, ran about 0.1% of payments by check.

Meanwhile, across the seas, the electronic revolution really had worked as Fenwick & Co. thought it would in San Francisco in 1972. Something more than half of all British payrolls and a quarter of all consumer payments go through an ACH electronically, and the figures are comparable in Scandinavia and in Japan. (The British payroll figure is especially impressive, given the long-standing Andy Capp tradition of not telling the wife what you make. British banks and employers *made* it happen: Northern Gas in Manchester, for example, gave each worker a £50 bonus for opening a bank account and agreeing to direct deposit.) The German banks are talking—not really seriously—of an end to branch banks and tellers and checks by 1995; and the French, as we shall see presently, are pioneering a technology that takes ACH convenience out into the heart of everyday life.

In 1983 NACHA and those of its member banks that are paying attention decided to break out of their prison by offering ACH services as a way for companies to pay their vendors. The 1983 NACHA annual convention, at which this reporter was a (paid) speaker, was devoted mostly to the creation of a Commercial Trade Payables (CTP) category in ACH processing. Rather different codes and procedures are necessary for this service, because the payments message must include data like invoice numbers and the format must be such that the information can be fed directly to and from the computers of the companies paying and billing: the greatest single attraction of paying by ACH entry rather than by check is that it will (or should) eliminate much of the generation of paper by both buyer and seller.

This program has something powerful going for it: the support of Sears, which starting in fall 1983 began to pay all its vendors—that's *40,000* manufacturing companies—by ACH credits. Sears is a sufficiently important customer for these suppliers that they cannot object to the change in payments procedure, which means that the roster of companies in the ACH files must at least double from the 21,000 in that status as 1983 began. Perhaps even more important to the future of ACH, the Sears payments are so vital to these suppliers that they will be willing to switch their banking business to a bank that participates in ACH if their present bank does not. A number of other high-voltage companies participated in the committee that designed the CTP program—the names included American Airlines, Xerox, Westinghouse, Exxon, Procter & Gamble—but at the ACH convention Sears was clearly the bellwether. The bankers were a little itchy about that because Sears has been in so many of their nightmares as a provider of financial services in its own right, but ACH, which ought to be the centerpiece of the banks' planning for the last years of the century, remains in such parlous condition that it needs all the help it can get.

2

Why did consumer electronic banking, so successful in Europe, perform so poorly in the United States? The list of reasons is long and instructive. Let us sample:

(1) *The SCOPE conception was wrong.* From the beginning, the banks and the Fed looked for an electronic funds-transfer system that would do exactly what checks did, only cheaper. Thus ACH was structured originally not as a system that would move credits (like FedWire and the European giro banks), but as a debit-transfer system. Instead of moving the customer's check through a payments mechanism, the insurance companies, power-and-light companies, et al., moved their *bill,* which was functionally the same thing as the consumer's check: it triggered a transfer out of the consumer's account and into theirs. It also triggered return items, which were communicated by mail and were an immense burden. The Chase ACH policy premium payments scheme generates no fewer than 90,000 return items a year.

James Hopes, the shirtsleeved, matter-of-fact manager of the Chase ACH effort, took me around his shop on the tenth floor of 1 New York Plaza, overlooking the harbor and the Statue of Liberty. Women were sitting at CRT screens, converting packets of handwritten paper return items back to electronic records that would tell the insurance companies that all these people had failed to pay their premiums, because the account was closed (dead people keep getting billed in this system, in addition to all the mobile policyholders who forget to tell the insurance company they've changed banks), or because there were insufficient funds in the account. In 1981 the average time elapsed between the day Chase submitted the debit tapes to ACH and the day the paper return appeared at the door was no less than eighteen days. In early 1983, after herculean efforts, Chase had got it down only to twelve days.

By the terms of its arrangements with the insurance companies, Chase had credited their accounts the day after the debits were sent out; now the return items had to be subtracted from those balances—and credits had to be conveyed to the bank that sent the paper return to cancel the electronic debit. By the rules of ACH, the bank bouncing the debit did *not* automatically get credit at the Fed for that amount (as it does when it bounces a check): Chase had to accept the rejection first. Some return items were so stale—more than forty-five days old—that Chase refused to give credit for the return. The time required in the subsequent negotiations was a cost item, too.

Because ACH entries were seen as a substitute for checks, the system was organized to a remarkable degree around the physical transportation of information. Let us, for example, consider the automated-payment gas-pump system created by Michael McCann, the bearded proprietor of International Payments Systems, Inc. of Los Angeles, with the help of General Electric, using a microcomputer made by the Engineering Systems division of Square D. In 1983 this system was up and running at half a dozen Phoenix service stations. Regular customers of these stations could arrange to get the cash discount when buying their gas without using cash, by prearranging an automatic debit to their bank accounts. They could use any credit card with a magnetic stripe. IPS would doctor the mag stripe with its own customer identification and give the customer a Personal Identification Number (PIN number) to punch in at a microcomputer box hung on the gas pump.

The card and the number unlock the pump for one use. The microcomputer registers the sale on a memory chip. Every evening a GE central processing unit not otherwise occupied (usually Rockville, Maryland) calls each microprocessor and takes the data off the chip. The CPU prepares a message for Union Bank in Los Angeles, which makes a reel of tape for ACH use, crediting the bank where the service stations have their account and debiting the customers' banks. The reel of tape must then be *walked across the street* to the Los Angeles branch of the Federal Reserve Bank of San Francisco because the ACH accepts inputs only in the form of tape reels. The data on the tape are transmitted electronically to San Francisco, where the ACH computer is, and then from San Francisco to Phoenix for distribution of the debits to the cardholders. It has occurred to GE that there are cheaper and better ways to process such transactions.

Between many pairs of locations, the electronic ACH actually moves money more slowly than the paper-based system it is supposed to replace. Corporations find that while outside services like Automatic Data Processing can get paper checks to employees for a Friday payroll, the bank offering payroll services through an ACH often cannot. The new business slide presentation by NACHA in 1980 presented a Q. and A.:

QUESTION: I can't meet your input schedules. What are my options?

ANSWER: You have two options. Advance your processing cycle by one day, or delay your payday for SurePay [the ACH slogan] participants by one day. Most have found that these adjustments, when necessary, were readily accepted—and the benefits received more than compensated for the adjustment. (Even when direct deposit payday becomes Monday!)

The exclamation point is in the original, and well warranted. It is hard to imagine a vote on a factory floor that showed a majority (or even a smattering of ayes) for taking direct deposit on Monday in preference to a check on Friday.

(2)*There was little understanding, either at the Fed or among the bankers, that ACH, by its nature, was a communications utility that would become more useful to everyone as the range of participants increased.* This is no one's fault. The basic insight on which Theodore Vail built the Bell System— that the value of every telephone was enhanced by the wiring of every new telephone—is not a fashionable notion these days. "Cross-subsidization" is presented on the left as a ripoff (some people are paying more than they should have to pay), and derided on the free-market right as an inefficient allocation of resources. At the 1983 NACHA convention, ACH promoters were asking each other how to handle the corporate customer who was concerned that half his 200 suppliers couldn't be paid efficiently with ACH credits because their banks couldn't receive the information in electronic form. It did not occur to any of the speakers that anything could be done about this problem other than waiting in hopes it will go away.

When the ACHs were formed, the Federal Reserve was a club that gave free services to its members once they paid their dues in the form of sterilized reserves. Its instincts were exclusionary and parsimonious. Though the Fed was willing to process for all ACH members, whether or not they were Fed members, it was not willing to extend its services to S&Ls or credit unions. In 1976 the New York Clearing House ACH, because it was processing independently of the Fed, did permit thrifts and credit unions to join, on the commonsense argument that direct-deposit payroll made no sense in the era of the NOW account unless the items could be entered wherever those who were being paid maintained their accounts. But it was not until the Justice Department sued the Rocky Mountain ACH on antitrust grounds that the Feds approved the entry of thrifts or credit unions into the ACHs for which it processed. Most of the banks, looking at ACH as an extension of their check collection for correspondents, were happy to see the thrifts and credit unions required to send and receive ACH messages only through the agency of a bank. In January 1983, when virtually all thrifts were offering checking accounts, only 15% of them were ACH members—and almost 4,000 of the nation's 15,000 banks were not participants.

But payments could be made to people and companies that banked with nonparticipants only by cutting a check; companies that might otherwise have been attracted to direct-deposit payrolls or trade payments felt, correctly, that the need to keep dual payments systems going ate up the savings that might be hoped for from a move to electronics.

Bill-paying by telephone was a salable service that should have been made viable by the ACH but was crippled by the failure of the associations to reach out for universal membership and maximum acceptance by ultimate recipients. "Pay-by-Phone" was a brainchild of Howard Phillips, a Boeing aerospace systems designer, who decided in 1971 that there was money to be made by bringing computer services to the home through the telephone. "Computer gear was expensive then," Phillips recalls. "We offered six services to the Seattle market—bill payment, income tax preparation, home budgeting, a calendar of events, records retention (you'd call in the purchases when you bought something, for insurance purposes), and the telephone as a calculator—a popular service. Those were the days when a handheld calculator cost $150. We called it 'In Touch,' and Seafirst purchased an interest in us in April 1972. We brought up the service in June 1973, and it fell on its face in six months. We had gone at it the way aerotech engineers would go at a problem, with no consideration of marketing, with a brochure in aerospace black and white, and a manual an inch thick. Seafirst said, 'We're ten years too soon,' and after an ugly shouting match, I became the sole owner of the company again."

What made Phillips's TCS (Telephone Computing Service) a viable enterprise was the desire of the S&Ls to get into the transactions business. Phillips designed a turnkey package, "hardware and software, systems and procedures," by which an S&L or a bank could offer telephone bill-paying. He also designed a large-scale system for syndicating these services for the Massachusetts Automated Transfer Service, and then for the Carolina Financial Services Federation. "They convinced us," he says, "that in this business the economies of scale were critical." In 1978–79 Phillips turned his company around from a systems-and-hardware company to a service company and began offering to perform all the functions of telephone bill-paying for any bank in the country, from his own offices in Seattle. Automatic Data Processing acquired TCS (and Phillips) in 1981. As of fall 1983 Phillips had about 85 banks using the service and was processing about 175,000 transactions a month, involving about $300 million of payments every year, about 30% of all the telephone bill-paying in the country. Thirty people work the keyboards and CRTs in little booths from 6:00 A.M. to 9:00 P.M. Seattle time.

The system relies on WATS service. The telephone number the bank gives the customer to call when paying a bill cuts the customer directly into a booth in Seattle, where the operator answers pleasantly, gives his or her first name ("Thank for calling Pay-by-Phone. This is Bill"), and asks for the customer's code number. The number generates a page on the terminal with the customer's name, address, bank, and list of accounts (each with a code number) to which he has previously paid bills through this system. ADP/TCS has a list of 75,000 "merchants" to which it can make payments without further instructions from the customer. The operator then greets the customer by name and asks for his security code. When this matches, the operator inquires whether the customer would care to pay any bills today and carefully repeats for each bill the name of the company or individual being paid and the amount. Every word said on both sides is recorded, for evidence in case of future disagreements. The error-rate, in fact, Phillips says, is only about 0.3%. When the recipient's name and number are confirmed, the operator pushes a key to close the transaction and asks if the customer has any other bills to pay. When the customer says, No, he's finished, the operator thanks him for calling _____ Bank, reading the name off his screen, and there cannot be more than a few dozen users of the service who realize that up to now their bank hasn't heard of this transaction at all. If he has a touch-tone phone, the customer can do all of this himself, speaking to nobody but a computer-generated voice saying, Thank you. But making the first transaction requires him to hit fifty-two numbers in correct sequence, and not everybody will be up to that.

At the close of each day, ADP sends an electronic message through an ACH to each of the banks with customers who have made a payment, telling them to debit these customers for this amount of money paid this day—and to send funds to cover the customers' total expenditures before tomorrow morning at 11:00 (Pacific Coast), when ADP will begin the work of paying the recipients. Payments are sorted, so that all those to a single recipient (which can be Sears, regardless of the store) can be printed out as a list and paid in a lump sum. This list is mailed to the recipient regardless of the means of payment. For the 10% to 15% of recipients who have authorized payment by ACH, ADP sends a series of electronic blips to their bank. For the rest, ADP prepares a check for the total sum, stuffs it in an envelope with the list of payers, and mails it out.

For each such payment, ADP/TCS charges a bank 40¢ (35¢ for a touch-tone phone payment without operator assistance). And ADP gets the float from the moment the banks' payment arrives on the wire until the moment three or four days later when ADP's check (written and mailed from faraway Seattle, remember) returns to ADP's account. At that, ADP is not the worst float-grabber in this business: its only significant rival, TymShare, performs these services from an office in Lewiston, Maine.

Meanwhile, the bank charges a fee to its customers. Because the advantage to the customer is perceived (on all sides) as the saving on the 20¢ stamp, about the most the banks can charge is a dime, splitting the value fifty/fifty. The reader will probably feel that a bank paying ADP 40¢ for a service that it sells to its customer for 10¢ is not getting rich in the process, and the reader will be right. Banks may save a lot on the paper processing that pay-by-phone eliminates, and they may gain market share through offering a new service, and it may improve their image—but they don't make money. Thus the turnover in Phillips's customers tends to be pretty high.

But the list has included some very big banks—Citibank, for one (Citibank sent out to Seattle books of Citibank check forms for ADP to use instead of its own checks, just in case the recipient of the payments might know the payers were Citicard customers and might find out that mighty Citibank, father of banking technology, inventor of all that moves, was using the services of a data processing company). In 1983 the new customer Phillips was especially proud of was Security Pacific, which had turned over the marketing job to ADP/TCS. "They're very happy," said Phillips. "The service has been a big success, and they're making money on it." Bob Thaler of Security Pacific heard this claim with some surprise. "There are a thousand customers on telephone bill-paying," he said. "We're not *un*happy with it, but we're certainly not making money."

Still, there might well have been a good business here for the banks, with savings on processing more than sufficient to pay the costs of the telephone service, if all the recipients could have been keyed to an ACH.

(3) *The refusal of the banks to regard the Automated Teller Machine as a public utility deprived the ACHs of what should have been a major source of volume while diminishing the value of the innovation to the public.* Though one should never underestimate the economic illiteracy of the Justice Department, it seems a reasonable assumption that the bankers' associations, the thrifts, and the Federal Reserve could have joined together to develop ATMs on the model of the telephone booth, as a general public service. (In Iowa, state law commanded shared ATM terminals, and there were no problems.) But banks liked the idea of the ATM as a promotional

tool—if your ATM and yours alone was in the local hospital or university or factory, presumably you got a lot of new accounts from those workers. The bank that made the first investment in machines would seize the best locations, *ad astra per aspera* with the Docutel and NCR and IBM salesmen.

When ATMs first came in, they were off-line devices that generated the customer's Personal Identification Number by an algorithm from his account number as presented by his card, and such machines could be "jackpotted" by someone who knew the algorithm and stole or copied a few cards. Under those circumstances, machine sharing put a bank at risk of inadequate security by one of its partners. But now virtually all the machines are on-line to the bank that issued the customer's card, the PIN number is encrypted at the machine, and the bank's verification and okay to pay are encrypted at headquarters. (During the Falklands War, the Commerce Department denied Docutel a license to export ATMs to Argentina because the built-in encryption system might have military application.) Jackpotting is further impeded by an additional pair of messages, also encrypted, through which the ATM and the bank's computer agree on how many bills are still in the machine's stock.

All this could have been done via switching machinery in an ACH with on-line capabilities. Even under the narrow limits in force, a few imaginative banks have found ways to use the interregional ACHs as a link to ATMs. In Burlington, Vermont, for example, the Howard Bank serves a college community with a "Money From Home" program, by which the parents of college students can order an ACH entry from their home town banks on one day, and cash can be drawn through an ATM in Burlington the next day.

Mostly, the banks abdicated. To the extent that ATMs are shared locally, the operators of the switches are data processors like National Data, Nationet, Decimus, and ADP, which can offer the service equally to all. In a number of smaller cities, most of the banks and the S&Ls run their machines through on-line processing owned and operated by ADP, which means that all the machines *could* service customers of all the banks and thrifts simply by a minor change in the card slot and a push on a button at the processing center. But the banks and thrifts cling grimly to proprietary machines, each with its own cute name, with a loss of business to all. In 1983 Manufacturers Hanover, which had been very slow off the mark in the New York ATM sweepstakes, decided to take partners in expanding its network, first NCR for the machinery and the computers, then the city's savings banks and any little commercial bank that cares to join: all would be welcome to Manny Hanny's Matrix network. Interestingly, Manny Hanny soon discovered that it lacked the machinery in place, the software and maybe the will to make this sort of thing go, and by the end of the year it had dropped the NCR connection and joined with Chemical Bank in an effort to build a shared ATM network that would include The Bank of New York and Goldome (a Buffalo-based savings bank that had acquired two of New York City's largest thrifts in the shambles of 1982) in the continuing effort to compete with Citibank.

ATMs have been a significant success: despite the inconveniences of proprietary machines usable only by the depositors at a single bank, in 1983 Americans met more than 20% of their need for cash by drawing from the 35,000 machines emplaced around the country. ATMs have not, however, been a source of profit for the banks. They do enable banks to cut down on the tellers behind the windows (and to use more part-time people as tellers, which is a considerable saving), but the machinery itself has a cost, and so does the wiring that links it to the bank's computer. The software package for ATM service runs into six figures, and the expenses of maintaining the terminal are nontrivial. There are homely problems (the cash has to be ironed to make sure the dispenser gets it out one bill at a time) and sophisticated problems: "*I* can't understand what happens between the ATM and the computer," says Hugh Barrett, a fortyish refugee from Citibank who became the chief systems designer and technological planner for Houston's First

City. "I have to pay a man $60,000 a year to understand it."

ATMs should be the cutting edge of imposing fees for services in consumer banking—machines should offer the banking services available to the lower middle class (deposit and withdrawal) at no or minimal charge, while access to the tellers and payment by check should require a fee, which will be more than covered, of course, by the interest earned on larger balances. Denying access to tellers by low-balance depositors is not a viable procedure, as Citibank found out the hard way in New York: people do not like the idea of being restricted to machines for their banking business. Larry Johns, president of the Isabella Bank of Mt. Pleasant, Michigan, told a nice story about the wife of a friend who had just heard that his bank was going to upgrade a shopping-center post in her neighborhood from machines only to a mini-branch with a teller and a loan officer: "I'm glad to see you're going to put tellers on the East Side," she said, "and stop treating us as second-class citizens." But customers would not resent machines if they were a shared utility, rather than part of "their" bank.

By insisting that a machine is, in effect, a branch of one bank, the banks may have lost ultimate control of the ATM network. Some Texas banks saw this coming: led by Mercantile of Dallas, they arranged with Safeway (which cashed more checks than the banks) to install 130 ATMs in supermarkets around the state. Mercantile's IMPACT card was franchised by four other major Texas bank holding companies and some scores of independent banks, but it wasn't enough to deliver Safeway the volume Mercantile had promised. Meanwhile, under the leadership of Houston's Interfirst (using the computers of First City), the other seven major Texas bank holding companies challenged with a shared PULSE card that would access their machines and some machines used by S&Ls and credit unions, around Texas and Louisiana. In the end, Safeway will probably kick out all the banks and offer its own ATMs, in which the banks can in effect buy shelf space.

This route was pioneered by the Publix chain in Florida, which has put in ATMs that can be used with any card from any participating bank. The supermarket charges the bank 56¢ per transaction in the machine, sweet revenge for all the years when the banks charged 5¢ to 15¢ to the supermarket for every check it deposited. "We'll use the Publix ATM," Charles Zwick of Southeast Banking Corp. said grimly. "Charge the customer fifty cents per transaction at Publix. We'll have our own machines in the same shopping center, no charge, and Publix will do the business because it's more convenient." Grand Union, Seven-Eleven, and Kroger lead a torrent of others on the Publix route. In fall 1983 a group of independent supermarkets in the Los Angeles area ordered 500 ATMs from Burroughs, the largest order ever placed for such equipment. National Transactions Systems, a California company, has arranged with Safeway to provide ATMs to that chain in California, and the first fifty such were installed in 1983. The charge for a withdrawal is 75¢, and the big five California banks all boycotted the system. (Each doubtless made its own decision—you wouldn't suspect them of violating the antitrust laws, would you?) In November, however, Citicorp broke the logjam, arranging for its Visa cards to be accepted for cash withdrawals at the California Safeways—and also, incidentally, at the Publix stores in Florida, presumably in anticipation of its subsequently announced acquisition of Biscayne Savings. In early 1984, Merrill Lynch added insult to injury by arranging with Safeway for cash withdrawals through the CMA Visa. The California giants will doubtless follow. In any event, National Transactions was confident enough to place an order with NCR for another thousand ATMs.

In 1982 First Interstate in Los Angeles, as part of its campaign to unify public perception of its subsidiaries in eleven western states, made the ATM machines in all of them accessible to cards issued by any of them. This built on the check-verification communications system the bank had already installed, which allowed customers to cash checks at any of the branches. It also built on the historical anomaly that had grandfathered the interstate operations of this holding company when the Douglas Amendment in 1956 forbade the further formation of companies that would own banks in more than one state. By 1983 Plus Systems of Denver was making the ATMs of thirty-five large banks (including Bank of America and Chase) available to customers of any of them across the country; and Cirrus, a network of 619 banks including First Interstate itself, Mercantile in Texas, Manufacturers Hanover, and Pittsburgh's Mellon Bank, was in partial operation through a switch run by the National Bank of Detroit. Locally, however, each ATM accepts only the card issued by its proprietor: the supermarkets will run them ragged.

All these travelers' services will be outmoded, anyway, by a Visa interchange program permitting a cardholder to use the machines of out-of-town banks that issue Visa cards. Visa runs the switch that feeds the machine to the issuing bank's memo file to verify that the customer is good for the money, and the debit to the issuing bank is merged with the other debits on the cards it has issued in the daily Visa clearing. One notes with interest that before agreeing to this plan, Visa's board of banks demanded that each bank have the right to exclude two out-of-town issuers from the use of their machines. The two most popular candidates for exile, by far, have been Citibank, which makes no bones about its desire to be a national operator in its own right, and Banc One, to get at the Merrill Lynch card. Citibank's agreements with Safeway and Publix can be seen as an effective riposte, not to say revenge.

Refusal to share was even more debilitating to the development of point-of-sale terminals: electronic cash registers in stores, which theoretically could have received bank debit cards instead of cash. This, too, should have been an ACH-based service, with terminals that would accept cards issued by any bank. It is hard to get a handle on how great the potential for this service is. Most people who are sent a debit card already have a credit card. Purchases made with the debit card are paid for that night, with deduction of the money from the bank balance; purchases made with the credit card don't have to be paid for something more than a month. Still, the supermarkets, which is where the original POS terminals were installed, have never accepted credit cards. An electronic transfer initiated with a debit card is the equivalent of cash for the store, and for the customer who would otherwise write a check it's a time-saver.

In 1984–86 POS will get a full tryout, in Los Angeles, where five of the largest California banks—Bank of America, First Interstate, Security Pacific, First California, and Wells Fargo—have joined together to design and install a system by which debit cards issued by any of them, or by any depository institution in Los Angeles that wishes to participate, can be used to pay for merchandise in all the city's major department stores and supermarkets. All five banks will compete for the accounts of the merchants, and each will run its own switch to allocate the debits to the cardholder's banks, collecting from them on a bilateral basis. The shared feature will be the card-verification system, which will query the cardholder's bank about the legitimacy of the card and the PIN number—and the presence of sufficient funds in the cardholder's account—before the transaction is authorized at the store. Outside firms have been invited to compete for the contract to provide this service, with a list of specifications—"wishes, really," said David Aaronson of General Electric, among those receiving invitations—that included a one-second response time on 800,000 queries a day in 1984, 2.5 million queries a day in 1985.

As the time neared for this system to go into pilot testing, the banks had still not decided who should pay for it—the customer, who probably wouldn't use it if the debit card cost money and a check did not; the merchant, who felt clearly that the most that could be asked of him was the purchase of equipment to modify his electronic cash register for the purpose; or the bank. The value for the bank lay first in the elimination of check processing, second in the float that would be generated by debiting the customer's account before the merchant got the credit. This value was greatest when the debit was "on us"— when the cardholder was a depositor in the same bank as the merchant or in one of the bank's respondents—which made the plan particularly simpatico at Bank of America, the region's largest consumer bank. The others could partially compensate by securing more than their share of the merchant accounts, which argued for the emergence of a bidding war among the banks. While this worried the banks, it gave perhaps the most solid reason for believing that POS would work in Southern California—if the merchants are bribed heavily enough, they may sell it to the consumer. What was lacking in the banks' plans, as usual, was any coherent strategy for making people wish to use such cards.

All this would have been much easier, of course, if the Cal-West ACH had been in shape to handle the inputs from the merchant's banks generated by the POS terminals in the stores. Moreover, the use of an ACH, with its now-established principle of open membership, would have been a prophylactic against the Justice Department, which has grumbled about the denial of "potential competition" in the Nebraska NET system, which hooks 80% of the state's depository institutions together through one POS computer. Instead, the five organizing banks all had to gear up to handle payments on an old-fashioned basis of bilateral settlement.

(4) *The banks allowed the Federal Reserve System to become much too dominant a factor in the planning and operation of the ACHs.* Indeed, they regarded ACH as essentially the Fed's baby. The district Federal Reserve Banks provided hardware, software, and delivery systems, and made virtually all the investments over the first ten years. And when Congress required the Feds to price their services, creating the remarkable competition we shall consider in the next chapter, the Fed kept the ACHs alive by setting prices far below what they considered their costs. It was not until the Feds announced a phasing out of this subsidy—at a rate of 20% a year, with full cost recovery at the end of 1985—that the banks began to consider seriously establishing privately owned and operated ACHs with more modern communications and more ingenious software than the Fed was providing.

139

The difficulty was that the Fed remained bound to the misconceptions of the initial SCOPE report: it considered the ACH as neither more nor less than an electronic version of the checking system. Instead of passing ACH entries to member banks in the form of electronic messages, the Feds sent them off as rolls of tape. "There are lots of people at the Fed," says an operations wallah at a major bank, who has served in executive positions for the National Automated Clearing House Association, "who think that if you have to get information from New York to Watertown, you send it on a truck."

Payments entered into an ACH normally produced available funds for the banks on precisely the same schedule the Feds established for checks. Indeed, because ACH entries at all but the Cleveland and Chicago Feds had to be put into the system by midafternoon while checks were accepted for processing until midnight or later, an ACH entry might produce usable funds for the bank receiving it a day later than a payment made by check. Though there were vague promises that FRCS 80 (Federal Reserve Communications System for the 80's) would open more channels for the electronic communication of ACH information—and even a suggestion of new ACH software by sometime in 1984—the Fed had no plans, and no interest in other people's plans, to make ACH payments faster than checks.

In 1982 the banks of two states—Arizona and Hawaii—established their own privately operated ACHs within the framework of CACHA (the Cal-West Automated Clearing House, operated by the Federal Reserve Bank of San Francisco). Working through computer facilities provided by First Interstate, which had bid for the job, these private ACHs were able to involve more institutions and sell more corporations than the Fed-based system had reached, at prices comparable to those the Fed said represented a 60% subsidy to the service. In mid-1983, both CACHA and NEACHA (the New England Automated Clearing House) put out tenders for bids by private processors to replace the Fed. As award time neared in California, Bank of America seemed certain to be the winner with a bid of 2¢ per item processed in a system that would move its information by wire rather than by hand delivery of tape rolls.

State Street Bank's James Lordan, a compact, energetic Bostonian who was president of NACHA in 1982–83, foresaw a future when the Fed would continue to deliver subsidized ACH services to banks that lacked the equipment to process electronic receipts, while private ACHs would take the cream of the market. Actually, for other reasons, the Fed was pushing the smaller banks to acquire electronic capability, lending them dedicated terminals for the receipt of FedWire in the New York district or leasing microcomputers to them at bargain-basement rates in the San Francisco and Dallas districts. The cooperation of the Fed in making its links to these banks available to private ACHs, for some minor fee, might be all the bankers would need to make the system universal—provided they were ready to make investments in the service.

Not many people believed that readiness was there. James Hopes of Chase Manhattan, who provides the New York ACH with four-fifths of its business and really believes in the principles of the thing, was eyeing rather wistfully a pile of checks processed by the Todd printer that can MICR–encode IBM–card checks to "counterfeit" (legally) the checks of any bank in the country. Chase still prepares these checks for those policy-holders of the insurance companies who feel strongly about getting checklike instruments rather than notices of pre-authorized electronic payment in their monthly statements from their banks. "Those cost us between two and three cents each. When the Feds lift the price of an ACH entry above five cents . . ." He made a face and shrugged his shirtsleeved shoulders (people in operations do not wear jackets at work). At the Fed, a number of operations vice-presidents (whose work force, after all, is concentrated heavily in check processing) commented that once "full-boat pricing" is set for the ACH, this little institution will just disappear.

Except that it won't disappear: it will simply move out of

the ambit of the Fed and the banking system. Both POS and home banking—of which, more in Chapter 10—require an efficient, fast, inexpensive, credit-transfer payments system to make economic sense. If the Fed and the banks do not provide this service, others will—perhaps Visa, which began an all-electronic ACH for eleven participating banks in 1983, or the S&Ls, which are, on the average, more automated than the banks and are undergoing more rapid consolidation; or the data-processing companies, which are already in this business through their payroll divisions and the networks by which they service ATMs; or Sears and Penney; or the equipment manufacturers like NCR, IBM, GE, or AT&T. "You have to be able to administer the value-transfer system inexpensively," says Bank of America's Thomas Wood, a large, thoughtful computer expert with disappearing blond curls who has been Bank of America's point man on automation since the early 1970s. "Whoever does this will have the business. Bankers are going to be forced to look again at giro-type ACH systems because the only way for the American banking business to survive is to reduce the cost of doing business."

3

Most Americans make contact with electronic banking through the Visa and Interbank (MasterCard) systems that make the rules and play the games of the credit cards. Between them, they have 120,000,000 cards outstanding in the United States (i.e., many Americans carry both), issued by perhaps 15,000 depository institutions, "honored" by more than 2,000,000 sellers of goods and providers of services. Ostensibly these plastics are offered by banks, and it is banks that extend the credit and bear the risks. Visa has its origins in the Bank-Americard pioneered by Bank of America and franchised around the country; Interbank, in the co-op of California banks formed to fight Bank of America for this business. But both (Visa especially) are now independent bureaucracies that dominate their bank-appointed boards, make their own plans, and run their own show.

The Fed talks wistfully about truncating checks—capturing the information on the check's first pass through the reader-sorter and then carrying on the rest of the value-transfer process by automated means. Visa and Interbank have done it. Visa's credit-card slip goes to the merchant's bank and is processed once (more often by a correspondent bank or a data-processing company than by the issuer), producing credits for the store or the airline or the restaurant and debits for the purchasers, either at the same bank (an "on us" item stripped from the system and recorded simply within the bank) or at some other bank, local or far away. Because the information moves electronically, there is no need to segregate claims on local banks. All debit messages move to a Visa processing center, where claims *by* a bank on behalf of its merchant accounts and claims *on* a bank to pay for its cardholders' purchases are netted out once a day. The result is a settlement sheet listing some thousands of banks (many of which receive and pay for correspondents). The settlement sheet is communicated electronically to Chase Manhattan in New York, which pays the banks with numbers on the left side of the ledger and collects from banks with negative numbers. For some of the banks, this transfer is accomplished by changing the numbers on their correspondent account at Chase; for others, Chase sends out messages alerting the bank to an upcoming receipt of funds by FedWire or demanding immediate payment. For handling an electronic item, the two credit-card systems charged 1.2¢ in 1983.

Historically, what the public has seen of this process is a carbon-set of flimsy paper slips, but the electronic nature of the operation has now spilled over to public consciousness with the expensive unveiling of Visa's new "electron card." In fact, the new card was devised less to facilitate the movement of money than to make the system more secure by removing the embossed name and number from the card and compelling merchants to demand a PIN number from the customer. Fraud losses in the credit-card business have been mounting exponentially because anyone with a child's toy printing shop can duplicate the raised printing, and anyone with a casette of blank audio tape and a steam iron can copy a mag stripe. In 1982 the credit-card system suffered a plague of "white card fraud," involving merchants in cahoots with criminals who prepared slips for entry into the system from blank cards embossed with the names and numbers of legitimate customers (which can be taken from discarded slips in trash cans).

Supposedly, Visa's new electron card will be a universal instrument. Printed on its face will be a mag stripe, an Optical Character Recognition number (for some chain stores), and a Universal Product Code set of thin and thick bars (for Penney's and the supermarkets, which already have machinery that can read the UPC). Whichever system the merchant uses, the Visa receptacle, hard-wired into a communications net, will check the bona fides of the card as the customer punches in his identification number. This is going to be a headache—merchants have resisted the effort to put PIN numbers into the card network because anyone who forgets his PIN holds up a whole line of patrons at the cash register (and people who write their PIN number on their card frustrate the security of the system). For the smaller stores, it will be no more of a headache than the present system in which someone has to call Visa or Interbank to get an authorization—but they will have to invest in a card reader and a telephone line.

Both these requirements are significant for a small store. Visa hopes to get its suppliers down to $500–$600 for a smart terminal with a "PIN port" that will automatically call headquarters when the mag stripe is swiped through it, communicate the contents of the stripe and the PIN number inserted by the cardholder, and print out paper slips as a hard-copy record of the transaction (required by Federal Reserve Regulation E) for both merchant and purchaser. Over time, the dedicated telephone line connecting this terminal to the Visa network may be even more expensive than the terminal, given the probability of greatly increased telephone communications costs during the second half of the 1980s.

Visa will try to minimize its own communications and mainframe computer costs by distributing the processing through a large number of regional nodes with IBM System One computers, but the installation of this system will be expensive—especially since the company expects to use it worldwide (more than a third of the 100 million Visa cards are issued outside the United States). In spring 1983 Visa's board gave management authority to sell $200 million in bonds—the company's first venture into debt—to pay the internal costs.

Though designed initially to stop the hemmorhage of fraud in the credit-card links, Visa's electron card and its associated network are easily adaptable to ATM and POS operation. Robert Irwin, an irreverent systems engineer recruited from IBM to work at Visa's San Mateo headquarters on the implementation of the electron card, believes that ATM networks cannot generate enough volume to sustain themselves unless they are also used for POS—"and when we are done here, we will have put in place a national POS network." Irwin envisages a future when Visa will settle accounts through "worldwide windows: we start at Greenwich time and settle every two hours, through the day and night." Such settlements would not go conveniently through Chase Manhattan; Irwin envisages heavy use of improved ACHs. Though nobody is talking about it, Visa would seem to have longer ends in view in its bids to be the processing agent for privately owned ACHs on the Pacific Coast and in New England.

"The merchant isn't the big problem," Irwin says, thinking of the mountains the electron card must climb before Visa reaches its 1985 target of 20 million transactions a day preauthorized through terminals. "Once he has a terminal, he's as happy as a pig in the mud. But the banks hate to get into a new business. It all goes back to how banks think—that's why the near-banks will eat them for lunch."

4

What the banks should want—but don't—is a system that moves as much of the processing as possible out to their customers, and then gathers the results once a day (or, rather, once a night, when the communications systems that handle other jobs are free to take this one) for posting to the accounts. There is something very strange in the notion that the merchants and Visa and the banks must be on line for transactions that average about $40 each. "The economies of operating off-line are several magnitudes of difference," says David Aaronson of General Electric. "But banks don't want to take the chance. Banks want to do a credit check on every transaction, to make sure it's a good card. That's the only reason you have to be on-line. It's crazy—but it's a psychology with them. Banks have a total lack of trust of the general public."

To date, then, American banks have neglected the most interesting piece of new technology for consumer payments: the "smart card," a tiny microprocessor-cum-memory-chip encapsulated in a standard-sized credit card. American researchers had been looking for some years for a memory device that would be more capacious and more secure than the mag stripe—which can hold at most 1,200 digital bits on three tracks—and both Fairchild Instruments and IBM had patents on devices using a semiconductor memory chip before 1970. But the first workable standard-sized plastic chip card was produced in France in 1974 by a journalist and tinkerer, Roland C. Moreno, in a home workshop where he and his friends noodled over odd notions that might be sold by a venture they had started under the name Innovatron, grandly described as the *Société Internationale pour l'Innovation.*

At the start, the chip card was distinctly a tinkerer's technology: a solution, as is still said of it, looking for a problem. Moreno had conceived it mostly as a substitute for the mag stripe on the bank card—more secure, because the password registered on the chip couldn't be copied, and more capable of retaining a record of activity because its memory capacity would be greater. Coupled with an electronic cash register to capture the data about the customer and the transaction—and then with a communications device to read out to a bank and to an automated clearinghouse at the end of the day how much should be credited to the merchant for his sales and how much should be debited from the accounts of each of the purchasers—the chip card could substitute for checks at the point of sale. This was important for France, where checks are slow, costly (Henderson of the New York Fed estimates a processing cost of $1 a check in France)—and, to everyone's horror, increasingly popular.

The big French banks were not interested in Moreno's chip card. They were planning a future American-style, with highly automated check processing and debit cards controlled by on-line verification arrangements using giant central computers. For their purposes, the magnetic stripe seemed satisfactory. But a handful of smaller banks, and their trade association, saw in Moreno's card a way to offer retail services comparable to those of the big banks, with much smaller up-front costs and greater flexibility.

More important, Smart Card caught the fancy of the government's Director General for Telecommunications, parent of the state-owned PTT (for Post-Telegraph-Telephone). PTT was up to its eyeballs in Videotex, a French technology, and was projecting a future in which every home would have a Minitel terminal with screen and keyboard that would allow the householder to tap various databases PTT would supply (starting with the telephone directory, which would no longer be printed). With Smart Card as a secure access device and personal record-keeping tool, PTT could proceed more rapidly to offer mail-order purchasing, home banking, electronic mail, and the like, on its Minitel terminals.

PTT also saw in Smart Card a way to solve two mundane but nontrivial problems: the nuisance of coin-operated telephones and billing for long-distance calls. A reader for a chip card could be made cheaply enough to be used in lieu of a coin slot in a pay phone. Tourists could buy a card with, say, $10 worth of message units on it, and the credit would run out of the card with use. Regular customers of the PTT would have a card that would access their account and set up automatic billing for long-distance calls made from any phone.

With PTT on board, it was no great trick to interest CII–Honeywell–Bull, the Franco-American, public-private partnership set up by Charles de Gaulle in his search for a plausible French challenge to IBM. But Honeywell–Bull saw much greater possibilities here. Moreno's memory card could be made an *intelligent* memory card by adding a microprocessor chip that could generate its own algorithms and access different areas of the memory for writing or reading, according to need and the cardholder's instructions. In 1976 Honeywell–Bull took the first license of the Moreno patents, blended them with some patents of its own, and began to produce CP8, "a portable computer for the '80s." The cards were twice as thick as normal bank cards, the banks couldn't see what use they had for the microprocessor, and commercial planning ground to a halt.

Now to the rescue rode Schlumberger, the petroleum equipment company, which had a subsidiary, Flonic, that made water meters, parking meters, and the like. With help from Moreno and from Siemens, the German company that would supply the chips, Flonic designed a system with a preprogrammed, hard-wired microprocessor, which was much cheaper to make, and gave the banks a proposal for a market test. When this project foundered in 1978 because the big banks still weren't interested, the government intervened: in late 1978 an interministerial council declared Smart Card one of the items of French high technology that should be supported.

Dragging the state-owned banks behind it, the telecommunications ministry put out a request for proposals from French manufacturers of electronic equipment, for cards and readers and registers to be used in shops and supermarkets. Seven bids were submitted, and in July 1980 awards were made for three pilot projects: to Flonic for the simple card, to Honeywell for a card with a complex chip that combined microprocessor and memory (and had been squeezed down to fit the 30–mil thickness of a bank card), and to Philips of Holland for a card in which microprocessor and memory chip were separately encapsulated and wired together.

By fall 1980 the locations for the three experiments had been chosen: two small cities, Caen and Blois, plus the commercial renewal project in downtown Lyon, looking for a demonstration of its modernity in its competition with the giant suburban shopping centers. *All* the banks in each city would be involved, large and small, so that a customer of any bank could get a card permitting him to play the new game and no merchant would be frozen out because he banked with the wrong institution. The numbers would be large: 125,000 cards altogether, and 650 terminals in the shops.

DGT and the manufacturers formed INTELMATIQUE, a society to exploit these experiments and promote Smart Card worldwide. In earnest of internationalism, Roy Bright, Jr., an English specialist in electronic banking, was hired as managing director. The French banks then took the lead to establish INTAMIC—the International Association for Microcircuit Cards, which in mid-1983 had more than 100 member banks in 11 countries. The U.S. delegation consisted of only two banks (Chase Manhattan and Bank of America), plus American Express through its London office.

In the emerging mythology of this subject, Smart Card came to America at an international telecommunications show in Los Angeles in late 1980. Arlen Richard Lessin, a stout, rather Dickensian New York communications consultant, was at the show on other business. "In an obscure area of the building," he recalls, "was a subdued and missable small exhibit of Honeywell–Bull, with a cardboard reader on display. I stopped and knew this was something of immense importance—instant awareness—I can't tell you why."

Lessin moved on to an appointment with DuWayne Peterson, a senior vice-president of Security Pacific, and "told him I had just seen something that was going to revolutionize banking." He got Peterson sufficiently excited to cancel afternoon appointments and put together a team of senior executives at the bank to hear a presentation from the French team at the show. Security Pacific was not convinced it needed Smart Card, but Roy Bright in Paris, who was not having much luck with American banks, decided INTELMATIQUE needed Lessin. "Within one month after I first saw the card," Lessin says, "I was a consultant to the French government. That doesn't happen."

In fact, of course, Lessin merely took Smart Card public: unspoken, in the bowels of the corporate research divisions, much work was already being done on chip cards. IBM's French subsidiary knew all about Moreno's invention. Honeywell–Bull was half-American from the start. AT&T was up on the activities of the French PTT, and Bell Labs was fooling around with a chip card for the long-lines division. Battelle Memorial Institute had done a study on chip cards and distributed it to its clients. Before Lessin went to the telecommunications show, Citicorp had a team working on chip cards at its Transactions Technology subsidiary. Bank of America's Tom Wood remembers that he began tracking Smart Card in 1979.

Probably the most thorough exploration of microchip cards in the United States was done in 1982 by Wood's Bank of America "task force" with Intel and Malco Plastics, a Maryland subsidiary of Britain's EMI–Thorn that is by far the largest American producer of mag-stripe cards, with an output of 200 million a year—and has its own patented "magnetic watermark" system for inproving the security of mag stripes. This project was much more ambitious than anything the French had on their plate. It was tied to Intel's development of a 256K memory chip at a time when the French were struggling to make cards around an 8K chip. Malco was involved mostly because Smart Card had caught the fancy of its president Larry Linden, a soft-spoken, meticulous, gray-haired Southerner who likes to talk about retiring to a farm he has converted to a one-man research lab in computerized telecommunications. But there were business reasons, too: "Smart Card represents an incredible opportunity for the first guy who learns to make it cheaply," Linden says, "and an unbelievable threat for everybody else." As of late 1983, the verdict at all three companies was still: not yet—let someone else solve the problems of reliability, manufacturability, and durability.

Perhaps because its promoter in the United States was a go-getter like Arlen Lessin rather than a government or a bureaucratic corporation, the chip card roused the instincts of a generation of electronic tinkerers. "I've been an enthusiast for Smart Card," says William Moroney, executive vice-president of the Electronic Funds Transfer Association, "since I saw Mr. Spock put his card in the computer in *Star Trek*."

The first use of Smart Card in the United States was for encryption purposes. First Bank Systems of Minneapolis was running an experiment in home banking using French Minitel terminals placed in 250 farmhouses near Fargo, North Dakota. Farmers have lived with party-line telephones. "They were concerned about security," says Stuart C. MacIntire, who ran this pilot program for the bank by arrangement with J. C. Penney, which bought the "First Hand" system and his services in 1983. "It was three hundred miles back to the bank. We bought the Honeywell CP8 card and programmed it for a home terminal environment. The card triggered encryption on a random-number table, and our computer locked into the signal from the chip. Because of the excess capacity on a 4K chip, we could capture all the farmer's financial activity on the card memory so he had a record of it that could print out."

Recordkeeping is the most promotable feature of the memory chip. A Smart Card, for example, could be supplied with every new automobile and would keep a record, in the car, of all maintenance work performed on the vehicle—any mechanic could plug the card into a reader and secure the history of its physical and psychiatric ills and their treatment. The airlines already do this with a centralized database for each aircraft, but even they might find it useful to have such a record inside the cockpit.

At the New York Stock Exchange, floor brokers write slips of paper saying they have bought so many shares from or sold to such-and-such a broker for this or that price. A clerk at the post time-stamps the pieces of paper and puts the sale on the ticker. Then everybody argues later about who made what mistake. In a brave new world, the brokers could insert their Smart Cards into a writer-reader with two activating buttons. Details of the sale—stock, price, quantity—would appear on a display screen, and when both brokers hit their buttons, the sale would be registered on the ticker, on a communications device that confirms to the brokers' offices, and on the Smart Cards. The identities of the buying and selling brokers would communicate automatically from one card to the other. If there was a dispute, the data would print off the card. "It feeds into the development of an audit trail," says Erik Steiner, head of the product analysis lab at the Exchange, very approvingly. "It's not on our list of things currently in progress, but it's on the list of 'mays.'"

Some of the paper Smart Card can eliminate is fraudulent paper. "I can't imagine why anyone still counterfeits currency," the president of a Federal Reserve Bank said conversationally. "The bank looks at currency. But nobody ever looks at food stamps, and you can counterfeit them with a color Xerox. There are brokers in every slum who will give cash for food stamps, even if you don't know anyone who works in a supermarket." The fact that a chip card can be loaded with an initial credit that works its way down with use—and can be updated automatically on the first of the next month—makes this technology a natural match with social-welfare programs. In recent years the United States has suffered from a growing flood of fraudulent documents. Counterfeit driver's licenses, Social Security cards, foreign nationals' green cards—such items are available from your friendly street-corner underground economist about as easily as a joint of marijuana. If the day should come when Congress is ready to move to establish a national ID document, a high-capacity Smart Card would clearly be a strong contender for the job. A single chip card could serve as everything from birth certificate to medical insurance record, driver's license to bank account number, each section of the card kept private by the microprocessor from any but specially authorized and equipped readers.

What's holding it up? If he's so smart, why ain't he rich? In part, the problem is the incompatibility of the three French card systems and a disagreement about standards between the French and the potential licensees and competitors elsewhere. The French manufacturers agree on the geography of the card, with the chip in the upper-left-hand corner, and on the location of the electrical contact points. But the Germans have been promoting a card with the contacts on the edge rather than on the face. The Americans feel they don't have enough information. In mid-1983 the French urged at a meeting of the International Standards Organization in San Francisco that standards for the placement of the chip and its electrical connections be established right now. Jerome Svigals, the tough-minded and worldly-wise manager of growth planning for IBM and head of the working group on Smart Cards of the American National Standards Institute, insisted that he needed more time. His schedule called for standards to be adopted by steps, the last of which would not be taken until late 1985. "By 1985," said Jean Boggio of INTAMIC, the French-sponsored bankers' group, "IBM will be ready to manufacture." Nothing, of course, prevents the French from adopting their own standards without reference to ANSI, as the PTT apparently has done with card-activated telephones—except the fear of cutting themselves off from the American market, which would frustrate half the purpose of the French government's investment.

In December 1983, Intelmatique announced what may have been a breakthrough: a decision by Carte Bleue, the largest of the French credit-card systems (not very large, be- cause the Banque de France has held down such activity, fearing its impact on monetary control, but still 3 million cardholders) that it would follow up on the p.o.s. experiment in Blois by issuing its members in that city a chip card rather than a stripe card. This is the Honeywell-Bull system, and both parties announced that if all went well in Blois early in the year, Carte Bleue—a Visa affiliate—would proceed to national use by the end of 1984, keying the introductions to the spread of the PTT's electronic telephone directory.

Still, it must be said that the French have blown an American media event that was one of the most spectacular opportunities for a marketing triumph ever offered by the goddess of chance. In summer 1983, newspapers and television and Congressional committees made much of a story about some high school kids with home computers who had been roaming data bases in hospitals, banks, even NASA. Smart Card was a proved and inexpensive strategy for controlling access to computers, with read-only terminals so cheap to make that the PTT was putting them in pay phones. The chip card had come to America originally as a security device in the First Bank Systems home-banking pilot. Representatives of Smart Card could have got on every TV news and talk show for weeks, and could have sold not only cards but systems. It never occurred to the French government or its U.S. advisers that they had such an opportunity, and the moment passed.

Beneath all this smoky argument is the real fire that the existing Smart Card is just not good enough. The cards in use in Blois, Caen, and Lyon contain an 8K PROM (Programmable–Read–Only–Memory) chip that cannot be erased. Even with a bare minimal entry for each transaction—date and amount and

nothing else—there is room for no more than perhaps 120 transactions (omitting date: 200). If the record on the card is to
include an identification of the store—which would seem necessary if people are to use their cards outside their own neighborhood—storage capacity of an 8K chip would sink to perhaps
50 transactions, and the card would have to be replaced every
few weeks. Discussing the possible use of Smart Card at the
New York Stock Exchange, Erik Steiner noted that an 8K card
wouldn't get a floor broker through a full day's work.

Two well-marked paths lead out of this corner: the memory can be made larger, or the memory can be made erasable.
INTAMIC's Boggio says blithely, "I'm sure in five years we
will have a million bits," but not many people agree. Honeywell's Nora, after pointing out that "16K is no problem," admits that "over 16K there is a problem of size"—that is, the
chip assembly becomes too big to fit conveniently on a card
only 30 mils thick. A putative American competitor called
Smart Card Systems (which does not accept the validity of the
French patents) has promised a 64K card anytime if some investor will put up the money. Both Bank of America's Wood
and IBM's Svigals think Smart Card Systems can make such a
card because its parent company, International Micro Industries, employs a much-admired patented process for bonding
microchips on a very thin film. But as of this writing the readers
and writers for this card do not exist even in prototype form.
And the standards for this system would be quite different from
anything now being considered by ANSI. "They kick us in the
teeth," said marketing director Philip Rima; "we're just little
guys, you know." Meanwhile, the 256K chip card that Intel
was working on for Bank of America remains on the horizon.
In summer 1983 Intel had a 256K PROM chip in production,
and a spokesman said it could be shaved to fit into a bank card
"in a year or two."

Making a rewritable memory would be easier. The French
resist it, allegedly in fear of a widespread computer sophistication that would enable crooks to "clone" Smart Cards if their

content could be altered. Steven Weinstein, chief scientist of American Express, who has been pushing his company toward experiments with Smart Cards (the Amex bank in London began issuing chip cards in January 1984), feels that "the security of a rewritable memory is a red herring because access to the memory is controlled by microprogramming within the card. If a competent person designs the microprogramming, there's no way an unauthorized person can get in." Bank of America's Wood observes that when the French began planning Smart Card, the E–2 PROM Weinstein would like to use (E–2 stands for "Electronically Erasable") did not exist. He believes that once the current tests are done, the French will realize how much larger the market for an erasable memory would be and will drop their objections.

There is an American challenge to chip-card technology: the laser card, made in Silicon Valley by Drexler Technology Corp. Lacking a built-in microprocessor, the Drexon Laser Card cannot quality for the encomium "smart," but like the idiot savants of the big-ticket quiz shows twenty-five years ago, it makes up in brute memory for what it may lack in intelligence. A strip of reflective material about as wide as a magnetic stripe on a credit card will hold 7,000,000 bits of information, or about 160,000 words of text. The material on which the laser incises the information is the invention of Jerome Drexler, a ruminative veteran of Bell Labs whose basic business is "micro-imaging"—his company makes the glass masks used for etching integrated circuits on silicon. He can turn out Drexon cards in batches of 100,000 to sell for about $1.50 each, and it is hard to imagine chip prices or card manufacturing technology that could bring the price of a Smart Card below $3. The laser card lacks the security the microprocessor gives the chip card, but its memory is so enormous that very positive identification of the user (a digitalized record of the dynamics of his handwriting, for example) can be hidden on its surface. As of late 1983, SRI was developing reader-writers for laser cards, using components much reduced in price thanks to the recent development of the laser audio disc, and seven customers had purchased licenses to make the machines when they are ready: NCR in the United States, Ericsson in Sweden, Elbit Computers in Israel—and four Japanese manufacturers. These licenses cost $250,000–$300,000 each. Toward the end of the year, five Japanese bankers bought their own Drexon licenses.

Though the technologies are quite different, the systems effect of the chip card and the laser card would be roughly the same: both would function as "Smart Cards." And one or the other is all but certainly coming. "Five years from now," Paul Finch of Valley National Bank in Phoenix said in early 1983, "everybody will have a Smart Card. It gives me a way to get away from the customer's chart of account numbers for his ACH payments. It can't be tampered with. I can imbed a credit score on it, limit the card, expand it. I can serve all my depositors and all my merchants. Of course, I'm an engineer," Finch added—he is another man in shirtsleeves. "I'm not really a banker, I've just been in banking since I went to school. I segregate the transactions business of banking from the funds business of banking, and that's hard for traditional bankers to do."

Smart Card will work through an Automated Clearing House or something like it—one would expect the ATM microcomputers out in the field to do the preliminary sorting and batching before messages were sent out. If the traditional bankers can't learn to think like the Paul Finches in their back offices, the economy will generate a separate institution to handle Smart Card, and the banks will no longer be central to the new payments system. The threat is especialy grave because the banks stand now in danger of losing control of the existing payments system, not to the technologically agile, but to their old friends and regulators at the Federal Reserve.

6

THE FED AS COMPETITOR

When the rich bankers met on Jekyll Island off the coast of Georgia to plan the Federal Reserve Act," said a distinguished if irreverent monetary economist and banking historian, "they had two things on their minds. They wanted to do something to restore public confidence in the banking system after the Panic of 1907 and the failure of the Knickerbocker Trust—and they wanted to set up some sort of neutral arbiter who would keep them from screwing each other all the time on out-of-state check collection."

1

Before 1913 neither the government nor any quasi-governmental agency had been involved in the American payments system—and to this day no governmental agency has anything to do with check clearing in Britain or Canada or in parts of the European continent. But in the United States, with 20,000 banks scattered over thousands of miles, and a history of undercapitalized banks that wound up unable to meet their own or their customer's obligations, it had not been possible to set up a nongovernmental system that allowed all bank depositors to use their checks all over the country. Prior to the creation of the Federal Reserve, checks drawn on remote banks were typically accepted only for "nonpar collection"— that is, the depositor received something less than the face value of the check from the bank where he deposited it: the bank charged a commission. Sometimes there might be more than one commission: a payment in Harrisburg, Pennsylvania, with a check on a bank in Butte, Montana, might involve several "exchange fees:" the bank in Harrisburg would collect for a fee charged by its correspondent in Pittsburgh, which would be collecting for fees from the Butte bank's correspondent in Helena and *its* correspondent in Chicago. Banks scratched each other's banks and might route checks in ways that maximized friends' opportunities to collect fees.

Among the missions Congress gave the new Federal Reserve Board was the establishment of check collection at par between any two points in the United States, using the facilities of what would be twelve partly independent district Federal Reserve Banks. In 1916 the Board insisted that checks presented for collection to and by a district Fed had to be honored at face value. If a bank refused to grant full value for a check presented through a Fed, its own checks would not be honored at all at any of the Federal Reserve Banks. Some states tried to protect nonpar collection commissions as a source of revenue for their banks, and as late as 1970 there were still 500 banks in the country that charged a fee for accepting out-of-town checks. But over time the Federal Reserve was too strong.

One of the beauties of the "reserve" system was that the Feds would never be at a risk in check collection because they held the reserves of the banks to which they were giving credit for the checks. When the Federal Reserve Bank of Cleveland gave the Harrisburg bank credit for the check drawn on a member in Butte, it knew that the Federal Reserve Bank of Chicago had funds from the bank in Butte that could be used to pay off. FedWire was created initially to move shares in the system's Gold Settlement Fund from one Reserve Bank to another in such situations.

Now, check collection (and payments) was always the primary service a "correspondent bank" offered to its "respondents." And the second most important service was credit in tough times—the money-center correspondent would help its country cousin by "discounting" some of the respondent's loans and providing cash. Each Federal Reserve Bank had a "discount window"—and the system as a whole had a charge from Congress to act as a "lender of last resort" and see to it that banks with sound loans on their books did not get in liquidity difficulties.

In theory, then, there was a dual system of correspondent banks in the United States from 1913 on, because the twelve district Feds offered an alternative (indeed, superior) source of the two most valued correspondent services. As the system worked out in practice, however—which is doubtless the way it was projected at Morgan's estate on Jekyll Island—the district Feds became the servants rather than the competitors of the big-city correspondent banks. State-chartered banks, always the large majority, preferred to keep balances at their correspondents, rather than reserves at the Fed, partly because the correspondent offered services the Fed couldn't match (introductions and bona fides for customers of the small bank seeking to do business in the big city, tickets to the ball game, the best dinner in town, and Heaven knows what else when the president of the correspondent bank came visiting), partly because state charters mostly allowed banks to earn interest on the reserves they kept with their correspondents while reserves at the Fed were sterilized. And the Fed provided check-clearing services (free, after 1918) not only for the checks on and to the big-city member banks, but also for all the checks such banks presented or accepted on behalf of their nonmember respondents. In hard times, moreover, correspondent banks found it much easier to lend money by discounting paper for their respondents when they knew they could rediscount *it* if necessary, at the Fed.

Among the other major purposes of the Federal Reserve Act was the provision of a more elastic currency and the substitution of Federal Reserve Notes for the notes of commercial banks that had previously circulated (also subject to "nonpar" redemption outside the immediate neighborhood of the bank that issued them). Among the causes of the long recession of the 1890s (not a "gay" period in the economy) had been a decline in the quantity of paper money issued by nationally chartered banks, which could print such paper only against government bonds in their vaults—and the government through this period, under Harrison, Cleveland, and McKinley, was doggedly reducing the national debt. (Fancy that!)

Following the theories of Adam Smith, the Federal Reserve Banks were empowered to issue currency (legal tender, no less) against holdings of various forms of short-term commercial paper. (They also had to have "cover" in gold amounting to 40% of their total note issue—for the Federal Reserve Note was a gold certificate, redeemable in bullion until Roosevelt slammed the gold window shut in 1933; and even then the note itself continued until 1964 to carry the legend that it was a gold certificate). The Feds would thus, in theory, expand their note issues when business was borrowing and needed money, and maintain the money supply when business was repaying its debts and the supply of commercial paper shrank. In the early years, the problem the Federal Reserve faced was that the prosperity induced by World War I and a massive inflow of gold from Europe reduced business borrowing, choking off the supply of commercial paper and thus cutting the Fed's capacity to issue currency. Benjamin Strong of the Federal Reserve Bank of New York found an ingenious way to bull through the restriction, using the Fed's gold to buy

paper from the commercial banks, and then issuing currency against the commercial paper to buy back the gold, which could be used again to buy paper from the banks, and so on ad infinitum. Half a century later, Federal Reserve Board Chairman William McChesney Martin found himself constrained by the other side of the requirement, as American gold drained off to Europe and Asia during the Vietnam War. This time there was no way to resolve the dilemma, and in 1968 Congress repealed the requirement for gold "cover" for the Federal Reserve Note issue.

The other problem the Federal Reserve Banks faced in the early years, so strange in retrospect, was a lack of earning assets to pay their own bills. The Federal Reserve Act had specified that every member bank had to purchase stock in its district Fed in the amount of 6% of its capital and surplus (only 3% actually had to be paid: the other 3% could merely be pledged; this was part of the general rule of the day that bank stockholders were liable for twice the par value of the stock they owned). The district Fed was enjoined by law to pay an annual dividend of 6% on that stock. The earnings for that purpose would presumably come from the interest member banks would pay at the discount window, plus the interest on the commercial paper the district Feds would acquire when issuing currency. The shortage of commercial paper that impeded the note issue therefore put the district Feds into financial embarrassment. They charged for their check-clearing and other services before 1918 because they damned well needed the money. In fact, life was pretty hand-to-mouth around several of the Federal Reserve Banks through the 1920s. It was not until the Glass-Steagall Act of 1932 permitted the Federal Reserve Banks to issue notes backed by their holdings of Treasury paper that the system really began to prosper—and not until 1947 that the revenues of the banks grew so great that the government began to "tax" the note issue.

In the years since 1947 the twelve Federal Reserve Banks, "owned" privately by their member-stockholders but controlled publicly through the entirely governmental Board of Governors, have become far and away the most profitable "enterprise" in the United States. They make their money the old-fashioned way: they print it. Every time they issue a banknote, they acquire on the other side of their ledgers an interest-bearing asset, usually a short-dated Treasury bill. The combination of inflation and high interest rates has meant their earnings have risen beyond the dreams of avarice. In 1982 the bottom line of the Federal Reserve Banks showed a record $15.4 billion profit for the year's work. But the marginal tax on that income reaches 100% almost immediately: of that $15.4 billion, the Feds could keep only $210 million for the expenses of the national Board of Governors, dividends on their stock and an increase in their surplus. All the rest had to be turned over to the Treasury.

Meanwhile, the effective costs of Fed membership had increased dramatically with the rise in interest rates. It was one thing to keep 18% of one's demand-deposit base sterilized at the Fed when interest rates were 2.5%, which meant that the cost to the bank of Fed membership was 0.45% of its demand liabilities; something else when interest rates were 12.25%, and the cost was 2.25% of demand deposits. The pinch was especially tight at the smaller banks, which had to keep balances at correspondents anyway to handle their nonlocal business. State-chartered banks that were not Fed members could use these correspondent balances as reserves and could earn interest on such balances over and above what the correspondent required as a payment for its services. Gradually, Fed membership declined, from banks with more than 80% of the nation's deposits in the 1960s to banks with only 70% of the deposits as the 1970s closed.

The Fed tried to hang on to members by increasing the range of services offered without charge, including FedWire, ACH, and improvements in check collections. There was some suspicion that the ballooning of Federal Reserve Float in the 1970s, to the point where it reached one-fifth of the required reserves, was tolerated by the Board of Governors because it reduced the effective price of membership. (Fed Float—checks on which the Fed has given credit before debiting the accounts of the bank on which they are drawn—turns up in the balance sheets as extra bank reserves.) But the march of dropouts continued, some of them banks as big as $1 billion in assets, some of them banks that had to switch their charters from federal to state to get out of their membership. Ultimately, the Board went to Congress seeking a law that would make Federal Reserve membership compulsory for all FDIC-insured banks. The argument was that the Fed's power to control the money supply was being eroded by the growth of the nonmember sector, which did not have to report its activities to the only central bank the United States had.

Congress moves in mysterious ways, especially when a lot of people are pushing on it at once. The Fed's demand for universal membership coincided with the need to legitimate the automatic-transfer services banks had established to give customers savings-account interest on demand deposits (a practice that a federal court had ruled a violation of the 1933 banking acts), to extend NOW-account powers nationwide, to get the inflation under control, and so on. As usual, Congress was annoyed with the Fed, which insists on asserting its independent powers at all times, though it is constitutionally an agency of the legislature. (Only Congress has the power to coin money, as it has the power to tax: the Founding Fathers were entirely conscious of the fact that inflating the currency is a form of taxation.) So when Congress acted in March 1980, the Fed got something quite different from its request.

Not only banks, but all "depository institutions" that offered transaction accounts—including the S&Ls with their NOW accounts and the credit unions with their share drafts—would be required to keep reserves against such accounts at their district Federal Reserve Bank. The fraction of their deposits banks would have to keep at the Fed as reserves was reduced to 12% (it had been 18% for the bigger banks), and the

Fed's power to vary the ratio was restricted. The Fed was instructed to charge the beneficiary banks when it created reserves by generating float. And it was told to disband the twelve regional clubs, to make their services available to all depository institutions—and to stop giving them away. Starting in September 1981, by law, the Feds were to price their services "explicitly," charging separately for check collection and FedWire and ACH and cash delivery and custody of securities. Prices were to be set so that for each service offered the fees would pay all out-of-pocket expenses and allocated overhead, plus a "Private Sector Adjustment Factor." This PSAF would account for the fact that the Federal Reserve Banks got their money free and were excused from corporate taxation (they do, however, pay local real estate taxes) while private concerns that offered similar services (mostly correspondent banks) had to sell stock or borrow money and pay various franchise and corporate taxes.

Under these circumstances, Congress thought it at least possible that private suppliers might be able to provide better services for less money than the Feds would charge. The Board of Governors was ordered to see to it that the district banks shrank their payrolls if private-sector competitors cut down their business. There was a loophole—the Act permitted the Feds to "give due regard to competitive factors and the provision of an adequate level of such services nationwide"—but it was intended to be a small loophole. The law bluntly ordered the Board of Governors "to require reductions in the operating budgets of the Federal Reserve Banks commensurate with any actual or projected decline in the volume of services to be provided by such banks. The full amount of any savings so realized shall be paid into the United States Treasury."

Prior to the Depository Institutions Deregulation and Monetary Control Act of 1980, selling had been a meaningless concept at the district Feds, which gave services to the 5,500 members and made them available to nonmembers only in special situations and in the most restricted and grudging way.

Suddenly the district Feds had a market, with 44,000 potential customers. But those customers were already being served—essentially, by the 5,500 members, who were in the habit of putting much of their correspondent work through the Fed because the Fed did it for nothing. Now the members would have to pay for the work done not only for themselves, but also (unless they changed their own institutional arrangements) for the banks and thrifts and credit unions they served as correspondents. The history of mankind argued that when the member banks found they had to pay for what they used to get free, they would look for ways to do the work themselves. If that happened, the district banks, which were organized around their operations functions (well over half their employees were in the operating divisions), would fall between the rock of their own bureaucratic necessities and the hard place of congressional mandate.

All this came at a rather awkward time for the district Feds, most of which had recently completed or were in the process of completing large building projects, including architecturally striking headquarters sites in Minneapolis, Boston, Richmond, Philadelphia, and San Francisco. It was painful even to think that this physical expansion would be followed by severe contraction in the numbers of employees and the work accomplished. The Board of Governors turned over the problem of marketing Fed services to the individual district banks. They operated in different labor markets, paid different local taxes, incurred different costs related to the differences in the banking markets they served—most banks in Iowa are smaller than the smallest banks served by the Federal Reserve Bank of New York. Each of the twelve Feds was told to set its own prices for check processing and ACH and custodial and transportation services; only FedWire would be priced nationally. And each was told to develop its own selling programs.

The shift in emphasis at the Feds was dramatic. "It's like taking a bunch of zebras and telling them that because they have stripes, they're tigers," said the president of one of the district banks. "They have to learn to pounce instead of trot."

2

In its early stages, this transmogrification was not very well done. The Board led the way gallantly, pricing the one national service, FedWire, in January 1981, nine months ahead of deadline. The price originally proposed was 80¢ per message, to be paid by the sender. The New York Clearing House banks, asked to comment, suggested that the fee was too low, though it was in fact 20¢ higher than the cost of a CHIPS entry, and noted that CHIPS policy was to divide the fee fifty-fifty between sender and receiver. This looked self-serving to the Board because the New York Clearing House banks were much more likely to be senders than receivers of FedWires (they took money in through CHIPS and SWIFT transfers, and sent it out by FedWire), and the initial schedule was put into effect as written.

Then it turned out the New York banks had been right: the receipts on FedWire ran $800,000 a month below estimated costs, and the Fed found itself in the embarrassing position of having to tell originating banks that the charge for their message would have to be increased because the receiving bank required telephone notification and couldn't process an electronic input. (Payment by sender only was also crazy as a matter of public policy, which seeks to encourage banks of all sizes to acquire electronic capabilities: by making it possible to receive FedWire payments through telephone calls, without charge, the original FedWire pricing schedule gave the laggard banks no incentive to perform.) By the time FedWire pricing had shaken down, in early 1983, the charge was 65¢ to both sender and receiver of an all-electronic message—with a $15 surcharge to a receiving bank that couldn't handle a wire transfer.

In planning their prices for check processing, the district Feds miscalculated either their own costs or those of the correspondent banks. What takes machine time in check collection is sorting down to specific banks the mass of checks that come through the teller's cage each day. Schematically, one does a first sort for checks "on us," on other local banks, other banks in the same Federal Reserve district, banks in the eleven other districts, government checks, traveler's checks. From the individual pockets, the checks run again, and again, until there are piles divided by the individual banks on which the checks are written. Some banks simply sent checks to the Fed in big, amorphous bundles, and the Fed itself sorted them down by address. Others did their own breakdowns and sent the Fed neat bundles that could be put right on the airplane for delivery to the clearinghouses and RCPCs out of town.

Pricing their services, the district Feds charged a very low fee for these "package sort" shipments, a fairly high fee for unsorted bundles. The price per check ran from 0.42¢—for a package-sorted shipment submitted by a bank in the Boston district to be collected from other banks in the Boston district—to 5.3¢ for unsorted checks deposited in the Federal Reserve Board of New York for collection outside the New York district. "The price reflects the work," says J. Richard Smoot, first vice-president of the Philadelphia Fed. "You have a low price for city checks because we can kill that in one sort; an RCPC costs more because it's two passes through the machine."

The switch to priced services occurred in August 1981—and volume at the Feds dropped like a stone, with revenues falling even faster than volume. Banks began using courier services to present checks directly to the out-of-town banks on which they were written, saving Fed processing and transportation charges. And of the checks that did go through the district Feds, a far higher proportion were package-sorted to take advantage of the bargain prices.

Volume fell by 17% for the system as a whole, different district Feds suffering to differing degrees. (It ranged apparently from 9% in Atlanta to almost 40% in Philadelphia). Philadelphia National Bank and the First National Bank of Boston were particularly aggressive in seducing away suburban banks that had previously used Fed services. Mellon Bank in

Pittsburgh stole business from the western edge of the Philadelphia district, which was in fact closer to Pittsburgh, anyway. In a report to Congress in spring 1982, the General Accounting Office estimated that the Feds' receipts were running behind expenditures on check clearing at an annual rate of "about $50 million to $150 million," in violation of the congressional mandate to operate on a break-even basis. If prices were raised to cover these losses, the GAO thought, the result might be a further decline in volume and even greater losses. The GAO commented grimly on "the importance of striving to make costs as responsive as possible to changes in volume."

Confronted with a real threat, the district Feds became real tigers. The GAO thought the Feds' only choice was between raising prices and cutting costs. The district Feds thought there might be a third way: boosting demand. Some hired marketing vice-presidents, some went to consultants. All created sales staffs who could go out and talk with the bankers of the district and tout Fed services. They recruited, bluntly: for a while, James Boisi of Morgan Guaranty carried around in his wallet a want ad from *American Banker*, in which one of the district Feds advertised for a "correspondent banking specialist."

For those who knew the old operating manuals that were what the district Feds supplied to member banks as descriptions of their services, the new brochures were a wonder to behold. Artistically, the prize had to go to the Dallas Fed, which issued a set of six small brochures, boxed tastefully in a cardboard folder, under the general slogan "Service Built on a Foundation of Experience." Each of the brochures was printed on heavy coated paper. Most pages had printing on only one side, and on something like a third of that. The heavy stock covers had gorgeous, dramatic photographs—glowing wires, their tips wrapped in twenty- and fifty-dollar bills, to illustrate electronic transfers; a shower of coins falling onto a golden light for currency and coin service; checks flying into the pockets of a processing machine, and so on. "SECURITY

AND EFFICIENCY hallmarked by experience," the wire-transfer booklet enthused. "Our experience in handling wire transfer transactions is unsurpassed. Our people have served as the architects of a system that is secure, efficient, and backed by experience."

"Have You Considered a Clearing Balance?" inquired a much plainer leaflet from the Federal Reserve Bank of Boston. "Did you know," the leaflet begins, "that a clearing balance can . . . facilitate access to Federal Reserve Services? . . . earn service credits to pay for Federal reserve services? . . . provide better management of your funds?"

The Kansas City Fed, also a plain Jane, put out a little brochure on its "Unsorted Deposit Program," selling its mixed check processing service like a printer selling personalized stationery:

"No Job Is Too Small for Us

" . . . Whether you're getting 400 or 40,000 items per day, we can arrange a processing program that provides you with timely credit availability and high-quality work at an affordable price. . . ."

The New York Fed, selling "Securities Services for the 1980s," warned of the "day-to-day realities that confront financial institutions" that hold investment paper: "Limited vault space. Thefts. Mysterious disappearances. Coupon Collection. Fails . . ." But the banks of the New York district could "resolve these and other difficulties" by leaving their paper with the Fed: "FedClass^{SM} service quality is designed to meet your ever growing and changing needs through the decade of the 1980s." A footnote warned sternly that "FedClass is a service mark of the Federal Reserve Bank of New York."

At the San Francisco Fed, electronic funds transfers were marketed under the logo "FedLine." For $175 a month, Fed-Line customers could lease a package from the San Francisco Fed: an IBM Personal Computer, including printer, guidance in how to use the thing, maintenance, and line charges for connection to the Fed. And the gadget would be useful: "Applications software is available to help you with: Daily Management Activities, Problem Solving, Financial Forecasting, Accounting, Word Processing, etc. . . . One of our representatives can demonstrate and explain the FedLine concept. Call or write today. You can't afford not to know about FedLine."

After its catastrophic first year, the Philadelphia Fed went out and got fully professional help, which decided that the big selling point for the Feds was the existence of what insiders call "the Fed airline"—the forty-odd chartered jets that fly checks back and forth around the country every night to and from the Fed processing centers. "New for 1983" was the heading on the large-format brochure: "Improved Availability Through The Federal Reserve." The illustration was an executive jet in the sunset, flying over mountains. The inside cover listed the cities where the Fed has processing centers, and asked, "In which of these 48 cities do your customers do business? . . . Our Hub-to-Hub connections let you reach these 48 endpoints . . . and hundreds of other cities and towns nationwide. . . ."

In most of the district Feds, however, this promotion, red in tooth and claw, was in fact done by the old zebras. "We hired an outside firm for photography, but we did the layouts and wrote the copy ourselves," said an old-timer at the Dallas Fed. "It's been some change. It's like, for sixty years everyone kind of sat around here and did what they wanted to do, and now everybody's watching."

The promotion was effective: late in 1982 the numbers began to turn around. In part, it was merely a matter of reaching out to the small "community banks" and the thrifts and S&Ls that had not fully realized they could access Fed services directly rather than through correspondents. (The U.S. Savings and Loan League helped this phenomenon along by launching a money-market mutual fund for its members, under the management of Philadelphia's Provident National Bank, to replace the investment facilities offered by correspondent banks to thrifts that cleared their NOW drafts through correspondents.) The new pricing schedules put into effect in summer 1982 were more attractive to respondent banks and reduced the gap between packaged sort and unsorted. But the real motive was the certainty and speed with which checks processed through the district Feds became "available funds" to the banks, thrifts, and credit unions that had relied previously on correspondents.

If the truck that picked up the bundled checks from a small bank got into an accident or the driver neglected to deliver the bag, that was tough luck for the bank when it dealt with a correspondent—but the Fed took responsibility from the moment its chartered transportation service took possession. And the Fed availability schedules were advertised and guaranteed. Fairly or otherwise, the respondent banks and thrifts believed that correspondent banks often held back on giving them credit for collected checks—just as they hold back on ordinary customers who want to draw funds from new deposits—to give themselves a day or two of free use of the money. "Availability is always more important than unit pricing," said Larry Johns, chairman of the Community Bankers Council of the American Bankers Association. "The correspondents—and some of them are very good friends of mine—have a credibility problem with some of the respondent-type banks."

As late as December 1982, the Feds were still in violation of the law. Reporting to the Board of Governors that month, E. Gerald Corrigan, who was chairman of the system's Pricing Policy Committee as well as president of the Minneapolis Fed, noted (in a footnote) that while the district banks were meeting their out-of-pocket and overhead expenses on the new pricing schedules and volumes, they were not covering the Private Sector Adjustment Factor. During the next two months, however, new rules were set for the check-clearing system that pulled the district Feds into the black for the first time since pricing began and took a considerable volume of work away from the private sector.

3

Correspondent bankers' reaction to Fed aggressiveness was mostly unprintable, both as to content and as to source, because not many bankers are willing to pick a fight with the Fed. "You know what it's like?" said George D. Norton, executive vice-president of the Philadelphia National Bank, a rather severe, older man in gold-rimmed glasses who is one of the few public antagonists. "It's like you're the defensive captain in the Super Bowl. You look across the line at the other team, and you see this big, husky quarterback in a football helmet, but he's wearing a black-and-white striped shirt." Even Norton, who had inspired a lawsuit to prevent the Fed from changing certain procedures, was concerned about how far it was safe to go: his bank had a merger application pending, and the same people who were making the rules on check clearing were going to have to vote yea or nay on the application. (They voted yea.)

The correspondent banks question the accuracy of the cost estimates that underlie Fed prices. They especially suspect the PSAF the Feds are supposed to add to their calculated costs to compensate for their advantage in not having to pay income tax or interest on invested capital. In the first cut at pricing, the Board proposed to set the PSAF for the system as a whole at 12%, and after much argle-bargle with a consultative committee of bankers the surcharge was raised to 16%. Charles Bates, who ran the American Bankers Association's section on electronics and operations, insisted that the Feds' formula underestimates the value of the space and equipment they use. "We know it's too low, based on our costs," he said. "It should be around thirty percent. The Fed did all this because Philadelphia National and First Boston had taken business away from them. Their forty percent share of market was gone. They'd lost status and members and Hay points [the reference is to a measurement of bureaucratic performance developed by a Philadelphia management consultant and taught at the Harvard Business School]. What they've done is clearly predatory—and you can put my name on that in lights and blaze it over Washington."

"Nonsense," said E. Gerald Corrigan. "You can put that in lights, too. Anybody's cost accounting has a sizable margin of error, but the allocation of Federal Reserve assets to the priced services, including the buildings, is done by as systematic and rigorous a method as we can do it. And even after you give every benefit of the doubt, our costs and our prices appear to be lower."

Nobody is going to resolve this argument. The Federal Reserve PACS (Planning And Control System) Expense Report, issued quarterly, carries a legend: "This report has been prepared for use by Federal Reserve personnel who are familiar with the data reported and the instructions under which it is gathered. The significance of reported data is not self-evident to persons who are unfamiliar with these matters." The legend is arrogant, but true: people with experience in commercial-bank cost accounting have a lot of trouble making sense of the PACS reports. And bank cost accounting is enigmatic, anyway: "You're telling me," said the operations chief of a big New York bank, "that Corrigan has learned in eighteen months what we haven't learned in fifty years."

Different district Feds handle the check-processing work differently and there are variations within single districts. The Jacksonville RCPC of the Atlanta district, for example, sorts checks to the data-processing companies that handle the demand-deposit accounting for groups of banks, rather than to the banks themselves, and makes banks deliver bundles to airports rather than picking them up by truck at the bank for transportation to the airports. As a result, its costs are 30 + % lower than those of the New Orleans RCPC in the same district—but both are bundled together to establish a single district-wide price for check-processing services.

Most of the district Feds now live in spanking new, costly buildings and do their check sorting on computer-driven IBM 38–90 machines, which even the biggest banks have found too expensive: they do not believe that the Feds' cost figures properly show the amortization on the buildings or the equipment. Some elements of Fed service are clearly more expensive than what the correspondents use—the "Fed airline," for example, by comparison with the commercial flights that carry most of the checks the banks send out for direct presentation. (There has been a kind of freemasonry of bank operating officers in the transportation area, helping each other move the paper: "People will call," says Alan Silberstein of Chemical, "to say, 'Look—did you know?—there's a new American Airlines flight . . .' ") BankWire is unquestionably cheaper to operate than FedWire: "We use multipoint lines instead of their point-to-point," says a BankWire director, "and they have the twelve banks with duplicative facilities, brings their costs up." But this is reflected in the costs—a FedWire funds transfer costs more than twice as much as a CashWire message. The problem is that the Fed won't grant final settlement on Cash-Wire payments until the next morning.

"The Feds *own* settlement," said Charles Bates of the ABA. "They control the funds of every banking entity." The man in charge of correspondent services at a big New York bank says darkly that the New York Fed discourages the use of correspondents by the country banks by delaying the posting of items to respondents' accounts: "Then they say it's the correspondents' problems; if you dealt directly with the Fed, you wouldn't have this problem."

A lot of this is just hate mail, and the Feds can respond in kind. "We've restrained ourselves," said the president of a district Fed, "not to do special deals with any individual customer, which the banks do all the time. Private institutions can change prices at any time, and nobody knows; we have to set our prices in a fishbowl of publicity." There is no question that what respondent banks pay for correspondent services from the commercial banks is a matter of how badly the big banks want that business. Some banks get much better prices than others, and the innocent country banker, who doesn't know what things ought to cost, has often been—to put it strongly but not unfairly—swindled.

"The large banks feel we are overcharging them for the benefit of the smaller banks," says Richard Smoot of the Philadelphia Fed. "And we do consider what we believe to be the elasticity of demand for a service. We never cross-subsidize funds wire or securities wire and checks. We calculate true unit costs, including all the overhead, support and direct—special equipment, centralized data processing, space charges, audit, human resources, legal. No price for any class of service is less than total. Checks in total recover all overheads—but we may apply them in a market-sensitive way. We think we can collect from customer A but not from customer B." There is direct congressional mandate for this approach: the Monetary Control Act does provide that "pricing principles shall give due regard to competitive factors"—but there remains an irreducible discomfort about a situation where a regulator is also a competitor.

Opposing the demand by the Board of Governors that daylight overdrafts be reduced and eventually eliminated, the New York Fed complains that such a step would drive business to CHIPS. Any discussion of future controls on FedWire overdrafts quickly moves to the Fed's felt need to impose equivalent or stronger controls on high midday debit positions in the Clearing House computer. The BankWire case is worrisome, especially in the light of the difficulties the district Feds have placed in the way of proposed local electronic clearing mechanisms on the CashWire chassis. Such a service was approved for Chicago, but when the San Francisco banks requested a settlement facility for a similar service, the Federal Reserve Bank of San Francisco replied: "Each Reserve Bank has been advised by the Board of Governors that we are not to enter into any new net settlement agreements without approval from the board . . . [G]aining approval for such a request is likely to take some time. . . ." Instead, the San Francisco Fed proposed, the local banks might consider applying for an extension of hours on FedWire (which closes down at 6:00 P.M. New York time, 3:00 P.M. on the West Coast) for local use only, a service that "could conceivably carry a different price. . . ." In other words, plan to do your business with us; we're not going to allow you to do it with anybody but us.

4

These disputes came to a head in 1982, on the issue of how the Fed proposed to carry out the congressional mandate to price Fed Float. Loading an interest charge for float onto the unit prices for check clearing, at the float levels and interest-rate levels of 1981, would have nearly doubled the per-item charge—and, says George Norton of Philadelphia National, "The Fed would have been clearly noncompetitive." So the Fed took the Monetary Control Act as an order to eliminate as much float as possible and only then price the rest. "The Fed's problem," said Smoot, commenting on the float issue, "is not to put itself out of business."

Like everything else, float was supposed to be priced, at least on a first-cut basis, by September 1981. The Fed missed that deadline, announcing that in December it would offer for comment proposals to eliminate or price float by mid-1982. (In fairness, the law can be read another way. It says that "not later than the first day of the eighteenth month after the date of enactment . . . the Board shall begin to put into effect a schedule of fees for [its] services." One of the seven specifically listed services covered by this sentence is "Federal Reserve float." The Fed argues that because of the ambiguous phrase "begin to put into effect," it was not required to list fees for *all* the listed services and could pick and choose from the menu. A more persuasive reading would be that the Congress wanted the Fed to take a first crack at the lot, but recognized that fees might have to be changed with experience.) When they came, the Fed's proposals were based mostly on the concept of "fractional availability": the Fed would give credit on its announced availability schedule for only a portion of the checks presented within the deadlines. This would save the Fed the cost of pinpointing which checks had not been debited from the paying banks' accounts before they were credited to the receivers, and assessing the tiny interest charges bank by bank. Eventually, the Fed said, all float problems would be resolved through Electronic Check Clearing—check trunca-tion—that would communicate payments information electron-ically from district to district as it was taken off the checks on their first pass through a sorting machine. The banks went through the roof: their contracts with their big customers, which included availability schedules, did not permit fractional credits, and the American Bankers Association estimated that equipment to receive payments data through Electronic Check Clearing would cost the banks $240 million. (The real objec-tion, of course, was that such procedures would reduce the float the banks generate for themselves, which is worth many times $240 million to them every year. Not being ready to provide the service itself, the Fed was not in a position to argue the question too strongly.)

When the General Accounting Office examined the com-pliance of the Fed with the terms of the Monetary Control Act, it was highly censorious of the failure to price Fed Float: "We believe the Federal Reserve Board should move faster to elimi-nate the costly check clearing subsidy to depositing institutions that float represents. . . . By providing interest-free advances to banks when clearing checks, the Federal Reserve is pricing its check clearing service below cost. Other competitors who must operate at a profit are not in a position to advance funds in the same manner."

But the availability schedules that generate float were the prime selling tool the district Feds had in their dealings with the community banks and the thrifts. The uncomfortable choice before the Fed was to delay availability schedules or increase prices to reflect interest charges on the float created by prema-ture availability. In either case, business—quite a lot of it—would move out of the district Feds to the correspondent banks. Through 1982 the Feds sweated their people to bring down the float: the Fed airline schedules were "reconfigured" to move more paper to and from processing centers on a more exact schedule, IBM 38–90 reader-sorters were installed throughout the system, operations staffs were retrained intensively and in some places reorganized with an emphasis on higher productivity. (In New York, the back office was formed into competing teams, each with responsibility for the entire process on one group of machines.) Float came down from about $4 billion a day in 1980, to $2.7 billion in the second half of 1981, to $1.5 billion toward the end of 1982. That was the best that flesh and blood and computers could do. In February 1983 Corrigan's committee told the Board the district Feds would have to bite this bullet.

"Of the $1.5 billion," Corrigan said shortly before submitting that report, "$1 billion is in interdistrict [i.e., the availability schedules to remote points were too generous]. That we will eliminate by changing credit procedures—if it ain't there, you don't get it. That takes care of the lion's share. The balance is mostly holdover float [checks the Fed processing centers received on time but could not process and push through in time]. That's maybe $300 million, and that we will price. It will raise our unit prices five to seven percent. Another $100 million to $150 million will be eliminated by the move to noon presentment."

The move to noon presentment. . . . It is a little technical phrase with very large implications. Until early 1983 the Federal Reserve Banks as collectors of checks for their members and then for others had "presented" items for collection to the banks on which they were drawn according to the schedules of the local clearinghouse. Indeed, the checks processed by the Fed were presented as part of the local clearing, though the Feds did not *accept* checks at the clearing: this was a one-way ratchet. In New York, presentation at the clearing meant, in fact, deliveries through the night, with a last sack for the ceremonial settlement at ten in the morning. Not quite 30% of the Fed's presentments were in that final 10:00 A.M. batch.

At the RCPCs, which were essentially clearinghouses themselves, processing for presentation to banks in the region was done at the same time as processing for shipment on the Fed airline, with completion at 3:00 or 4:00 A.M. and checks presented to the banks of the region itself well before the start of the business day. (This, you will recall, was why the RCPC banks were used for controlled disbursement accounts.) By the terms of the Uniform Commercial Code, however, banks are permitted to present checks to each other at any time up to 2:00 P.M., for credit that day. (This is done occasionally for high-value items and is one of the reasons corporate treasurers are unhappy with disbursement through big-city banks.)

The last $100–$150 million of Fed Float mentioned by Corrigan was generated by checks that dribbled through the Fed processing systems after the presentation deadline at the big-city clearinghouses but well within the limits set by the Uniform Commercial Code. In spring 1982, as part of the antifloat crusade, the district Feds had announced that beginning that July they would make a final presentment of checks to big-city banks at noon, and urged the clearinghouses to revise their schedules accordingly. Coupled with the changes in the Feds' transportation schedules, noon presentment would not only wipe out this piece of the float, it would also allow the Feds to improve availability schedules on its standard services, both intra- and interdistrict. If a bank in Philadelphia took checks on San Francisco banks to the Philadelphia Fed by 10:15 P.M. for example, the Fed could give credit for those checks the next day—indeed, there were only three processing centers in the country (Charleston and Columbia in South Carolina and Helena in Montana) for which any delay beyond the next day would be imposed, provided checks came in by 10:15. Even a check that didn't come to the Philadelphia Fed until 1:00 A.M. would get credit that day unless its endpoint was served by a processing center in one of those three cities, or on the West Coast, or in Texas, Oklahoma, or Arkansas.

These schedules deprived the correspondent banks of the timing advantages they had previously enjoyed through direct presentment by courier. "We see ourselves abandoning all our friends," said Alan Silberstein at Chemical Bank, "all the private-sector alternatives we developed when the Fed began pricing." Because delivery times could be moved to later in the night at all the RCPCs, the Feds could offer out-of-town banks an availability the correspondents could not match unless they revised all their processing schedules, which would be hard for them to do. The banking day, after all, still ran from 10:00 to 3:00; checks being debited from accounts at the bank still had to be posted during the day so the machines could be used to sort and read checks being passed on for collection that night. And it seemed clear that with the new Fed transportation and availability schedules, much more than dribs and drabs would be presented at noon.

"What it means," said George Norton, "is that the Fed will have more time to process its items, while the private sector has less time to process *its* items. They're simply shifting costs, providing economic gains to the Fed at the expense of the private sector. They haven't done any research to prove this is in the public interest. We think it's an abuse of their rule-making powers, and the reason they wished to do it was to recapture the volume they'd lost." In July 1982 Philadelphia National and other banks in that city sued to prevent the district Feds from changing presentation schedules, and the Board of Governors agreed to withdraw the new regulations pending further consultation.

Meetings between Corrigan's group and an ad-hoc bankers' "Committee for a Level Playing Field" produced one major change in the Feds' plans. The original proposal had called for noon presentment only in the cities; as revised and submitted again in December 1982, the proposal contemplated noon presentment to the RCPC banks, too, to take away what would otherwise have been their insuperable advantage in soliciting further disbursement accounts. Another bone was thrown to the correspondent banks by taking the move to noon presentment in two steps: first to 11:00 A.M. in late February, with noon to follow in the summer. The big-city banks did not feel they had gained much, and as the first deadline neared, they inspired a lawsuit by some air courier services that carried checks for commercial banks, alleging that the Feds, in violation of the antitrust laws (yet) were conspiring to put them out of business. Neither the Cincinnati district court where the request for an injunction was made originally (presumably because somebody thought he had a sympathetic judge in that district), nor the appellate court that heard argument on an emergency basis, thought much of the air couriers' case, and the change in schedules went into effect on February 24, 1983.

While the move to noon presentment was pending, a number of bankers offered doleful predictions that the correspondents would simply be driven out of the check-collection business by the Feds' rule-making blunderbuss. In the event, they sweetened their own pots, undoubtedly at considerable cost, revising their processing and availability schedules and offering their more important respondent banks extra services or better prices. After all, they have a long list of other services, from home banking to brokerage to investment planning, that they expect to sell to or with their respondent banks, and check clearing has always been the cement in the structure. Even the Chicago banks, which had built their processing centers to serve respondents—Illinois law had not permitted them to acquire the branches or the holding-company subsidiaries that feed the processing machines of the banks in the other big cities—seemed to be retaining enough business to keep the operations division employed.

Competent witnesses testify to a belief that over the long run the banks can more than hold their own in this competition with the Feds. George Mitchell sees a future when "the concentration of processing is going to be much greater than it is now. We'll be down from three thousand to two hundred places where bank records are being kept." This much smaller group of banks will be able to communicate with each other electronically—as they do now in SWIFT ("a *super* system," says Mitchell, who remains an enthusiast at age seventy-nine)—with enough correspondent accounts to handle most transfers on the books of the banks themselves rather than at the Fed. After all, the banks do have major systemic advantages over the Fed: they understand payments as well as collections, and if they wish (this is not guaranteed), they can acquire a much better grip on what the end users, who will finally control what happens, really need from a payments system.

But somebody is going to have to pay attention and spend money. It is because the district Feds made the investment in the IBM 38–90s (the taxpayers' investment, of course) that the banks were so poorly placed to compete when the rules were changed to permit noon presentment. There *are* benefits to the public in the tighter articulation of the payments system. If it appears that the district Feds deliver those benefits and the banks don't—especially if the banks continue to appear to be more concerned about what's in it for them than about values to their customers—the future George Mitchell envisages will not come to pass. And because the Fed has such powers of ultimate control, even the best bankers may shy away from the intellectual and financial investments that future would require of them.

George White, once a banker and now a consultant and publisher of *White Papers,* argues that the Fed has been cheating, that float has been greater than the estimates on which the charges have been imposed, and that the reason is the Fed's insistence on giving availabilities faster than it can, in fact, move and process the paper. He writes: "The Fed is using its regulatory power to inhibit marketplace selection of payment alternatives by giving faster . . . availability in order to maintain its own major payments processing role. By artificially making the check collection system more attractive than other payment alternatives (e.g., the electronic automated clearing house system), the Fed negates the incentives that would exist in a truly free marketplace for changing to more effective alternatives." If the Fed offered realistic alternatives, White grumbles, "it would lose processing volume to the private sector and would become only the processor of last resort."

The facts would seem more complicated than that. With

Fed Float running less than 5% by value of total daily clearances through the Fed, and with different cities affected on different days, systemwide postponement of availabilities would mean denying collected funds to many more banks than now benefit from premature access. Still, there is a hollow sound to all the Fed's righteousness, and the matter could bear further inspection. The General Accounting Office has visited once again, and its report will become available between the day these words are written and the day they are published. The Fed says GAO will give it a clean bill of health—but Volcker maintains that the first report supported the Fed rather than its antagonists, because that's what his staff told him. (He didn't have time to read it: Volcker is not—and there is no reason why he should be—an operations expert.) In any event, the Congress that set the district Feds loose to compete with the commercial banks has an obligation to assure that its tiger fights fair.

III

---

*The
Banking
Business*

7

FINDING THE MONEY

Banks as we have known them earned their income by making loans and getting them paid back, with interest. What they lent was, of course, other people's money: they were "intermediaries." They got their money by providing services—"safekeeping" in the mythology of the London goldsmiths, from the time when city streets were *much* more dangerous than they are today, then transaction accounts, as the linchpin of the payments systems. When interest rates rose in the 1960s and people learned to economize on cash, the banks were increasingly compelled to purchase the money they lent, through interest-bearing time accounts, certificates of deposit, and the like. Since 1980, when Congress legitimized the interest-bearing checking account, banks, both large and small, have had to purchase virtually all their funds.

The bank that makes a living by lending other people's money incurs three different kinds of risk:

(1) *Funding risk:* the danger that the depositors whose money is being lent will demand the return of their funds. Because that money has been put out to the borrowers, it may not be available on demand to the original depositor. The bank could then suffer a liquidity failure. Virtually every law chartering a bank anywhere in the world forbade a bank to continue to accept deposits after it denies a prior depositor contractually guaranteed access to his funds: if a bank can't repay a depositor, it has to close its doors. Rumors that a bank might not be able to pay could sweep through a community, producing a run on the bank that might shut even the most soundly managed institution. If the panic grew general, the banking system as a whole would be crippled and could be destroyed.

(2) *Credit risk:* the danger that borrowers will not repay. The social justification of bank profits is that banks run the credit risks. Presumably, interest rates are set high enough to assure the profitability of the bank even though some loans turn sour. Still, the organizers of banks are required to put up their own capital as part of the funding of the bank, so that losses on bad loans too large to be absorbed by the profits on good ones would eat up the owners' capital rather than the depositors' deposits, which are supposed to be risk-free. Given the insistence of today's international bankers that "sovereign risks"—loans to nations—are always safe, it is probably worth noting that in the years before the industrial revolution multiplied the need for credit, banks went broke most often because of defaults by sovereign borrowers: the kings and princes and municipal authorities whose permission was required before a bank could operate, and who charged for that permission by compelling banks to lend them money.

Later, the chartering authorities attempted to protect depositors by limiting the loans a bank could make to any individual borrower. In the United States, that limit was set as some fraction of the owners' investment plus the accumulated prior earnings the owners had left in the capital accounts of the bank. That fraction was 10% until 1982 and became 15% with the Garn–St. Germain Act of that year. By diversifying the loan portfolio among a large number of different borrowers, presumably the bank reduced the degree of its credit risk.

Small banks that served individual localities might find a high proportion of their loans going sour at once if something awful happened around the home base. A drought could destroy a country bank or (to bring matters up to date) a collapse in oil prices could devastate a bank in the oil patch that had concentrated its loans in the energy-related enterprises dominating the local economy. And in a major nationwide depression accompanied by a deflation—which meant that borrowers had to repay in money worth more than the money they had borrowed—a big bank with loans scattered around the country in dozens of different industries might find all its customers pinched for cash at the same time. In effect, this is what happened in Latin America in 1981–82, when the extremely strong dollar compelled companies that borrowed in dollars to come up with much greater sums in their own currency to buy the dollars they needed to service their debt.

(3) *Interest-rate risk:* the danger that rates on short-term funds, which are what a bank normally buys, will rise to such a level that the bank's longer-term loans, written at the lower interest rates of an earlier time, will become unprofitable. Theoretically, it is also possible for a bank to get in trouble by entering into long-term funding contracts that require it to pay higher interest rates than it can earn with short-term loans. Irving Trust was less profitable than its sister New York banks in the second half of 1982 because it had committed to longer-term funds in the expectation that interest rates would continue to rise. In the language of the trade, the bank had "got on the wrong side of the rates." But the normal "maturity transformation" function of a bank leads it to borrow short and lend long.

Interest-rate risk is a creation of modern banking practice, and even in the 1980s, most bankers really comfortable with it are still a little young to be at the top of the banks. Much—maybe most—of what is happening in the maelstrom at CHIPS and the flooding at FedWire is banks buying funds from each other on a one-day basis. Petros Sabatacokis, the thirty-six-year-old Columbia-trained, Greek-born treasurer of Chemical Bank, reports that when he comes to work in the morning, he finds that his bank has only about half the $45 billion it will have to pay out that day; his job is to buy the rest, at what will work out over some short time-horizon (probably one week) at the lowest possible rates.

It was interest-rate risks that virtually destroyed the savings-and-loans and the savings banks in the early 1980s. They had entered into long-term mortgage contracts at rates more than adequate to cover the interest they had to pay on long-term savings accounts, plus expenses. Then it turned out they didn't have any long-term savings accounts to speak of because the holders of those accounts insisted on more interest for their money. Deregulation of interest rates is widely regarded as a cousin of deregulation of airlines, trucking, and other industries, but it was a beast of another species, an inescapable rather than a willed action. If the government had not invented high-interest certificates for the S&Ls to offer their depositors, the S&Ls would simply have gone under, unable to pay off their depositors fleeing the old low-rate passbook account.

2

The ineffable, terrifying risk is the funding risk—indeed, the other two forms of risk become crucial because public perception of losses from bad loans or mismatched interest rates produces the withdrawal of funds.

A bank's first line of defense against insufficient funding was, simply, cash. During the nineteenth century, most banks kept gold coins in the vaults to cover anywhere from 10% to 40% of their deposit liabilities, depending on the sophistication of the market served and ,the prudence of the management. Historically, this was the real meaning of the word "reserves." The Federal Reserve System did not make reserves sterile: they were sterile by nature. But a bank that had a higher porportion of its assets in sterile form would have to charge a higher interest rate for its loans than a rival that put a higher fraction of its money into interest-bearing loans or investments. Competition betwen banks therefore tended to drive down the level of reserves. Among the purposes of government supervision of banks was the assurance that reserves would be kept at a level the government thought necessary to avoid any danger of a liquidity failure.

The second line of defense against funding trouble was the easily salable investment or the very short-term loan—basically, government paper, call money, and "bankers' acceptances," which financed trade and self-liquidated rapidly. The banknotes issued by national banks before the creation of the Federal Reserve had to be backed by government bonds, partly because it was convenient for the government to have a guaranteed market for its paper, and partly because government bonds were easily salable for gold if holders of the banknotes came to the tellers' windows demanding gold. Classically, because bank deposits were demand deposits, banking theory held that *all* bank loans should be very short term, to avoid the danger that money to which the depositors were entitled whenever they wanted it might be tied up in loans that could not be sold or called and would not be repaid for some time.

But once a banking *system* became reasonably well articulated (i.e., once there was a clearinghouse with members who knew each other and each other's business), an individual bank did not have to worry quite so much about liquidity. One bank's withdrawals were, in normal times, another bank's deposits. Even before there was a Federal Reserve to act as lender of last resort, the House of Morgan and its friends served as an effective source of short-term money for smaller banks temporarily embarrassed, but essentially sound. (Interestingly, Morgan assumed that function again in summer 1982, when the money-market mutual funds refused to roll over their certificates of deposit at Continental Illinois, and the Fed wished not to get involved, if possible. Morgan went into the market to borrow money on its own name, then passed it on, night after night till the crisis ended, noblesse oblige—no charge—to keep Continental Illinois afloat.) There grew up a new banking theory: that depositors might come and depositors might go, but for the system, as a whole—to use the phrase preferred by the Bank of England—"current account goes on forever."

Except that there might be a panic. If a bank failed—if the depositors in one bank found they could not get their money back, or use their checking accounts to pay bills—people might rush to take their money out of other banks. During the days when money had a metallic base, when circulating paper could be redeemed for gold, there were sudden and dramatic shrinkages of the banking system as a whole. Reserves would drain out of the banks and into people's mattresses, the banks scrambled to call their short-term loans or sell their investment paper, and businesses found that banks could not make new loans because they didn't have the money to lay out for that purpose or couldn't risk not having the funds the depositors might call for at any moment.

In a fundamental sense, the change from metallic money to credit money meant that this sort of panic could never happen again. Because the reserves of the banking system are now nothing more than a government's promise to pay (and what is to be paid is not specified), money can be created at will and the banking system can be kept solvent however great the panic. If people want to hold cash rather than bank balances, the government simply prints more bills (and this isn't even inflationary because the extra cash will simply return to the banks and the government's vaults when people trust the banks again). If the Arabs decide they would rather hold gold than dollars, they buy gold from people who own gold. For the banking system, the result is a wash: funds in the banks are transferred from Arabs to sellers of gold.

When the United States froze Iranian assets following the hostage seizure, the ostensible excuse was that the Islamic Republic had threatened to remove all Iranian deposits from U.S. banks around the world. But as Assistant Treasury Secretary for International Affairs C. Fred Bergsten admitted openly, this threat (which, incidentally, may not even have been uttered) was not very important to the banks because the only thing the new depositories for Iranian funds could do with the money was to put it in another bank. That bank thereupon could (and would—with electronic speed) lend it back to the banks that had lost it, at an interest rate only a few hundredths of a percentage point higher than what was being paid to the Iranians. What contracts the banking system now is not the depositors' demand for funds but the bankers' inability to lend because the potential borrowers seem incapable of repaying their loans—or, rather, if 1982 is any guide, because the potential borrowers throw up their hands when confronted with the interest rates they are told they must pay.

However safe the system, there were still funding risks for an individual bank, which might not be able to borrow enough from its sisters to stave off worried depositors (especially when the information that worried the depositors was also worrisome to the banks on which the troubled institution might call for loans), and might not be able to command sufficient support from the Federal Reserve. In the aftermath of the bank failures of the Great Depression, the government protected the smaller banks against any risk of a run on them by their depositors through the device of deposit insurance, placing the full faith and credit of the people who print the money behind the bank's ability to repay depositors, up to a certain maximum. (The original figure in the deposit insurance law was $2,500; by 1983 it was $100,000 and a lot of banks and S&Ls were pushing to get it raised to $250,000.) This was a New Deal "reform," and most commentators regard it as a measure to improve the economic security of the citizenry. In fact, as Roosevelt (who had opposed it) understood, it was a protection for the country banks, to enable them to start up again and keep deposits that might otherwise have gone to the big-city banks, which, with very few exceptions, had paid their depositors on demand, one hundred cents on the dollar, through the depths of the Depression.

Deposit insurance was triggered by bank failures, and as such it was cold comfort to the bank's stockholders and management. (As it still is, by the way. At a time when top executives in nonfinancial corporations vote themselves "golden parachutes" and perks to make sure they will be cared for lavishly if another company absorbs theirs, FDIC and FSLIC always see to it that in a merger where government assistance is required, the officers of the failing bank are not offered jobs by the bank that absorbs it and are in no way specially recompensed on their way out.) For thirty years after the passage of deposit insurance, banks continued to defend themselves against funding risk by "asset management." They kept portfolios of easily salable short-term government paper, reducing the proportion of their assets held in that form when business was brisk and loan demand was high and increasing it when loan demand dropped. In the aftermath of World War II, which the government had financed mostly by selling paper to the banks (budget deficits supplied the deposits the banks could use to buy the paper), all banks practiced asset management willy-nilly—in 1945 government paper made up roughly half the assets of the U.S. banking system. But the sale of Treasury paper to fund private loans ran down the portfolio in the 1950s, and by the early 1960s the banks could fund new loans only by increasing their liabilities—by going into the money markets deliberately to buy what they would then lend.

For the banks that led this march to "liability management," the experience was liberating, and among the problems from which they thought they had been freed was concern about funding risk. Citibank especially elaborated a theory that a bank's liquidity in the modern world was a function not of its cash or easily sold holdings but of its access to credit in the world's money markets. So long as a bank could sell its certificates of deposit—and the holding company that owned the bank could sell its commercial paper—there was no funding risk. And a big bank would always be able to buy money that way because the government guaranteed implicitly that the bank would pay back. In point of fact, between 1934 and 1982 the government never liquidated a bank with uninsured certificates of deposit among its liabilities. Whenever an institution large enough to have such paper outstanding was seen to be failing, the FDIC arranged a "purchase and assumption" by which some other bank, with government subsidy, took over responsibility for all liabilities—except, of course, the shareholders' capital and the "subordinated" bonded debt that counted as part of capital.

But the truth was that liability management had brought back the old funding risk and the danger of a liquidity failure. When the Federal Reserve Bank refused to approve Franklin National Bank's acquisition of Talbot, a cash-heavy finance company, rumors spread through the markets that the refusal was based on a negative analysis of the bank's net worth—and suddenly the bank was short more than a billion dollars a day of the money it had to buy to fund its loans. Before the FDIC finally made a deal with the Fed to divide up the potential losses from the bank's overvalued assets (Franklin had kept itself apparently profitable by fraudulent foreign-exchange transactions, and FDIC refused to guarantee any successor bank against losses of that kind), the Fed was compelled to lend Franklin as much as $1.75 billion through the discount window, every day, to keep the bank from collapsing before a safety net was in place.

Repeatedly, from the mid–1970s through the early 1980s, the Fed was called upon to supply funds to banks because the market had closed on them. Indeed, the Fed could scarcely avoid this responsibility because the shortfall occurred in the form of a reserve deficiency, when the illiquid bank could not cover for the checks its depositors wrote or the payments it had entered on their behalf at CHIPS. At that moment—which was a pretty scary moment—the Fed had the choice of preventing a day's clearing, which would throw sand in the wheels of the payments system and thus of the real economy, or finding a way to extend credit to the failing bank. This was a difficult decision with a foreordained result. The reluctance of other banks to sell Fed Funds to a troubled colleague, the unwillingness of the purchasers of CDs or commercial paper to risk their money with a bank that seemed to be experiencing serious losses, was in reality a "run on the bank" quite as devastating as the lines of depositors waiting to withdraw their money that had signaled the bank failures of the 1930s.

When John Heimann was Comptroller of the Currency, his regional administrators were under orders to report all evidences of what was called "tiering." If all banks were equally safe, all banks should be able to buy Fed Funds or sell CDs at more or less the same interest rate; when the market separated banks into "tiers" by differentiating the interest demanded from them, Heimann knew there was trouble, that some banks were being regarded as less safe than others. Like the first evidence of depositors in unusual numbers seeking to withdraw their funds back in the days before deposit insurance, such tiering in the rates could have a snowballing effect as brokers, analysts, purchasers of the paper passed the word. Whatever a bank's troubles, a need to pay higher rates for money exacerbates them. Yet the regulators could not proclaim openly that in the event of a bank failure they would guarantee the purchasers of large CDs: they had no legal authority to make such promises, and no defense against subsequent charges in the Congress and elsewhere that their pledges of safety had promoted unsound and unsafe banking. "Why not run a portfolio of risky loans if the feds will backstop any difficulties?" the *Wall Street Journal* inquired editorially.

The FDIC, arranging for a more solid bank to take over the failure, would purchase the weakest assets in the portfolio, giving the buyer of the bank a relatively "clean" balance sheet. In the days when the most admired and profitable banks were those with rapidly expanding networks of branches, which could deliver inexpensive "core deposits" in checking accounts and passbook accounts, the acquiring bank was often willing to pay in new money (once the insurance corporation had cleansed) for what had been an unprofitable institution, restoring the capital position of the failed bank while assuming all its liabilities to depositors and lenders.

If the bad loans had been made honestly, the FDIC stood a reasonable chance of recovering a good share of its subsidy through a workout or (if necessary) the forced liquidation of the borrower. In the Franklin case, the Fed got lucky on the failed bank's foreign-exchange position and actually made money on its Franklin support operations—and the economy turned around enough for FDIC to recover from its presumably high-risk piece of Franklin's loan portfolio all the outlays in connection with the bank's insolvency. But this was not guaranteed, and there were other "purchase and assumption" deals where the insurance fund was hit substantially. The FDIC's agreement with California's Crocker Bank to keep the doors open at the failed U.S. National of San Diego, for example, held Crocker harmless for any losses related to loans made to the business interests of E. Arnholt Smith, the bank's chairman. It turned out that Smith's enterprises had commandeered almost half the bank's loan portfolio, in one way or another, and the loss to FDIC approximated $250 million. Every year there are nits and bits, some of them quite colorful. In spring 1983, for example, FDIC shut down Commercial Bank of California, paying the bank that took it over $14 million for assets with a face value of $16.2 million and a real value of very much less. Twenty percent of the bank's stock had been owned by Johnny Carson and his lawyer; and in 1982 there had been an admitted loss of $2.5 million on loans to Jack M. Catain, Jr., one of those people identified in the media as "an alleged organized crime figure," who at the time of the bank's collapse was awaiting trial in Los Angeles on charges of counterfeiting. That sort of thing is interesting to work on.

In 1981 the Reagan administration installed Todd Conover and William Isaac, very able young men who happened to be free-market ideologues, as Comptroller of the Currency and chairman of the FDIC. As a matter of principle, both men believed that bank behavior should be policed by the market rather than by government regulators, that "tiering" was a *desirable* phenomenon: a warning to shape up that was more effective than any amount of lecturing by a bank examiner to management or to the bank's board of directors. Both believed also that market discipline would never be imposed upon banks until there was a case where uninsured depositors—the big lenders to a bank who bought CDs for more than $100,000—lost their money in a bank failure.

In spring 1982 the Lord delivered up to Conover and Isaac a middle-sized ($500 million) bank in the Oklahoma oil patch, which had been managed abominably but had nevertheless been able to sell million-dollar CDs around the country. (One of them had been sold to the Wright Patman Credit Union in which the congressional staffs and some congressmen had their savings—you can't fault Conover and Isaac for courage.) This Penn Square National Bank, which had grown in five years from a $30–million shopping-center sort of operation, also had accepted contingent liabilities of such size that no bank would willingly undertake them as part of a purchase.

"Closing down Penn Square was entirely Todd's call," Isaac said cheerfully some months later. "Plus the Fed had to decide whether to continue funding. Ordinarily the Fed will fund an institution with a liquidity problem if it's a viable institution. That Fourth of July weekend, the Fed and Conover talked it over, and Todd decided to close it down at seven o'clock Monday evening. The Comptroller *must* close it down if there's a book insolvency. Of course," he added, sipping a Diet Coke, "the decision to pay off depositors or do a purchase-and-assumption is entirely ours. Penn Square had sold participations of $2.1 billion, and when we do a merger, we have to indemnify the purchasers. There was another $900 million in the bank in standby letters of credit and loan agreements. We couldn't justify assuming that responsibility."

John Heimann, who had moved back to the private sector and was co-chairman of the banking and brokerage house of Becker–Paribas, was appalled by this action, which he thought constituted reckless endangerment of the banking system. "You shouldn't change the rules that way on an ad hoc basis, in the middle of the game," he said. "You're driving the suppliers of deposit liabilities out of the smaller banks. Treasurers of corporations now have to say, 'What size bank will the government *not* allow to fail?' " Paul Volcker, who in effect had to approve the liquidation of Penn Square, was almost equally disturbed, but saw no choice: "We looked at it for a long time. It was too complicated, too many contigent liabilities. There wasn't anything you could do but close it down."

What made the blowup at Penn Square so resonant in the banking system, however, was more than the change in the rules of the game. The failure of this previously obscure Oklahoma bank directly involved the fortunes of five major institutions: Chase Manhattan, Chicago's Continental Illinois and Northern Trust, Seattle's Seafirst, and Michigan National. All of them had lent their own money to Penn Square's borrowers, relying on the alleged expertise of the officers of Penn Square. These were a flamboyant lot, given to extravagant gestures like drinking beer out of a boot in a local pub. One of them had been implicated in a nursing-home swindle. Penn Square itself had been limited in the size of the loans it could make in the oil and gas fields by the relatively small size of its own capital and had arranged for these large national lenders to take participations considerably larger than what the Oklahoma bank put up itself. By trusting Penn Square, the larger banks saved the costs of hiring experts in Oklahoma energy to vet such investments on their behalf, which seemed to make the loans more profitable.

Except that a lot of these loans were wildly optimistic

about the extent of the reserves to be recovered by oil and gas production. (In some instances, it didn't matter how much oil and gas was there because Penn Square had neglected to follow through with the legal formalities that secured the assets as protection for the loans.) Even the less-reckless loans made sense only on an assumption of steadily increasing prices for oil and (especially) gas. Continental Illinois bought more than a billion dollars face value of these loans, a sum equal to 60% of its capital; Seafirst, more than $400 million, which was more than 70% of its capital.

Nine months after the collapse of Penn Square, a quarter of these loans had been written off as a dead loss by the lenders and three-quarters of the remainder was "nonperforming"—that is, the borrowers weren't meeting their interest payments. In April 1983 Seafirst's outside auditors forced writeoffs so great that the bank's capital fell to 3% of its assets, an impermissibly low ratio. The bank, the largest in the state of Washington, had to be sold off to Bank of America in a complicated transaction that left the selling shareholders still liable for up to $112 million of additional losses. The Washington legislature had to meet in special session and pass a law allowing the out-of-state purchase.

Continental Illinois, the sixth largest bank in the country, had been a very fashionable bank, much admired by bank stock analysts. Keefe, Bruyette & Wood, the largest brokerage house specializing in bank stocks, had rated it second only to Morgan. When the Chicago Board of Trade started a futures contract in bank CDs, Continental was one of only eight banks whose paper was acceptable in satisfaction of a contract if the purchaser demanded delivery. The bank lost that distinction immediately—and presently, despite everyone's knowledge that the Fed would not let Continental Illinois go belly-up, despite the bank's willingness to pay a premium for money, the market closed on Continental CDs. Senior members of the bank's management went around to the money-market mutual funds, hat in hand, and were turned down. "Look," said the manager of one such fund, "*I* think Continental CDs are safe, but I'm not paid to express such opinions. The institutions who buy our fund want absolute safety. They run their eye down our list of investments, and if they see something they don't like, they take their money somewhere else. Safety is worth more to them than an extra eighth."

Before the crisis, Continental Illinois had bought on a very short-term basis more than a third of the funds it needed to continue operating; Seafirst probably had bought more than a quarter. In the first days after Penn Square blew up, there can be little question that much of this money came from the Fed. (Some damn fool at Seafirst told the press blithely late that year that the bank was going to earn more money in crisis than it had before because the cost of funds from the Fed was so much less than the costs it had been incurring in the market.) Thereafter, with the Fed acting as guarantor, in effect, syndicates of large banks were formed to supply funds these two banks could not raise any other way. The consortium was announced publicly for Seafirst, managed privately by Morgan for Continental. Because of its strong position in Europe and on the Arabian peninsula (it was, after all, "David Rockefeller's bank"), Chase Manhattan was probably able to replace on its own initiative the funds lost by the reluctance of the usual CD and commercial-paper buyers to take the paper of the friends of Penn Square.

For the banking system as a whole, the Penn Square fiasco raised the price of money: the differential between what the federal government had to pay to sell Treasury bills and what the banks had to pay to sell CDs widened considerably. It then widened again, to an average gap of more than a percentage point, when (only six weeks after Penn Square) the Mexican debt crisis emerged.

3

What made the international debt problem so severe in the last months of 1982 was not the danger to bank assets—which can always be carried more or less at par by convenient definition, given some help by tolerant bank regulators, pliant auditors, and external accountants—but the funding crisis at Banco do Brasil on December 9. Both Mexico and Brazil had concealed the depth of the red ink in their balance of payments by sending their banks out to borrow short-term funds in the U.S. market and roll them over every night. By nationalizing the banks and applying the proceeds of government borrowings to the reduction of their overnight debts, (one piece of this repayment was apparently done on a temporary basis *by the Federal Reserve System itself,* for the account of the Mexicans), Mexico had prevented its insolvency from knocking out the pillars of the international monetary system, but the Brazilians gambled that their banks would muddle through.

There was a major systemic difference between the sort of borrowing the Brazilians were doing and the normal short-term (90-day, 60-day, even 30-day) financing that occurs in the international nexus. Banks made their funding plans expecting certain payments on certain days, but if something looks shaky, contingencies can be readied—and there is usually a few days' warning from the debtor that he may have to "delay." When Bolivia missed a payment to Bank of America in early fall 1982—because Argentina had failed to make a payment due to Bolivia—the U.S. bank was able to cover the shortfall with only minimal annoyance, though the failure occurred late in the day. What the Brazilians and Mexicans had done, however, allowed for no warning and jeopardized not only the agencies and branches of their own banks, but the entirety of the international payments system.

Brazil's abuse of the American overnight money markets seems to have covered at least $5 billion of that country's accumulated debt. Every morning, Banco de Brasil would make enormous entries to CHIPS to repay the previous day's borrowings; during the course of the day, it would arrange for new borrowings to bring its CHIPS position back to balance before 4:30 P.M. Most of these borrowings were through the Fed

Funds market. As the dimensions of the Latin American debt burden filtered through the community of banks, increasing numbers of regional banks instructed the Fed Funds brokers not to make their money available to the U.S. branches and agencies of Latin American banks. The Brazilians had to pay mounting premiums on their borrowings—tiering with a vengeance—and finally the staff economists and planners at the major international banks convinced the credit officers on the line (who liked the apparent profits) that a ceiling had to be put on Brazilian takings from the overnight market. As noted earlier, the shortfall on December 9 seems to have been about $360 million, and CHIPS had to be kept open late until Bankers Trust, the settling bank for Banco do Brasil at the Clearing House, rustled up funds to permit the system to balance and close for the night.

A "liquidity problem" for a nonfinancial borrower is no great shakes for a banking system: that's what credit is all about. But an illiquid bank is a failed bank: there is a difference of kind—not just degree—between the liquidity problem of a nonfinancial borrower and the funding problem of a bank. What was so shocking about the developments in the international lending business in 1982 was that the bankers involved—and the bank regulators—had no understanding of so fundamental a point. The costs of permitting sovereign borrowers to use their banks as a life raft could have been—almost was—far greater than the money (mostly taxpayers' money) that was lost. And these are the people in whom we are now supposed to place our "confidence."

4

With the passage of the Garn–St. Germain bill in 1982, Congress inadvertently and stupidly removed the discipline of funding risk from the concerns of dishonestly operated banks.

Prior to December 1982, interest-rate ceilings had prevented banks from competing for funds except in pieces of $100,000 or more, and anything over $100,000 was not insured. Money-market funds had agglomerated such pieces for small investors and had thrived on the competition to sell large-denomination certificates. But they had to publish their CD holdings at regular intervals and could not afford to load their portfolios with paper from dubious banking entities. No money-market fund held Penn Square paper: the losers were credit unions, S&Ls, corporations, and rich individuals seduced by money brokers to "take advantage" of the higher rates Penn Square had to pay as the bank careened out of control. And the funds rapidly abandoned Continental Illinois, Seafirst, and even Chase in their hour of need.

With the removal of interest-rate restrictions on smaller deposits, it became possible for any bank to raise funds by giving people *the government's* promise to pay them premium interest rates on their money. For deposit insurance covers both principal and interest.

Prior to fall 1982, a bank with too many bad loans on its books normally began to shrink on both sides of the balance sheet. It might be willing to write new loans (indeed, it probably was willing to write new loans other banks wouldn't touch because it was looking for high yields to absorb the losses on the existing portfolio), but there were enough savvy depositors who moved their business elsewhere because they didn't like the look of things. There was an amusing interchange at a Senate hearing between Senator Jake Garn of Utah, chairman of the Senate Banking Committee, and William Isaac of the Federal Deposit Insurance Corporation, who was advocating publicity for unfavorable findings by bank examiners. That could destroy a bank, Garn objected, especially in farming towns like the one where he was brought up, where the residents would panic at the news and take their money out of the bank. Isaac inquired how many people had lived in Garn's home town, and got the answer; six hundred. Well, he observed, he'd been brought up in a country town with five hundred residents, all of whom knew exactly what was going on at the bank. There wasn't anything any bank examiner could tell them that they didn't already know. Garn, sensibly, moved on to other subjects.

Since fall 1982, a bank in bad trouble has been more likely to expand than to contract because it can draw new funds from all over the country. It can not only pay more than the going rate for deposits (with the deposit and the interest insured fully by the government), it can pay commissions to brokers who steer in the funds. This is something nice a customer's man in a brokerage house can do for a customer who has some idle cash: find him a bank that pays on insured deposits considerably more than any money-market fund—and, meanwhile, pays the customer's man a commission, which the money-market fund does not do. (And the customer doesn't even know the customer's man is getting a commission.) Shadowy firms have formed to move these relatively small pieces of paper to where they are most wanted and to break down larger pieces into $100,000 chunks that qualify for deposit insurance.

In spring 1982 FSLIC had been forced to shut down Oakland-based Fidelity Savings and Loan because rumors that the thrift was in trouble had provoked deposit withdrawals running up to $70 million a week; nine months later, FSLIC had to move fast to close down Chicago's Manning Savings & Loan, an $80-million institution that *grew* by $20 million in the forty-eight hours before the regulators moved in. Early in 1984, FDIC and FSLIC moved together to change the rules on eligibility for insurance, requiring brokers to make deposits in their own names rather than those of their principals. This would put the ceiling on insured accounts at $100,000 per bank per broker, and put an end to that business, which in the second half of 1983 had attracted some eminent Wall Street firms. Treasury Secretary Regan—perhaps unwisely, given his Merrill Lynch background—denounced the action, and for now it's business as usual.

"It's made life a lot easier at the discount window," said the president of one of the Federal Reserve Banks with cheerful cynicism. "Nobody comes around any more—they'd all rather get funds from the money broker than mess with their regulator." Eventually, well-run institutions pay the freight in the form of increased premiums for deposit insurance—which means that their old depositors get lower rates, or their borrowers pay higher rates, to support other people's fraud. Occasionally, the prevailing atmosphere of catering to "hot money" creates situations where the depositors do lose. Thanks to a Tennessee law that permitted finance companies to use the name "bank" if they had used it before the restrictive legislation of the 1930s, C. M. Butcher's Southern Industrial Bank was able to maintain its funding line by advertising high interest rates in the weeks before it sought the protection of a bankruptcy court (something a bank can't do). Many who lent money to this institution believed they were insured at Southern Industrial Bank as they had been in brother Jack Butcher's United American Bank, which had failed a week or two earlier without loss to depositors (large or small: the FDIC arranged a takeover by First Tennessee Bancshares, which honored all liabilities). But the people who had "deposits" in Southern Industrial Bank will get their money back slowly, if at all, as the courts grind through the rituals of bankruptcy.

One cannot remedy this situation by returning to the days of interest-rate ceilings on deposits, which would simply "disintermediate" the banks—that is, force them to buy more of the funds they need at rates above the ceiling, from the money-market mutual funds and similar institutions that would take possession of what would otherwise have been bank deposits, because the interest rates they can pay are uncontrolled. Nor is it possible, despite the urgings of right-wing theorists at the Heritage Foundation, to recast the banking system without deposit insurance. When ordinary people put their money in a bank, it should not be at risk.

In spring 1983 FDIC chairman Isaac proposed a two-part

attack on the problem. First he suggested fractional insurance on deposits over $100,000, with agreement that a successor bank acquiring a failed institution with FDIC help could write down such liabilities to perhaps 75% of their face value. Such a provision would indeed extend market discipline over the activities of all but the dozen or so largest banks. (The perception that the government would not let the giant institutions fail would persist, and would be correct.) Isaac's second suggestion, however—to charge higher insurance premiums to banks with riskier loan portfolios—would not help because it would not affect the behavior of depositors or discourage the failing bank from reaching out for money it shouldn't get. (A bank willing to pay more than the going rate for deposits will also be willing to pay more for deposit insurance.) What is needed is something closer to Isaac's proposal for the large depositors: an insurance scheme that would reduce the coverage on deposits to the extent that a bank paid more for them than some benchmark rate. Such a rate could be set without any exercise of governmental judgment, by reference to the average rate being paid by all the banks as a class. What market discipline must mean in the banking system is that the people who supply the funds are compelled to recognize a relationship between risk and reward.

Neither half of Isaac's remedy could be put into effect without Congressional approval, and deposit insurance is like apple pie and dairy price supports in Congress: only the very brave and very knowledgeable, two small minorities even smaller at the intersection of the sets, will even consider any proposal that harms it. As an alternative, Isaac began to throw his weight around. Because the insurance corporation is liable, he argued, FDIC examiners—who had previously accepted the Fed's opinion of the stability of state-chartered member banks and the Comptroller's evaluation of national banks—should be empowered to participate in *all* bank examinations, and to deny insurance coverage to any banks they consider unsound. FDIC may indeed have this authority in law, and Isaac may have the disrespectful gall to exercise it. If he does, the arguments over the shape of bank regulation, which we shall examine in Chapter 11, will acquire a new urgency and a new nastiness.

What is certain is that the effort to eliminate funding risk from the banking system has failed—as, indeed, it had to fail. As Hyman Minksy of Washington University in St. Louis has been pointing out for twenty years in a series of brilliant papers, the alternative to forcing the recognition of funding risk is increasing financial instability as government feels compelled to validate careless, greedy, or just foolish behavior by banks. Penn Square was truly the crack of doom for the paternalistic banking regulations the United States has known for half a century. The laboriously constructed bailout that rescued the banks from the carelessness, greed, and folly of their foreign lending was the last effort of its kind that the authorities will have the *capacity* (let alone the will) to mount. Conover as Comptroller and Isaac as FDIC chairman may have been ideologically motivated appointments by the most reactionary element in the circle around Ronald Reagan, but even ideologues may be right in their analyses. In the years ahead, bankers will have to accept the burden of managing their credit risks and interest-rate risks as though the future of their banks depended on it because that's the way it's gonna be.

"The fail-safe system worked well in the first fifty years," Isaac explained. "Now we're moving into a deregulated climate, broadening the activities permissible to banks. In the old days, an ordinary bank *couldn't* fail, had to be incompetent or crooked first. Now all you have to do is to make some dumb decisions."

8

PICKING THE
BORROWERS, AT HOME
AND ABROAD

Lending is the activity of the banks most charged with the public interest—"We decide," John Bunting declared magniloquently while running the First National Bank of Pennsylvania (running it almost into the ground, as it happens), "who shall live and who shall die." It is also the most private of banking activities because borrowers usually would prefer not to let the world know how much they are in hock. Recently, the quality of the privacy has deteriorated. The practice of "syndicated" loans, with a number of banks lending together to one borrower, has meant that some loans are public knowledge from the start; and whenever larger credits go bad, the newspapers find out the identity of the major lenders to the defaulting borrower. In 1982 the Securities and Exchange Commission compelled publicly held banks to reveal their exposure in foreign countries whenever loans to a nation and its businesses total more than 1% of the loan portfolio. In late 1983, voting on an increase in the U.S. quota at the International Monetary Funds, Congress instructed the banking regulators to require the exposure of a bank's loans to a foreign country and its residents when the total exceeds $20 million.

Still, the vast bulk of bank loans remain secret, in some states by law; neither the stockholders in nor the lenders to a bank know where their money has been lent. Corporate proxy statements tell stockholders the legal fees paid to any lawyers on the board, but they do not provide any information about the borrowings from the bankers on the board; nor are banks required to tell stockholders about loans to companies whose officers sit on the board of the bank. (Lending to their friends, Walter Wriston and Bert Lance are sisters under the skin. Thanks to Mr. Lance, the Financial Institutions Regulatory Act of 1977 requires Citibank as well as little Georgia banks to print each year an aggregate, though still not the specifics, of all lending to outside directors, though still not to their companies.) Sometimes all this secrecy produces a major embarrassment, as when a bank is lending both to a corporation seeking to take over another corporation and to its intended prey. As lenders are privy to the business condition of their borrowers, the company fighting a takeover bid must make a considerable leap of faith to believe that its banker has not passed confidential information to the shark.

Such incidents are rare—indeed, very little of a bank's lending is newsworthy or unpredictable or in any way interesting. Consumer lending is actuarial: the lending officer queries income, assets, other debts, family status, credit rating, employment, length of time at current address, and so on. The result is a numerical score: over a certain number of "points," the loan is made, and below it the application is refused. (Unfortunately, the same data provide an acceptable score for the issuance of several credit cards, each of which can be exploited to the hilt because the credit-card issuers never share information; so a consumer, like a Third World country, can borrow himself into bankruptcy before the banks realize it.)

Mortgage lending is even simpler: if monthly payments will not exceed a certain percentage of income—one-quarter used to be the standard (and wives' income was not included, bankers' wisdom being that wives quit jobs), but in the 1970s most bankers would go to 30% (of total income for both spouses), on the grounds that home ownership is savings as well as housing—then the borrower is "qualified." Commercial and industrial loans are primarily for the purpose of financing inventories or sales and providing working capital; assets or future receipts are pledged specifically, by formulae of great antiquity, to the repayment of the loan.

For years, the automobile dealer was the local banker's biggest and best customer: he borrowed to "floor plan" the cars in stock (for dealers had to pay the automobile companies for the cars shipped to them), and he sent his customers to the bank for car loans. Dentists borrow for dentist's chairs, doctors for X-ray and electrocardiogram machines, restaurateurs for glassware and china and chairs and tables and carpets and ovens, drillers for oil rigs, builders for land and lumber and labor. For builders' loans, banks like to be sure that the "take-out" financing—the long-term mortgage—is arranged before construction begins. The federal government has pretty much guaranteed this for moderate-income single-family housing through the FHA and VA programs. For apartments and office buildings, the builder has to make his own permanent arrangements first.

These days one forgets what a good business this was. In a small town, the interest rate a bank charged was a classic administered price: the banker set it at whatever level paid his bills and yielded him a profit of the size he thought proper. Meanwhile, he gave depositors whatever banking services he thought they deserved. Most borrowers from a small-town bank did too little business to justify the time of an out-of-towner who would have to investigate the situation not only before he made the loan, but repeatedly; there is no such thing as a safe loan that can be left outstanding so long as the interest payments are current. (Well, maybe a home mortgage is the exception that proves the rule.) Even where all the numbers were larger, in a big-city context, it was by no means easy for a medium-sized borrower to change banks: at the least, the process took a lot of time and might well involve some disruption of the business. Sometimes because of personal contacts and relationships, sometimes because of history (events long forgotten that had established patterns), sometimes for reasons of simple convenience, banks had franchises. What this meant on the other side was that borrowers paid monopoly rents and depositors received services far from commensurate with the earnings a bank produced from the deposits. "Coming from industry, where it's hard to make a buck," said chairman George Haigh of Toledo Trust, who had been with DeVilbiss Company until 1977, "it shook me, the way a lot of banks were run. It hasn't been hard to make a buck in banking."

Yet it was always possible for newcomers to break in. Bank of America's Giannini became a significant lender to major industry despite his location in California and the distasteful fact that he was an Italian who had not gone to the right schools; thanks to his many branches, he always had money to lend, even when the money-center banks were dry. In the 1970s Edmond Safra built a major banking institution in New York under the noses of the giants and in the teeth of disapproval by the government regulators. His Republic National Bank traded in gold and silver at a time when Wall Street disapproved (and, anyway, knew nothing about the subject), offered the contacts of Safra's network of European private and merchant banks, went after board directors who were well placed in New York political life. Always the lending relationship was the key: it's the man who borrows money who guarantees the bank's revenues. The *arriviste* banker hungry for business retains his awareness that whatever a bank can do to make a borrower's business more successful—except cut the interest rates—will increase the profits of both parties.

In the 1960s and early 1970s the sophisticates of the banking business decided that lending was a secondary activity as a creator of profits. The growth of a national money market and the spread of the administered prime meant that interest rates had become relatively standard. The best customers were conglomerating; most of the largest did business with scores of banks and would not pay one of them more than it paid the others. "I wouldn't want to run a big bank," says Ernest Deal of Houston's Fannin Bank. "You're dealing all the time with corporate treasurers who have a staff of people hired to make sure you don't make any money on the account."

In an efficient market, one bank could earn greater interest income than another only by taking more risky loans, which presumably washed out the apparent added profitability when a higher portion of the portfolio went sour. What would make a bank more profitable was not higher prices for its loans or a better loan loss record, but cheaper funds to lend. The banks with the large branching networks—in California, North Carolina, in New York City (which has more population and much more money than most states)—were the ones that showed the best return-on-assets. It was in response to this record that the reserve city bankers mounted their campaigns to change the laws that forbade banks to open deposit-taking offices out of their own state. "The name of the game is the expansion of consumer deposits," said Richard Hill while chairman of the First National Bank of Boston. Once the deposits were in the bank, the money could be pushed out in a relatively routinized way by young recent MBAs who could be sent out as traveling salesmen, "calling officers" who had a quota to fill.

Yet even in the heyday of this approach to banking, the spectacular success stories were the people who held fast to tradition. Ernest Deal came to Fannin in Houston in 1971, forty-two years old, a deceptively easygoing Alabaman who had supervised consumer banking for Texas Commerce Bank. ("I set up their credit-card plan," he said reflectively some years later. "A valuable experience. No bank I'm ever associated with will have a credit card; the credit card is a hand grenade in the pockets of the banks, and the pin is pulled.") When Deal arrived, Fannin was a $60-million bank—"dormant," he said; "a good staff, but never had much management. Those days all you heard about was retail banking; we decided we didn't like retail banking."

Restricted by Texas law to a single office near Houston's great hospital complex, Deal pegged the future of Fannin to becoming *the* bank for a relatively small number of customers with considerable borrowing needs. "We isolated five areas of the market," Deal said eight years later, when Fannin was a $400-million bank. "We're all natural gas, real estate, construction, middle-market commercial—fifty thousand to five million dollars—and executive and professional. What the banking customer wants is a man of integrity, understanding, capability, and constancy. Our people have been here ten, fifteen, twenty years—we have the lowest officer turnover in Texas. And the lowest loan losses, which saves management time, means you're looking at opportunities, not problems. Our demand deposits go up every year, and we don't have any hot CDs; all our CDs are to people with whom we do business." Fannin charged more for loans than most Texas banks—and could get away with it because it gave more service: as chief executive officer, Deal was involved personally with most of the larger accounts. In 1978 the bank earned 1.5% on assets, half again the average profits for banks its size; and though the capital ratio was unusually high (more than 8% of liabilities), Fannin earned 21% on equity.

That such results were not a Texas fluke was demonstrated in Los Angeles by a very different bank in a very different situation, led by a very different man. Leonard Weil left California's Union Bank in 1963 with the view that Los Angeles needed a bank that wasn't anybody's branch and would be dedicated to improving the prospects of that city's decaying old downtown. He opened his Manufacturers Bank near the loft district on a corner that already had branches of Wells Fargo and Bank of America, and he directed his attention to the city's struggling clothing business, a welter of small shops below the notice of the big banks. There were lawyers who needed libraries, clustered around the courthouse not far away; and doctors and dentists; and accountants beginning to acquire machinery. The breakthrough came when Manufacturers began to finance small builders of commercial properties, acting as intermediary (no charge for the service) to secure the take-out financing before the bank began lending on the construction. Weil did only short-term lending—"My total portfolio turns over every six or seven months"—and he funded the bank out of the deposits of his borrowers. It was like something out of the nineteenth century. "We don't require compensating balances," Weil said, "but we ask for our customers' *entire* banking relationship. Our loan officers look to our total business with each borrower and see that it's profitable."

Weil recruited retired bankers from other California banks to help build Manufacturers—he advertised his senior executives in the *Wall Street Journal* as the "over-the-hill gang"— and spread his activities through the city, always concentrating on the "middle market." "The big banks went chasing after big export-import business," he said, "and ignored the guy who needed $250,000. We issued him letters of credit, bought the yen for him. Ten percent of our people are in import business." Even after the bank crossed the half-billion-dollar level in 1978, Weil continued to run it in a small-town way, sitting stocky and crew-cut and informal at a desk open to the public just to the right of the door as people entered the bank. Sometimes he and his customers would exchange waves as the customers went to the tellers. Like Deal, Weil never offered a credit card, "which has kept us from losing a lot of money."

The central principle of Manufacturers, Weil said, was that

"we always have money." More than 30% of the bank's assets in a normal month were in short-term securities and Fed Funds sold to other banks. "It used to be," Weil said cheerfully in 1979, when short-term interest rates had gone into double digits, "that liquidity implied a sacrifice. This year, it's offered a premium. Maybe people will learn." As a result, Manufacturers gained business in every credit crunch: in one month of 1975, it actually made more construction loans in Los Angeles than Bank of America (not more money, but a greater number of loans). Through the 1970s, profits ran better than 1% of assets and approached 30% of equity. By 1980 the bank had $800 million in assets.

Fannin weathered the hard times in the oil patch almost unbelievably well. In spring 1983, out of assets of $540 million, its nonperforming loans just touched $300,000. Return on assets had peaked at a remarkable 2.1% in 1981 and dropped only to 1.8%—over twice the national average—in 1982, when return on equity was 23%. "We are a relationship lender," Deal said. "Mostly, we do not do business with people who do business with other banks. People have their wives' accounts here, their children's accounts, their wills. They're not leveraged. People get in trouble around here when they're dealing with big banks and with youngsters who've never been through bad times." Weil, too, reported in spring 1983 that Manufacturers' earnings were "better than the average California bank," but the circumstances of his growth to $1.8 billion in assets prevented him from maintaining his ratios.

Those circumstances were, briefly, that in 1981 Mitsui of Japan acquired the bank, now known as Mitsui Manufacturers, and folded in its own previous California banking operation. Weil continued as president and CEO and continued to sit in his old space on the Ninth Street banking floor. (Actually, Manufacturers now has two banking floors on its original street: Bank of America closed its branch across the way, and Weil took over the property.) He maintained a six-to-seven-month total turnover of portfolio and mostly continued to fund the bank from deposits, though he said in 1983, "We've dipped our toe into the national money market." Unlike most Japanese venturers in the United States, Mitsui had decided that it wished American management for its bank; indeed, that was the reason why it bought Manufacturers. Weil was happy with the Japanese, but he thought that if his bank had not been bought up, he could have continued to grow and continued to show his startlingly good return on equity.

Fannin's Deal thought the glory days were over. In 1982 he merged his bank into the Interfirst holding company at a satisfying profit for himself and his associates. Even Deal's depositors had begun to insist on interest on their checking accounts. "There was no way our profit ratios could have been maintained in the face of narrowing spreads. If we'd been in Midland or Amarillo," Deal said, "I'd have stayed independent, but I was somewhat pessimistic on the long-run viability of a large independent bank in a city like Houston. Interstate banking is coming. A Citibank or a Chase will come in here and put in an operation across the street. They'll start a loss-leader operation, and they'll get away with it. We feared Houston would be a place where dumb people would come in and do dumb things and wreck the house."

There was also a deeper concern. "There's a man named Kenneth Schnitzer, a developer here, shopping centers and office buildings, no housing. Jerry Hines has the reputation in the East, but he's not the hitter Schnitzer is in Houston. He's done his personal banking with me for a long time and paid higher interest than he would have paid elsewhere. Once I asked him why he did it, and he said, 'You've handled me with grace and style. When I call bigger banks, I deal with young officers who don't know me from Adam's off ox.' But now he's borrowing more, and he has to go for the cheaper price: he can't afford the luxury of dealing with the chairman of Fannin. That sort of thing changes the business you can do."

Weil is more optimistic about the future of the sort of bank he and Deal ran. "We've had an explosion of banks in California, and they're finding new market sectors. There's still a place for what we call niche banking. Find your niche and you can have much better earnings than the bank that tries to be all things to all people." There are several success stories of fairly large and rapidly expanding banks to back Weil's optimism. New York's Key Banks, for example, an upstate operation that has made money on 50 branches acquired from Bankers Trust and Bank of New York (which found they couldn't make money upstate), has grown to be a $5 billion bank by offering services (including electronic banking, leasing, and discount brokerage) to the small businesses of small cities. A specially intensive examination of the holding company on the occasion of its acquisition of a Maine bank in 1983 found only a handful of loans for $1 million or more—and virtually no nonperforming assets. Similarly, General Bancshares of St. Louis, with $1.8 billion in assets, has specialized profitably in mortgages and local commercial lending. Chairman Jack W. Minton told John Curley of *The Wall Street Journal,* "I don't want to get into anything I don't understand."

2

A better word than "niche" is "expertise"—no doubt a bank can make money on expertise. Consider, for example, the situation in Providence, Rhode Island, the home base for most of America's costume jewelry industry, which requires gold for gold plate. In March 1968 the finance ministers and central banks of the world agreed to stop selling or buying gold except to and from each other, to staunch the outflow of monetary gold from the United States during one of the earlier crises of the dollar. The result would be a two-tier market in gold, with a pegged price for official transactions and a free price at which nongovernmental producers, holders, purchasers, and users would deal with each other.

The economic theory behind this was rather murky. Gold is a commodity, identical for monetary or nonmonetary purposes; James Tobin of Yale observed that it was as though the finance ministers had decreed that all the gold in their vaults should be painted blue, and only gold not painted blue would continue to be "gold" for private and industrial use.

The practical effects on American industries using gold were dramatic. A law from the Roosevelt era still forbade Americans to hold gold except for ornamental or manufacturing use. Industrial users had bought their gold under strictly controlled conditions directly from the assay office of the Treasury. Now, pursuant to international agreement, the Treasury stopped selling—without lifting its requirement that any private purchaser from abroad would have to get a license to import. Those licenses were hard to come by. No one in the Johnson administration seems to have thought that this would make some trouble out in the great nongovernmental world where people earn the living that permits them to pay taxes. When the private markets in gold opened ("Appropriately, it was April Fool's Day," says Jack Fraser of Hospital Trust National Bank in Providence), the volume available was nowhere near the needs of industrial users.

Hospital Trust was the banker for much of the costume jewelry industry on a straight inventory-financing, sales-facilitating basis. Now the industry was in trouble because of the shortage of gold and the Treasury's fear that wholesale issuance of licenses to import would encourage people to hold bullion in violation of law. "We thought it appropriate to bring order to the market," Fraser says, "and we applied for a license. Treasury was willing to give us a ten-thousand-ounce license, which would have taken care of the needs of one client—they were really hung up on the possibility that people might speculate. We finally convinced them that we could control speculation from Providence better than they could from Washington." Fraser also had to convince the board of his very traditional bank, for whom "gold" was a shady world of international operators. He pledged that at no time would the bank own an unsold inventory of more than 400 ounces, and he structured the bank's dealings in such a way that in fact the inventory has rarely risen above a total of 50 ounces, $40,000 at the peak of the market—not much exposure for a $2–billion bank.

At first, Hospital Trust simply bought in London for immediate resale in Providence at the London price (plus about 50¢ per ounce, for the bank). "But a lot of companies here sell by catalogue," Fraser says, "watchbands and such. They have to price in advance. We went to them and said, 'Wouldn't it be appropriate for you to pay us a premium to insure your cost?'" On May 3, 1968 Hospital Trust put an ad in the *Providence Evening Bulletin,* offering gold to industrial users for delivery on their schedule, at the price on the day they decided to buy plus 22¢ per ounce per month for the life of the contract. The big business for the bank, of course, was the loans written for the manufacturers to carry the inventory Hospital Trust was acquiring for them. "The carrying charge is a little over prime," Fraser says, "because there is no compensating balance, and because we do have a credit risk when the price of gold goes down." Meanwhile, the bank acquired a secondary business in the borrowing and (especially) lending of gold all over the world, because the inventory of a commodity need not be kept in physical form. "Gold," Fraser says, "is like a foreign exchange." As with foreign exchange, the inventory risk is controlled essentially by selling in the forward market what is purchased at spot, keeping Fraser's exposure below the limits set by the board.

Three officers and a staff of ten run the gold business for Hospital Trust; they import 2.5 million ounces of gold a year, "a tad more than half of all the gold brought to the United States for industrial use." At a guess, they contribute something like one-sixth the profits of the bank. It's a nice niche.

There are other niches in which expertise may bring satisfaction, but not much money. The most obvious of these is a racial niche. Take, for example, Mechanics & Farmers Bank of Durham, North Carolina, one of the nation's largest black-owned-and-operated depository institutions. It was organized in 1908 with the help of North Carolina Mutual Life, the largest black insurance company, still a significant source of deposits and other help. The bank's footings are about $50 million, and it has branches in Raleigh and Charlotte—eight branches in all.

Even in the heyday of the money-market funds, Mechanics & Farmers didn't lose deposits. "I've got pretty good loyalty among my accounts," says president James Joseph Sansom, sitting in his small windowless office behind the banking floor a block off the main drag of Durham. "We have a lot of accounts and most of them don't have a lot of money. They won't move for fifteen or twenty dollars. We want this institution to continue. We know our customers and they know us; we've been through a lot of things together. But a lot of that loyalty is from the older people.

"We feel competition from the big banks. The blacks who have jobs, they're bankable people now, and the big banks are going after them. It's better for the black businessman's status to be at NCNB or Wachovia—he'd rather be well regarded by them than by us. Banking is like a lot of other businesses: the white businessman has the advantage of both markets. It's hard for the black businessman to get white business." Mechanics & Farmers concentrates of necessity on mortgages ("that's what our people needed—they needed homes") and on installment lending, where it winds up with too high a proportion of those for whom this bank is the lender of last resort.

"We've got a lot of additional expense from all these regulations. We are examined by both the FDIC and the state banking commissioner. It used to be one joint examination, but then the North Carolina court ruled that certain records had to be public records, and the FDIC couldn't live with that. And now we've got a special compliance examination, over and above the FDIC, the banking commissioner, the trust examination. There are all those changes—you get the forms, then they change the rules and you need new forms—Truth in Lending, RESPA [Real Estate Settlement Procedures Act], Equal Credit Opportunity. The motive behind it is good, but Sears Roebuck doesn't have to go through all that. I've had to hire a compliance officer."

William Kennedy, chairman of North Carolina Mutual Life, who is still on the board of Mechanics & Farmers (until his company bid for a television station, he was on the board of RCA, too), feels that the bank must expect trouble ahead. "We're losing black customers. We can't serve them. We have no credit card, no automated teller machines. Can't afford them—that's banking house and fixtures, and there's a limit to the share of assets you can have in that. The big banks have branches in the shopping centers and teller machines for after hours. Go look at the lines standing outside the Wachovia machines at Duke University Hospital. Half of them are blacks and would be doing business with Mechanics & Farmers. And, of course, the bank has the problem we have—the number of accounts you have to service to get the same dollar numbers the big banks and insurance companies get with half as many accounts, or even fewer."

3

And sometimes banks get into niches where they have no expertise, and the niche becomes a trap. The danger is especially great for money-center banks that feel themselves uniquely placed to finance the fast-moving operations of the money markets. There is money to be made in this business, but not very much, because the banks' customers know the angles better than the bank does; and the risks are much larger than a bank management may understand. To wit:

Drysdale Government Securities, a name the Chase Manhattan Bank dearly wishes it had never heard, was formed in February 1982 as an offshoot of a long-established small Wall Street brokerage house called Drysdale Securities. (It had been Joe Kennedy's broker.) An indictment filed in New York Criminal Court in July 1983 alleges that the spin-off was motivated by huge losses in the government's trading department of the brokerage house, which were transferred out to the new firm.

The guiding star of Drysdale Government was David Heuwetter, a fortyish bachelor, a swinger, a trader in government bonds, who had been with Drysdale Securities since 1980 and had made enough money to put up $10 million equity from his own resources. (The indictment says, Hogwash: there was no capital: Drysdale Government was $150 million under water on the day it opened.) Another $10 million of subordinated capital was raised, $5 million of it from Drysdale Securities in the form of a preferred stock issue with an option for conversion to equity—and Drysdale Government Securities was in business as a dealer in the New York market, buying and selling (and borrowing and lending) government bonds, bills, and notes for its own account. Within two months, Drysdale's position in governments was nearing $10 billion. It had moved its offices into the splendid old New York Chamber of Commerce and Industry building on Liberty Street, which Hewetter and two colleagues from Drysdale Securities had purchased (to the despair of urban preservationists). Another month, and Drysdale Government Securities was bankrupt, with losses of $285 million suffered by Chase, almost $30 million by Manufacturers Hanover.

The government securities market is the heart of the cash-management services banks provide for their customers (and, indeed, for themselves). Initially, this market was an artifact of the prohibition on the payment of interest on demand deposits: banks arranged for their customers to earn interest on money not needed today by making a short-term purchase of government securities for them, on a basis whereby the seller agreed to repurchase the securities in a day or a week or whenever the bank's customer expected to need the cash. The transaction was done at the face value—the redemption price of the bond. The seller continued to be the beneficial owner of the interest accruing on the bond, which would be returned to him at the close of the transaction. He paid interest for the use of the purchaser's money—that is, when he bought back the security he paid face value, plus an interest charge arranged before the original sale.

Rather than charge its customers a fee for this service, the bank conducted such transactions as a dealer. It might supply the bond from its own investment portfolio, or it might buy the bond in the market, entering into its own matched repurchase agreements with third parties. If the interest rate in the market was 10% and the repo was for twenty days, a $1,000,000 bond would be sold to the bank by a dealer for $1,000,000, with an agreement to repurchase for $1,005,479.45. The bank made money by charging a markup—perhaps 0.25%, annualized. On the transaction where the original seller was paying the bank $5,479.45 for twenty days' use of the money, the bank would pay its corporate customer only $5,342.74. That's not much— but it's an infinite return on assets because the bank doesn't put up a penny. It uses the million dollars it receives from the corporate purchaser of the repo to pay the dealer who supplies the bond.

The repo market became the normal means by which the Federal Reserve operated in the open market to increase or decrease the supply of money to meet what are considerable fluctuations in demand for it. By purchasing securities under an arrangement by which the seller would repurchase them in a few days, the Fed could inject reserves temporarily into the banking system and control the prices in the Fed Funds market. Later, the Fed developed a "reverse repo" market, by which it could drain reserves temporarily from the system by selling securities under an agreement to buy them back. The Fed "recognized" a group of primary dealers—usually between two and three dozen of them—with whom it conducted such

224

operations. About half of these primary dealers were major banks; about half were securities houses. In return for their privileged position at the Fed, these firms kept the Fed informed of all their activities in the market. But they were by no means the only dealers in the market—indeed, could not be. Banks and securities houses all over the country were buying and selling every day.

The purchaser of a government bond was the legal owner of that bond even though he had agreed to sell it back in twenty days. In the meantime, he could sell it himself in the market and get his cash back. In fact, he would get more than his cash back because the bond on a straight sale (no repo) would be priced at face value *plus accrued interest to the date of sale.* Coupons on government bonds are redeemed twice yearly. A $1,000,000 bond with an annual 10% interest rate would have two $50,000 coupons to be paid each year. If one of those coupons were ready for clipping on December 1 and the sale was made on October 1 (and the market interest rate was the same 10% as the bond interest rate), a purchaser would pay $1,033,333.33 for the borrowed bond.

We live in an age of wire transfer: these sales can be made the same day as the repo, with all the paper changing hands in both directions before the accounts are posted that night. Actual bonds—pieces of parchment—no longer move: like money itself, a government bond appears in the world only as an entry on the books of the Fed, and ownership of Treasury paper is transferred, like money, by FedWire. The borrower's sale could be made as a short sale before the repo was arranged. The net effect would then be to give the dealer who played this game twenty days' free use of $33,333.33.

When the bond dealer has to close out such a transaction, he is out of pocket, but not by much. To buy back this bond in the market twenty days later, assuming no change in the interest rates, will cost him $1,038,797.81. Offsetting that $5,400 loss is the interest paid by the original seller of the bond as part of the repurchase agreement. So the net loss to the dealer is about $121, in twenty days. That's an interest cost of about 6.6%, annualized, on the $33,333.33 he had been playing with for twenty days. And meanwhile he had been able to speculate, using other people's money, on the chance that the bond market might fall. If the price of the bond dropped by 2.5% in the market during the twenty days (which on a bond with a year to run would be caused by a rise in the interest rate from 10% to 10.3%, something that in recent years has often happened in a single week), he would have a profit of $25,000 on the transactions. And we have been talking about a lousy million-dollar short-sale covered with a repo. Drysdale was operating in the billions. On a $1 billion repo book, a 2.5% drop in bond prices is worth $25 *million*.

But into each life a little rain must fall: it may happen that instead of falling by 2.5%, bond prices *rise* by 2.5%. Now the short sale and repo man has a $25 million loss if he seeks to clear his account, a development to which the obvious riposte is to keep the account open: roll over the repo to avoid buying the bond. At some point, however, the speculator runs into the negative aspect of the system that permits him to price the paper he borrows at its face value. If he keeps the bond through the day when a coupon matures, he must make the payment on that coupon himself. Let us return to our example of a bond with a December 1 coupon purchased October 1 for $1 million subject to repurchase at the same price plus interest, but make the repo a 90-day rather than a 20-day transaction. Between October 1 and December 1, the repo artist has the use of $33,333.33 of other people's money. On December 1 he has to come up with $50,000 for the original owner. Instead of gambling with money from the house, a Drysdale finds that on a $1 billion "book" it must pay out $17 million.

Should this happen, the banks could find themselves in the middle. They were the intermediaries who bought the bonds from the original owners in the repurchase agreements, and then executed similar repo agreements with dealers like Drysdale. They would be expected to pay off on those coupons—

and to replace the bonds even if the price went up—whether or not the Drysdales of the world lived up to their contracts with their banks. The owners of the bonds might not have been willing to enter into direct repurchase agreements with pipsqueaks like Drysdale; they felt safe because they were dealing with a big bank, a "recognized" primary dealer whose activities were monitored by the Fed.

For ease of accounting, the banks carried these transactions on their books as loans, but it should be noted that the accounts were inevitably misleading. Cash had gone from the bank to the owner of the bond, and from the dealer (who sold the bond in the market) to the bank. The *real* loan had been that of the bond itself, from the bank to the dealer—but that was secured so firmly by cash that the bank didn't worry about it. In fact, the bank did not necessarily know what had happened to that bond—whether the dealer had sold it or repo'd it to someone else or used it as security for a loan from somebody else. Once it had agreed to do business with this dealer, the bank turned over the handling of the account to the cash-management or investment service people, who were used to handling these floods of government paper.

U.S. Trust had been the main intermediary for Drysdale in the government bond business, before the separate firm was spun off to accommodate Heuwetter and his trading, because individuals at Drysdale had long-standing relations with that bank. Heuwetter added Continental Illinois and First Interstate, for which he had worked when it was still United California Banks. The clearing account—the handling of the Federal Reserve confirmation that investment paper had moved in one direction and money in the other—was handled by Chemical Bank.

It is not clear who first introduced Drysdale to Chase. Perhaps Chase solicited the business: its Investment Services Group had been structured to reward its executives with a share of the profits, which were largely a function of the volume of business that passed through this corner of the

227

bank's machinery. Chase certainly had no doubts about the firm. According to Chris Welles, who detailed the Drysdale story in *Institutional Investor,* the partners in the two Drysdales were approved as purchasers of the Commerce & Industry building by David Rockefeller, chairman of the Chamber, who assured its board that the Drysdales were solid citizens. Others, however, watching the market operations of Drysdale Government Securities, decided Heuwetter was building much too big a pyramid on his capital base of (at most) $20 million, and one by one they withdrew as intermediaries in Drysdale deals. Chemical's withdrawal was accomplished with consummate skill, for the bank continued to do Drysdale's clearing, and it is difficult for an operations staff to make absolutely certain that the bank is *never* carrying some debt in cash or securities for a dealer during the course of the clearing. But strict orders had been issued, and were followed, that no securities were to be accepted for Drysdale unless the cash was in hand (and vice versa). On the day Drysdale Government crashed, Chemical had no obligations.

Later, when the situation was unwound, three elements of Chase's fecklessness were simply incomprehensible to the regulators and to other bankers. The first was simply the size of the operation the bank had allowed Drysdale to conduct on the basis of the bank's name—for, after all, it was Chase that initiated the repos. Drysdale had quickly become a well-known if not well-regarded name in the government paper market, but it was very small potatoes outside those narrow confines. One of the senior executives of the Federal Reserve Bank of New York was in Washington meeting with Federal Reserve Board chairman Paul Volcker on the day the story broke. Volcker (who had once worked for Chase) was trying to figure out what was going on. He asked his visitor (a former colleague, for Volcker had run the Federal Reserve Bank of New York) what he knew about Drysdale, and received the bewildered response, "You mean the pitcher? For the Dodgers?" A government-bond dealer never recognized by the Fed, with a name not known to its senior executives, had been permitted by Chase to acquire almost $5 billion of securities on which the Chase Manhattan bank was the primary obligor.

The second element of incredulity arose from the fact that Chase, unlike the banks that had cut Drysdale off, had never noticed Heuwetter's pattern of trading, which was a clear tip-off that he was getting into desperate trouble. Drysdale Government's bond borrowings had increasingly involved securities nearing their coupon date, which steadily increased the cash flow the dealer derived from the mismatch between payment out at par for the repo and payment in with accrued interest when the borrowed security was sold. This pattern, quite evident to the market, was what persuaded U.S. Trust that despite its continuing business relations with Drysdale Securities, it wanted no part of Drysdale Government Securities.

But the most serious problem was the revelation that Chase simply had not understood the business it was in. The first indication (to Chase) that Drysdale was in the soup came on a sour Sunday in May when the firm reached Chase executives at their homes to reveal that it would not be able to meet payments required on Monday to deliver the interest represented by the bond coupons on its borrowed holdings, and to return securities now due for repurchase. Heuwetter requested a loan of $160 million—and for the first time, the credit side of Chase took a look at Drysdale's condition. Without realizing that Chase could not walk away from Drysdale's obligations, the lending officers advised the Investment Securities Group to wash their hands of Drysdale. Though Chase continues to insist that the law is murky and that the bank was on strong ground in contending that it had been acting simply as Drysdale's agent in arranging the repurchase agreements, the market distinctly thought otherwise.

At a meeting summoned hastily at the Federal Reserve Bank of New York, Chase essentially offered the owners of the bonds a loan facility to help them ride out the disruptions of their operations that would be caused by Drysdale's failure—

and was informed in very strong statements that the owners had no relations with Drysdale. Their contracts were with Chase, and they expected Chase to put up the money whether Drysdale paid the bank or not. In the end, Chase swallowed the losses, though it continued to threaten to sue the government-bond dealers who had known perfectly well why Chase was buying the securities involved in the repurchase agreements and whose claim therefore, Chase insisted, should lie against the bankrupt Drysdale. But the only suit Chase actually brought was against Arthur Andersen, Drysdale's accountant, for certifying some implausible books.

Chase chairman Willard Butcher sent an embarrassing memo around the bank, trying to buck up the spirits of people whose morale had been damaged considerably by the revelation of the incompetence management had permitted (and the loss of hoped-for bonuses from 1982 profits). "I liken us," he wrote, "to a superbly trained and physically fit boxer who clearly dropped his guard—momentarily perhaps—but he dropped it and he got slugged. He got floored and he's got a black eye. But he is not out for the count. In fact, he isn't even knocked out. Certainly, it wasn't a fatal injury. Now, that boxer has a choice. He can quit the ring, or he can get back up and fight. The quality of a champion is one who can get decked, crawl back off the canvas, and then go back to his game plan, which is sound, and fight and win." This memo was published in an article by Jaye Scholl in *Barron's* magazine, and the ring of disgrace was closed.

The Drysdale episode was multiply revealing. It gave the first indication of what was to be demonstrated that summer after the Mexican collapse—that the Fed was not using the information it gathered routinely from the banks and the market to exert any but the mildest deterrent to unsound practice. It demonstrated the drastic decline of the influence of the banks—and among the banks, especially of Chase—in deciding what other people must do. In 1974, when Herstatt went under, Chase was one of few American institutions that had any of

Herstatt's assets in its custody; the bank promptly seized those assets to offset against Herstatt's liabilities to Chase itself and Chase only, greatly reducing Chase's exposure and the other banks' chances for recovering losses. In 1979, when the Iranians threatened to withdraw their deposits from American banks, Chase (and Citicorp) had enough influence in Washington to persuade the Treasury Department to approve the offset of Iranian assets against Iranian indebtedness to the banks— something Chase, in particular, needed, for it had been the lead bank on a $500 million syndicated loan to the Shah that had never been approved by the Iranian legislature, as required by that country's constitution, and thus might well have been repudiated by Khomeini and his friends with the approval of American and international as well as "Islamic" courts. But by late 1980, when Poland was forced to renegotiate its loans, Chase was unable to make the banking syndicates separate its secured loans to the Polish copper mines and had to throw this exposure into the general unsecured pot, from which few—if any—repayments will be made. And in 1982 the bank's vulnerability to the market with regard to the source of its lendable funds forced it to buckle immediately when others refused to accept its insistence that it had no liability for Drysdale's fails.

Merrill Lynch was among those to whom money and securities were owed by Chase on its Drysdale activities, and Merrill Lynch had something like a billion dollars of Chase liabilities in the portfolio of its Ready Assets Fund. Neither Merrill nor Chase admits that a direct threat was made to dump this paper on the market and drive up Chase's cost of funds if the bank disclaimed responsibility on Drysdale; perhaps the threat did not have to be spoken. Ultimately, rather than Chase's shoring up the market, which was what Butcher offered graciously at the first meeting, the Fed had to shore up Chase; and with Chase the community of large banks (and the dealers) as interest rates rose on the CDs of the money-center banks which were known to act as intermediaries in the repo market.

Chase's troubles were far from over: the Penn Square collapse was only two months away. And there was another government-bond dealer to go: Lombard–Wall, a long-established house that had been off-and-on a Fed-recognized primary dealer. As such, Lombard–Wall had access to direct repos from the owners of the bonds, and when it defaulted, the losers were mostly institutions and one large government agency: the New York State Dormitory Authority. This time the Federal Reserve Bank of New York claimed that it had tried to help, circularizing the government-bond dealers to remind them that in many ways a repo was an unsecured loan of the interest on a security, and lenders should be sure they knew the condition of the borrower's business. The Fed couldn't mention Lombard–Wall by name, a Fed spokesman argues, because that would put the house out of business and subject the Fed to possible libel suits—but everyone in the market should have known who was the target. Because the repos were direct, the Lombard failure wound up in the courts, rather than in a conference room at the Fed, and the judge who first heard the case greatly muddied the repo market by ruling that the bonds in question were part of the estate of the bankrupt and could not automatically be reclaimed by repurchasing sellers before other claims against Lombard were adjudicated. Among those who had sold to Lombard and now had to wait to get their securities back was . . . Chase Manhattan.

4

The 1970s were a time when many banks thought they had found safe and profitable niches for themselves in places far from the costly regulations of their domestic supervisors and the grasping manners of the corporate treasurers. By the second half of that decade, international lending accounted for more than half the reported profits of the giant money-center banks. The problem, which did not come to light until 1982, was that these were not real profits, and the activity was not real banking. A Leonard Weil in Los Angeles ran a real bank in which the portfolio turned over in its entirety every six or seven months: loans were repaid and profits were pocketed. But a Walter Wriston in New York ran a phantasmagorical bank in which profits were merely reported and never earned; the loans never were and never would be repaid, and the borrowers could not afford to carry them. Increasingly, the interest on these foreign loans, which Citicorp reported as revenue, was merely another loan from the bank to the borrower, building reported assets faster than reported liabilities, but yielding no cash flow. "Ponzi finance" was the term used to describe such lending by Hyman Minsky of the University of Washington at St. Louis, the outstanding American theoretical economist in the banking field. And Ponzi schemes, as everyone knows, collapse.

The failure of the foreign borrowers to produce cash interest payments on their loans meant that the giant banks were, in fact, paying the interest on their own funding by borrowing more from the market. Through the fall of 1982 and into 1983, the banks and their regulators sought to transfer at least some of these exponentially growing loans to the International Monetary Fund, which can create assets indistinguishable from money, to improve the proportion of bank earnings derived from receipts rather than from bookkeeping. Everyone became deeply conscious of the degree to which banking is a matter of people's confidence in the banks. Great leaders of world finance, both private and governmental, became, in the fullest sense of a familiar term, "confidence men."

There is nothing new about foreign lending. The classic banking documents, the letter of credit, and the banker's acceptance, still powerful financing tools, were created to facilitate foreign trade. In the first of these, a bank arranges for a customer to draw funds abroad from the bank's foreign correspondent banks. The most common situation is an order for merchandise, to be shipped to the bank's customer, with payment of the proceeds of the loan to be made to the manufacturer or wholesaler when the bill of lading is received at the port of entry. In the second, the manufacturer's own bank makes the advance to him, on a promise that the purchaser's bank far away will stand surety for the repayment in thirty, sixty, ninety days.

Letters of credit have come to serve diverse functions, including performance bonds; it is "standby" letters of credit that back the commercial paper that corporations sell to each other to adjust the business community's cash positions without the intermediation of the banks. Because they don't have to lay out any cash when they sign the client—and rarely have to part with money at any time under such contracts—banks have a tendency to behave as though that standby letter of credit does not involve a credit risk (an attitude the government regulators encourage by not including such standbys as part of the exposure to a single corporate borrower limited by law to 15% of a bank's capital). But a standby letter of credit is a pure example of credit risk, as banks find out every so often when the letter is used *because* the borrower is no longer creditworthy—or, in the international context, because a Khomeini and his brigade of imams wish to strike out at all things American.

The banker's acceptance is another way for banks to do business without committing their own resources. The bank with the customer who signs for the loan (Manufacturers of Los Angeles guaranteeing the credit of the store importing videotape machines) stands at risk for the money but does not advance it; the bank with the customer who receives the proceeds of the loan (Fuji of Tokyo, paying JVC for the VHSs) pays out the money but can recoup its cash position instantly by selling the acceptance in the market. The bank will be able to sell the paper for more than it paid out to the exporter because banks pay lower interest rates for money than their borrowers do. One speaks of "names" in banking largely because of, historically, acceptances sold on the market at prices determined by the reputation of the bank that guaranteed them.

Merchant banks, so-called—distinguished from commercial banks by their reliance on their partners' rather than on their depositors' capital—might do considerable foreign business of a different kind, helping a country to raise funds in the money market of a country not its own. The American railroads were built by loans from British merchant banks and bond sales arranged by British merchant banks; the London financial crisis Bagehot writes about in *Lombard Street* (and Marx in Volume III of *Das Kapital*) began with the failure of a crooked U.S. railway company. The misconduct by the U.S. banks of the 1920s that really pushed the Glass–Steagall Act through Congress in 1933 (prohibiting commercial banks from underwriting securities and selling them to the public) involved Latin American bonds the banks dumped out of their investment portfolios into the hands of their unsuspecting customers when the banks found out the paper was no good. It might be noted in passing that the international financial crisis of 1982–83 took the form it did, with the banks at risk, only because the public was protected by Glass–Steagall. The National City Bank of New York had been the worst villain in the bond scams of the late 1920s; its successor, one suspects, would have "placed" quite a lot of Brazilian paper with investors in 1980–81, if the law had not prevented it. In his last issue for 1983, editor Gerald T. Dunne of the *Banking and Law Journal* noted a "competition between supervisor and supervised alike to junk Glass–Steagall, a process the historically minded may well analogize to a peasants' dance on the slopes of Vesuvius."

For a bank to lend depositors' money to borrowers far away was always regarded as questionable banking. After all, a bank lends not to balance sheets, but to real businesses and (more important) real people: it's hard to know in any depth the people who take your money or the condition of the businesses in which they use it if they are many miles away. Though the money mainly wound up abroad, the letter of credit and the banker's acceptance were written essentially for the benefit of the importer who was the local bank's local customer. If a bank *did* lend money to remote places, it would work through correspondent banks, whose judgment it had reason to trust, who had money in the deal themselves, with whom the bank did enough reciprocal business to keep the correspondents careful and honest. American banks were slow to get into foreign lending after World War II—this is one of the reasons the Marshall Plan was necessary—in part because they were reluctant to jeopardize profitable relationships by going into competition with their correspondents.

But the dollar had become the world's currency: key commodities were priced in and sold for dollars, wherever they were grown or mined or pumped and wherever they were to be consumed. During the long reconstruction after the European war, U.S. policy was to make dollars more available to foreigners, and not only by AID and government loans. To give an example quite incredible from the perspective of the 1980s, cargo rates were set so that shipping to the United States was considerably less expensive than shipping from the United States. The U.S. balance of payments ran in steady deficit for decades, first because of aid programs, then because capital flowed abroad to take advantage of what until the late 1970s were always higher interest rates abroad, finally because the American merchandise balance of trade, positive in every year in this century until 1970, fell into persistent and enormous deficit.

Some of these dollars shipped abroad returned in purchases of U.S. government securities (the basic storage for other countries' foreign-exchange reserves: in 1983 the Treasury securities held by the Federal Reserve Bank of New York for foreign governments and central banks topped $120 billion), or in investments by foreigners in American industry or real estate. And some of the dollars simply were held by foreigners as the transaction balances of the world economy. Dollar-denominated transaction balances are what American banks do for a living. Payments in dollars clear through New York, whether they are made in Tokyo or Bahrain or London or the Cayman Islands. And any dollar-payments system requires the participation of banks that relate to the Federal Reserve, the only continuing source of dollars.

So one by one the American banks dropped their correspondent relations, opened their own branches, subsidiaries, or agencies abroad, and launched "consortium banking" in which they were partners with their former correspondents. At first the banking authorities of foreign countries were deeply suspicious of this dollar-denominated lending going on right under their noses. After a generation of flight from other currencies to the dollar, the governments feared that any dollar market in their midst would simply smooth the path for the continuing devaluation of their own currency. But what they found was that American banks had come primarily to lend money to American multinational corporations starting or acquiring businesses in the host country. Such investment by foreigners raised GNP, improved job opportunities, increased exports, and so on. It would take the pressure off local capital markets and allow for more investment without squeezing the poor or stimulating inflation.

The package was irresistible. Especially in countries where the government sought to control the money supply by restrictions on bank lending (the British "corset," the French *"encadrement du credit"*), central banks might encourage local businesses to do their borrowing in dollars; at first for export-oriented production that would yield the foreign exchange required to service the debt, later as a way to keep production growing without requiring more savings from their own public, finally as a way to pay for desired imports that simply increased domestic consumption. Until the late 1970s, dollar interest rates were consistently lower than domestic rates elsewhere, so such loans were a bargain to the borrowers. And because American banks did not have to keep sterile reserves at the Fed against their dollar deposits abroad, their cost of funds for

237

foreign lending was (and is) lower than in the United States. By charging a little more for their loans than they could get in the American market and (in effect) paying a little less for the dollars they lent, American banks operating abroad would improve their "spread"—their real return on assets. Presently there were more than one hundred banks with London branches, selling and buying Eurodollars. In late 1983 there were almost *five hundred* foreign banks operating in London.

Still living under an international monetary regime that required the United States to redeem its currency in gold on demand from foreign governments or central banks, the Kennedy administration grew concerned about all this lending when the numbers were still small, and in 1963 imposed an Interest Equalization Tax to reduce the banks' spreads on Eurodollar loans and diminish the lure of the foreign borrower. When this didn't work, the Johnson administration created a Voluntary Credit Restraint Program, soon made mandatory. But by now the balance of trade was beginning to deteriorate. In 1971 Nixon closed the gold window; in 1974, for reasons we shall examine presently, all restraints on foreign lending were removed. By then, the international foreign exchange market was all but unrestricted—with the unintended result that the suppliers of vital commodities (especially oil) were able to demand payments in dollars from all their customers.

The tenfold growth in the Eurodollar market between 1971 and 1982 is an oft-told (though often not very well-told) story. It is usually said to begin with the oil-price explosion that followed the Egyptian attack on Israel in October 1973 and the reaction of world markets to the Arab boycott of the United States and the Netherlands. A more likely point of origin is the decision by all the industrial world's finance ministers and central bankers to bull their way out of the recession of 1969–71 by slamming the gas pedal to the floor. The explosion of money creation following Nixon's removal of the gold constraint produced an immense rise in *all* commodity prices in 1972–73 and the beginnings of the inflation that would wrack the democratic societies for a decade. When the oil producers began leapfrogging their prices, the money was there. Given the centrality of energy as an input in industrial societies, and the inflexibility of the plans both governments and corporations had made to expand energy use in the 1970s, the quintupling of energy prices between summer 1973 and spring 1974 met virtually no resistance from consumers.

Now the banks moved center stage in the world economy. Cash-rich and quite at a loss to know what to do with their money, the oil producers deposited their receipts in the international banks. They expected interest on their money; to pay that interest, the banks had to lend the money, and the countries that needed oil saw no way to keep going other than to borrow. The carousel of "petrodollar recycling" began, picked up speed, and soon came to seem a natural aspect of world trade.

But it was not natural at all. There was never any question that developing countries would have to increase their external debt in the process of development. One cannot build harbors and dams and airports and roads without borrowing, and these societies did not generate internally the volume of savings for the builders to borrow. In most of them, for reasons ranging from plausible to thievish, the state would also build and own the country's heavy industry. All this would have to be borrowed for. Nations are entitled to a national debt—the United States has quite a large one—and there is no reason why such a debt cannot be owed to foreigners, as much of the U.S. debt is. If private foreigners are prepared to hold a nation's debt, that is their concern. In this century, national debts usually do not get repaid. (They represent mostly the cost of wars, which it is considered proper to push off to future generations.) If the investment of the borrowed money generates enough cash flow to pay interest on the debt and keep the infrastructure in good repair, holders of a nation's debt who wish to change the assets in their portfolios will have little difficulty in finding third parties willing to purchase the income stream.

Petrodollar recycling had nothing to do with that. The borrowers were spending the proceeds of their loans not for investments that would later produce an income stream to service their debt, but on gasoline that burned up and was gone forever. And once nations got in the habit of borrowing to increase or sustain this aspect of current consumption, there was no reason why they could not budget the use of borrowed funds for other nonproductive purposes, from housing the poor to modernizing the military. Such projects would not throw off an income stream to service the national debt held by foreigners. As those payments came due, the borrowers would have to squeeze domestic consumption (especially of imports)—or borrow more, in what soon would become an exponentially accelerating spiral.

Of course, nothing is that simple. For most developing nations, borrowing to buy oil—even borrowing to maintain social services—could be defended as the only way to preserve the plans to build an infrastructure and secure a base of heavy industry. (The only other choice, if one was to keep the plan, was socialism-in-one-country a la Stalin, and even the Russian satellites were not willing to do that.) The argument could be made that servicing the debt later would require only a slightly greater diversion to debt service of the revenues from what would be a rapidly growing production. What Barbara Ward had called the revolution of rising expectations could not be turned off simply because oil prices had risen.

Indeed, the reaction in the Third World to the rise in oil prices was, idiotically, a whoop of delight. The political leaders of those countries felt that the success of one raw materials cartel presaged the creation of others. They saw a future in which real resources would be transferred in ever-increasing quantities from the industrial nations to the less developed, partly through political maneuverings in the United Nations, mostly through the newfound economic muscle of the poor. Under such circumstances, a small rise in the debt now—to tide them over to their brave new world—was not something about which anyone had to worry unduly. Especially in a period when the interest rates in the market were below the rate of inflation in the industrial countries, which meant that the real burden of even a mounting debt would be steadily reduced.

The banks were only too willing to buy these arguments: they needed a place to put the oil producers' money. Particularly in the mid-1970s, when the United States in recession ran a balance-of-payments surplus and domestic demand for investment funds fell through the floor, the call for capital in the mature economies fell far below the money the banks had to offer. Banks, like countries and giant corporations, worked on a master plan that called for so much growth a year. Lending officers were given quotas to fill. Quite literally, they went out in the world to sell money. In his book *The Money Lenders,* Anthony Sampson has brilliantly described the scene at the annual meetings of the World Bank and International Monetary Fund, when bankers worked the corridors and the cocktail parties to persuade finance ministers and central bankers from countries they would have been hard put to find on a map that they were "underborrowed," that they could improve the lives of their citizenry and thus their political standing by taking and spending some of the banks' money.

If the banks had not multiplied their loans to the developing countries, those countries, the international financing organizations, and the governments of the industrial nations would all have had to confront true dilemmas. *Some* increase in the national debt of the poor countries was inescapable: there was a limit to how much they could reduce what were already minimal imports of energy and high-priced raw materials. The international agencies did not have the resources to take them very far, and by the terms of its charter, the IMF could make only short-term loans, to help the recipients achieve the very "adjustment" to life at a lower standard of living that the poor countries had to avoid—especially those that were industrializing most rapidly and had made the largest promises to their people. The governments of the industrial countries, com-

241

ing slowly to the realization that they would not be able to keep the promises of growth and social services *they* had made to their people, were not prepared politically to increase their budgets for foreign aid and foreign loans on anything like the scale required. The oil exporters were no more prepared politically than the industrial nations to undertake the burdens of lending or granting to the oil importers they were impoverishing. And even if they had felt a deep need to be generous (which they didn't), they lacked the institutional structure to express their generosity.

Only the banks could have carried the world economy over the hump of the first oil shock, and they have been no more than truthful—if a little whiny—in their complaints that their governments urged them down this primrose path of high-risk lending. They structured their loans to make everything appear quite safe, with relatively short terms and interest rates that floated just above the rates they had to pay their depositors. Because there was so much competition for this business, the spreads narrowed dramatically with the passage of time, down to less than 0.5% of the money borrowed, increasing the willingness of the borrowers to borrow without much reducing the willingness of the banks to lend. (They still had all that money coming in, the spread on any loan was better than what could be made laying the money off in the interbank market, and the lending officers had those planned quotas.) But the profits remained considerable, especially for those giant banks with their skilled treasurers who had client contacts in the Persian Gulf, who could buy money at the lower end of the range of the London Interbank Offered Rate, and who could play the maturity schedule of their own borrowings to take advantage of rate changes they were better able to predict than others. And then there were the origination fees, which many banks, in violation of all respectable accounting practice (but with the connivance of their accountants) took down to profits as they were paid.

As the loans grew more risky, the big banks pulled the

regional banks into the game. In February 1982, for example, Bankers Trust of South Carolina was encouraged to take a $5 million piece of a six-month "syndicated credit" to the Banco Nacional de Mexico, which eventually had to be rescheduled for eight years. Richard Fearrington, in charge of the bank's new foreign lending division, remembered that he checked with several New York banks about the loan, and that these giants, already trying to hold down their Mexican exposure, were the "most avid recommenders." Smaller banks by the hundreds—Treasury Secretary Donald Regan estimated 1,500 of them—were pulled into international lending, most of them quite late in the game, by big-city correspondents who assured them everything was safe as houses. These syndicated loans were presented to the boards of these banks as easy profits: as former Comptroller John Heimann told S. Karene Witcher of *The Wall Street Journal*, "Somebody else was presumably doing the work."

This system required a formidable constituency: the banks themselves, the governments of the industrial countries (given a way to ignore the demands from the poor countries for direct official aid), the governments of the borrowing countries (enabled to shove off to the future the cost of the programs for which they could claim the benefits now), and, where they existed, the private enterprises of those countries (given access to world capital markets at rates apparently far below those at home—though only apparently, for if their home currency depreciated with reference to the dollars they were borrowing, they would have to earn much more in their own currency to meet the payments called for by their loan contracts).

Given two conditions, the scheme could work. The output of the borrowing countries (and probably their exports, though this is arguable) would have to rise at a rate faster than the continually rising interest payments on their loans. And the industrial nations (especially the United States) would have to be willing to endure the social strains of a constantly increasing rate of inflation, based on negative real interest rates that would encourage domestic as well as foreign borrowing, so that the real cost of servicing loans would diminish over time with the decreasing purchasing power of the money. Presumably, the oil producers, the ultimate creditors of the system, whose money in the banks would lose value in this process, either would not know what was happening to them or could be forced to stand and take it. This was an interesting speculation, but it was not banking.

When the second oil-price jump came in 1979—ostensibly the result of the chaos in Iran, actually a response to the 1977–79 inflation in the United States—the game was clearly near an end. But the great banks, now vitally dependent on their international business, rallied round with a call that they had done it before and they could do it again. The Cassandras of the 1976–78 had been proved wrong. Not so. The last time around, the borrowers had been relatively unencumbered with prior debt and debt-service obligations; this time around they were already stretched to make their payments. The last time around, the economies of the borrowing countries had been less tightly articulated, their cities less cancerous, their failures at self-government less damaging. In the early 1970s the rich and/or powerful of the Third World had not been so capable of transferring their country's wealth, plus any aid or loans that arrived, to the extensions of their own pockets they had created in Switzerland, France, and the United States. The last time around, the chairman of the Federal Reserve Board had been Arthur Burns, who was definitely against inflation but could see why a politician (especially a Republican politician) might sometimes need lower rates than an anti-inflation policy might dictate; this time around, it was Paul Volcker.

The banks were indiscriminate. Brazil was borrowing to build a capital base for a stronger domestic product in the future. Mexico was borrowing to spend now, for the benefit of its growing middle class, the oil riches promised for tomorrow. Argentina was borrowing to buy toys for its military government and to enable its upper classes to maintain and increase their holdings of foreign assets. ("If you were an Argentinian," said a U. S. banker who had worked there, "you, too, would want to keep your savings, your family's security, abroad, as a matter of prudence.") All three were permitted to incur obligations totaling more than $2,000 per head for every resident over the age of fifteen.

Poland had a "centrally planned" economy. Bankers lending to Poland inquired, pro forma, about the country's economic situation and what their money would be used for. Poland said its planning agency didn't have most of that information. The banks lent anyway. Yugoslavia was experimenting with competition among worker-owned enterprises. Bankers lent to them individually, and to a gaggle of independently operated Yugoslav regional banks, and were then amazed to find how high the totals had gone.

Sudan was encouraged by its bankers to plow ahead with gigantic cotton and sugar projects that could never be competitive in the world market. The unspeakable Mobuto of Zaire—the world's richest man, because any hard currency that arrives in his country soon departs for his accounts in Switzerland—received loans from both American and European banks and thumbed his nose at the International Monetary Fund without suffering any serious consequences. (Eventually, though—in 1983—the IMF caught up with Mobuto and forced Zaire to cut the government budget.)

Nobody seems to have done economic analysis: the east bloc countries were somehow covered by a "Russian umbrella"; Citibank's exposure in Mexico was safe, the vice-president in charge of it said at a public forum, because with 7,000 borrowers, the portfolio was diversified soundly. (Citibank did not realize until August 1982 that all these borrowers had only one source of dollars, the Mexican central bank). Loans to governments were risk-free because "countries don't go bankrupt." The Asian economies flourished under the steady sprinkle of money; the African economies percolated with corruption and collapsed; the Latin economies grew erratically in ways that required ever-increasing imports and implied ever-growing deficits.

By mid-1981, with real interest rates at terrifying levels and both Europe and America in recession, the dollar strengthening steadily, and commodity prices falling steadily, the game was clearly over—but the banks kept hoping that something, somehow, would turn up. Though world trade stagnated, international lending actually accelerated. The American banks seem not to have read the warning signals at all. In December 1981 the Group of 30, a very influential think tank funded by the Rockefeller brothers and led by Johannes Witteveen, the former head of the IMF, conducted a poll of 200 banks active in international lending. Of the 29 large North American banks responding to the questionnaire, only 7 thought there would be a "substantial" increase in lending risks over the succeeding five years (and 6 thought there would be a decrease in risk or no change). By contrast, 26 of 55 European banks saw substantial increases in risk, and only 4 thought risks would be steady or declining. The group as a whole thought banks were almost as likely to get into trouble through losses in foreign-exchange trading or maturity mismatching (i.e., funding the bank with short-term money and lending long in a period when short-term rates rose above long-term rates) as through loan defaults or large restructurings.

Yet by then the pattern of borrowers' behavior, especially in Latin America, had begun to send the clearest of messages. Desperate for money, the Latin countries were taking ever-increasing loans in the form of "trade credits" beyond the volume of their trade, interbank lines, and overnight borrowings in the London market and in Fed Funds. This activity drew into the net any number of lesser banks that had never been involved in foreign lending to any great extent, but went for the lure of very short—apparently very safe—loans at better than market rates.

The big banks were the great villains. "Why did you keep selling them Fed Funds?" asked the inquiring reporter of the treasurer of one of the ten largest banks, referring to his dealings with Mexico and Brazil. "Well," he said, "they were paying an extra eighth." A corporate officer of another bank said he almost had to physically restrain his treasury people from selling funds to the Latins because the spread on such transactions qualified the department for the bank's incentive bonus program.

The Fed was inattentive. Necessarily, the New York Fed as the operating arm of the Open Market Committee monitors who is taking what in the Fed Funds market. The increased short-term takings of the Mexican and Brazilian branches and agencies were "noticed—but nobody thought through what they meant."

When the boat sank in summer 1982—when first Mexico, then Argentina, then Brazil had to confess themselves unable to continue paying interest on their debt (let alone repaying capital), the lesser banks went overboard and began scrambling for the shore. For several sickening weeks, the major New York banks and the Federal Reserve kept finding new examples of previously unknown indebtedness by what came to be called the "MBA" countries (Mexico, Brazil, Argentina). A situation that would have been painful but manageable a year before had become a full-fledged "crisis."

The U. S. government scrambled to keep the Western Hemisphere borrowers from going into flat default. Money was lent from the obscure Exchange Stabilization Fund, created in 1933 to hold the government's profits from Franklin Roosevelt's 60% increase in the price of gold. A hurry-up "bridging" loan to cover the time until the ponderous International Monetary Fund could wheel up its artillery was arranged from the Bank for International Settlements in Basel, the central bank of central banks (juridically, incidentally, still a private institution, with shares traded on the Paris Bourse, a source of constant fury to the knavish bureaucrats of the United Nations). The Treasury and the Federal Reserve financed 50% of the BIS loan by means of "swaps" (God knows what was swapped).

The U. S. Department of Energy made an advance purchase of a billion dollars' worth of Mexican oil for the national reserves. Representations were made in Tokyo to get the Japanese bankers, who had fled Latin America with practiced haste as the tidal wave rolled in, to put their money back into Mexico and Brazil. Similar representations in Europe were less successful. The Swiss just laughed. Some months later, the Swiss would refuse to participate in balance-of-payments lending to socialist France; there's a lot wrong with Swiss banks, but they are run by real bankers.

Early on, Mexico nationalized its banks, which made their grossly exaggerated short-term borrowings a direct obligation of the Mexican government. The day before it declared a moratorium on repayments, Mexico also paid off all its commercial-paper borrowings: the numbers were relatively small (less than $100 million in a total indebtedness of more than $80 billion), and the investment bankers who would have been hurt were very influential. Brazil, conscious that its economy was less beat-up than Mexico's, tried to brave the waves, but was forced quickly to seek help from the official international agencies. Argentina simply didn't pay its bills, an old Argentine habit. It was conscious of the fact that the banks could continue to accrue interest on the loans in their books for ninety days before their failure to collect triggered an accountant's demand that they stop treating these nonexistent payments as part of their profits. Among the little bits of assistance the U. S. bank regulators gave the big banks in 1983 was a suggestion for a law that would permit banks to credit themselves with continuing profits for six months before they had to acknowledge that a foreign loan in arrears had gone sour.

The man placed in charge of keeping the international banking system afloat was the managing director of the International Monetary Fund, Jacques de Larosiere—slight, bespectacled in rimless glasses, a littly fussy, firm, enigmatic, honest, a distinguished graduate from the elite corps of the French Inspecteurs des Finances. De Larosiere came to the meetings of the creditor banks (there were literally hundreds of creditor banks), and told them that if the IMF was to devote resources to helping these debtors pay their bills, the banks would have to put up still more money.

Except, I think, for Morgan, which was (I think) privy to this planning from the beginning, the banks were appalled at this demand that they throw good money after bad. They were moved, but not to action, by the argument that there was so much bad money involved now that they could not afford to back off—and the governments and international agencies could not find enough by themselves to make the private lenders whole. IMF would impose an austere economic regime on the borrowers to increase the chance that they could recover their creditworthiness over time. And the U.S. government was prepared (reluctantly, but "what else could we do?") to offer its banks a bribe. The examiners would not question these loans, no reserves would have to be taken against them, alleged profits could continue to accrue, and, despite the extraordinarily negative implications of such conduct both politically and economically, the banks would be permitted to increase their interest charges on renegotiated loans and to pocket gigantic "rescheduling fees." It was Alice in Wonderland; the extra interest charges and the fees were simply piled on the borrowers' indebtedness, but if the government okayed it, the private auditors would not ask questions.

What was needed in international borrowing was what the banks did for domestic borrowers in trouble: some arrangement to reduce the burden of debt. This is not something the banks do well. A survey of 99 big banks by Charles Williams of the Harvard Business School presented to the 1983 International Monetary Conference in Brussels showed 87 of them with the belief that (in the words of the *Wall Street Journal*'s Peter Truell) "bank analyses of troubled loans are often superficial and remedial action often unimaginative . . . banks are often willing to 'hope for the best' and ignore hard realities." Still, if it's Chrysler, International Harvester, or

Massey-Ferguson, the banks arrange to take some of their loan repayments in the form of equity shares in future profits, to reduce interest rates, even to take partial write-offs that penalize reported profits. In the case of sovereign borrowers, the banks insisted that the borrowing governments could, in time, squeeze the money for them out of the workers and peasants (maybe even, with real strong governments, out of the local rich and politically powerful). Anyway, if everyone was very lucky, the problem could be put off until the next generation of executives took over the bank. Meanwhile, the present generation would be able to show magnificent apparent profits from its stewardship.

This will not work: there are real losses here, to be borne by the lenders as well as by the borrowers. The measures taken so far to "resolve" the crisis will do harm. Even if an improvement in the world economy makes these loans look sustainable in 1984–85 (which is possible, but unlikely), the result will merely be a worse, potentially unmanageable threat to the banks and the banking system the next time the business cycle turns down. By restating and reducing their profits for the period 1980–83 and accepting reduced income from their loans to severely troubled borrowers for another few years, the banks might restore the viability of their environment—and, incidentally, make a major contribution to the revival of world trade and employment, for the money the borrowers save in interest will be available to pay for imports.

The German banks have taken the first steps, doubtless under the urgings of the Bundesbank. In reporting their results for 1981 through 1983, the German banks showed excellent profits—and paid no dividends because they were building reserves against the losses that would have to be charged eventually against these profits. By the fourth quarter of 1983, Deutsche Bank in Luxembourg had accumulated reserves against losses that worked out to 6% of the bank, 40% of the loans to Third World and East European borrowers. In the United States, by contrast, Congress had to force the regulators to require reserves against the most hopeless sovereign loans, and the banks moaned piteously about it.

Morgan has made a start. In the first half of 1983, Morgan Guaranty doubled its provision for loan losses, bringing the total to double the amount the IRS accepts as a tax deduction, in an effort to contain the damage to the bank. But Morgan stands virtually alone. Some of the smaller banks have specially reserved against their foreign loans—North Carolina's Wachovia, for example, reports a "special reserve" of $22 million to reduce by about 16% the reported value of its relatively small portfolio of Latin American loans (noting in passing in its third-quarter 1983 statement that it had placed $9 million of Brazilian loans on a cash basis—posting income from them only as the money was received, not simply "accruing" unpaid interest—even though "under regulatory guidelines" it could have considered all its Brazilian assets "current"). In the third quarter of 1983, by contrast, as the unwillingness of Argentina to pay its debts becomes obvious to all, Chase Manhattan actually *reduced* the proportion of its Argentinian assets that it classified as "nonperforming" to avoid admitting a major reduction in its profits.

Among the more astonishing spectacles of late 1983 was the way the banks shared the pleasure the rest of us felt at the election of a social-democratic majority government in Argentina. From their point of view, the change in government was dangerous. President Alfonsin could survive in the snake pit of Argentinian politics only by driving a much harder bargain with the banks than anything the military junta had arranged—and it would be all but impossible for the banks to resist the pressures from their home governments to help this attractive man and his admirable policies. Alfonsin is right and the banks are wrong, and the deal that will be struck with Argentina (inherently the strongest of the over-burdened borrowers) could provide an opening through which the international financial system might escape the consequences of a decade's folly. But that's not the way the banks see it.

Certainly there must be major changes in the management of the debt crisis. This tourist testified before Senators Heinz and Proxmire and a subcommittee of the Senate in favor of the planned $8.4 billion U.S. contribution to the increase in IMF resources that permitted the original fairy tale to be written. I now regret it. As late as early 1983, the losses from imprudent foreign lending could have been written off over a period of years out of bank profits. Without IMF and U.S. governmental intervention, the banks would have been compelled to strike a deal with the Third World debtors, reducing their interest rates well below the banks' own cost of funds, and giving the hard-pressed governments of the borrowing nations the politically effective proof that the lenders were sharing—rather than profiting from—their people's agony.

As 1984 began, there were signs that the banks were beginning to realize that in the end neither their governments nor the IMF could protect them from loss. The regional banks in the United States and many of the European internationals were indicating a willingness to reduce considerably the interest burden on the debtors and to write down their current profits, to maintain some fraction of these loans as plausible assets. Most of the largest American banks still seemed to believe that somehow Big Daddy would provide, that some mixture of creative accounting and regulatory flimflam would enable them to continue pretending that everything would come out all right. Given the great reluctance of the American regulators to lean on the giant banks, it may well be that the theatricalities of 1982–83 would continue to play out on the world stage. If so, we are all of us—not just the banks—in for some hairy times. For the situation structured in the 1982 emergency, and solidified in 1983, simply assured that at some future time, that when the loans collapsed, the banks would suffer an impairment of capital, and the borrowers would be saddled with governments even more distasteful than those they had in 1983. Then the only hope remaining is that when the time of truth arrives the private banking system will no longer be so vital a prop to the real economy of the world.

9

LIVING LONG TERM IN A SHORT-TERM WORLD

Among the pieces of cheap wisdom floating around the newspapers and the business schools in recent years has been the line that banks get in trouble by borrowing short and lending long, and there is just enough truth in it to keep the professors and the columnists employed. "A man highly dependent on short-term funds is living on top of a volcano," says George Mitchell. And it *is* a sign of a bank in trouble that its loan officers are reaching out for longer maturities because it argues that credit risk is being, if not ignored, at least played down as a major factor in loan decisions.

The short run is always more predictable than the long run.

Thus, in principle, the "yield curve"—the graph that plots interest rates against length of loan—should slope upward. Other things being equal, the longer the loan, the higher the interest rate. Banks that keep large portfolios of liquid assets—interbank loans, broker's loans, short-dated Treasury bills—are regarded as run conservatively; banks that lengthen the average maturity of their portfolios are perceived as taking extra risks in hopes of extra earnings, which often means there are problems they are trying to cover up. And if there aren't problems now, the world expects that there will be before the next business cycle hits bottom.

But "maturity transformation" is what financial intermediaries—especially banks—do. Historically, bank liabilities were demand deposits, the shortest possible obligations. The cost of such funds was the noninterest cost of providing transaction services. From these days, there survives the populist myth that banks like high interest rates. But today the world is much more complicated because banks have become borrowers. When interest rates rise, costs are imposed on banks as well as on their debtors.

In a sense, of course, any deposit in a bank is a borrowing by that bank from the depositor. And banks have always done some explicit borrowing, too—from each other, usually but not exclusively to settle accounts at the clearinghouse (later, in what is really the same phenomenon, to maintain required balances at the Fed), from the public through issues of subordinated bonds, and from their corporate customers through arrangements later formalized as Certificates of Deposit. Banks have always done most such borrowing on very short terms—by the week, in the days when messengers ran securities and cash around Wall Street; by the day, since the telecommunications network made fast transfers inexpensive. Their preference for the short term derived partly from their distaste for uncertainty and partly from the expectation of profits from the maturity transformation. It was reaching out for such profits that was the sin of borrowing short and lending long.

In theory, inflation should make no difference in the shape of the yield curve; in fact, it does. Short-term interest rates adjust rapidly to the rate at which money is losing value. Borrowers are eager to take funds they can expect to repay in money that is worth less; lenders are reluctant to take what Keynes called "titles to money" unless they see an interest rate high enough to compensate them for what they lose through the deterioration of the currency. Looking at the longer term, however, both borrowers and lenders tend to resolve their uncertainties about the future course of prices on the side of stability—i.e., on the assumption that the present inflationary burst will wear out and price movements will return to whatever the rate was in recent years. So short-term interest rates rise much more rapidly than long-term rates and the slope of the yield curve becomes "negative"—the longer the term of the loan, the lower the rate. Conversely, as 1982–83 demonstrated so vividly, a deceleration of inflation after a long siege of it will bring down short-term rates fairly quickly, while the expectation of inertia, the belief that the inflation rate of the past few years will return, keeps long-term rates high, creating a yield curve that slopes upward sharply.

The later 1950s were a time of slow, persistent inflation. (One of John Kennedy's campaign arguments against the Eisenhower administration was that it had permitted a horrendous 3% inflation rate that was making American exports uncompetitive abroad and distorting investment decisions.) The inflation slowly pushed up the costs of operating the bank, reduced the value of the longer-term loans and the Treasury notes in the investment portfolio, and cut the profits of the bond-trading department by creating a negative yield curve. Worst of all, it began to erode the footings of the banks. With cash losing value, people and corporations shifted out of demand deposits in the bank to interest-bearing short-term investments ("cash management"), and holders of bank time deposits looked for assets that would yield them more than the government allowed the banks to pay.

Thrift institutions, free to pay any interest rate they wished, subject only to the generalized rules of their regulators (which, in effect, said they were not to lose money on their operations), could easily outbid the banks for consumer savings, which historically had never interested the banks much, anyway (they typically offered time accounts—until World War II the law had forbidden describing such deposits as savings accounts—on a contemptuous "safekeeping" basis, with interest rates below Federal Reserve limits, and well below the market).

Coming into 1960, then, the banks were pretty much dead in the water, controlled in their capacity to expand their lending by stagnation in the demand-deposit base and hobbled in their borrowing powers by government interest-rate ceilings. Then First National City Bank of New York (the future Citibank) found a way out of the funding dilemma—in effect, by avoiding the prohibition against the payment of interest on demand deposits. Citibank offered corporate customers a new negotiable Certificate of Deposit, which the purchaser could sell on the market when it wanted funds—and guaranteed that the paper would indeed be salable by arranging for Discount Corporation of America to make a market in bank CDs. These CDs were introduced at a time when the market rate on ninety-day paper was, in fact, below the ceilings the Federal Reserve had set on three-month time deposits. The bank could offer an attractive short-term investment: bank-guaranteed repayment at the commercial-paper rate, with assurance that the money would be available—a little less than the face value of the certificate if rates rose, a little more if they fell—whenever the purchaser of the CD needed cash. Then, in the mid-1960's, rates rose above the Fed ceilings on ninety-day paper, and the CD market closed down.

In fact, the money crunch of 1966 reflected an interest-rate risk assumed rather carelessly by Citibank and its imitators when they expanded the share of their footings formed by borrowed money. In appearance, however, the 1966 crisis reflected funding risks, and the banks energetically sought out new sources of funds. By then, many of them had reorganized as holding companies to carry on certain nonbanking activities in separate corporations, and the holding companies were able to sell commercial paper (which a bank cannot legally do), flowing the receipts through to the bank. There had grown up in Europe a separate "Eurodollar" market, essentially unregulated by anyone, where U.S. banks, like foreign banks or commercial borrowers, could put their hands on U.S. money. The banks staggered through 1966, met their commitments to borrowers, and mostly blamed the Fed for their troubles.

But the 1966 crunch taught the banks that their established modus operandi was no longer viable. They were no longer practicing asset management—shifting a portfolio of given size between investment paper and loans in response to loan demand. Instead, whether they knew it and liked it or not, they were living in an age of liability management, when the arts of profitability would include control of the size of the bank and the costs of its funds. In 1969–70 the problems of 1966 recurred, again as a crunch and an apparent funding risk—but now the extent of the banks' reliance on borrowed funds was so great, and the dangers of financial collapse so frightening, that the government was forced to back away from interest-rate controls. The proximate cause of this retreat was the Penn Central fiasco, which imposed losses of $82 million overnight on the holders of the railroad's unsecured commercial paper and dried up the commercial-paper market as a source of funds for all but the sturdiest industrial corporations. Chrysler was on the brink, heavily dependent on commercial-paper financing.To persuade the banks to replace Chrysler's unrenewable commercial-paper borrowings with bank loans, the Fed lifted all interest-rate limits on large-denomination (over $100,000) bank CDs. The fig leaf of the money crunch had been removed from the reality of interest-rate risk. From now on, when interest rates rose and the yield slope turned negative, the impact would be felt as a reduction in the earnings of the banks.

THE BANKING BUSINESS

To understand what has happened in banking in the last fifteen years, it is necessary to look at this sea change as it appeared from inside the bank. What was affected by the reversal of the normal yield slope was the gross margin of the bank, the difference between the total cost of its money and the total revenues from its assets, both interest payments and fees. Gross margin had to pay all the costs, from the chairman's salary to the janitor's soap powder. Most of the bank's costs were entirely independent of the gross margin earned, and if that margin shrank, profits automatically fell. The populist beliefs about banking were not entirely stood on their head—high interest rates per se remain rather attractive to banks because the same percentage of gross margin applied to a bigger base will yield a higher profit. But rising rates, which increase the cost of funds faster than they move the receipts from loans, become disastrous. Falling rates, on the other hand, become the bankers' delight: by reducing the cost of funds before they reduce the yield on loans, they widen the gross margins and rapidly boost profits.

The banks reacted to the emerging difficulty with their gross margins by establishing, at the center of the management system, a "sources and uses of funds committee" that gave instruction to both lending officers and funding officers. In the nature of the beast, the committee was dominated originally by people from the lending side, and the first reform to emerge was a drive to eliminate fixed-rate lending: if we have to pay more for the money, dammit, those bastards will have to pay more for their loans. The device chosen was the strengthening of the old and not very meaningful "prime rate," a posted price supposedly the rate charged for short-term (ninety-day) money to the most solid of borrowers. Writing loans that would not be repaid for more than six months, the banks began to set interest rates by reference to this prime rate ("prime plus one," or two, or whatever), with periodic readjustment, usually every six months, to keep the rate in a stable relationship to prime.

258

For various reasons, this system turned out to be a mistake. In an era when interest rates might move by a full percentage point in a single week, the semiannual readjustment on the time loan was too infrequent to solve the gross-margin problem—but the rate changes came too often for many industrial borrowers who had to know their money costs to make their plans. Worse, it gave the banks a chance to get greedy, moving the prime up rapidly as money-market conditions raised the rate they had to pay for the marginal dollar of their own borrowings (though the average, "blended" cost of their funds remained below that of the marginal dollar for some time), and then refusing to lower the prime as money-market rates came down, on the argument that the decline would have to be sustained for a considerable period before the reduction in their blended cost of funds justified a lower rate for borrowers. Administered prices like prime rates bring out the worst in all businessmen, including bankers. Within a few years, this greed boomeranged, and the most solid borrowers shifted an ever-increasing proportion of their borrowings to the commercial-paper market, where at least they wouldn't get cheated. "We've been idiots to let our natural market get blown away from us," said Alan Fishman, chief financial officer and strategic planner for Chemical Bank. Of course, it was easy for Fishman to say: he worked on the funding side of the bank.

With the passage of time, power on the sources-and-uses committee moved from the lending officers to the newly created "Treasury" department, where toiled the traders who borrowed funds for the bank to lend. The key year was 1974, when the ever-growing surpluses of the oil exporters inundated the Eurodollar banks with funds, and the extension of FedWire to third-party payments cut the costs of money trading to a fraction of what they had been.

All the money markets grew like weeds: Fed Funds, London interbank, commercial paper, Treasury bills, foreign exchange. With the arrival of floating currency-exchange rates in

1973 and the virtual elimination of exchange controls by the major trading powers, it even became possible to fund the bank by borrowings in foreign currencies, a very heady thought.

Increasingly, bank managements began to look on their Treasuries as profit centers in their own right. By 1974 the man who ran the Paris office of the Bank of America was furious about the policy that allocated two-thirds of the profits on a loan to the office that found the funds (normally London or New York, if not San Francisco) and only one-third to the office that found the loan. "If they know what they're doing in London," he said, "they should be able to make money on the funding without any credit from the loan." One could almost say that the young traders coming into the funding side of the banks in the 1970s saw the lending side as an excuse to make money by playing the funds markets.

Given the way their day went, such attitudes were natural. Told to borrow a billion dollars for the bank today, a man does not simply set out to find money. (Man is generic in this context: because funds trading does not involve customer contact and thus does not arouse atavistic fears of what the customer will think, this is an area of opportunity for women.) Calling another bank or a funds broker, he does not ask his interlocutor what the lending rate may be, but what rate is being quoted both for borrowing and for lending. If the trader on the other side of the phone call is quoting an especially attractive rate for his own borrowing, the man making the call may sell him funds overnight, even though that will increase his own borrowing needs later in the day. He expects that he will be able to borrow for less before he closes his book. If he senses that rates are higher in the morning than they will be at 1:00—and he is right—he may be able to lend $2 billion and borrow $3 billion over the course of the day for a considerably lower cost than he would have incurred if he simply borrowed $1 billion. A man gets bonuses for that.

A step above the trader, the economic analyst is judging whether the bank should "take a view" of where interest rates are heading in the coming days, weeks, or months. If rates are rising, the bank should seek to fund itself with longer borrowings—with thirty-day, three-month, six-month, even one-year Fed Funds or Eurodollars or holding-company commercial paper. If rates are declining, then the bank will be best off with a shorter maturity schedule on its borrowings. If interest rates are lower in Germany than in the United States and the bank expects marks to remain stable or decline in dollar value, the smart thing to do may be to borrow, say, DM 100 million and convert it to, say, $40 million, expecting to buy back the marks in six months and capturing the difference between the German and American rates into the bank's gross margin. It should be noted that there is no way to make this deal both profitable and safe. There is a large forward market in marks, and the trader can, in fact, purchase his DM 100 million for delivery in six months at the same time that he sells his DM 100 million today for dollars. But the market has already adjusted for the differences in interest rates, and forward D–marks are quoted as stronger than current D–marks by about the difference in the interest rates.

The fact is that you can't make this game safe for the players, almost ever. Funding a bank with market funds mismatched in maturity with the loan portfolio they serve is inherently risky. It's banking, all right, but it's not banking as our bankers have known it. Funding by borrowing on maturities different from those of the loan portfolio will come out right over the long run only if the bank's charges to borrowers include some premium to cover interest-rate risk. Because American bankers had been insulated from interest-rate risk by government regulators for a generation, they tended not to understand these risks and not to plan for them.

No small part of the appeal of the Euromarket to American bankers was that it looked so safe. The jumbo loans to foreign governments were written at some fraction of a point over the banks' cost of funds with rates to be adjusted every six months to maintain that differential. The basic borrowing by a bank in the London interbank market was a six-month borrowing. So there was no interest-rate risk in the big Eurodollar loan: the marginal cost of funds was always less than the marginal receipt from the loan. Any expenses the bank incurred in making the loan were more than made up by the up-front fee in arranging it, and thereafter the ⅝ of 1% (or whatever) difference between what the borrower paid and the London Interbank Offered Rate was not just gross margin, but pure profit. After all, there was no credit risk: as Walter Wriston himself said (often), "Countries don't go bankrupt."

Some banks participated in the Eurodollar markets for prudential reasons associated with their funding needs. Wachovia Bank in Winston-Salem, North Carolina, for example, roughly the fortieth largest bank in the country, has never had a London office, but its chairman John Medlin reports that he takes about $300 million out of the London interbank market every day, through his branch in the Bahamas: "It's a wash for us. We lay it off for about what we pay for it. But if the day comes when we need that $300 million, nobody asks, 'Why's Wachovia in the market?'" Of its $8.5 billion in footings in 1979, First City of Houston had about $900 million in its London branch—"about double our loans there," said chairman Nat Rogers, "to assure liquidity." Ben Love's Texas Commerce Bancshares had $1 billion of liabilities in London—"we put $600 million back in the market, lend $250 million in Eurodollars, use the rest domestically." The treasurer of one of the largest New York banks was asked about this way of handling the funding problem and shook his head sadly. "When you're in trouble, the whole world knows it," he said. But it's better than starting from scratch.

Outside the Eurodollar loans, the banks can't opt out of interest-rate risks. "We got on the wrong side of the rates in 1974," said Tom Storrs, the scholarly but deeply aggressive economist who runs North Carolina National Bank in Charlotte, the nation's twenty-fifth largest bank. "When it was over, I called in some of my young people and asked them what lessons they thought we should learn from the experience. I called them back a few months later to ask how their study was going, and they gave me their findings: we should restrict our intermediate credits to triple-A risks, our short credits to A-1 risks, and we should hold down our interest-sensitive funding. I asked them what their profit objective was, and they told me they hadn't got around to that yet." The professors advise the banks to hedge their interest-rate risks in the financial-futures markets, but you can't expect to do that for much less than 0.5% of the money you're protecting over a year's hedging, and the damned bank makes only about 0.7% on its assets.

2

Above all others, one industry had to live under the shadows of interest-rate risk, and was almost crushed by it: the thrifts, mutual savings banks and savings-and-loan associations. Their assets were concentrated in the longest-term investments: residential mortgages, structured by federal insurance programs as twenty-five-year and thirty-year paper. Their funding was supposed to be long-term, too, for Americans did not spend their savings except for very special purposes: down payments on a house or a car, weddings, college education, retirement, funerals. As Henry Wallich noted, Americans went into debt because they didn't want to "touch their savings." People who could pay full price in the showroom for a car preferred to take a loan because then they knew they would meet the monthly payments and "preserve their savings," which might yield them only half what they had to pay for the loan.

But the thrifts had always run funding risks. Mortgages were the most illiquid investments. If the economy turned down and people lost their jobs and had to "tap their savings," it was hard for the S&L, which might have nine-tenths of its portfolio in mortgages, to find the funds to pay them. In the early 1930s, especially, the S&Ls found themselves unable to roll over what were then their typical "balloon-payment" mortgages (i.e., they came due with one very large payment to be made at the end of five years; the name of the inventor of this crazy system of home finance is lost in the mists of time). Because the S&Ls needed the cash, people found their homes foreclosed from under them. They could make the monthly interest payments (though this was hard enough in the great deflation of 1930–33, when an increase in the value of money made all fixed-debt burdens much heavier), but the institutional structure of the thrift industry was such that the local mortgage lender could not afford to continue the loan. And, of course, foreclosing did the S&L no good. The repossessed house was unsalable, anyway—nobody could get the financing to buy it.

More than a third of the nation's S&Ls went under in the Great Depression. States passed mortgage moratorium acts to preserve people's homes. (The Supreme Court upheld them, though they were unquestionably unconstitutional on any reading of the Bill of Rights. In emergencies, even the Court has to consider the practical effects of its decisions.) The Home Owners Loan Act predated the New Deal and authorized a federal mortgage corporation that would buy mortgages from the thrifts to keep them in funds and their borrowers with roofs over their heads. In 1934 a system of federal support for housing finance was institutionalized, with the Federal Housing Administration to insure self-amortizing mortgages, the Federal Home Loan Bank Board to charter mutual savings-and-loan associations and supervise the dozen regional Home Loan Banks that would service and support them, the Federal Savings and Loan Insurance Corporation to insure "shares" (later deposits) in these S&Ls, and a federally chartered private corporation to establish a secondary market in FHA-insured mortgages, tapping the bond market as a source of housing finance. This last did not happen—eventually the government had to establish its own Federal National Mortgage Association, which held mortgages rather than trading them and was made a private corporation only in 1969, after the courts ruled that its borrowings were part of the federal deficit and could not be hidden away among off-budget items. Everything else worked like a watch.

This complex of federal housing and housing-finance institutions was the most successful and efficient venture of the New Deal. Supplemented by the Veterans Administration no-down-payment mortgages after World War II, it increased the proportion of Americans who own their housing from under 50% to over 66% and created financial intermediaries that by 1960 rivaled the banks in the total of their deposit liabilities and held more than half of all outstanding residential mortgages in the United States.

Interest-rate risk had not been a problem for the S&Ls and the savings banks because mortgages had always carried higher yields than corporate bonds (considerably higher than government bonds). Thrifts could afford to pay more than others for people's savings. Though banks were controlled in the interest they could pay on time deposits, S&Ls and mutual savings banks were not. For a long time they got money without much trouble because people wanted to save and had no other place to put savings. When the first increases in interest rates came in the 1950s, the thrifts easily were able to outbid the commercial banks, which at first weren't very interested, and then were restricted by the government in the rates they could pay.

Rising rates did begin to create problems in the early 1960s because an increase in the passbook savings rate would apply to the entire funding of the thrift, while all the mortgage portfolio—except the very newest loans—continued to carry the old rates. In response, the California S&Ls, which were growing the most rapidly, developed new instruments: fixed-maturity consumer certificates of deposit, which would pay whatever was necessary to draw money on the day they were issued, while leaving undisturbed the passbook rates that held down the blended cost of funds for the institution as a whole. In the words of Norman Strunk, who was for years the operating head of the U.S. League of Savings and Loans, they then learned that "they were dealing with the most avaricious sector of American society, the American consumer." Passbook savers who saw the ads for the new CDs switched their accounts in sufficient numbers to raise the cost of funds to the S&L so high that gross margins threatened to disappear. In 1966 it became necessary for the Federal Home Loan Bank Board to run to the rescue of the most aggressive of the California thrifts. (Oddly, it was State Savings, later resurrected as the S&L success story of the early 1980s, when aggressiveness paid off.) Congress thereupon extended government control over interest rates to the savings associations. To protect housing finance, however, Congress gave the savings associations a "differential," a higher ceiling on what they could pay for savings accounts than was permitted to the commercial banks. In 1966 this differential was as high as a percentage point; it was reduced to half a point in 1970, and to a quarter of a point in 1973.

The regulators were conscious of the fact that keeping the interest rate low on S&L deposits and certificates risked the disintermediation, the loss of deposits that had hit everyone in 1966 and 1969, and they lifted the ceilings as market rates rose. They also proved ingenious at devising instruments that would protect the thrifts against future disintermediation—two-year, three-year, six-year, and even eight-year certificates at slowly rising interest rates, with penalties to be applied in cases of "premature withdrawal." George Mitchell recalled from the vantage point of 1979, "I went around to the S&L people, and I told them to sell those six- and eight-year CDs. Forget about the deposits in the passbook accounts, lock up the money now. But all that most of them could see was that the new certificates cost them more, and they stayed out."

As early as the 1960s, a handful of consumer-oriented banks—most notably New York's Amalgamated Bank, owned by the Amalgamated Clothing Workers Union—had insisted that people did not have to be stuck with the relatively low rates the Fed allowed on bank deposits and certificates. Not many customers of a bank like Amalgamated had the $10,000 minimum required to buy a Treasury bill that paid market rates, but Amalgamated could put together pieces of $500 for its customers and then purchase a Treasury bill for them as a group. Each owner of the group would then be the beneficial owner of a piece of a Treasury obligation even safer than a bank instrument and yielding more than the top rates a thrift institution was allowed to pay.

In the early 1970s, after interest-rate limits were removed from large-denomination bank CDs, some mutual-fund managers and brokerage houses found they could do even better, offering "money-market funds" that would give the consumer access to what the banks paid the rich. Under the Investment Company Act of 1940, these funds were regulated by the Securities and Exchange Commission rather than one of the banking regulators. The SEC approved the open-ended issuance of shares in such funds, provided they limited their investments to bank CDs, commercial paper, bankers' acceptances, and Treasury bills of less than one-year duration; kept the average maturity of their investments below 120 days; passed through all their earnings (less the management fee) to the shareholders; sold by prospectus; and published the full list of their holdings at the end of each quarter. At first these funds priced their shares like any other mutual fund, with the investments valued every day, at the close of the market, share prices rising and falling according to the market value of the investments, with the interest they earned accumulated and paid out periodically. But Howard Stein of Dreyfus wanted something easier for his advertisements to sell and his customers to buy, and he worked out with his custodian, The Bank of New York, a scheme by which the value of the shares would always be $1 (originally $10) each. Changes in the market value of the securities and interest earned on them would be credited to the shareholder's account in the form of additional shares, which the customer could cash in at any time at $1 each. Indeed, Stein arranged with The Bank of New York to have shares in his Dreyfus Liquid Assets Fund redeemed in the most convenient possible way—by check. Above a certain minimum (the industry standard came to be $500), a shareholder in a money-market mutual fund (MMF) could sell his shares back to the fund (in effect) simply by writing a check, which could be—and sometimes was—used for third-party payment purposes. (The most common check, however, was the one drawn to the shareholder himself, for deposit in his checking account at a bank.)*

The money-market funds were formidable competition for savings accounts. Because they gave their share purchasers most of the advantages of their aggressive cash management, the funds credited purchases more quickly than the thrifts credited deposits (as much as a week faster, if the thrift was playing games, as most of them do). Withdrawal by check was infinitely more convenient than waiting on line at the S&L or the bank, or sending the thrift institution a form in the mail, to which it eventually responded by mailing a check that the customer then had to deposit in his checking account. When the thrifts got checking-account powers in 1980 (the New York and

---

*Actually, the process of calculating values to maintain a level $1 per share is not so simple. If all the arithmetic were performed, most shares in fact have a value slightly more or slightly less than $1. But the SEC permits the funds to pretend that paper due in less than sixty days is worth par, and income from that paper can be taken into the fund day by day, by dividing the total still to be accrued by the number of days until redemption. Paper with more than sixty days still to run must be priced on the market, however, and its value as of that day fed into the math by which it is determined that each shareholder has a touch more (every so often, a touch fewer) shares than he had yesterday. A separate calculation is made for the newspapers to show as an interest rate the annualized percentage of the increase in each shareowner's holdings over the previous seven days. An interesting side effect of this system came to light in 1979, when the First National Bank of Chicago, as adviser to an institutionally oriented fund operated by Discount Corporation, put its client on the wrong side of the rates, loading up with 270-day paper that had to be valued at market at a time when rising rates drove down the value of longer paper. A wave of redemptions followed. To prevent the asset value from falling below 99¢, at which point the shareholders' holdings would have to be reduced by SEC rules, the operators of the fund had to inject several million dollars of their own money, as a gift.

New England banks had been offering "NOW accounts" since the mid-1970s, under special dispensation), they could give passbook holders a service permitting transfer by mail or phone from passbook to checking account, but that involved only the very low interest rate passbook because the time certificates had been issued under government-required withdrawal restrictions. When market interest rates rose above the federal ceilings on deposit rates, the MMF was a considerably better product.

In 1974, when the maximum interest payable on passbook accounts at S&Ls was 5.25% (recently raised from 5%, to the fury of many S&L executives, who saw the quarter of a percent coming right out of their earnings), rates rose over 8.5% on six-month Treasury bills and over 9.5% on bank CDs. Money began to flow in what now looks like moderate quantities but was then terrifying floods (up to $18 billion by the peak in 1975) into the money-market funds, presumably out of the pool that would otherwise have fed savings accounts in the banks and S&Ls. Then the recession of 1974–75 drove Treasury bill rates down below 5%, the interest paid by the funds fell below the passbook rates (and well below the rates on longer-term consumer certificates), and the money flowed back to the thrifts. In 1974 the net deposit inflow to the thrifts had been about $4 billion (but those who blame the MMFs for all the trouble at the S&Ls should remember that net flows had been negative in 1966 and 1969, before such funds existed); in 1975 new money in the S&Ls rose to $28 billion, and in 1976 to $33 billion.

Hoping to protect the thrifts from another bout of disintermediation—and keep money available for housing—the regulators in June 1978, as interest rates resumed their flight to the stratosphere, gave the thrifts and the banks another piece of paper to sell to the public: the six-month money-market savings certificate with a new series issued each week at an interest rate fixed at a new level pegged to the results at the Treasury's Monday auctions of bills. The minimum size of such certificates was set at $10,000, to protect the passbook accounts at the thrifts, thus cheating the poor again. Eventually, the rate on these certificates was set at 50 basis points (0.5%) above the T-bill rate for S&Ls, and 0.25% above that for banks, maintaining the "differential" so long as T-bill rates remained below 9%. (If T-bill rates got above 9%, as they did, the S&Ls and banks would both be permitted to offer 0.5% above, presumably on the theory that when the cost of funds to lenders gets that high, nobody can afford to take a residential mortgage, anyway. This dividing line did indeed demonstrate the importance of the differential in funding the thrifts: when they had it, they took 60% of all the money spent on such certificates; when they lost it, their share dropped to 30%–40%.)

These rates, it should be noted, did not make the depository institutions truly competitive with the MMFs because the T-bill rate is a discount rate; 14% at the auction equates to 16.2% simple interest. The money-market mutual could also invest in bank CDs, commercial paper, Eurodollar deposits, and other instruments yielding more than the T-bill rates, and was required by law to credit the shareholders with all the interest earned, less a management fee that was typically 0.5%. When T-bill rates were 14% and the banks and thrifts' money-market certificates paid 14.5%, money-market funds might be paying 16.5%. Still, the rates on the certificates were attractive enough to move money by the hundreds of billions of dollars from passbook accounts to certificates.

The impact on S&L costs was dramatic. In fall 1979 Roy Green, president of Jacksonville's Fidelity Federal Savings and Loan, who still had almost 70% of his liabilities in passbook accounts and old-fashioned time certificates, reported that "our cost of money is moving up steadily at six basis points (0.06%) per month." In California the rise in costs was much faster. California Federal Savings and Loan, then the largest mutual S&L in the country (about $8 billion in assets) was an aggressive seller of money-market certificates and a borrower in the "jumbo CD" (over $100,000, no interest-rate ceilings) market. Its chairman Robert Dockson reported that Paul Volcker's actions of October 6, 1979, when the Fed shifted its rhetoric to control of the money supply, had driven up his average cost of funds by 29 basis points in that one month. Farther out on Wilshire Boulevard, William Montgomery of Santa Monica's First Federal S&L said his cost of funds had risen by 50 basis points (one-half a percent) in October 1979, and another 30 basis points in November. "If you take it seriously," Dockson said with considerable prescience, "and you begin to wonder where the hell you are going, you wake up in a cold sweat."

In 1978, as the housing industry boomed and rates on T–bills held under 7%, the nation's federally insured S&Ls averaged earnings of 0.82% of total assets. Despite the introduction of money-market certificates in midyear, four-fifths of the liabilities of the S&Ls still carried controlled interest rates: their average cost of funds for the year was 6.67%, and their average return on mortgages was 8.47%. Two years later, 42% of their liabilities were "subject to market-determined ceilings," their average cost of funds had risen to 8.94%, and the average yield on their mortgages had risen to only 9.31%. Their gross margin had dropped from 21% to 8%. Earnings were down to 0.14% of assets, en route to losses in the next two years. Valuing their assets and liabilities at market rather than book, Andrew Carron of the Brookings Institution calculated that by the end of 1980, the nation's thrift institutions had a negative net worth of $17.5 billion. By mid-1982, the liquidation of the thrifts as a group, selling their mortgages at market prices, would have meant that they had a net deficit of almost $120 billion. The insurance funds that were supposed to guarantee people the safety of their deposits in such institutions (and in the banks) had total resources of about $15 billion. It is remarkable that we got out of it alive.

But through the trauma of the inflation, as their losses grew and the market value of their portfolios disintegrated, the S&Ls never faced a funding crisis. There were 511 mergers of S&Ls in 1982, 75 of which required assistance from the Federal Savings and Loan Insurance Corporation. But this could usually be done without any major infusion of cash by the FSLIC, simply through the magic of "purchase accounting," by which losses on a mortgage portfolio could be transmuted to assets carried as "goodwill."*

One of the reasons an S&L could muddle through was the reasonably competitive insured money-market certificate and its cognate (lower rate) "Small Saver Certificate" for those with only $2,500 to switch, pegged to the rates on three-year Treasury paper. (Later, when the yield slope turned positive, consumers switched quite a lot of money out of what had become lower-rate money-market certificates into higher-rate thirty-month Small Saver Certificates.) Between them, by the end of 1981, these certificates accounted for about $380 billion of the roughly $770 billion of liabilities in the thrift institutions. Money did drain out of the S&Ls in 1981, but the net loss of deposits was a manageable $26 billion, or only 3.5% of total liabilities, because the certificates kept bringing money in.

Another reason was the nature of the S&L business, which

---

*The arithmetic of this bit of lying with numbers is rather interesting. Take a $50,000 mortgage written at 8% for a twenty-five-year term, of which ten years have elapsed. After ten years, the S&L has credited the borrower with amortization of $9,618 and carries the mortgage on its books as worth $40,382. Meanwhile, the market interest rate has risen to 15%. If that mortgage has to be sold on the market, the S&L will find that the monthly payment of $385.91, for fifteen years, is worth $27,573. Now, when an S&L purchases another S&L, it must calculate the value of the assets acquired as though they were being bought separately on the market. This mortgage therefore shows a loss of $12,809, in comparison with the book value at which the S&L being purchased has carried it.

The S&Ls the FHLBB was peddling in 1982 had so many such losses that their net worth was negative. Acquiring such an S&L without paying anything for it, the purchasing thrift (or bank) would have to show a loss on the transaction, unless the FSLIC made up the difference. The FSLIC didn't have that kind of money and didn't wish to spend what it did have in this manner. So the FHLBB authorized the purchasing S&L to take that portfolio loss as an asset—as the "goodwill" of the institution being purchased, under an arrangement by which this "goodwill" could be written off over a period of forty years. The acquiring S&L could now sell off that mortgage, and, to simplify the illustration, use the money to acquire a fifteen-year mortgage at the 15% market rate. This would produce the same $385.91 per month, but much more of it could be taken as income because new mortgages amortize generates large cash flows into the institution from the repayment of mortgages when houses are sold and from the steady amortization of the self-amortizing instrument, money that is available to repay depositors who want out. In 1981 there was a shortage of mortgage money that aborted many sales, and the inflow of funds to S&Ls from mortgage repayments was greatly reduced by the folly of some state courts and legislatures that prohibited the S&Ls from enforcing the due-on-sale clauses in existing mortgages. But the inflow of funds to S&Ls from repayments still reached a total of $34 billion.

Yet another reason for the continued liquidity of the S&Ls—very important—was that the outflow of deposits was motivated by greed rather than by fear: thanks to public belief in deposit insurance, there was no run on the bank.

But the crucial reason why the S&Ls never looked as if they might be closing their doors for lack of cash was the backing they received from the Federal Home Loan Bank Board.

---

much less rapidly than old mortgages. In this example, the old S&L, in accounting for its receipts of $4,631 on the mortgage, would have been able to allocate only $3,178 to income (with $1,452 to amortization). The acquirer, however, would be able to take $4,101 as income, allocating only $530 as amortization. Thus the income on its portfolio would appear to be $922.44 greater than what the old S&L would have earned. From this profit of $922.44, the new S&L would have to deduct one-fortieth of the "goodwill" acquired in the purchase, leaving an apparent net earnings improvement of $602.22, plus origination fees on the new mortgage. Assuming reinvestment of the amortization at 15% in both cases, the apparent return on the (diminished) portfolio would rise from 8.1% to 13.9%, the return on total assets from 8.1% to 9.5%, and what had been an unprofitable S&L before the acquisition would be a handsome contributor to the earnings of its acquirer after the purchase.

This improvement in current earnings would have to be paid for in later years—but the FSLIC was willing to undertake those future liabilities. What was important to the FHLBB and FSLIC, struggling to keep a drowning industry from going down for the third time, was a device to keep the game going until market rates fell. The Financial Accounting Standards Board finally put a stop to this scam by requiring that the write-off period for the acquired "goodwill" be related to the maturity of the asset being written down, but it was lovely while it lasted.

There is much talk about the Federal Reserve System as the lender of last resort to the commercial banks, but it is a rare crisis week when the Fed has as much as $2 billion out to its members in liquidity loans. In 1982 the Federal Home Loan Bank system had $80 billion out to the S&Ls—12% of their total funds.

The twelve federal Home Loan Banks and the Washington-based FHLBB that controls them were created to "promote" rather than merely charter and regulate S&Ls. Any S&L, whether chartered by the FHLBB or by a state—and any mutual savings bank—can become a member of the Home Loan Bank system by purchasing stock in its district bank to the extent of 1% of its mortgage assets. Together with various counseling services, membership entitles an S&L to borrow from its bank at rates only slightly greater than the cost of money to the FHLBB itself. As the FHLBB borrows by issuing bonds through the Federal Financing Bank, the rates it pays are only slightly higher than those paid by the Treasury, and thus considerably lower than those an S&L would have to pay in the uncontrolled jumbo CD market. Moreover, a new borrower gets access to the blended cost of FHLBB borrowings, which means, if rates are rising, a considerably lower rate than the current market.

Access to these funds is almost a matter of right. The Bank Board may restrict stock associations from increasing their dividends while they are in hock and can limit the acquisition of assets by mutual associations unless they reduce their indebtedness to the System. When the Home Loan Bank of San Francisco was run by Maurice Mann, a ruminative Bostonian who began his professional career with a decade as an economist with the Federal Reserve Bank of Cleveland, San Francisco instituted a policy of charging a punitive interest rate to S&Ls that appeared to be abusing their access to FHLBB money. The primary victim of this policy was Fidelity S&L of Oakland, which went bust noisily in 1982, partly because its net worth had been devoured by the penalty rates it was charged on Home Loan Bank borrowings. And it was the FSLIC decision to foreclose on Fidelity that created the auction of its assets won by Citicorp, giving the New York giant its foothold on the Pacific Coast. Thus do the decisions of economists cast their shadows into the future.

Meanwhile, the mutual savings banks of New York did experience something like a funding crisis. They had chosen not to join the Home Loan Bank System, though they could have done so (about 100 of the nation's 440 mutual savings banks did), in part because they were members of the Federal Deposit Insurance Corporation, which was for years a better selling tool than the FHLBB's Federal Savings and Loan Insurance Corporation, in part because they felt that the 6% return on the stock of the Federal Home Loan Bank Board was an inadequate yield for the investment they would have to make.

The New York mutuals were empowered to buy corporate bonds as well as mortgages and government paper, and their state legislature had maintained an unrealistically low ceiling on mortgage interest rates in New York. Moreover, they had learned a harsh lesson in 1975–77, when many of the mortgages they had written out-of-state at the high interest rates of 1973–74 were refinanced at a lower yield to the bank. (This had happened to the S&Ls, too: "a mortgage," Richard Pratt said when he was chairman of the FHLBB, "is a one-way option for the borrower"; but the S&Ls were stuck with mortgage investments by their charters and in many states by law.) In any event, in 1979 the New York mutuals decided to move out of mortgages and lock up what looked to them like the very high interest rates available in the bond market. When the big crunch came the next year, they did not have the same rates of cash flow from amortization of mortgages that eased the funding situation at the S&Ls. The bonds were way under water—if the mutuals had been forced to sell their bond portfolios in 1981–82, they would have recovered less than 85¢ on the dollar. By and large, then, FSLIC in merging troubled S&Ls could conserve its resources by assuming future liabilities; FDIC in arranging the purchase of busted savings banks by less busted savings banks had to make an immediate cash infusion of considerable dimensions—more than $3 billion in 1982.

The losses suffered by the thrift industry in 1981–82 were greater than those of the steel industry, the auto industry, and the agricultural-machinery industry combined. They were masked to a degree by a variant of purchase accounting, through which the FHLBB permitted S&Ls that sold their old loans at a loss to maintain their apparent assets by crediting the amount of the loss to the "goodwill" of the institution, a process facilitated further by the willingness of the FHLBB–controlled Federal Home Loan Mortgage Corporation to "swap" participation certificates in mortgage packages (which were easier to sell) for the S&Ls' old mortgages. As a result, the S&Ls showed a loss of only $2.7 billion in 1982—and an increase of $17 billion in "other assets," the great bulk of these assets being this fictitious "goodwill." The pressure from the S&Ls' losses was felt in the housing industry, which saw new mortgages by S&Ls shrink from $98.7 billion in 1979 to $48.7 billion in 1982—and in the legislatures, both state and federal, which had to come up with something, somehow, to preserve the savings of their constituents and the future of what is, after all, the nation's second largest industrial sector.

3

There was all but universal agreement in government, thrifts, banks, and academies that the collapse of the savings institutions was the government's fault. "We set these things up to get in trouble," said Frederick Schultz, formerly a Florida banker, who served as vice-chairman of the Federal Reserve Board for Jimmy Carter and a year's worth of Ronald Reagan. At bottom, the government was to blame; not so much for the institutional arrangements, which served the country well for a generation, as for laying the preconditions of the inflation that twisted the yield curve and made suckers of all investors in titles to money. Before proceeding to the remedies proposed and adopted, however, it should be noted that not all the thrifts were afflicted equally.

There was a chance for a medium-sized thrift to bull its way through even the worst of the interest-rate panic in 1980–82, following the example of State Savings and Loan, centerpiece of the Los Angeles-based Financial Corporation of America. FCA came into 1979 with less than a billion dollars in assets, profit ratios of just under 0.9% on assets, and 9% on capital. For four years, its young chairman, Charles H. Knapp, led it charging into every market where an S&L could make loans. By the end of calendar 1982, FCA claimed $6.6 billion in assets; though the return on assets was down to just over 0.5%, the return on capital was up to just over 14%. Earnings figures turned out to be somewhat inflated by clever practice. (Rather than take his loan losses when projects went sour, Knapp had developed a technique of selling off his delinquent mortgages at par, with FCA lending the buyer the money to make the deal on a basis that left FCA still at risk.) But even after the SEC stripped the revenues from such projects out of the associations' reports, FCA was profitable for a period when its rivals were out of the water, gasping, or under the water, drowning. In 1983, FCA acquired First Charter Financial, and at year's end had $22.7 billion in assets and fourth-quarter earnings of $56.3 million.

It is by no means clear that this tactic would have been available to many other thrifts, but very few of them tried. The fact is that the industry had got fat and lazy through a series of government-induced housing booms. S&Ls took government-insured deposits at a controlled interest rate; could write insured mortgages at a higher rate; and could boost their earnings while helping the profits of their board members through wholly owned "service corporations" that could do virtually everything associated with banking or real estate except make commercial loans or practice law. Mortgages were the safest of loans—William Ford, then chief economist for Wells Fargo, commented that "On the last $25 billion of home mortgages written by this bank, our losses have been $57,000." In inflation, the home was always worth more than the loan balance.

With all that comfort around, everyone slowed down. "When I was an appraiser," said William Mortensen of Santa Monica's First Federal, "you did nine or ten houses a day. Now a maximum effort is three. In the old days," he added, meaning the 1960s, "if a man called on Monday, we could close his loan on Thursday or Friday—at worst, in a week and a half. Now it takes six weeks. Partly it's legislation, Truth in Lending, RESPA [Real Estate Settlement Procedures Act], partly it's fear of litigation, mostly it's just declining productivity."

Most of what the S&Ls did to save themselves grew from their imitation of a competitor in the marketplace, the growing group of mortgage bankers, who dealt almost entirely in federally insured mortgages and sold them off, first to the Federal National Mortgage Association, then to FNMA and the Government National Mortgage Association established in 1969 when FNMA was turned over to the private sector. The mortgage bankers made their profits by fees when mortgages were originated and by servicing the paper, collecting the monthly payments, and passing them on to the investors in the mortgages, at so much per coupon plus the float on the funds.

Thrifts could be mortgage bankers, too; and starting in the early 1970s, the FHLBB encouraged them to increase their liquidity by selling their mortgages through a Federal Home Loan Mortgage Corporation that, in turn, offered the bond markets "participation certificates" in diversified mortgage pools. Especially when interest rates were rising, it was good business for S&Ls to sell off a lower-yielding portfolio, even at a loss, keeping the service revenues and freeing up money to be lent at the new, higher rates. A number of them, especially in California and Arizona, did keep selling mortgages and renewing their portfolios, some as a matter of intelligent policy, some by luck, because the demand for mortgages in their area was so far beyond the increase in their deposits. In 1979 Anthony Frank's San Francisco-based Citizens Savings wrote $750 million of new mortgages on a new deposit inflow of $50 million. Thus it was Citizens Savings, which was not burdened with portfolios of low-yielding old mortgages, that was in shape to take over failing thrifts in New York and Florida and form what Frank called First Nationwide Savings. This was one of the earliest of the takeovers; the FSLIC had not yet thought through its procedures, and Frank got a sweeter deal than anyone who came later. One should also remember, with awe, that just a year before the troubles struck, Frank had sold Citizens Savings (a stockholder-owned S&L) to National Steel, for $250 million.

4

The first official efforts to preserve the S&Ls from the magnitude of their interest-rate risk came from the Federal Home Loan Bank of San Francisco, which in 1978 authorized the West Coast federally chartered thrifts to offer Variable Rate Mortgages. Under the terms of the San Francisco arrangement, banks were permitted to write mortgages that would allow (but not require) them to raise interest rates by up to 0.5% at six-month intervals, provided that the average cost of S&L funds in the San Francisco district had increased by 0.75% in the intervening period. If money-market rates dropped, the S&L would be compelled (not just permitted) to lower rates on such mortgages, also by 0.5% at six-month intervals. The maximum change over the life of the mortgage would be 2.5%. In theory, and initially in practice, such mortgages would start from a lower rate than the conventional fixed-payment self-amortizing instrument that housing lenders had been offering since 1934.

The new mortgage was well accepted in California. Anthony Frank, who sold off all the fixed-rate mortgages Citizens Savings wrote after VRM but kept some of the new instruments, reported that he got only two complaints from 14,000 notices of rate increases the first time he sent out such bad news, in sharp contrast to the reaction when the bank increased people's monthly bills because their localities had raised their real estate taxes, "and twenty percent of the people would scream."

Soon there were proposals for all sorts of new instruments: a Graduated Payments Mortgage (GPM, with lower monthly payments early on, to enable more people to buy, and higher payments later, when presumably the inflation would have made the burden less, allowing the S&Ls to recover the interest lost at the start); a "Canadian rollover" (a five-year mortgage renewable every five years at the then-current interest rates; Mortensen wanted one-year rollovers); a Shared Appreciation Mortgage (SAM, with a reduced rate for the borrower, the lender to profit by taking a piece of the increased value of the house on resale); a Growing Equity Mortgage (GEM, with payments to rise every year by a prearranged percentage, usually 4%, the difference between the payment on a straight self-amortizing mortgage and the increase to be added to the homeowner's equity, retiring the loan in twelve or thirteen rather than thirty years). The thrifts' own favorite was an infinitely Adjustable Rate Mortgage (ARM), where rates would change automatically as the lender's cost of funds changed. Saul Klaman, president of the National Association of Mutual Savings Banks, said flatly, "We can no longer afford to guarantee to any borrower a fixed rate of interest on any instrument." That would take a customer out of the government bond market, too.

All of these mortgages presented problems. An infinitely adjustable rate of interest meant that a homeowner could not predict the future cost of his housing. People live like that in England, but it is simply unacceptable to American borrowers (and, nontrivially, to their elected representatives). Canadian rollovers looked far less attractive in the aftermath of Canadian experience in the early 1980s. The GPM has the disadvantage that the loan amount actually rises during the early years, which means that any disinflation in the housing market—and there was one in 1982—can give the borrower a rational incentive for walking away, which is the kind of thing that makes bankers and regulators very nervous. SAM has the quite hopeless disadvantage that at some point the lender must force the homeowner either to sell or to make what turns out to be the equivalent of a very large balloon payment to continue living in his house. (There is also no way anyone can write insurance on the repayment of such mortgages, and it's a very hard paper to sell in the secondary market.)

GEM is better. The economics committee of the President's Commission on Housing, of which I was a member, grew increasingly fond of this instrument as we studied the alternatives. Unfortunately, GEM does not have much appeal for the S&Ls, largely, one suspects, because its benefits are complicated. In fact, by accelerating the amortization of the mortgage, the GEM gives the S&L increasing quantities of money to sell at higher rates if the rates rise. Starting with an 11% mortgage, after five years the GEM will produce a greater cash flow to the S&L than a ARM with a cap at 13.5%. If rates have gone to 15%, the rapid shrinkage of the loan, which gives the lender more new money to invest, yields a greater total return than a capped ARM after nine years. And GEM gives the householder the indispensable security of knowing from the start what his mortgage will cost him at any point in the future.

Honesty compels the admission that the economics committee was unable to sell the idea to a housing commission on which the S&Ls were well represented. (GEM was offered as an alternative, but not recommended in the report.) As of eighteen months after the publication of the committee's report, it is hard to find thrift institutions that offer such mortgages. Pity.

5

The great change in the climate for the S&Ls between 1979 and 1983 was that they were made pretty much the masters of their fate. Legislation in 1980 and 1982 increased both their asset powers and their liability powers. All the varied mortgage instruments were made available to them. Congress preempted usury restrictions on mortgage interest rates and restored to mortgage lenders their power to demand the repayment of a mortgage when a house was sold. S&Ls were permitted to offer checking accounts and their lending powers were extended to permit personal and commercial loans of all sorts. An unintended side-effect of the legislation was that S&L charters became increasingly desirable to newcomers. Late in 1983, Household Finance, which had acquired a federally-chartered S&L in California, announced an intention to turn its two hundred finance offices in California into "banks" that would offer checking accounts as well as consumer loans—and to expand the service to all eleven hundred offices in forty-five states when the political climate permitted.

The immediate risks of insolvency in the thrift industry were taken care of by the Garn–St. Germain bill of fall 1982, which permitted the Treasury to swap its IOUs for depository institutions' IOUs, in sufficient quantity to bring the net worth of the thrifts to 3% of their assets. (The legislation provided that thrifts could count such Treasury paper as part of their net worth.) The FHLBB was ordered to use discretion in arranging such bailouts (following a recommendation of the Housing Commission, which proposed that the bank regulators instead of counting beans in the vault should make a judgment on whether or not this institution would be able to pull out of its money-losing habits if the market turned and the price of money dropped). It must be said, however, that the FHLBB is capable of peculiar use of the discretion it has always had: the decision to dissolve Biscayne S&L in Florida, later rebuked by a federal court that undertook the remarkable labor of unscrambling the eggs, wantonly ignored the prospects that the institution could be made well again by a combination of the sale of branches to Cal Fed—which already had offices in Florida and thus presented no delicate problems of interstate branching—and new capital from the homebuilders Kaufman & Broad, who already controlled the bank. An appeals court later returned control of Biscayne to the FSLIC, essentially on the grounds that in the deposit insurance nexus the government is allowed to operate capriciously: the appellate judges thought no better of the Home Loan Bank Board's behavior than the district court, but felt the law offered no remedy and thus no right. At some time, Congress and the industry will have to wrestle with the paradox that deregulation, while decreasing the detailed control government agencies exercise over the operations of financial institutions, increases their powers of life and death; but that time is not yet.

In December 1982 and January 1983 the government created two new instruments that banks, S&Ls, and credit unions could sell to the public: a short-term certificate of deposit with limited transactioon uses (no more than three checks a month, plus cash withdrawals and telephone payment orders), and an interest-bearing checking account on which banks and S&Ls could pay any rate they wished. The notion that one funds housing with money bought at an infinitely variable rapidly changing interest rate is one that would take people a long time to get used to, if they thought about it. Fortunately, they don't. And housing is indeed where the money went.

At first, the commercial banks outbid the thrifts by some margin in the request for this money, but late 1982–early 1983 saw the return of the positively sloping yield curve, with a vengeance: in July the rate on short-term Treasuries had been four percentage points higher than the rate on twenty-year bonds; by December, it was three percentage points lower.

By itself, the drop in interest rates would have driven money out of the money-market funds, as it did in 1976; coupled with the rates the banks offered on the new accounts, the greatly reduced attractiveness of direct short-term investments made the banks and S&Ls the intermediaries of choice. In their first six months, the new accounts garnered $350 billion, of which about $175 billion came from other accounts at the banks and thrifts, about $75 billion from the funds and about $100 billion from other investments and from the biggest burst of money creation by the Fed since 1972. The S&Ls

booked about $85 billion of the $350 billion. Swimming in liquidity, compelled to pay rates that made parking the money in short-term Treasuries unprofitable, quite unprepared to do any amount of commercial or other nontraditional lending (some of them did try to live an old Walter Mitty dream of becoming property developers, which was unwise; in October 1983 the FHLBB was driven to deny deposit insurance to some S&Ls California had foolishly chartered despite their open-and-aboveboard declared intent to use insured deposits as a funding base for speculative home-building), confronted with a public that wanted, above all, its old-fashioned self-amortizing fixed-rate mortgage, the thrifts resumed their old ways. The inflow of funds had enabled most of the industry to make a dash for profitability, expanding to increase the average return on assets, writing new mortgages at 13% to blend with a mortgage portfolio that averaged only 10.5%. By May 1983 a *Wall Street Journal* horseback survey indicated that three-quarters of the mortgage loans being written (in big quantities, once again) were fixed-rate, long-term instruments with few—if any—escape hatches for the S&Ls. "There's something about a positive yield curve that erases scar tissue," Anthony Frank told the *Journal* sardonically.

Inside and outside the industry, there was a good deal of head shaking about the renewed willingness of the thrifts to assume interest-rate risks and much muttering that one had thought the S&Ls had learned their lesson. Later in 1983 a number of S&Ls bit the bullet and expanded the proportion of variable-rate mortgages in their portfolios by offering the first year at interest rates below what they were paying depositors, with subsequent years to be individually calculated at market rates. This allowed mortgages to be written for many families who will have a hell of a time servicing them in later years, but it does show the S&Ls awakening to the need for responding to consumer desires.

In any event, the argument about learning lessons is backwards. The thing to hope for is that the government has learned its lesson. Before the disaster of 1980–82, Arthur Weimer, former head of the Indiana University business school and a consultant to the U.S. League of Savings and Loans, noted that "in an inflationary atmosphere, housing won't get any money at all, because after a while there isn't any long-term lending." The social phenomenon expressed by the negatively sloping yield curve is more important than the symptoms. All the economic activity that contributes to a prosperous future is contingent on the availability of long-term funds, and only the society that thinks of its children's future can be a sound society. "We're not going to write twenty-five-year loans at a fixed rate and hold them," said Alan Fishman of Chemical Bank. "We expect to be around too long for that. But how do you build America on floating-rate loans?"

Financial institutions are better equipped than others in the society to bear interest-rate risks. The magnitudes are such that it is folly to believe the risks can be hedged in some interest-rate futures market (which is what the more sophisticated S&Ls mendaciously say they are doing when critics ask them how they can return so soon to fixed-rate mortgages). The argument for pushing VRMs at people is not that they might preserve the thrifts in time of crisis (after all, who cares? The deposits are insured, and it doesn't matter much whether the Fed prints money to pay the interest on Treasury securities or to redeem people's savings accounts), nor that they might keep funds flowing to housing when money is tight (which may not be all that desirable, and if desired can be accomplished by selling government-guaranteed instruments into the market), but that they enlarge the constituency—now dangerously small—who really understand the menace of inflation.

If by some miracle we avert another bout of double-digit inflation, the S&Ls will thrive almost regardless of the powers they are given; if inflation returns, they will, to the extent that they survive at all, become very much like commercial banks, with a niche in mortgages. What can be hoped is that they will understand better what is happening to them and respond more quickly in ways that put more effective pressure for responsibility on our increasingly irresponsible governments.

10

MAKING THE CUSTOMER PAY

As traditional banking business goes elsewhere," said Judith Walker in the Office of the Comptroller of the Currency, "you have to find something for the banks to do."

1

As measured by most indices, the most successful of the hundred largest banks in the United States in the decade 1972–82 was State Street Boston. Over the ten years, total return to investors who held shares in this holding company—from dividends, stock splits, price appreciation—was 16.77% compounded. Its return on average assets in 1982 (leaving out a one-shot gain from a real estate transaction) was 1.02%, more than one-third higher than the average for the larger banks; its return on equity was 20.2%. It was one of a handful of banks in the *Fortune* 100 that could boast a stock price higher than book value. State Street's physical assets included one of the nation's great data-processing centers, a million and a half square feet in two austerely handsome white buildings in Quincy, south of Boston. Bank stock analyst James McDermott put State Street at the head of his list of five bank holding companies (the others were Provident of Philadelphia, Banc One of Columbus, Bay Banks in Boston, and Mercantile in Dallas) that "have already paid the bills for the technology."

Some of State Street's success is attributable to a strong record in conventional banking—a net margin in 1982 of almost 33% (i.e., the difference between what the bank got on its loans and what it paid for borrowed funds was a third of the gross receipts), a loan loss experience that actually showed a decline in losses as a proportion of total loans in 1982, a loan loss reserve of more than 2% to absorb shocks. But what sets State Street apart from other banks is the extraordinary percentage of its earnings that derive from fees. Excluding, again, the profits from the one big real estate deal, State Street reported noninterest income as 45% of total income in 1982. By contrast, Security Pacific, the most active of the larger banks in expansion of fee-earning activities, finished 1982 with only a little over 38% of its gross margin from noninterest sources; and Citicorp, for all its nonbanking subsidiaries and its heavy profits on foreign exchange and bond trading, showed noninterest income at only 34% of gross margin. The State Street 1983 annual report describes the corporation as "a unique combination of Commercial Banking and Financial Services." Fair enough.

At the head of the Financial Institutions division of the bank is Peter Madden, a youthful, long-headed marketing man who first arrived at State Street's doors in the 1960s as a salesman for IBM. His rapid patter, most unbankerly, illustrates the difference between people who do and people who don't have competitive instincts: "When I was an IBM salesman here," he recalled, "I knew when the NCR salesman was in the door—because I was afraid of failing." Such fears must now be safely behind Madden, who has driven his bank to a quite astonishing prominence in the areas he supervises.

State Street, as custodian for the assets of almost a third of all mutual funds, sends out statements to 3.4 million accounts; the names include Fidelity, Putnam, Rowe-Price, Scudder, Federated—and Sears and Merrill Lynch. Two laser printers squat in the Quincy building, working all day and all night, spewing out the green-and-white IBM paper with the perforated edges at a rate of 13,000 lines a minute. Men must be employed for each of the laser printers twenty-four hours a day to carry the boxes of paper from a storeroom and deposit them beside the machine on a schedule that ensures that each sheet will be acclimated to the temperature and humidity conditions of the processing room before it is fed into the printer.

State Street "clears"—arranges the physical delivery of the securities and the collection of the money paid to buy them—for about 10% of all the transactions on the New York Stock Exchange. For most funds, State Street also acts as keeper of the general ledger and transfer agent, registering the purchase and sale of shares in the fund itself. The staff is organized both by function (in direct relation to the machinery) and by fund. Long rows of men and women sit at CRT screens, each "account controller" (for the biggest funds, each little group) responsible for tracking developments in the holdings of one fund, crediting sales and dividends, deducting payouts. "They're all two-year or four-year accounting or finance majors," says James Lordan, another MIT alumnus, who runs the entire Quincy operation, speaking just a touch defensively in a Boston Irish way. They relate both to the management of the funds and to the shareholders, who think they are calling their fund when they use telephone services, but are really calling State Street. Calls for information about the value of holdings (or balances in the bank, for State Street depositors) are made to a separate number that feeds directly to a large green box, the essence of anonymity, which recognizes the account and code numbers punched into the consumer's phone, solicits the information from a computer, and generates a voiced response.

John Houlihan, yet another MIT alumnus, runs the mutual-fund-accounting end of Quincy Street and describes the round of the day: "The first thing is to verify how much investable cash the portfolio manager has today. Our people call the traders, who call back periodically and say, 'Here's what I've done.' Early afternoon is for ledger entries, checked up to the close of the market at 4:00. Then we have an hour to get closing prices times the number of shares owned by each fund. The transfer agent gives you the number of shares *in* the fund, and you divide. You must have the numbers ready for the AP by 5:20 or you wind up with a bunch of z's in the paper, and you get some phone calls.

"For stocks and bonds, there's usually a five-day settlement period. The trader can tell you what he did yesterday and you still have four days. In the money-market funds, the items you hold all settle either today or tomorrow, so everything moves on a much shorter time frame. To maintain the one-dollar price, you have to perform constant testing of the portfolio. In 1981 we brought into use an on-line machine, so you don't have to wait an hour to see what happened as the result of a transaction."

Servicing money-market funds and brokers' cash-management accounts (including Paine Webber's), State Street also supplies the Visa cards and Visa processing, plus the checks. "We are the *only* bank," says Peter Madden, exaggerating a little like any salesman, "that can do it all—custody and management, card processing, securities clearing, customer relations, governments transactions." Three thirty-foot-long IBM reader-sorters, each with twenty-four pockets, whir pieces of paper past magnetic recording heads and microfilm cassettes at a rate that in 1982 exceeded one billion passes a year. Scores of glum-looking middle-aged women and young men sit at the little screens that magnify Visa flimsies and punch in the transaction data, credits first to the merchants who use State Street as their Visa bank and then to State Street itself, debits to the customers' banks through the great Visa switch in Kansas City and the Visa clearing mechanism at Chase Manhattan. (The machines and the Visa section also serve the entire bank and a gaggle of more than a hundred correspondents: it was State Street that organized and processed the first NOW account for Consumer Savings in Worcester.)

The bank is custodian for the assets of the World Bank and the Harvard University endowment, and it serves as master trustee for pension funds that in 1982 totaled $34 billion. All told, counting the mutual funds, pension funds, insurance company funds, endowments, and personal trusts, State Street holds about $150 billion in custody, nearly four times the amount held by J. P. Morgan. (Morgan, however, does not take master trust accounts, in which the bank acts as custodian and agent for transactions directed by others; all Morgan's $16.5 billion of pension trusts was managed by the bank, while State Street managed only $8 billion. Morgan's income from fiduciary activities in 1982 was $190 million, as against State Street's $58 million—but Morgan is fourteen times bigger as a bank.)

As custodian, paying agent, and transfer agent for the funds, State Street is necessarily big in the wire-transfer business. It runs overdrafts at the Federal Reserve Bank of Boston every day as the money goes out in the morning and returns in the afternoon. Two separate computers process cash payments and receipts and securities sales and purchases through Fed-Wire. Among the more sophisticated services performed at the bank is the management of foreign-exchange exposure and transactions for the international investments of IBM.

"We've also been active," says Madden, "in developing consumer banking strategies. A lot of banks got into the credit-card business; the usual route was, they had some excess computer capacity. That didn't work, so they sold out their processing contracts to American Express. The key problem bankers had in the credit-card business is that they thought they were in the credit business, and really they were in the transactions business. We were the first bank in the country to charge a fee for a credit card—we were alone out there, charging ten dollars a year, for the first six months. We lost about fifteen percent of our accounts, but only two percent of the outstandings, and we had a notable decline in fraud, because if people pay for the card, they keep track of where it is."

A transactions orientation necessarily led State Street to an interest in point-of-sale terminals and Automated Teller Machines. The bank put its first lines out to supermarket terminals in 1976. In 1982 State Street set off on a joint venture with National Cash Register to provide a New England-wide shared ATM system, which was up and running by the end of the year at ninety-three banks in four states. "We can franchise it," Madden says, "or we can provide the elements of a system with which somebody else's system integrates." Following those principles, State Street has joined *both* Cirrus and Plus, the nationwide ATM networks that will allow depositors at any member bank to draw cash from machines operated by any other member bank, except in their own city.

The Quincy operation works twenty-four hours a day, seven days a week. It couldn't be more convenient for the clerical staff: a stop on Boston's newest and quickest subway line lies just across the street. There are two shifts, at 10:45 A.M. and 11:00 P.M.; each employee works three shifts a week. Not the least of the coordination problems is the division of labor between State Street and DST, Inc., of Kansas City, which share out Visa and mutual-fund processing and other chores and jointly own Boston Financial Data Services, housed in the taller of the Quincy buildings and performing processing chores for other banks.

Fees for this activity are calculated three ways: as a sliding scale against assets, based on the number of different assets in the portfolio, and based on the number of transactions. Except for the broker/dealer funds, which house money resting only briefly between the sale of one stock and the purchase of another, the charges per shareholder in a money-market fund are flat: average activity, says Houlihan, "is consistent and predictable over the year." Insiders report a range from $10 to $28 per account; in 1982 Howard Stein said he paid The Bank of New York $16 per shareholder in Dreyfus Liquid Assets fund. With Dreyfus and the Merrill Lynch Ready Assets fund (separate from CMA), The Bank of New York has held the leading position for such processing from the beginning.

There are other competitors, most of them biased toward slightly different services. Philadelphia's Provident tries for investment management on as many of its accounts as possible. It came into this business via a decision to follow Citibank in offering an equity mutual fund in 1970. The day the prospectus was to be published, the Supreme Court came down with the decision that Glass–Steagall prohibited such activity. "I kept reading the decision," says president J. Richard Boylan, who keeps the front page of this aborted prospectus behind glass on his office wall, to remind him of the vanity of human wishes. "It seemed to me the court had left an opening for a bank to manage a money-market fund, provided somebody else sold it." Provident went looking for a partner and found Loeb, Rhoades, which was later absorbed by Shearson, Hammill. Neither the bank nor the broker wanted to get into a mass distribution business, and their Temp Fund, the second money-market fund to be offered, was aimed at institutions seeking to maximize return on cash balances. "We've avoided the directly distributed funds," says Walter Knorr, who manages relations with broker/dealers, "where the transfer agent takes orders on the phone and opens checks in the mail. We don't like sweat businesses. Our ideal is the Liquidity Fund of the U.S. Savings & Loan League." This agglomeration of short-term moneys from the S&Ls started in October 1982, under Provident's management; by January 1983 it was over a billion dollars and rising, with only a few hundred customers providing all the investment.

Boylan gathered together a group of young bankers and data processors and set them to work looking for business Provident could do. They quickly came up with variants on the then-new and not very successful Merrill Lynch CMA. "We did a comprehensive study of all these pieces of plastic, trying to decide which was the best from the customer's point of view," said computer services vice-president Charles Zerr, "and came up with the American Express Gold Card. We were looking for somebody to dance with, and our contact was Shearson, because they'd bought Loeb, Rhoades. American Express didn't want to do business with Provident—we were a cockamamie little bank in Philadelphia. We said we could get them a lot of Gold Card customers. Sometimes I think we were responsible for the Shearson–American Express merger."

As of early 1983, Provident was responsible for one or another part of three large brokerage house cash-management accounts: Shearson's (for which the bank provides checking, overdraft services, and transfer), Smith Barney's (all of the above, plus custody), and E. F. Hutton's (checking alone). During the course of the year, the bank had its own internal adjustments to make following its merger with Pittsburgh National to form the new PNC Corp., but it gradually implemented a deal long in the making, with Automatic Data Processing, back-office subcontractor and clearer for most of the smaller firms on the New York Stock Exchange. As a result of that deal, any brokerage house with ADP services can offer a CMA: checks from what is now PNC Corp., credits cards from American Express, account maintenance by ADP. Incidentally, the profit for the bank is less in the processing than in the loans customers will take, which will be overdrafts on the broker/dealers' accounts with PNC. In this business, fee income and interest income intertwine.

2

A great deal of the banks' fee income is related one way or another to extensions of credit. The commercial-paper market could not have survived the Penn Central debacle without "backup" or "standby" lines of credit. Despite their short maturities (270 days maximum by SEC rule, 90 days on average) the corporate IOUs sold in the commercial-paper market are really a source of permanent financing for most of the companies that issue them. Schematically, they finance inventory or production costs (or loans to consumers, for finance companies); when the inventory or production is sold and the loans are repaid, the commercial paper is redeemed—and then reissued, to finance new inventory, new production, new loans. In real life, the proceeds of the sale of new commercial paper are devoted primarily to the redemption of the last batch: the paper "rolls over." What the purchasers want, then, is assurance that if they choose to get out rather than to roll over, the company will have a substitute source of funds. This assurance is usually provided by a bank, which reserves money for the commercial-paper issuer, to be made available if needed. In payment for this unused line of credit, the borrower in the commercial-paper market normally pays a fee of between 0.25% and 0.50% a year, on the entire line.

Numerous advantages attend this procedure. The fee goes straight down to profits in the quarterly statements because the operation is virtually without cost. If the commercial-paper issuer is also a heavy borrower from the bank, near its legal lending limit, the backup line permits the bank to continue serving an important customer because the regulations do not count such facilities against the lending limit. And the banks see virtually no risk in providing such guarantees, partly because they also trust the "names" that borrow in this market, partly because these lines are often hedged with "covenants" that permit the bank to withdraw them if the company has just the sort of bad patch that will make the buyer of the commercial paper wish to get out. Some bankers regard backup lines of credit for commercial paper as a folly of their industry, since it encourages the market to find replacements for bank loans. The answer, in this case conclusive, is that if the banks don't do it, the insurance companies will. Nothing improves anybody's profit picture like payments for giving comfort.

Other fee income is associated with actual loans, sometimes because there are costs to be covered, sometimes as a concealed increase in the interest rate. Mortgages fit in the first category, though in fact the fees banks and S&Ls charge to write a mortgage exceed considerably the costs of appraising the property and qualifying the borrower. Later the bank will earn processing fees for collecting the payments for the holders of the mortgage securities who actually fund the loans. And the timing of mortgage payments may be such that the collector enjoys a float before passing the funds on to the actual source of the money. In the second category—of fees unrelated to expenses—are the payments by international borrowers either for syndicating a large loan or for renegotiating it if the borrower gets in trouble. This can be big money: on a billion-dollar "jumbo," a 1% origination or renegotiation fee means $10 million.

The problem with such fees is that they are not, really, fees—they are add-ons to interest payments. No cash is paid by the borrower to the bank; instead, the money made available by the loan is reduced by the amount of the fee. This was especially obvious in the case of the government-guaranteed mortgage at a government-imposed ceiling interest rate, where the difference between that rate and the current market was expressed by "points": reductions in the cash actually paid out by the bank. (Among the genuine accomplishments of the Reagan administration was an end to this foolish system of easily evaded federal ceilings on FHA interest rates.) Because they are really interest payments—and are indeed received by the bank only through the repayment of the loan—such fees should not be taken as current income. Accounting for these fees as immediate profits not only presents the bank as more profitable than it is, but persuades management to go along with deals the bank might otherwise refuse, making the loan portfolio riskier than it looks and piling up future troubles.

A 1983 guidebook to bank accounting prepared by the American Institute of Certified Public Accountants calls explicitly for fees in excess of expenses (but why only those?) to be amortized over the length of the loan rather than reported as current earnings. As part of their effort to sell Congress an increase in the resources of the International Monetary Fund, needed to help developing countries pay the interest on their debt (or to continue vital imports while paying that interest: it amounts to the same thing), the banking regulators imposed a requirement that the banks follow the AICPA accounting rules. (The regulators' statement insisted that the rules had previously been ambiguous, which is hogwash—or whitewash, to cover the inadequacies of bank supervision.)

Since the nationwide introduction of NOW accounts (and the more recent money-market accounts and SuperNows), the most rapidly mounting source of fee income has been in the area of consumer service. First charges were raised for bounced checks; then fees were routinely imposed for "account maintenance" on checking accounts and low-balance savings accounts; then there was a return to the once-common charge per check (sometimes disguised as a price for fancily printed checkbooks). Initially, bank credit cards were offered to the public free of charge—that was, indeed, their selling point by comparison with the "travel-and-entertainment" cards like American Express, Diners Club, and Carte Blanche, which cost something every year. (A less-advertised difference was that the bank cards charged interest if payments were not made within thirty days of the receipt of the bill, while the T&E cards demanded instant payment and cut off the cardholder who was delinquent.) Since the mid-1970s, however, virtually all the banks have come to charge an annual fee for the use of their cards. Citicorp, in a brilliant stroke, added a maintenance charge of 50¢ a month for cardholders who pay their bills fast enough to avoid the imposition of interest charges. Assuming 15 million outstanding Citicards, of which half pay no interest charges, this gimmick would be worth $45 million a year—and few customers would even notice.

Banks also present as fee income the charges they make to merchants who present slips for credit to their account. These charges are a subject of negotiation between the bank and the merchant, and they vary widely, from 1.5% in the case of the airlines to 8% for the local haberdasher. The more the bank wants the merchant or the restaurant, the lower the charge; it is an unusually pure example of bargaining on the basis of bargaining power. The bank keeps only part of this fee. Paying the merchant 97¢, say, on the dollar, the bank either holds the slip and waits to collect (if the cardholder is one of its own customers), or passes an electronic signal to the credit-card clearing center to debit the bank that issued the card. Because that bank will not collect from its customer (or start charging him interest) for an average of forty days from the purchase date, it will not pay the merchant's bank dollar-for-dollar. The discount the customer's bank applies to the credits demanded by the merchant's bank is a function of the average length of the customer's float on the slip as calculated periodically by the credit-card company's machines, and the cost of money to the banks. And then the merchant's bank pays a collecting fee to the Visa or MasterCard co-op. If it's fast on its feet and lucky, the merchant's bank may keep 0.5¢ from a 3¢ fee.

Despite the 18%-and-up interest rates charged on credit-card accounts, such lending has been profitable to the banks only on the rare occasions when the spread between the CD rate and what the consumer pays is greater than 7%. The first forty days are free, processing fees and costs take a chunk from an average transaction of $40 that earns interest for perhaps six weeks, and credit losses are much higher in this business than in any other—up to 2.5% of total outstandings over the year, and that total includes a large dollop of bills the customer pays on time without paying interest. (When Citicorp "rolled out"— the bank's favorite phrase—its nationwide credit-card blitz in 1978, its losses ran 5% of outstandings: "Citibank," said a competitor dreamily, "has made itself the credit-card issuer of last resort.") Fraud has been eating the system alive, with estimated losses in 1983 approaching $1 billion. It should be remembered that, if a chemical pollutant made all plastic melt in people's wallets, a large portion of the loans the banks make on the chassis of the credit card would be made anyway, through somewhat different means—by arrangement with the department stores, or simple overdraft accounts. Reporting a spectacular increase in the profits of its "Individual Bank" in the second quarter of 1983, Citicorp credited the improved spread between the cost of funds and interest charges on home mortgages and consumer loans—and a whopping increase in fee income on the credit cards. That's where the money is.

There are many sources of fees, old-fashioned and new-fangled: charges for traveler's checks, for wire transfer of funds, for purchasing Treasury bills on a customer's behalf, for accepting bundles of checks from supermarkets as deposits, for letters of credit, for foreign exchange, for acting as agent, for investment advice, for planning and selling general-obligation bond issues for states and municipalities, for structuring corporate deals, for tax advice and tax shelters, for safe deposit boxes, for serving as trustee. International business is particularly rich as a source of fees. "Every bank ought to be involved in foreign exchange to a certain extent," says Aiden Harland, an English banker who left Chemical Bank in 1978 to form the Darien Consulting Group in Darien, Connecticut. "And it is, to a certain extent, even if it's only cashing a Canadian traveler's check accepted by a customer. Any bank within a hundred miles of the Canadian border can make $200,000 per billion of assets, and that's not bad. We help them realize they can open a branch abroad, sell their customers drafts on their own bank, make two percent at each end—that's nice business."

Many of these fee-earning functions are performed by a more-or-less separate "trust department"—more separate in recent years because the SEC has worried about commercial bankers conveying inside information to their trust colleagues. Until fairly recently, the courts took a highly idealistic view of trustees, who were in the rubric of English law to consider only the interests of *cestui qui trust,* not (never) their own interests. Banks found it convenient to say that their trust departments were unprofitable because the fees didn't cover the costs—

unless you counted in, as the internal bookkeeping did, the value of the deposits the trust accounts kept at the banks. Nobody admitted the resulting conflict of interest between the bank and the trust (which would surely be best off if all cash were kept in earning assets): what could the bank do, after all, confronted with a law that forbade the payment of interest on demand deposits?

Not the least of the contributions made by the money-market funds in the 1970s was an end to this little fraud: now income from trust assets (stock dividends, bond interest payments, receipts from securities sales, and the like) will be put to work promptly. The other side of that coin is that the banks now charge higher fees for managing trust assets and treat the trust department openly as a profit center. Honesty is the best policy. The volume of personal-trust business has grown substantially in recent years, with the growth of Keogh Plans, Individual Retirement Accounts, and the other devices by which the government has sought to increase the savings rate of the middle class.

Just as brokers and others have been looking greedily at the banks' business, bankers have been peering over the fence at the green grass of other financial sectors. The one that makes them salivate is insurance; either the sales-and-brokerage end or, more likely, the underwriting end. By comparison with money-market funds and commercial-paper dealers, bankers have become the high-cost providers of the kinds of service traditionally associated with banking—but they would be low-cost providers of insurance if it were offered as an ancillary in offices where the banking business pays the freight. One form of insurance—credit life (i.e., life insurance that pays out the remaining amount of a loan, mortgage, installment or personal)—has been a standard banking product for generations, and a very profitable one. To prevent gouging, the New York State legislature found it necessary to demand that the banks set premiums for such insurance at a level where at least 60% of what the customers pay gets returned to them as a class.

A number of midwestern banks—mostly not very big—had

started or purchased insurance subsidiaries—mostly brokerage firms—before the Bank Holding Company Act of 1970 ruled such behavior out of order in the future. In 1982 James Ehlen, chief bank stock analyst for Goldman, Sachs, told Lynn Brenner of *Institutional Investor* that many regional banks that retained this business "probably make more off the agencies than from banking operations." Banks have also been involved in the selling of insurance on the credit-card chassis, renting stuffer space in their billing envelopes to insurance underwriters of life and health coverage, for a price of 5% of the premium income the insurance company receives from such sales.

Citicorp has plunged into all sorts of businesses, letting the Federal Reserve Board evict it later if the Fed's lawyers disagree with Citi's about the relationship of this venture to banking. Some of these are dignified—like the sale by subscription of the bank's monthly economic analysis reports that had once been a freebie to customers. Some are remarkably downscale in their appeal—like the JTX Club, which offers its members discounts at every schlock tourist attraction in the country, and stickers saying This Stuff Is Protected by Identifax Nationwide Registry Traceable Anywhere by Law Enforcement Agencies ("Proven Effective in Keeping Burglars Out of Your Home"), and insurance that provides legal fees (up to $300 for a manslaughter charge) to a member driving a car who gets picked up on criminal charges, and discounts on purchases of everything from automobiles (through participating dealers) to prescription drugs (through a centralized, computerized dispensing service).

Other banks have been more sober, and perhaps less confident of their ability to compete against mainstream marketing companies. Moreover, others have been willing, as Citicrop has not, to recoup their investment in technology by franchising their systems to other banks. First Interstate has announced a willingness to franchise the entire bank—name and all—to bankers willing to tie into the Los Angeles holding company's computer and communications systems, and (like the neighborhood McDonald's) contribute to the advertising budget for the chain. Chemical has rented the use of its Chem-Link wire-transfer and cash-management system to banks around the world, under the name BankLink. The magazine *Euromoney* reported in 1983 that the result of this marketing strategy was to make Chemical the big gainer from the arrival of cash management on the other shore of the Atlantic—to the virtual exclusion of Citicorp, which offered its system only to corporate customers who kept their accounts at Citibank.

Perhaps the most interesting niche has been carved out by Security Pacific, the nation's tenth-largest bank and until the 1970s one of its stodgiest. (While others in California rushed to open branches, Security Pacific had cultivated its correspondent relations: its ambition was to be regarded as "the Morgan of the West".) The niche, oddly, was on Wall Street, across the continent; and the bank found it more or less accidentally. Robert H. Smith, who had run the somnolent branch network, had been put in charge of the bank's even more somnolent trust department by its incoming chairman and CEO, Richard Flamson, who gave a single instruction: "I want you to make money." A large, athletic man with broad shoulders and a broad forehead over pale blue eyes, Smith has a brisk manner spiced with a well-practiced conviviality. He did not much like his or the bank's prospects for expanding conventional trust business—"dependent on value added, which is a labor-intensive business. We needed new kinds of business."

Early on his new job, Smith met Thomas Conahan, a salesman for Bradford Trust, then the major clearing operation on the New York Stock Exchange. Conahan had been ordered by Bradford to sell the firm's West Coast operations, which Smith did not want to buy. But among Conahan's friends back in New York were the back-office leadership of Loeb, Rhoades, who were being displaced by their firm's sale to Shearson, Hammill. They were experts in municipals and governments ("munies and govvies," Smith calls them), and they needed employment.

Smith took them on, creating Security Pacific Clearing & Services Corp. to house them. "That was 1980," he says reminiscently. "It was eighteen people. Now"—he was speaking in May 1983—"it's three hundred and twenty. We began saying, 'What else can we do around Wall Street?'"

In May 1981 Security Pacific made contact with the discount brokerage house of Charles Schwab, which needed a loan or subordinated capital or both to finance its headlong expansion around the country. Smith went on the call because the trust department was a powerful potential customer for Schwab, and came back with other interests. "We set up a computer model to run projections on what we could expect in the brokerage business from a base of two million customers of the bank. I talked to my lawyers, said, 'Look at this old Glass–Steagall Act. It says banks can execute 'customer-directed securities transactions.' That's discount brokerage, isn't it?"

Security Pacific may have flirted with the idea of buying Schwab, though it seems likely that Smith always wanted the chance to pick up a much smaller house for starters and beef it up with new offices around the country. In the meantime, Bank of America came around with a fatter checkbook and bought the Schwab operation for roughly three times book value. Undiscouraged, Smith went to Fidelity Financial Services in Boston to discuss with them "what they might do with our two million customers." The upshot was an agreement for Security Pacific to be, for one year, an "introducing broker" that would funnel business to Fidelity and give both sides experience in a new relationship between banks and the stock exchange.

In February 1982, more than six months before the Federal Reserve got around to approving Bank of America's acquisition of Schwab, Security Pacific began offering stockbrokerage services, the first bank to do so in fifty years. In August the bank formed Security Pacific Brokers, Inc. as an independent subsidiary that would seek its own seats on the stock exchanges, offer brokerage services outside California at the holding company's out-of-state offices (what with its wholly owned finance companies and mortgage banking subsidiaries, Security Pacific by the end of 1982 was qualified to do business in forty states), and provide to other banks (70 of them had signed up by spring 1983) the services Fidelity had provided to Security Pacific the year before. For all its processing expertise, Security Pacific hired Automatic Data Processing to keep the accounts and clear trades for its little brokerage house.

In December 1982 Smith short-circuited some of the barriers to the bank's ownership of seats on an exchange by acquiring Kahn & Co., a Memphis brokerage house with offices in Houston and Dallas. He also took a step toward resolving one of the more awkward regulatory dilemmas posed by the banks' emergence as brokers: he asked the Comptroller of the currency to permit Security Pacific to seek National Association of Securities Dealers registration for its customers' men. Because it was assumed that banks were forbidden the brokerage business by Glass–Steagall, the Securities Act had exempted banks that executed securities transactions for customers from the normal restraints on stock salesmen. If the people who dealt with customers at the banks were less regulated than the people who dealt with customers at brokerage houses, the courts might well rule for the Investment Company Institute, the brokers' trade association, in their suit (which the Supreme Court has agreed to hear) to prevent banks from offering brokerage services. In fall 1983, Security Pacific purchased a seat on the New York Stock Exchange.

"We strategized," Smith says (unfortunately), "that we could be a winner; one, if we could always be the low-cost provider; and two, if we could get to a very high volume. And it was an interesting way to deal with high-net-worth people out-of-state." Another way of making such friends was developed by Smith's trust department through a division that prepares tax returns—"something between H&R Block [once a Citicorp property] and the accountants. You never get rich doing tax preparation. You make a little money, but you don't get rich. But you do get all that information about the customer, you learn what other services he needs. And we can provide services at a very low cost: mutual funds, insurance, deposits, loans, brokerage. I keep the database, the customer initiates the transaction, and we run it out of Memphis because it's a low-labor-cost market." Early in 1984, Security Pacific added to its list of products by arranging for a line of SP mutual funds to be handled by Dreyfus.

Meanwhile, Security Pacific has increased its New York and international presence considerably, acquiring two more stock and bond wholesale clearing operations in New York, a 29.9% share (the largest permissible under the London Stock Exchange rules) in a British broker/dealer, and a large interest in a Swiss bank specializing (as Swiss banks do) in the individual investments of the very rich. The Salomon Brothers research department projects that by 1987 more than two-fifths the profit of the "bank" will come from its nonbanking activities. There remains, however, a long way to go: Smith was talking about half a million brokerage accounts as the basis of his profit projections, and in mid-1983—counting the group that came through the Fidelity services, the Kahn clients, and the bank's own customers—the total was 67,000. The profits, so far, have come from the wholesale operations. "We've been a financial intermediary," Smith says. "Our future is to become a financial conduit and get paid for it."

3

The most spectacular run for daylight at any of the banks is being made by Chemical in New York, which has gambled $20 million and kept 130 people working full-time since 1981, on the proposition that a bank could become the premier conduit for the home-information services that will play an important role in an increasing fraction of American households as this decade proceeds, and may become a major industry in the 1990s.

These services involve the use of existing telecommunications facilities, either the telephone or the television cable or some combination of the two, to carry individually tailored messages and responses in the form of videotex transmissions. Through these wires, the family television set, or a home computer, householders can examine up-to-the-minute statements of their bank accounts, pay bills, make purchases, and pull up whatever information (about the stock market, airline schedules, the state of the world, the availability of tickets to shows, restaurant menus, the history of Kampuchea) has been put into the database by the proprietors and various service providers.

Consumer research and pilot projects to test the viability of such services have been going on since the late 1970s. Chemical was scheduled to go public with its "Pronto" system in New York in spring 1983. California's Crocker Bank would then offer Pronto soon after the New York system was up and running, and a dozen other banks would join the network by early 1984.

What Chemical hoped to get out of this expenditure was the ownership of—and thus the royalties on—a home-information system that could eventually generate immense amounts of money. John Farnsworth, director of the Pronto project, is a lively New Yorker in his early 40s with dark hair and the manner of an enthusiastic small boy; he seems much too young to have been manager of the bank's commercial lending operations in England before commencing his education in electronics. (Given Chemical's history as a white-shoe, Princeton bank, he also seems much too brash to be, as he is, a son of a former senior officer.) With minimal prodding, Farnsworth can be persuaded to project a future with 250 banks on his network, each with 25,000 customers, 6,250,000 end users, each paying a fee that will include $1 a month (which means $75 million a year) for the progenitors at Chemical. That would be a nice return on an investment of $20 million.

Farnsworth expected to offer a sizable array of services on Pronto. They would include an encyclopedia, to help Junior with his homework (price: a dime a page, or maybe an annual fee for unlimited access), advice from *Consumer Reports,* the Sears catalog (order directly by pushing the button), electronic mail (any two subscribers could send messages to each other through the system—and public utilities, department stores and such could send their bills electronically rather than through the post office); a chance to make restaurant reservations or purchase theater tickets or airplane tickets without leaving one's easy chair or picking up the phone; the power to buy and sell stocks without calling your broker (and to summon forth from the distant computer the value of your own portfolio, as of the market prices of fifteen minutes ago). Plus all the usual and some unusual banking features: not just bill paying, but bill paying on whatever day you specify, up to ninety days in the future, a record of all payments and deposits made recently, automatic transfer of funds among accounts, and so on.

At the beginning, Pronto services would be available only on the Atari line of home computers, which the bank considered the best bet in consumer hardware. With a lesser Atari available in discount houses for under $100 (and a modem to hook it to a phone line for another $100), the market would not be restricted by the cost of equipment. Shortly after introduction, Farnsworth said, Chemical would have Pronto software ready to run on IBM and Apple, with Texas Instruments and Radio Shack on the near horizon (the bank did not foresee the rise of Commodore)—and Farnsworth's goal was "to be terminal-indifferent within a year's time." Then the sky was the limit: "The Yankee Group in Boston says forty million homes in the United States will have a computer by 1990; they'll be impulse items. People will be buying these things not because they are computers but because it's a *service.* There are already eighteen million households that have a terminal in the home, a video game: they've learned you can interact with your television set." To get in on this market, the out-of-town banks offering Pronto would pay Chemical a $100,000 entry fee and pledge an annual $10,000 contribution toward the maintenance of the system—plus a $1-per-household royalty.

In the event, none of this worked as it was supposed to work. Spring 1983 came and went with no Pronto: the programming proved more difficult than Farnsworth's computer people had expected. Atari lost standing as the machine "early adopters" of this sort of consumer service were likely to own. Not many banks signed up: Farnsworth had expected to have twenty banks lined up to start the first year, but when the doors opened, he had only eight. "I underestimated the difficulty of selling the banks. I consider myself a sensational salesman, but this has been a very tough sale. I've been to two hundred and fifty banks. You've got to convince the data-processing guy that our Tandem computers are good equipment, convince the bank's planners that this is a good business, convince the retail people that they can sell it, and ultimately convince the president of the bank. In the end, we sell novelty . . . and fear: Citibank has a home-banking system, but they won't license it; Sears is coming onto our service as part of the database and as a receiver of payments, but it's clear they're doing it to get experience, they're interested in this business themselves. I tell the bankers, 'You'd better be the first in your area, or Citibank's coming, or Sears.'"

More seriously, Chemical didn't have the product. When Pronto was actually offered to the public in October 1983, it was still for Ataris only: IBMs and Apples were added in November, but many of the others seemed a long way off. Worse, *none* of the information and shopping features Farnsworth had outlined for Pronto was available, for reasons which are by no means clear. It had been generally agreed that plain vanilla banking would not be enough to persuade any large number of people—even people who already had a home computer and a modem—to spend the $12 a month Chemical charged for the use of Pronto; but that was the only flavor in the freezer. Even that was somewhat deficient in butterfat, for Pronto permitted the payment of bills only to four hundred or so merchants who had agreed to receive payments in Automated Clearing House format: to pay anybody else, the Pronto user would have to write checks, as he had always done. One early purchaser of Pronto told *The New York Times* that the only bill Chemical had let him pay through his computer was the one from American Express.

Chemical's best-advertised rival for home banking services was scarcely better off. Citibank began selling its "HomeBase" system to the public with demonstrations at Macy's and in computer stores in March 1983—on IBMs and Apples as well as Ataris, with Radio Shacks added in the summer. For $10 a month, the service offered a stripped-down version of the Dow Jones newswire as well as banking and permitted its users to pay anybody at all through entries in the home computer. Citi ignored the Automated Clearing House entirely: it executed the payments customers ordered through their electronic marvels by writing a check on their behalf and putting it in the mail. This involved ponderable postage costs when the payments were made to local stores, doctors, and the like (the postage costs on payments to the public utilities, the city, and such were slight, because a single envelope could pay a lot of bills), but gave the bank a float between the instant deduction of funds from the customer's account and the subsequent crediting of the bill collector's account.

After a successful introduction, Citibank pulled back and stopped offering HomeBase to new customers. According to computer wonks in the financial services business, some of whom had worked for Citicorp, the problem was an inadequate system. Citi had begun its planning for HomeBase with the thought that the terminals would be designed and manufactured, like the bank's special ATMs, by its own Transactions Technology subsidiary in California. When the home computer caught on, Citi transferred its attention to existing customer machinery and did indeed push ahead of Chemical in producing software for the more popular brands. But the central processing unit and the programming for it remained unchanged, and turned out not to be serviceable for any large number of home computers. Signs of strain developed after the first five hundred customers were signed up, and presently the entire project was relegated to demonstration status.

Putting on a brave face, Farnsworth defends Chemical's decision to go public with banking alone; it was, he says, a marketing ploy, "to win national distribution now, and dimension out the service later." He still expects to be offering a variety of information retrieval and shopping features once Pronto has established itself (as does Citibank: "My guys," says Pei-Yuan Chia, the vice-president in charge of HomeBase, "are talking about the same things as Farnsworth's; we're all going to the same conventions"). Meanwhile, Automatic Data Processing and a group of twenty regional banks are stealing a march on both of them with Home Banking Interchange, a full-featured banking-cum-information-cum transactions service (the information supplied mostly via the Los Angeles *Times Mirror,* the national shopping by J. C. Penney).

HBI began in 1982 as a joint venture with AT&T and CBS in a pilot project in Ridgewood, New Jersey, with two hundred upscale homes participating. The refined version, now a partnership between ADP and about twenty banks, went into its first homes (of employees of the banks involved) toward the end of 1983. Among the participating banks are Continental Illinois, Bank of Montreal, BancOhio, Connecticut's City-Trust, North Carolina's First Union, New York's Marine Midland, and First Wisconsin. What the consumer gets is in every way fancier than what Chemical and Citibank offer: not only are there many more things to do with the toy, but the information comes encased in fancy color graphics on the customer's own television set. To participate, however, the householder will have to buy a special conversion unit for the "Presentation Level Protocol" of AT&T's videotex communications system, and that conversion unit does nothing but provide access to the HBI computers.

In HBI, the banks have given up some portion of their processing revenues in return for ADP's ten years of experience in managing pay-by-phone services, which are systemically, of course, quite similar to home banking by computer. What they hope to retain is a share in the revenues a systems operator can earn by running toll bridges ("gateways," in the lingo) between the community of service providers—stores, publishers, travel agents—and the consumer at the videotex terminal.

Another group of banks considers that hope quixotic and has tied on as the tail to a kite being flown by newspaper publishers—Knight-Ridder in Miami (and seventeen other cities, if the introduction goes like gangbusters), Times Mirror in Los Angeles, Sun-Times in Chicago. The publishers had come to videotex in the belief that information services alone would persuade people to spend the money for adaptors, take time before the terminal, and buy what advertisers would pay to put forth in messages on the new medium. The reality of the costs rebuked belief, and they began building a package of consumer services. Unlike Chemical Bank, they finished what they had started. In early November 1983 Viewtron, the Knight-Ridder home-information and transactions system, went on sale in Miami with a dazzling array of goodies that can be summoned to a television screen through a $600 AT&T hand-held remote terminal.

Using this new "Sceptre" terminal, Floridians since late 1983 have been able to pull to their screens any of an estimated seven million pages of news and data, price and purchase goods and services ranging from bank CDs to theater tickets to sweaters to a visit by the exterminator—and then pay electronically without writing a check or licking a stamp. Using the same device, the children can access reading lessons or math drills, or cram courses for the Scholastic Aptitude Test, or the text of a Grolier encyclopedia. Or they can play video games supplied by the Viewtron computer. Grown-ups when not playing games can call to the screen the latest from the AP or local papers or the *Washington Post*'s Washington analysis, or the price of stocks they own or follow, or up-to-the-minute race results and ball scores, or a nautical maps with the location of all the nearby shipwrecks (where, presumably, fish are lurking), or classified ads from the *Miami Herald,* or product evaluations by *Consumer Reports,* or the police blotter of the local precinct, or . . . but you get the idea.

Subscribers can also send messages to each other through their Viewtron hook-ups—among the services offered, indeed, is a collection of videotex Hallmark cards to which the sender appends his own greeting. The recipient finds a "message waiting" signal when the machine is turned on, punches the appropriate button, and is wished a happy birthday or a sent loving Valentine on the TV screen. In another mode of message retrieval, an E. F. Hutton customer (Hutton bought the only Viewtron "gateway" offered for sale to a stockbroker in the introductory year) can find out by pushing a button whether a trade he had commanded has gone through and can leave his broker some words of commendation or complaint. And all this is presented on the TV screen suitably illustrated in living— well, computer-generated—color, at a monthly fee of $12 plus about $1 an hour for telephone company line charges, 10¢ per message for electronic mail, and specific fees for banking services, the airlines guide, and other pay-for-use providers.

Very similar services will be offered beginning at various times in 1984, under different names, by *Times—Mirror* in Orange County and in Chicago by KeyCom, a consortium of Centel (a midwestern telephone company), Field Enterprises (Chicago *Sun-Times*), and Honeywell (which will make terminals rather different from AT&T's Sceptre). Concerned about asking customers to plunk down $600 or more for a terminal that does nothing but receive and send videotex, they will package terminal rental with the service, at about $30 a month. Terminal prices will come down, of course. Charles Anderson of Southeast Bank Corp., working with Knight-Ridder on Viewtron, expects that within a year or two adaptor boards for home computers, enabling them to receive AT&T videotex and plug it into television sets, will be available for $150 or so.

Home banking is supplied on all the publishers' home information systems by VideoFinancial Services, a company formed and owned by three large regional banks and one international giant: Southeast in Florida, BancOne in Ohio, Wachovia in North Carolina, and Security Pacific in California. Each put in a million dollars, which was not enough money, to get VideoFinancial started. Any bank, S&L, or credit union in an area serviced by one of the publishers' systems will be able to offer home banking through the VideoFinancial computers in Orlando, Florida. Three additional partners, including the State Street Bank (where the *Globe* hopes to get on the Knight-Ridder bandwagon), were added to the original consortium early in 1984 to complete the system's regional coverage and provide the remaining $4 million that VideoFinancial required to finish its software.

Asked how the partners were going to make money marching in the publishers' parade, John Fisher of BancOne, a feisty marketer who is VideoFinancial's chairman, answered quickly, "Processing fees." BancOne, which had gone early into this business on the Warner/Amex Qube two-way cable-TV system in Columbus (and gone out of it after discovering that the cable-TV operators couldn't guarantee the necessary levels of accuracy and security), solicited Chemical as a partner when VideoFinancial was forming, and got turned down. Citibank then asked to join, and the smaller banks refused, believing that the New York giant, with its nationwide ambitions and its reputation for unscrupulous behavior, would simply use whatever information it picked up to improve its competing service. "Nobody," Fisher says sourly, "wanted Citibank."

Embarrassingly, VideoFinancial was not ready when Viewtron went on sale in November 1983: the software didn't work. (The problem, uncovered by bank employees who were "friendly users" in the pilot phase, was a terrifying glitch. During the four hours or so when the banks' computers were posting customer accounts, entries through Viewtron were simply lost: there was no buffer to hold the information on customer payments or transfers when the machine was out of direct contact with the accounts in the banks.) "The first transaction" by a Viewtron customer was handled by VideoFinancial in late January 1984, but it is not clear that all the banks were included in the service.

And it may be that all these elaborate devices are quite unnecessary. Little Toledo Trust went public in summer 1983 with its "Vista Banc," a home-banking system offering everything Chemical or VideoFinancial had on tap, at a cost to the bank of only $16,000—a payment to IBM for a software package. This tourist ran into the existence of Vista Banc while visiting California First Bank in San Francisco. Charles Pedersen, the bank's rotund, mustachioed, earnest vice-president in charge of fancy projects, took me upstairs to the PCs, pushed a button on the Hayes Smartmodem, and summoned to the screen a sample account from Toledo. While Chemical and Citibank were struggling to get their systems operative on more than two or three home computers, the IBM package for Toledo Trust was up and running on all the Apples and Ataris, Commodore, Heath/Zenith, IBM, Osborne, Texas Instruments, Radio Shack, Xerox, and "most CPM based computers." In October 1983, Toledo Trust licensed the system nationwide (except for Ohio, Michigan, and Indiana, which the bank kept for itself) to Quadstar, a Dallas Electronic Funds Transfer network with a transponder on a satellite. The announcement said—and I believe it—that Quadstar would customize Vista Banc for smaller banks around the country and expected to have exemplars scattered about the continent by mid-1984.

Similarly, CompuServ, a computer-communications concern operated from Columbus, Ohio, can offer its customers anywhere in the country home banking from Huntington Bank in Columbus, or Shawmut in Boston. These systems will run on virtually any computer that has a communications port that links with CompuServ. Research indicates convincingly that "home banking" alone will not sell a videotex service—but if people already have a computer with communications capability and subscribe to an existing linkage service, banks may have a built-in market they can reach at minimal cost to them and to their depositors. No color, no graphics, no theatrics—but the same service, for less.

And the banks will not be alone in offering "banking" via videotex. E. F. Hutton's participation in Viewtron will include bill payment from that broker's version of the cash management account. Independently of any of the fancy packages, Dean Witter will offer all account services (except the actual registration of orders to buy or sell securities—the customers' men wish to maintain their contact with their customers) via a telephone dial-up line to almost any home computer. Merrill Lynch has plans to take all its services to the home via a hybrid system that will deliver information from the broker via broadcast teletext (picked up by the television set's antenna on the "vertical blanking interval"—the black line that shows up between frames of the TV picture when the vertical hold goes out of whack) and accept instructions from customers through a home computer hooked to a telephone line. Test runs of this system to Merrill offices were carried out through summer 1983 on the facilities of the Public Broadcasting System.

Standing in the wings, almost dancing with impatience, is J. C. Penney, which acquired an existing pilot home banking project from First Bank Systems in Minneapolis in early 1983 and closed it down after eight days when the maker of the computer mainframe involved, who had lent his machine to the bank, demanded that Penney either buy the product or return it. Penney has taken a gateway on all the publishers' services and in HBI, on an unusual basis: while the other sellers of merchandise will process payments for their goods through the banks, Penney will do all the financial processing itself, through its own credit-card operation or its Visa and MasterCard services. Starting in mid-1983, Penney went into negotiations with a number of large banks across the country, hoping to establish partnerships that as the year ended were still elusive. In its initial planning, the retail chain had expected to use the French-made terminals inherited from First Bank Systems' "First-Hand" pilot, with an enormous collection of IBM System Ones to distribute the processing. By the end of 1983 Penney was uncertain about the equipment it wished to use: "There are other technologies we expect to come along," said executive vice-president Ralph Henderson with deliberate imprecision.

Chase Manhattan, which has been fiddling for several years with a poorly judged telephone-based home-banking system that would give the customer only a tiny one-line screen above the home handset, has apparently decided to take partners for a new technology. The first partner is to be Cox Cable, which pioneered a videotex banking system via American Can Company's now defunct HomServ venture in San Diego. Rumor says the first installation of the system is to be in Tucson; rumor does not say whether Chase is going to solicit accounts for the big bank in New York or franchise through local banks in Arizona, and at this writing no one is talking for the record.

Between 1980 and 1983 half a dozen pilot tests of home banking and home information systems were run in various parts of the United States, and the companies that ran them were optimistic about the prospects. "We were all surprised," said Harry Smith of CBS, "at the extent to which people went into the ordering process. They *liked* to do it. They didn't say, 'It's convenient' or 'It's easy.' They said, 'I *like* it.'" James Holly of *Times Mirror* in California reports that when people who had been given his company's service free for four or five months were told they would have to pay for it in the future, more than 40% of them put up from $10 to $40 a month to keep it. Those who had the service for the full nine months of the *Times Mirror* test used it for more hours in the last weeks than they had before and said they were sorry to lose it. But revenues from subscribers alone can never carry the costs of this business, and whether advertising or transaction commissions can be generated in sufficient amounts is still something that can only be guessed—and the guesses go both ways. The initial offering of AT&T Sceptre terminals in Miami was startlingly successful: the first 2,500 went out of the stores, at $600 each, in the first two weeks. Some of them, of course, were purchased by AT&T competitors (notably IBM and the Japanese) for reasons unrelated to Viewtron.

The long-term appeal of these services will depend on their

quality and—in the banking area—on the pricing both of what the consumer can do with his terminal or his computer and of the alternatives. All the systems now in operation have annoying inefficiencies, as the consumer chooses among services, files within services, sections within files, items within sections—and the computer typically delays a response to each command while it churns through the queue. It may be difficult to avoid what the telephone company calls the Mother's Day syndrome, when the systems crash because everbody wants to make a call at the same time. Especially if the system requires a special data transmission line over and above the normal telephone company twisted pair (and Knight-Ridder says it does), line charges may make the monthly costs much higher than the marketing experts have bargained for. At best, moreover, reading text on a television screen is rather unpleasant.

Money is important to people, and there are concerns about the security of the system. As noted in Chapter 5, the farmers of North Dakota gave Smart Card its start in the United States because they wanted encryption of their messages and the chip card was the cheapest way to get it. AT&T's Sceptre terminal does encrypt messages, but Pronto is *en clair*—the phone can be tapped. Consumers will be reluctant to move money about without some audit trail that gives the depositor a record of what he's done. All the systems require people to double-check on the screen before executing a transaction, but that may not be enough. Farnsworth reports that one of the householders in the Pronto pilot group hooked in his videotape recorder and made his own record of every transaction—"I told him that was great, maybe he'd catch us in an error." Farnsworth put his people on urgent rush to program the Coleco Adam for Pronto because of the new computer's standard-equipment printer, on which householders could generate their own bank statements. Still, a new generation may have fewer of these hangups. "You interview kids sixteen, seventeen," Farnsworth says, "and the concept of writing out a paper check—writing the numbers twice—they think that's crazy." (For their elders, interestingly, the check format seems to provide comfort. In the Ridgewood test of the ADP system, consumers were given a choice of simply punching a button to pay a bill as listed on the screen, or writing out through their terminal a check form displayed on the screen beneath the bill: pay to [blank] so-much money, signed [blank]. Almost 85% of the users chose to make out the imitation "check.")

What will sell home banking over the long run, Farnsworth argues, is what he calls "behavior-modification pricing"—that is, the bank will charge a good deal more for checks (quite apart from postage costs) than it does for entries through the home computer. Access to Pronto will be kept relatively cheap—$12 a month for unlimited banking. Because Pronto uses the consumer's standard 9,600-bit telephone line, there will be no line charges, but each service provider may of course impose a price for his services. (Some won't: the ticket vendors, mail-order sellers, and restaurants displaying their menus and taking reservations will probably be glad to offer free access.) But the bank can keep home-originated entries cheap enough to justify the pricing only if the subsequent steps are also electronic—again, the banks are crippled by their failure to support the Automated Clearing House. "Banks," Farnsworth said in an unusually pensive moment, "are going to have to share technologies a lot more."

IV

---

*Public
Policy*

11

THE POLITICS OF BANKING

Congress doesn't like to deal with banking legislation," said Frank Morris, the genial president of the Federal Reserve Bank of Boston, "because the big banks and the little banks and the thrifts never agree."

"Why . . . should state banks be burdened by two layers of regulation while national banks operate with one?" FDIC chairman William Isaac asked in an article in *The New York Times*. "How can we justify a separate regulatory system for savings and loans now that they have commercial lending and checking-account authority? Why should mergers be subject to antitrust review by both the banking agencies and the Justice Department? Why should the banking agencies enforce the securities law for banks when the Securities and Exchange Commission has responsibilities for bank holding companies

321

and other businesses? Why should the banking agencies enforce consumer laws with respect to banks, while the Federal
Trade Commission oversees nonbank companies? Why is it
permissible for a securities firm to own a bank, but not the
reverse?

"A short answer is that the regulatory system is no longer
rational, a condition that should be addressed through comprehensive reform."

Of course, the U.S. banking regulation system never was
rational. The greatest historian of American banking, Bray
Hammond, wrote in the 1960s in his book *Sovereignty and an
Empty Purse* that the National Bank Act of 1863 and its administration had "fostered what is probably the greatest mass of
redundant, otiose and conflicting monetary legislation and the
most complex structure of self-regulating powers enjoyed by
any prominent country anywhere . . . [The conflicting state and
federal jurisdiction] has made insistence on proper practice
most firmly exacting only when the authority concerned is embarrassed by institutions that it wishes would for God's sake
creep into a rival jurisdiction to die . . . Its lasting result is the
stultifying bureaucratic complex of matchless redundancy with
which the country is still blest."

1

Three forces lock banks and politics together in a tight em-
brace: the role of banks in creating the money supply of a place
or a nation, the importance of lending decisions in determining
what businesses can be carried on where, and the profitability
of bank charters.

The power to control the money supply is a central attri-
bute of sovereignty, which means that chartering banks is an
unusually significant and serious governmental action. Other
businesses can be conducted as partnerships, without government license, and incorporation for purposes other than bank-

ing is a routine operation: the necessary forms can be bought at Woolworth's. But only some special authority can give a person or a company the right to open a bank, to take deposits and issue checkbooks full of pieces of paper that can circulate as money. Interestingly, though banking is a licensed activity, it is not a licensed occupation: anybody, regardless of training, may legally run a bank, and you can find places where anybody does. Restrictive bank chartering is in the interests of the state itself, not the people.

By limiting the number of banks that will be chartered and controlling their activities, a nation presumably can manage the price level (including the interest rate, which is the price of money), or can assure market receptivity to its own borrowings. It will be noted that these two goals are mutually exclusive: a state that wishes to use its banks as a device for funding government deficits will lose control of the money supply and the price level. John Law's Bank of France in the early eighteenth century was the first example; Paul Volcker keeps gnawing at the president and Congress about the budget deficits for fear that the Fed in 1984 will become another.

The banks' power to get businesses started and help them grow (or stay afloat) is a steady source of pressure on politicians from those who want the government to make borrowing easier or cheaper. It is also the source of popular desire to keep banking a local activity. Not unreasonably, people want their bank chartered locally, owned locally, operated locally, and subject to pressure from the neighborhoods. The McFadden Act of 1926 and the Douglas Amendment to the Bank Holding Company Act of 1956, which narrowly restricted the deposit-taking offices a bank or a holding company could control, expressed the weight of the nation's experience. The Community Reinvestment Act of 1977 was only the most generalized and idealistic of many political efforts to make local banks and branches of distant banks lend their money where they got it.

There is a great difference to a community—often a visible difference—in whether a bank lends its depositors' money to local enterprise and farms or ships it out for use in far places.

By the same token, communities are forever being tempted to set usury ceilings, limits on what the local banks can charge for their loans to small businesses, consumers, and homebuyers, who cannot easily shop a wider market for lenders with more attractive rates. (But the result is that remote deposit-takers or borrowers can offer more for money than the local bank, and the community protecting itself from paying high rates finds its businesses and homeowners unable to borrow at all because the same people who get government to protect them against the market's high rates when they borrow insist on receiving the market's high rates when they lend.) The crucial importance of bank lending decisions also leads to restrictions on the ownership of banks, on lending by banks to their officers and owners—and on what banks can own, to protect businessmen from having to compete with rivals who always have first call on funds from the bank.

The profitability of bank charters has meant that people who wish to start banks are forever leaning on their contacts in governments to find them charters. In the nineteenth century, state legislatures retained to themselves the power to charter banks, one at a time, by legislative action duly approved by the state governor. This was a prime source of corruption in American political life for several generations. Twentieth-century reforms have taken most of the corruption out of bank chartering, though it still helps someone seeking a bank charter if he has the right friends or has made a contribution to the right campaign. But all the other problems remain, some in attenuated form. Consumers can borrow from Citibank on the chassis of its nationally distributed Visa card as easily as they can borrow from the local bank, and homebuyers can get mortgages from nationwide mortgage bankers as easily as they can get them from the local S&L. The small business and the farmer are still largely dependent on the local bank, however—indeed, now that deposit insurance is amongst us, the losers when a bank fails tend to be the borrowers, who, to some degree, will be tarred with the bank's brush and may find it difficult to replace what had been a vital source of credit.

Competing with a business owned by a bank is still a difficult corner to be in, as the travel agents can testify in Toledo, Ohio. (State law permits Toledo Trust to operate what is by far the city's largest travel agency, though the holding company that owns the bank would be forbidden by federal rules to own such a business.) Banks that own businesses—or are controlled by businessmen who borrow from the bank—pay less attention to the needs of others in their community than banks that have to look for lending opportunities on a purely commercial basis. The Bank Holding Company Act Amendments of 1970, which restrict such entities to business "directly related to banking," expresses a truth long apparent to both bankers and businessmen.

So does the Glass–Steagall Act of 1933, which prohibits banks from underwriting nongovernmental securities for sale to the public. If banks had been empowered to package their sovereign risk loans into bonds, they would have had no Third World debt problem in 1982–83—they would long before have unloaded the junk on the public. One notes with interest the timing of the S&Ls' entry into the participation-certificate business (and Bank of America's first venture into mortgage-backed bonds). It is nontrivial that under present law such paper can be sold to the public only by an independent underwriter, whose standing with his customers is to some degree affected by the quality of what he sells. No doubt the law has been interpreted in ways that deprive banks of legitimate business opportunities, especially the chance to sell mutual funds to and manage them for the general public as well as the trust department customer. But the thrust of the law was and is sound, and if it deprives banks of a "level playing field," it protects the public from being flattened by the juggernaut.

There is also a fourth link between banking and politics that nobody likes to talk about: the fact that since 1933 government in the United States has stood as guarantor of bank deposits and, indeed, of the solidity of the structure of the banking system. The belief that "the government will never let a big bank fail" underpins the market strength of our money-center banks. More subtly, by permitting banks in trouble to use "Regulatory Accounting Procedure" rather than "Generally Accepted Accounting Procedure," the government has encouraged what can be a fundamentally false portrayal of the strengths of financial institutions. Nonbanks that hold securities among their assets must "mark to market" in their annual reports, revealing the extent of their investment gains and losses; only depository institutions can carry at par value paper that could be sold only at a considerable loss. If that doesn't work, there is always "purchase accounting," as discussed in Chapter 9.

Sometimes, the SEC itself is the villain. In 1983, for reasons difficult to discover, the Commission ordered bank holding companies to present their P&L statements with securities transactions included rather than (as in the past) segregating profits into categories of "before" and "after" securities sales. Every bank has enough old paper in its vaults from loan work-outs to jazz up a bad quarter if needed, and enough low-priced, low-yield bonds to create losses as desired. When the fourth-quarter reports for 1983 came out the bank stock analysts were in a state of shock and fury: it seemed clear enough that the banks hadn't done very well, but nobody could be sure how poor the results had been.

Among the worst elements of Regulatory Accounting is the treatment of bank capitalization. No sensible bank would look at a borrower's reserve for bad debts as part of its capital, or consider its bonded debt the equivalent of equity—but the regulators allow the banks to take their loan loss reserve and their subordinated debt as "primary capital." This enabled the regulators to tell Congress with a great flourish in spring 1983 that they would in future prevent the banks from getting overstretched by requiring them to maintain their capital ratio (the percentage of total liabilities represented by investments in the bank) at a minimum of 5%. In fact, as of the close of business in 1982, only four of the top ten banks had stockholders' equity (which is what most people would consider capital) totaling as much as 4% of total liabilities: Morgan,

Chemical, First Interstate, and Security Pacific. And, of those, only Morgan even approached 5%. But the regulators' new rules could be carried through without forcing the banks to sell any great amount of stock on the market because the government had encouraged accounting procedures that made the banks look far more solid than they were. "It's like any kind of control system," said Frank Morris, president of the Federal Reserve Bank of Boston, genial and a little world-weary. "No matter how logically you've written the rules, you produce ridiculous results."

To the extent that the banks meet the new capital-adequacy regulations through the issuance of preferred stock, incidentally, it will be important to look at their per-share earnings rather than total profits in comparing their performance. Essentially, preferred stock substitutes a required dividend for what would otherwise be required interest on a borrowing. The latter is a cost deducted from gross earnings before profits are claimed; the former is paid out of profits. All the textbooks say a bank is better off issuing debt than issuing preferred stock because the interest paid on debt is deductible, but in the modern world—where banks can shelter earnings with tax credits in the United States against taxes assessed (not always collected) by foreign governments, or in leasing deals, or through the purchase of tax-exempt securities—the tax break that counts for a bank may be the one corporate customers receive on income from dividends paid them. Morgan was able to sell preferred stock (at least to Merrill Lynch, which got stuck with something like $200 million of it) at a dividend rate 4.875% *below* the rate paid on intermediate-term Treasury paper.

Every so often, a big bank gets itself in such bad and public trouble that the market won't take its paper even though everybody knows the government will somehow keep the place functioning. Seattle's Seafirst, one of the nation's thirty largest banks and by far the biggest in the Pacific Northwest, could not have survived as an independent company in 1983 because everybody also knew that this bank had too many bad loans on its asset books. Such giants as Chase and Citibank had real troubles in 1974 (and were on the "watch list" of banks in trouble at the regulators in 1975, as someone inconveniently told the *Washington Post*). Though nobody is more contemptuous of government regulations than Citicorp, the fact is that without the certainty of government help if needed, Walter Wriston's empire would have unraveled in the late 1970s, when its unanticipated $250-million-dollar loss in its consumer ventures became more or less public knowledge, or in the early 1980s, when its ludicrous overexposure in Brazil (a country that had accounted for up to a tenth of its alleged profits in recent years) became a subject of cocktail-party conversation. "How many of the banks," Paul Volcker asked rhetorically, "could truly stand on their own feet?"

The climate of opinion thereby created is sour and needlessly variable. By and large, the regulators consider it their job to save the banks from themselves; the banks, believing themselves to be grown-up now, can see only that they are being denied profitable opportunities by archaic laws. (The attitude is not quite universal: "Banks to some extent," says Wachovia's John Medlin, "*do* need to be protected from themselves.") Questions relating to the conveniences and necessities of customers—depositors, borrowers, consumers of service—arise in this climate only when outside pressure is applied, usually through Congress, and usually in ignorance of the real sources of the evil the pressure seeks to erase.

This book began as a study to serve as underpinnings for the work of the Task Force the Twentieth Century Fund expected to form in 1980, to study whether (really, what) banking legislation would be needed in this decade. The project was aborted after Congress passed the Depository Institutions Deregulation and Monetary Control Act of 1980, a much more extensive reform than anyone had expected a few months before. This legislation had been made necessary by a federal court decision declaring certain practices all banks had adopted (with the consent of the regulators) to be in violation of the 1930s banking acts. (The most important of the practices was the Automatic Transfer Service, which permitted depositors to use their savings accounts as checking accounts, drawing interest, in effect, on demand deposits in flat violation of the deposit-insurance acts.) The court recognized that Congress did not in fact oppose these practices, and that their immediate abolition would make more trouble than it was worth, so it permitted them to continue until the end of 1979, to give Congress time to write a new law. Congress couldn't do that, and instead passed a three-month legitimization measure, which probably would have been rolled over for years except that Henry Reuss, chairman of the House Banking Committee, serving his last term, wanted to get the damned thing done with in his time and recognized the great strength he had as a legislator from the very fact that he was not standing for reelection.

The result was the bill that amalgamated regulation of banks, S&Ls, and credit unions with reference to their transaction account function, categorizing them compendiously as "depository institutions"; ordered an end to controls on the interest rates banks could pay (to be phased in by 1986 at the latest); preempted all state legislation restraining the interest rates on mortgages; removed most of the Fed's discretion in setting reserve requirements; and in general established a policy of more competition and less restraint by government on the operation of depositories. Murray Rossant, president of the Twentieth Century Fund, looked at the new law and decided that Congress would not wish to enmesh itself with banking legislation again for at least ten years, and that a Task Force would thus be a waste of everybody's time. He was right as rain about what Congress wished, and right also as to the utility of the document I had prepared, which had assumed that Congress would do a great deal less than it did and underestimated the force of the technological revolution already sweeping the barracks of financial intermediation. Very little of that report has survived into these pages, though this book was commissioned initially as its expansion. But Rossant was wrong about Congress, which was dragged into action again in fall 1982 and will scarcely be able to avoid further legislation before 1985.

2

One must distinguish between the objectives of public policy and the institutions created to achieve them. What government had intended is defensible; what it has achieved is more or less nutty.

For example, local control was to be maintained mostly by "dual banking": twinned systems of bank chartering and supervision. Some banks would be chartered by states and supervised by state banking commissioners. Other banks would be chartered nationally, supervised by the Office of the Comptroller of the Currency. (OCC, a division of the Treasury Department, self-supporting through bankers' annual fees, is now housed separately in a rather Hollywood, very ungovernmental office building in L'Enfant Plaza. The Comptroller's little private office just behind his public office, with its nicely framed view of the river and the airport, is one of the most pleasant spaces in Washington.) Though policymaking is highly centralized in this national headquarters, where Congress can get at it, operations are conducted through a dozen regional offices averaging about 250 employees each.

Dual banking almost automatically produced what James Robertson, a former FBI man who became vice-chairman of the Federal Reserve Board, once called a "competition in laxity." (This competition was illustrated recently in living color on a slightly different screen, when the Federal Home Loan Bank Board was first authorized to charter mutual savings banks and the state-chartered New York thrifts used the threat of switching to a federal charter to bully various concessions from state legislators, most of whom never did understand why the leadership no longer cared what favors members wanted from banks and thought only about the goodies the state could give to banks.)

Because banks could shift their charters from state to national or vice versa, banking regulators were forever fighting for the hearts and minds of bankers. In 1926 Congress began to control aspects of this competition, ordering, in the McFadden

Act, that nationally chartered banks should have no greater powers than those given to state-chartered banks with home offices in the same states. If California or North Carolina permitted unlimited branching to their state-chartered banks, then national chartered banks in those states could branch ad lib; if Illinois restricted state-chartered banks to a single office, or New York to a single county or city, nationally chartered banks would have to play by the same rules. Moreover, unless the state they wished to invade gave its consent, nationally chartered banks would not be permitted to branch into states other than the one that held their home office.

But the United States was a common market. Banks in all states used the same dollar, and as the railroad and the advertising industry nationalized American purchasing habits, the banks' customers increasingly sold all over the country. To serve these customers, local banks became dependent on their money-center correspondents, who were susceptible to panic. The Federal Reserve System was created in large part to provide a Big Daddy of a correspondent that would nationalize the transactions system without impinging on the independence of local banks. In earnest of the continuing stress on local control, the law provided that no two of the Fed's seven governors (each chosen by the president and confirmed by the Senate for fourteen-year terms) could come from the same Federal Reserve District (of which there are twelve: Boston, New York, Philadelphia, Richmond, Atlanta, Dallas, Cleveland, Chicago, Minneapolis, St. Louis, Kansas City, San Francisco—guess which state had a senator whose approval was indispensable to the passage of the bill).

All nationally chartered banks automatically would be members of the Federal Reserve, which would not be responsible for assuring their safety and soundness—that would continue to be the responsibility of the Comptroller. State banks could join the Fed if they wished, but would have to accept dual supervision, with separate examinations of their condition by their state supervisor and by the Fed.

When deposit insurance came, a third layer of supervision

was poised above the banking system. Clearly, the FDIC could not insure deposits in banks unless it had authority to examine them. But once again by a custom quickly established, the Comptroller's powers were left undiminished; if the Comptroller's examination said a bank is okay, FDIC had no role. (The Comptroller is one of the three directors of the insurance corporation.) State-chartered member banks of the Fed were also permitted to escape FDIC supervision, because the Fed was examining them. But nonmember state-chartered banks— never less than three-fifths of the total number of banks in the country—became subject to the rules and regulations of the FDIC. Some states allowed joint examination by their own supervisors and the Fed or the FDIC; others required that the state auditors perform their job in solitary majesty. Among the unanticipated results of deregulation has been a great increase in the powers of the FDIC and its examiners, who now poke where they wish: if banks are to be more at risk, the insurer had to become more than a bag-holder.

Localism was threatened not only by branching, but by the bank holding company, which could own the stock of a number of separately chartered banks, in-state and across state lines. The most daring venture of that sort was A. P. Giannini's. He reached out from California with his Bank of Italy in the 1920s, acquired the Bank of America in New York, changed the name of his old bank, formed Transamerica Corporation to run both (and others), and hired to run the holding company a young Frenchman named Jean Monnet, who would later be the architect of European unity. (He was not an architect of unity for Giannini, who waged a bitter war to get him out of Transamerica after the entire empire staggered to the brink during the Depression.) From the 1920s, there survive a small number of interstate banking companies, most notably First Interstate in California and ten other Western states, Minneapolis–based Northwest Bancorp and First Bank Systems. Interstate holding companies were Franklin Roosevelt's preference as a way to get the nation's banking system moving again after the awful days of 1932–33, but Congress opted for deposit insurance instead because it would preserve the integrity of local banks.

Once deposit insurance had made possible the revival or replacement of all the little banks that had collapsed in the Depression, the holding-company idea receded in the general gloom of the 1930s. It revived after World War II, but only a handful of states, most notably Montana and Iowa, were willing to approve the transfer of charters into out-of-state hands, or to grant new charters to out-of-state incorporators. In 1956 Congress took into its own hands the regulation of bank holding companies, and an amendment by Senator Paul Douglas, the only professional economist in the Senate, applied McFadden restriction to multibank holding companies as part of a general restriction on their activities. (Existing interstate holding companies were permitted to continue as they were; Transamerica and Bank of America had already reached a parting of the ways.) Enforcement of all these restrictions was placed in the hands of the Federal Reserve Board, which for the first time acquired leverage on the behavior of banks. The holding-company act also gave the Fed the power to review the decisions of state banking commissioners and the Justice Department on the propriety of *intrastate* acquisitions by holding companies, a power the Fed used to increase bank competition, compelling holding companies that wished to reach into new areas to start their own banks "de novo" or confine their purchases to mom-and-pop banks rather than buy substantial existing institutions.

But the 1956 act had left a loophole in the rules limiting the businesses other than banking that banks could enter: there were no restrictions on *one-bank* holding companies. This form of organization was useful to the small-town banker, who really made his money out of his insurance or real estate agency, and everybody was better off if his various interests were all available for inspection in one shell. Only two larger banks—Winston-Salem's Wachovia and Los Angeles's Union—had or-

ganized themselves as one-bank holding companies, and they
had been relatively modest in what they reached out to do.
Then Citicorp was formed in 1967, with Citibank as its crown
jewel, and began pouring troops through the loophole, acquiring everything from finance companies to travel agencies.
Citicorp's change to holding-company status was instantly
profitable. Among the bank's long-standing businesses was the
issuance and sale of traveler's checks. Federal Reserve regulations require a bank to sterilize a fraction of the proceeds of
such sales in reserves, on the grounds that payment for travelers' checks is really a kind of deposit. When traveler's check
issuance was spun off to a separate subsidiary of the holding
company, the bank got the use of all the money. This put Bank
of America on the holding-company bandwagon almost immediately. Within a year, newly formed one-bank holding companies controlled one-third of all the assets in the U.S. banking
system.

Late in 1970, Congress gave the Fed authority to define the
activities that could be considered "so closely related to banking or managing or controlling banks as to be a proper incident
thereto"—and restricted one-bank holding companies to the
activities the Fed approved. Though George Mitchell complained that the duty to regulate holding companies had made
the Fed "like a public utility commission," Paul Volcker said
some years later that he was glad to have the chore: "It forces
us to get out of monetary theory for a while and look at what
the banks are doing out in the real world." It should be noted
that the big banks got something for themselves in the jockey-
ing that produced the 1970 act (which passed on New Year's
Eve, just before the 91st Congress disappeared into history).
"The benefit," said Donald Rogers, operating head of the Association of Bank Holding Companies, "was the chance to go
across state lines." A bank holding company could not own an
out-of-state bank, but it could own a finance company that
operated nationwide, a leasing company, a Real Estate Investment Trust, even (by 1983) an out-of-state S&L. The Fed's

approval or disapproval of a holding company's ventures in such business could be and was conditioned by its view of how well the basic bank was being operated. For the banks organized as holding companies, then—and by the end of the 1970s, they held three-quarters of all the nation's bank assets—the Fed became, as Rogers put it, "the supreme regulator." But not by any means the only one.

There remains a crazy quilt of banking regulation. The Fed supervises the holding companies and state-chartered member banks. The Comptroller supervises the nationally chartered banks regardless of what the Fed thinks. If the Comptroller says, as he did in the 1960s, that a nationally chartered U.S. bank can borrow Fed Funds overnight without counting the money as a borrowing, or can buy stock in a foreign bank, the Fed may continue to prohibit state-chartered member banks from making such purchases, but can't stop the nationally chartered bank. This is why Chase Manhattan, which had operated with a state charter since the early 1950s, when it acquired the Bank of the Manhattan Company by a legal maneuver through which Manhattan juridically absorbed Chase, switched to a national charter in the 1960s. If the Comptroller awards a national bank charter to Dreyfus Corporation, a mutual-fund manager, the Fed can't prevent it—and, as insult to injury, will have to accept Dreyfus Bank as a member.

Since the days of James Saxon, Kennedy's Comptroller, who liked to extend the powers of national banks to see what would happen, the competition in laxity has been less between federal and state and more between different federal agencies. In 1983 the Fed was the pliant regulator, helping banks deny the reality of their losses on foreign loans though both the Comptroller and the FDIC wished to require write-offs. "We have an obligation to call them as we see them," FDIC chairman William Isaac growled. "If there is a foreign-policy problem, let the government increase foreign aid." But when push came to shove, Isaac went along with the very minimal restraint on international accounting the Fed suggested to Congress as the quid-pro-quo for increasing the lending powers of the International Monetary Fund, and Isaac purred like a pussycat, concealing his discomfort almost throughout the questioning, at the congressional hearings on that subject.

The state commissioners supervise state-chartered banks and may approve their engaging in activities the Fed has forbidden—thus Toledo Trust can run a travel agency under its bank charter, regardless of what the Fed says about travel agencies in bank holding companies—and maybe Citicorp can operate an insurance company if the Fed allows it to purchase a state-chartered bank in South Dakota, where a new law permits a bank to underwrite insurance. (The legislature loves Citicorp in South Dakota and wants to keep it happy.) The FDIC examines state-chartered banks that are not members of the Fed and can shut them down by withdrawing their deposit insurance if it finds them unsound, whether the state commissioner likes it or not.

The crazy quilt not only covers the country, but can cover a single institution. "We have layers of examination," said Guy Botts, chairman of Florida's Jacksonville-based Barnett Banks. "We have thirty-one banks [this was 1979]. Some are nationally chartered, some are state member banks, some are state nonmember banks. And the holding company is regulated by the Fed. There's no need for all that, but everybody's afraid of monolithic enforcing, worships the sacred cow of dual banking." And Botts operates in only one state. Joseph Pinola's First Interstate owns banks in eleven states and must relate not only to the overlapping federal agencies but also to eleven different state banking commissioners enforcing eleven different sets of state laws. It takes a lot of his time.

Meanwhile, if I may (may I?), there is the oddity of the fifth wheel that grew up to be a Trojan horse. S&Ls were separately and far more loosely regulated than banks, because their business was less complicated—and less important. They were restricted by their charters in the kinds of loans they could make; they did not offer transaction accounts; they played a far less significant role as financial intermediaries. Nothing in the Federal Home Loan Act prohibited interstate S&Ls or the ownership of S&Ls by nonfinancial corporations. Indeed, nothing prohibited the ownership of an S&L by a bank. But until the 1970s the FHLBB could charter only mutual S&Ls, which meant that the holding-company form of organization was impossible, and a wholly "foreign" S&L would be hard put to penetrate the web of interrelations in a local real estate market that provides the necessary lending opportunities. The state authorities that chartered joint-stock investor-owned S&Ls were no more likely to let out-of-state institutions come into their savings market than the (usually separate) banking commissions were to accept applications from citizens of "foreign" states who wished to start a bank.

When California allowed Sears (which had controlling investments in both) to amalgamate the Hollywood and Metropolitan S&Ls into Allstate Savings & Loan, it required a formal undertaking by the giant retailer that it would never seek to expand the operations of its house thrift beyond the state borders. "It was an investment," said Sears's Clayton Banzhaf smoothly, "like our investment in Control Data. Very successful." But the only legal restraints are on lending powers: many states permit the mortgaging of property in the first instance only to financial institutions with home offices in that state, purely for reasons of turf control. (There is and can be no control on the subsequent sale of the mortgage to out-of-state investors.) California's restrictions on Allstate have become meaningless in the new environment. The six hundred "financial service centers" Sears will open in stores across the country in the next decade will sell Allstate paper of various kinds to customers who want some part of their funds in government-insured investments.

In 1974 S&Ls in the New England states and New York were authorized to offer consumer transaction accounts, and in 1976 the Justice Department forced the Automated Clearing Houses to accept S&Ls as members, so they could participate in programs for direct deposit of payrolls. As home banking operates through the ACHs, Sears in planning its entry into that market has no need to buy a bank and get involved with banking regulators; its long-established S&L will do.

In 1980, when the legal distinctions between types of financial intermediaries were breached by the general definition of "depository institutions," the S&Ls got access to FedWire and the check-clearing services of the Federal Reserve. At this writing, they still must rely on correspondent banks for access to the clearinghouses that process checks, but it can be only a matter of time before the courts rule that the banks' monopoly on check clearing is an illegal restraint of trade. In 1982 the Garn–St. Germain bill allowed S&Ls to invest up to 20% of their assets in commercial loans, and in 1983 Western Savings & Loan of Phoenix and Great American S&L of San Diego, the latter headed by the elegantly courteous, soft-spoken but formidable Gordon Luce, organized consortia of S&Ls with pools of funds totaling $4 billion for that purpose. If the S&Ls are to make commercial loans, they will eventually demand and receive the right to accept commercial deposits; as noted, their wholly owned service corporations can already perform "cash concentration" functions for companies seeking to invest their short-term funds most efficiently.

The first depository institution to touch both shores was an S&L—Anthony Frank's First Nationwide Savings, with offices in California, New York, and Florida, wholly owned, as it happens, by National Steel. Cal Fed, which went from a mutual to a joint-stock form of ownership in spring 1983, in the largest first public offering of a company since that of Ford Motors, owns S&Ls in Florida and Georgia, has purchased the trust business of Ticor, is among the major organizers of INVEST (the S&Ls' brokerage co-op), owns a mortgage company that has qualified to do business in fifty states, and will offer electronic funds-transfer services to commercial borrowers at very competitive rates. It is big in the jumbo CD market and plays with Eurodollars; its money desk (and computer) recalculates the S&L's blended cost of funds every day—"sometimes," says chief economist Jerry St. Dennis, "twice a day"—for communication to the lending officers. George Rutland came to Cal Fed early in 1982 to launch a commercial-lending division, after seven years with Crocker following twenty-three years with Citibank. "This," he said late in 1982, "is by far the most fun, because of the opportunities. Two things have moved us up: Penn Square and its revelation of the banks' heavy concentrations in energy; and the international loans, which we don't have. I can show you a lot of people who would rather buy Cal Fed CDs than bank CDs."

The watershed event in most people's minds was the acquisition of Fidelity Savings of Oakland by Citicorp. Before being granted access to the auction of that crippled thrift, Citicorp had to promise on various peoples' mothers' graves that it would continue to operate the place as an S&L, would not let the proportion of mortgages in the portfolio fall below 62%, would not flow deposits upstream to Citicorp, and so on. But "Citicorp Savings" depositors will of course receive Citicorp Visa cards, allowing them to access the cash machines of the Pulse network, and will be offered Citibank's imitation of the Merrill Lynch cash-management account, and eventually the Citicorp home-banking service. Citibank will be Savings' correspondent bank for its remote check clearing. In the course of time, Citibank's California finance companies and mortgage banking centers will be coordinated with the Savings operation, and the "products" developed by Citibank for its New York customers will appear in the California market through Citicorp Savings' statewide branches. And, in this section of its operations, Citicorp will be regulated not by the stern supervisors of the Comptroller or the conservatives of the Fed but by the friendly folk at the Federal Home Loan Bank.

Shortly before he left the chairmanship of the FHLBB, Richard Pratt thought S&Ls "might become more like merchant bankers . . ." It will not be easy for the banking regulators to deny their wards whatever Citicorp can get from the FHLBB. What lies ahead is not just a new ball game, but a new kind of ball game, for which nobody has yet written the rules.

3

Attempts to rationalize bank regulation in the United States stumble first over the unique position of the Federal Reserve. The other agencies regulate an industry or some part of it; the Fed regulates the economy. Its Chairman sits with the Secretary of the Treasury, the Director of the Office of Management and Budget, and the Chairman of the Council of Economic Advisers as the "Quadriad" that advises the president on economic matters. For the others, the honest and sensible operation of the credit-generating financial intermediaries is an end in itself; for the Fed, the issue is always the relation between the generation of credit-money and the economic health of the community—the stability of the value of money, the size of the Gross National Product, the employment (or lack of employment) of the productive resources of the society, the growth of savings, and the growth and nature of investment. Few archaeological finds tell us as much about what was happening in prehistory as the changing quality and composition of the coinage.

We must control the money supply, keep it from expanding too fast in good times (enabling people to buy more than there is to buy, creating inflation) or shrinking in bad times (making it impossible for people to pay their debts, creating a downward spiral of depression). In the United States these days, about two-thirds of the transaction-available money supply has been created, one way or another, by bank loans, which appear in the economy as the demand deposits of the borrowers and then of the people they pay (their workers, suppliers, etc.). To get a handle on this money, the state can control either lending by the banks or the banks' creation of the liabilities they lend. In Britain up to 1972 (and in France to this day), the central bank rationed the banks in the loans they could make; the United States took a crack at this system in Harry Truman's time, when the Fed restricted the kinds of loans banks could make, and again in Jimmy Carter's last-ditch efforts to beat inflation painlessly in early 1980. The normal

American procedure (to which we returned in summer 1980) seeks to control the banks' creation of liabilities by compelling them to keep a reserve against their deposits. When the government wishes the money supply to expand, the Fed increases the reserves available to the banks by increasing its own liabilities; when the government wishes the money supply to contract, the Fed reduces its liabilities by selling off assets, making money tight for the banks.

This is a rather subtle procedure. Its advantage is that it rations credit through the actions of thousands of private actors in the marketplace rather than through bureaucratic decision. (This is a real advantage. The British "corset" tightened the rein on the banks that had good ideas for making loans while leaving money lying around at the banks that had no ideas; the French *"encadrement du credit"* allocated loans to lame ducks in steel, textiles, and chemicals, with a general loss of efficiency in the economy. For all the moaning and groaning, the Unites States came into the 1980s far better prepared for a high-tech future than any of the European economies, in large part because funds had been allocated to the exciting ideas by people with their own money at risk and by bankers looking for profit.) Its disadvantage is that the central bank is hard pressed to keep a handle on what is happening. The effective money supply can rise while the central bank is not looking if an increase in velocity compensates for restrictions on the creation of new liabilities (and this will happen automatically when interest rates rise), or shrink when a decline in velocity negates the increase in bank liabilities made possible by increased reserves ("pushing on a string," in the language of the 1930s).

Velocity is a derived figure: statisticians calculate the Gross National Product (not very accurately) and some defined money supply (not very meaningfully) and divide the former by the latter to get a number expressing how often money has to change hands to produce the results. But to the extent that bank credit creates money and other lending does not, velocity must be a function of the proportion of bank credit to total credit, and this has fluctuated in recent years, as Frank Morris of the Boston Fed likes to point out, between 21% and 43%. As the Fed's policies drive borrowers to sources other than banks, in other words, velocity necessarily rises; as the Fed loosens, it necessarily declines. This makes fine tuning all but impossible, and gross tuning very difficult.

The Fed is bewildered by the variety of near-moneys created when it is holding down the creation of bank liabilities, and has great trouble determining an index to use as a guide to its activities. For a generation, the Fed tried to use interest rates in the interbank market as both its policy tool and its guide to events, and the normal trope for stability in the market led to dangerous expansion when the economy was booming. (If loan demand is rising rapidly, a Fed seeking to keep interest rates from rising too fast keeps pumping out reserves.) But the switch in 1979 to the use of monetary aggregates as the policy tool and guide foundered on the system's ability to create near-moneys—and, meanwhile, interest rates fluctuated abominably as people rushed from one side of the boat to the other. Led by Milton Friedman and his acolytes—one of whom, Beryl Sprinkel of Harris Trust, became Under Secretary for Monetary Affairs in the Reagan Treasury—the monetarists complained that the problem was caused by technical deficiencies in the Fed's procedures.

This argument is worth considering, not for its own sake, but as an illustration of the triviality that has come to characterize discussions of these profound and difficult subjects. The Federal Reserve's week ran from Thursday to Wednesday. Under the 1980 act the reserve requirement applied to depository institutions is 12% of their average transaction balances (plus 3% of their corporate time deposits) during the course of a week. But the week for which reserves are counted and the week for which the balances are measured have not been the same week. For the week ending next Wednesday, the depository institutions had to keep reserves reflecting their balances in the week ending the Wednesday before last. Thus each bank came into a week knowing in advance how much money it will have to leave in its account at the Fed (or keep as cash in its vaults overnight, which counts as reserves) to meet requirements—and the Fed knew roughly how much paper it would have to purchase in the market to create the necessary total reserves. (Only roughly, because cash—a separate Federal Reserve liability—counts as reserves, and the public's preference for cash vis-à-vis demand deposits fluctuates from week to week; as we are dealing with perhaps $165 billion in circulating cash and one-week changes of perhaps half a billion dollars of required reserves in a very volatile week, the probability of error in the Fed's calculations is pretty high.) By making purchases, the Fed "accommodated" the bank-generated money supply of two weeks before. By refusing to make purchases—or by selling paper instead of buying it—the Fed created a situation where the banking system had to borrow at the discount window to meet its obligations.

To keep the banks on their toes, the Fed has made borrowing at the discount window a rather painful and very uncertain experience: access to the window is a privilege, not a right, and any bank can be turned down at any time. Thus banks needing reserves will buy Fed Funds in the market from banks with excess funds (or with customers whose excess funds the bank can tap). If the Fed is being grudging about increasing the reserves, interest rates in the Fed Funds market rise; if it is being generous, they fall. Presumably, the more aggressive banks, making the most new loans, are the heaviest purchasers of Fed Funds. ("The Fed regards Fed Funds as hot money," said Frank Gentry, the smart young financial planner for North Carolina National Bank, speaking in the soft accents of the deep South with the attitudes of hard New York. "For some of us, that's core deposits.") Thus rising rates in the Fed Funds market restrict the total lending of the banks much more than the magnitudes of the change might indicate. Or so the Fed believes.

To the monetarists, all this pales before the simple fact that because the books had to balance, the Fed had to provide one way or another the reserves the banks were known to need this week; the only question was whether the reserves were provided through the system's open-market operations or through the discount window. Thus, the Friedmanites argue, "lagged-reserve accounting" facilitate irresponsible expansion of the money supply. Only "contemporaneous-reserve accounting"—applying the reserve requirement to the banks' transaction accounts in the current week—can *really* influence the behavior of the banks, which would have to operate more conservatively because they would never know for sure where they stand.

So in February 1984, the Fed began assessing reserves on the basis of contemporaneous accounting (well, *almost* contemporaneous: the books will close on Monday to determine reserves required through Wednesday). But it will be just as true as it was before that the Fed (now overwhelmingly on Wednesday, when it gets some grip on the current week's numbers) will have to supply the reserves needed to balance the books. Because banks' relations with their customers are continuous, and because they don't know on which day a borrower will take his credits or use them (indeed, given the division between the lending side of the bank and the operations side, the lending officers to their fury often don't know when the money they have sold to a customer will become available to him), because an individual bank has no way to predict how much cash the public will deposit or withdraw on a given day, it is most unlikely that the change can make the slighest difference in the way banks behave. But an academic pressure group with great influence in the Reagan administration will have been appeased.

The Fed itself has explained the startling fluctuations in the various measured money supplies as an artifact of the new instruments that banks and S&Ls have been able to sell their customers, especially the various accounts without interest-rate limits introduced since December 1982. (The one that limits checks to three a month does not have to be reserved

against; the "SuperNow" interest-bearing account with unlimited checking requires the bank to sterilize 12¢ of every
deposited dollar by shipping it off to the Fed.) Earlier, there
had been exculpatory grumbles about the effects of the decline
in Federal Reserve membership by large state-chartered banks,
which resigned in some numbers in the 1970s as rising interest
rates pushed up the cost of sterilized reserves. (It was this
concern that stimulated the portmanteau definition of "depository institutions" in the 1980 act, and the requirement in the act
that all institutions offering transaction accounts keep reserves
at the Fed against such balances). But none of this could have
been anywhere near so important as the rise of FedWire as an
instrument for third-party payment and the consequent change
in the *function* of the large banks' reserve accounts at the Fed.

Reserves are calculated by the Fed once a day, very early
in the morning, before the banks open for business. In the old
days, they were used once a day, to settle accounts at the
clearinghouse, in most cities between 10:00 A.M. and 11:00
A.M. If a bank did not have sufficient funds at the Fed to meet
its bill from the clearinghouse, it was in deep trouble and would
be forced into the discount window immediately for a well-
collateralized overnight loan, presumably at a penalty rate, and
for a lecture about how to run a bank.

Today, reserves are *primarily* the transaction balances of
the banks themselves. In the middle of every day, the books of
the Federal Reserve Banks now show enormous liabilities in
the form of payments to FedWire recipients not covered by the
balances of the paying banks. At noon, these unsecured
intraday loans to banks probably exceed the system's liabilities
in the form of reserve deposits. Though the Board of Governors has made disapproving noises about this practice, nothing
has been done to stop it—or will be done, for fear of driving the
business to private competitors. If reserve requirements and
overdraft privileges were both eliminated from the Fed's tool
kit, the banks would, *force majeure*, keep larger reserves at the
Fed every night than they do today, or they would change their

operating practices significantly. No doubt the reserves held overnight and reported are more important than the daylight overdrafts that wash off the books by early afternoon. But it is quite impossible to believe that Federal Reserve credit influences real monetary aggregates only when everyone is asleep, not during the day when people are actually conducting their business. For these daylight overdrafts, which facilitate the huge growth of financial markets, are a nurturing ground for the generation of the near-moneys that increase velocity whenever the Fed gets tough.

I think it is fair to say that the implications of daylight overdrafts and electronic funds transfer through FedWire have not been analyzed at all, except perhaps as part of the collection of uncertainties that has made the Fed neurotic. In sum, these uncertainties have made the Fed most reluctant to give up the various supervisory chores it performs under the bank holding company acts. If the only weapon the Fed is to have to stop inflation is the elevation of interest rates to levels where they discourage borrowers (an optimistic lot who turn desperate when they are not optimistic), then monetary policy becomes a dangerously inefficient and costly means for macroeconomic control.

From the Fed's point of view, the debate that should be raging about the future regulation of financial intermediaries is not today's imbroglio about who should be allowed to compete how and where, but a more fundamental discussion of the tool kit a central bank requires at a time of computerized communications, liability management, and wire transfer of funds. No doubt there is something distasteful about the Fed's love for control for its own sake; no doubt, too, that the Fed, in Richard Pratt's parting shot, is "very cumbersome, ponderous; it has a big board and the board and staff slow it down; they get paralyzed by their own approach to problems." And certainly no doubt that, as Frank Morris of the Boston Fed said, "The tide of change is overwhelming; nothing you can do will hold it back." But that scarcely justifies dealing with these vital questions as though what matters is whether Citicorp can do everything Sears or Merrill Lynch can do. Still, that's where the political money is, so that's what the argument is about.

4

The tide that kept imposing new regulations on the banks—that carried in the Truth in Lending Act, the Community Reinvestment Act, the Real Estate Settlement Procedures Act, and the Financial Industries Regulation Act, all very time-consuming for both the banks and the agencies—reversed quite suddenly, almost mysteriously, in 1978. The true cause of the reversal was the new technology that was changing the banking system whether Congress liked it or not; the catalyst was the invasion of the American markets by foreign-owned banks and the fundamental unfairness in the legal treatment of U. S. banks and foreign banks operating in the United States. The former, whether nationally or state chartered, could have branches only in their home state (unless other states specifically okayed their expansion and accepted their offices). But the latter could operate, in effect, in any state where a state-chartered bank wished to have an operation in the foreign bank's home country. For the international rule was "reciprocity"—your bank can have an office here if our bank can have an office there. Thus Bank of America would have an office in London only if California agreed to charter the activities of, say, Barclay's Bank in California, while Morgan Guaranty could operate in London only if Barclay's was permitted to open branches in New York.

The new legislation grandfathered in all the foreigners who already had interstate operations, but put a stop to any further exploitation of this peculiarity of American shared sovereignty. To redress the balance just a little, Congress permitted U. S. banks to increase the number and functions of their "Edge Act" affiliates—in effect, foreign trade branches—that had been permitted for fifty years and could be housed in any major port regardless of the state to which the parent bank was otherwise restricted. (This produced an immense boom in banking in Miami, fed by drug money from Colombia, Ecuador, and Jamaica, and flight money from Venezuela and Central America.)

Congress also instructed the president to prepare a report on the advantages and disadvantages of eliminating restrictions on interstate banking, to be delivered on the last day of 1979. That last day came and went without any report by the president (though in fact the document was complete) because Jimmy Carter had lived through an election campaign in Georgia in the year that state abandoned its old unit-banking rules and allowed holding companies to operate statewide, and he wan't going to live through that again. The report that was finally delivered to Congress, after election day, 1980, recommended allowing an experiment in branch banking in contiguous states. The details were not very important (and nothing came of the report, anyway). What mattered was that Congress and the president had begun to look at banking with an eye to deregulation and assistance rather than control and repression.

By March 1980—one notes that this was some time before the election or even the nomination of Ronald Reagan—the deregulation tide had risen so high that Congress had no hesitation about giving its landmark banking legislation the title "Depository Institutions Deregulation and Monetary Control Act of 1980." The key institution created by the act was a Deposittory Institutions Deregulation Committee, with a first job of deciding on the timetable for the elimination of Regulation Q, the Federal Reserve Board's instrument for the control of interest rates. The members of the committee, each with an equal vote, were the Secretary of the Treasury, the Chairman of the Federal Reserve Board, the Chairman of the Federal Home Loan Bank Board, the Chairman of the Federal Deposit Insurance Corporation, and the National Credit Union Administrator, whose wards had taken to giving their depositors "share drafts" that would circulate as checks. The Comptroller was to sit on the committee without a vote, essentially because John Heimann, who was then Comptroller, had managed to offend members of the banking committees by unwise demonstrations that he was smarter than they were, and members of the Carter administration by refusing to certify that Bert Lance was as clean as a hound's tooth.

DIDC was not the first attempt within the government to bring the banking regulators together to make shared decisions. As early as the Lyndon Johnson years, the White House had started an Inter-Agency Coordinating Council to bring together the banking and S&L regulators and the Treasury Department for periodic consultations—but after the first few meetings, the heads of the agencies did not attend. The Financial Institutions Regulation Act had created a more formal Financial Institutions Examinations Council, involving the Fed, the Comptroller, the FDIC, the FHLBB, and the Credit Union Administrator.

After the perils-of-Pauline days of 1975, when giant banks appeared on the "watch list" at the Comptroller's office, the Fed had led the way to joint evaluations by the regulators of "shared national credits"—syndicated loans to big companies involving more than one bank—to make sure that everybody agreed on definitions of riskiness. The Examinations Council made the procedure formal and permanent. Also in the time of the Ford administration, the Comptroller had sought help from other regulators after losing a battle with the State Department over its authority to pass negative judgments on loans to foreign governments and governmental entities. (In that first battle, the diplomats managed to remove the stigma of "classification" by the bank examiners from loans to Italy, which was borrowing on a grand scale without any apparent attention to how the loans might later be serviced.) The Examinations Council extended the joint evaluation of shared credits to foreign loans, and presently the State Department decided to leave credit judgment to the experts, while the experts agreed not to make too many waves. In 1983, Congress ordered the regulators to make the banks reserve against loans to obviously hopeless debtors, and in early 1984, the Examinations Council placed its seal of bad housekeeping on Poland, Sudan, and Zaire. In retrospect, it can be argued that the need to achieve consensus in the Examinations Council may have prevented any one of the regulators from speaking bluntly enough to the banks that were digging themselves so deep a hole by their careless international lending in 1979–82.

Perhaps the most remarkable achievement of the Examinations Council, however, was something it did not do. The Federal Reserve has sufficient clout in the government, and sufficient responsibility for the supervision of bank holding companies, that it could probably have stopped the Securities and Exchange Commission from requiring the publication of more and more information about how those banks owned by holding companies (all the big ones) were conducting their business. And the Fed's normal position on disclosure, FDIC's Isaac reports scornfully, was that "the best way to protect bank depositors is to keep secrets."

But through the second half of the 1970s, the Comptroller's office was in process of changing the nature of bank examination. As Ford's Comptroller, James Smith had commissioned a study of bank examinations by the accounting firm of Haskins & Sells, which in effect had recommended that OCC move its emphasis from the balance sheet—the adding up of all the assets and all the liabilities to make sure everything was really there—to the profit-and-loss statement, the question of how well the bank was being managed. By establishing a database of bank profiles in the computer, the Comptroller could quickly spot "anomalies," major differences between this bank and others of its size and type and location, and major changes of policy with regard to the composition of a bank's funding or its assets.

It was not a popular change. "When I first got here," said

John Heimann, Smith's successor, "I heard a hell of a lot of criticism from the bankers—'I don't need a policy statement to run my bank; my board knows our policies.'" (The criticisms were not entirely unjust: Barnett Banks' Guy Botts spoke sarcastically of the examiners "trying to find out if your people know what they're doing.") And the Comptroller's new system of examination has obviously been something less than a triumph: the computer could tell you that Seafirst or Continental or National Bank of Michigan was rapidly expanding its energy portfolio, and the management could tell you why it had embarked on this adventure. Still, in the absence of the old-fashioned loan-by-loan sort of bank examination, the Comptroller might not find out that the borrowers were taking the banks for a ride. Because Colonial Bank in Waterbury, Connecticut told the examiner it was making all those shipping loans to Greeks as a matter of deliberate growth policy, the Comptroller let nine figures of such loans pile up untended and uncriticized in the vaults of a middling-sized ($1.2 billion) bank.

The new examination procedures, however, provided information of the kind that stockholders are entitled to know. Like Volcker, Heimann retained a sense that confidence in the banks might be fragile; but as a man whose background was in investment rather than commercial banking, he could see that the SEC had a point. Once Isaac had come to power at the FDIC and Conover had taken over the Comptroller's job, voices were heard within the Financial Institutions Examination Council itself that disclosure was the necessary reverse side of the coin of deregulation. Without backing from the other regulators, the Fed was not prepared to go to the mat with the SEC, even on so delicate a matter as the SEC's insistence in 1982 that the banks publish the extent of their exposure in individual foreign countries if their loans in a country grew to be more than 1% of their total loans. This did not tell the potential purchaser of a bank stock all he might need to know. It did not tell him, for example, what proportion of the foreign loans were guaranteed by an agency of the U.S. government, what proportion were to divisions of multinational companies, to foreign private companies, to foreign governments. And it did not say anything at all about off-the-books risks like the bank's contingent exposure under letters of credit that foreigners had used as guarantees when borrowing from others. But it was a good strong start. In 1983, by consensus, the Examinations Council went a step further down the disclosure road, agreeing that the three bank regulators would publish semiannually the "call reports" in which banks detail for their regulators where they stand with reference to all classes of creditors and debtors.

But for all its accomplishments, the Examinations Council was basically a talking society: each agency could go its own way—as, indeed, Conover and Isaac did in approving the sale of banks to brokerage houses, insurance companies, furniture chains, industrial conglomerates, and the like. The Depository Institutions Deregulation Committee was something else: it was a mini-legislature, and its votes were binding on all the agencies. And because the Comptroller did not have a vote, the banks had to live with the fact that three officials who had neither responsibility for nor contact with banking could make decisions that grossly affected all bank planning. There were indeed a number of votes, including the one that authorized SuperNow accounts, in which the Chairmen of the Fed and the FDIC found themselves an impotent minority of two.

What was most striking about DIDC as an institution was that the participants did not attempt to achieve agreement before their meetings, which had to be held in public, under the general provisions of the "sunshine" legislation of the 1970s. Nobody knew before a meeting what the committee might do, and the discussions were often acerbic. At the start, the committee attempted to hedge each relaxation of the rules, and bankers grumbled that the output of the Deregulation Committee was a stream of ever more abstruse regulations. But increasingly, with the passage of time, the committee's decisions were influenced by Treasury Secretary Don Regan's strong if simpleminded faith in deregulation per se. By mid-1983 the only controls that survived were those prohibiting payment of interest on commercial demand deposits (which were almost entirely the product of bank loans, anyway) and those limiting the interest that could be paid on passbook accounts (a monstrous unfairness to the mostly lower-middle-class and elderly holders of these accounts, but a necessity if the S&Ls were to retain some low-cost money to see them over the hump of their losses).

In theory, DIDC will go out of business when all interest-rate controls are lifted, but it will be surprising if Congress does not keep the institutions alive in some form to make the hard decisions on the depository and lending "products" that various institutions will be permitted to offer as technology bulldozes the barriers between the credit providers. Even if DIDC disappears, it will have made an extraordinary change in the relations of government and banking in the United States: it has put flesh and muscle on the conceptual bones created by Congress with the compendious description, "depository institution." As Richard Pratt said on his way out of FHLBB, "You used to be able to use the varying types of institution as a way to allocate credit. What DIDC has done means you can't do that anymore." Once all the depositories are authorized to offer the whole range of liability instruments on an equal footing, the government cannot, over time, restrict them to limited categories of assets. If the congressmen who voted for the 1980 act had known that this is what they were doing, the bill would have been shouted down without a vote.

Meanwhile, a White House committee involving the vice-president, the chairman of the SEC, and White House domestic policy staff as well as the banking regulators and the Treasury has been considering what new legislation should be proposed to rationalize government regulation of financial institutions in the next generation. The first shot out of this howitzer came in July 1983, with a general recommendation for major modifications of the holding-company acts and minor changes in Glass–Steagall, permitting banks to perform the entire range of financial services—including insurance, real estate brokerage and leasing, full-service stockbrokerage, mutual-funds management—with the single exception of corporate underwriting. By extension of the same principles, all financial-service institutions (but no others) would be made acceptable as proprietors of banks. As the companies that would be permitted to enter the banking business all operate without geographical restriction, there is a clear implication in this recommendation that the Douglas Amendment should go on the dustheap of history, but nobody is saying that in public.

On January 31st, 1984, the vice-president's task force reached agreement, more or less, on a thorough restructuring of the bank regulatory apparatus. The push is for the creation of a Federal Banking Commission to take over all the functions of the Comptroller of the Currency and many tasks now performed by the Federal Reserve and the FDIC. Holding companies, except for the twenty largest, would become the responsibility of this commission rather than the Fed, and the FDIC would cease to perform its own examinations. To the fury of the state Banking supervisors, the Fed would be given some amorphous authority over all state-chartered banks. S&Ls with more than a certain percentage of their assets in the form of mortgages would continue to enjoy the indulgent regulation of the Federal Home Loan Bank Board (as would some thousands of small country banks), but those which take more uninhibited advantage of their new powers would become wards of the Banking Commission. The Federal Reserve is fighting against any diminution of its regulatory authority (the blow to "non-bank banks" in December was a preemptive strike on the attempt by the task force to limit its authority over bank holding companies), and no one can tell what Congress will do in an election year when so many Political Action Committees with such rich treasuries are interested in the outcome. The likely result should be a kind of DIDC writ large: a Commission whose members will be expected to represent constituencies of the different kinds of depository institutions, with a unified staff and a wholesome respect for the powers of the state banking authorities. A great deal would depend on how such a Commission is structured (the relative powers of its chairman and mere commissioners), and on the individuals appointed to the jobs. Congress could easily make the regulatory structure less clumsy without making it more relevant.

5

In the first months of 1983, the nation's community banks produced what looked like an awesome display of political power. In response to a newly imposed withholding tax on interest payments to depositors, they persuaded 22 million Americans to write their congressmen and senators and demand its repeal even before it came into effect. The rights and wrongs of this situation take more disentangling than the intrinsic importance of the incident justifies. Briefly, the banks were right to be mad at the government for loading on them the costs of an operation much more complicated than the Internal Revenue Service, a bunch of lawyers who live in a fantasy world of their own devising, could begin to imagine. Day-of-deposit to day-of-withdrawal accounts with daily compounding of dividends do not lend themselves easily to withholding. Consumers were hornswoggled into believing that they shared the banks' grievance at the tax, which had little to do with them except to the extent that the billion-plus dollars it would have cost the banks every year to comply with the new rules would have come from the pockets of the small saver. And the president and the furious Republican Senate leadership displayed in stereophonic high-fidelity the fact that once somebody goes on the federal payroll, whatever his ideology or politics, he begins looking for ways to lay the costs of his programs on anything but his budgeted appropriations.

The fact that the banks could tap wells of resentment against the government and the tax system does not mean they can promote their own interests effectively in Congress. In fact, the banking industry rarely has a unified set of interests.

"There are the ten percent of the banks that control seventy-eight percent of the assets," John Heimann said while Comptroller, "and then there are all the others. That's the *real* dual banking system in the United States." Willis Alexander, the genial head of the American Bankers Association, asked what position his group had taken on an issue before Congress, said cheerfully, "We came down so hard on both sides of that one, you couldn't possibly guess where we stood." And on those occasions when a unified banking industry does stand against the insurance agents, the realtors, the home builders, or even the stockbrokers, it tends to get nothing or little from Congress: the playing fields remain tilted.

The banks do better in the states, where they can promise jobs and competitive advantages vis-à-vis some other state. A number of states have passed "Merrill Lynch laws" limiting the banking activities of brokerage firms. Delaware has all but eliminated taxes on giant banks to lure their data-related activities down from Philadelphia and New York. South Dakota gave Citibank tax breaks, the abolition of usury ceilings, and a new banking law permitting a South Dakota-chartered bank to enter the insurance business. To all intents and purposes, Maryland abandoned banking regulation so far as it affected the out-of-state operations of its own or others' banks. In New England, state governments, preparing for the end of geographical restrictions on banks and anxious to assure that their own banks will then be large enough and strong enough to fight off New York's, have established a more-or-less common market in which a bank chartered by one of the six states can open offices in any or all of the other five. (In December 1983, Citicorp sued to enjoin the application of this legislation, arguing that the New Englanders were subverting the commerce clause of the Constitution.) For the same reasons, Pennsylvania, which once rigidly separated the Philadelphia and Pittsburgh markets for banking services, has not only permitted but encouraged the large banks in the two cities to join forces.

Still, the fact is that the revolution in banking has been channeled less by state or national lawmakers than by regulators, who are operating at the edge of their authority, or beyond it. Congress acts, Frank Morris of the Boston Fed said, "only to ratify what the market has done, simply because it's too difficult to try to reverse it." There are, after all, limits on what laws can do when they seek to control how people handle money, which knows no home and feels neither geographic nor institutional loyalties.

The future of banking is up for grabs now not because the rules are changing, but because the technology of delivering financial services is changing. Buffeted by competing demands, ignorant of both the economics and the practicalities of the situation, Congress waits for things to become so desperate that the competitors find it easier to compromise than to function within a legal order that has become largely irrelevant. But that compromise will almost certainly reflect what has already happened rather than what will or should happen—and will probably have little to do with the public interest in the functioning of this market that affects all other markets.

Seeking to put logic and experience behind Paul Volcker's "instinct that there's something special about a bank," E. Gerald Corrigan, president of the Federal Reserve Bank of Minneapolis, wrote in his 1982 report that "the case for segregating *essential* banking functions into an identifiable class of institutions is every bit as powerful today as it was in the 1930s." But in the 1930s these functions, which relate mostly to the maintenance of liquidity in the economy and the operation of the payments system, could not be performed by any institution other than a bank, and that made segregating easy. It will not be easy, and may not be possible, today. Adjusting regulation to reality requires first an understanding that reality cannot be adjusted to regulation, and then the further understanding that market forces cannot be the sole determinant of the creation and use of what is the only government-made commodity. Everybody has a lot of work to do.

12

THE FUTURE
OF BANKING

I grew up in the Depression, saw all those banks converted to bowling alleys," said Frank Morris, president of the Federal Reserve Bank of Boston, sitting in the president's office on the upper level of the two-story executive suite atop his bank's glamorous new building. "It's going to happen again."

"I don't think banks are going to die of bad loans," said George Mitchell, formerly governor and now consultant at the Federal Reserve Board in Washington, thumbs hooked under his waistband as he prowled his office overlooking Virginia Avenue in the new wing of the Fed. "I think they're going to die of old age."

"I used to think the banks would just disappear, like the brontosaurus," said James McDermott, head of a staff of forty-five bank analysts at Keefe, Bruyette & Wood, the leading broker/dealer in bank stocks, gazing over the Hudson from his office in the World Trade Center. "But I don't believe that anymore."

1

In late 1982, being in Los Angeles on other matters but working on this book, I checked into the Beverly Wilshire Hotel (the other matters were paying the expenses) about an hour before I had an appointment with Stuart Davis of Great Western Savings & Loan, which also had an address on Wilshire Boulevard in Beverly Hills, a couple of thousand digits lower. Fresh off an airplane, I felt a need to stop sitting down and decided I would walk from the hotel to Great Western's free-form glass tower. This was a mistake: I was dogged for months by the asthmatic complications of a three-mile walk down Wilshire Boulevard on a mild Los Angeles day. But the walk was instructive, as a demonstration of how dependent on retail banking urban real estate has become. Two-thirds of the occupied storefronts on this stretch of Wilshire Boulevard (which is not where the action is in Beverly Hills) were banks and lavish S&Ls. I mentioned my observation to Davis, who made a face and nodded and agreed that at least half of those storefronts—he thought three-quarters—would be abandoned by their tenants before this decade ends.

"Why should a man go to a bank?" George Mitchell inquired rhetorically in 1979. "I don't go to my insurance company. I don't have to go to a bank to get cash. We have a credit union here in this building"—the reference is to the Federal Reserve Building, and the idea of the Fed's credit union competing successfully against the banks is a very nice touch. But the point is certainly well taken, even more certainly five years after it was made.

It is insane for people to stand on lines before bank tellers to deposit their paychecks when the technology not only exists but has become routine for the direct deposit of payrolls. Cash machines at the workplace or the supermarket or out on the street supply cash at least as conveniently as a teller. As point-of-sale terminals become more common, there will be less need for cash, anyway—and the clerk in the store will have all the equipment needed to accept deposits from a customer while debiting his purchase. In an age of credit cards and overdraft privileges, people can—and increasingly do—arrange any lines of credit they may need by filling out forms at home and mailing them in. Elaborate but inexpensive computer software permits householders with personal computers or videotex receivers to access their bank accounts—and none of that paraphernalia will really be needed in the future, if all people wish to do is check their accounts or even pay their bills: with fiber optics, voice-and-data lines, electronic switching, and a twelve-button touch-tone pad on the phone, the rudiments of home banking can be provided even if the customer can't afford or doesn't want to purchase or rent fancy equipment. Why go to the bank? And if people don't go to the bank, what is the point of all those offices?

To what extent, indeed, do the forward-looking banks want depositors? Morgan Guaranty, the most admired American bank, has long chosen to fund itself almost exclusively with corporate deposits, trust account spillovers, and purchased money. In the mid-1970s, Bankers Trust, unable to compete with Citibank and Manufacturers and Chase in the retail market in New York (its slogan, "You'll find a banker at Bankers Trust," may have been the most ineffective selling pitch of the decade), reversed course entirely, sold off almost 100 branches, closed a couple of dozen that couldn't be sold, and emerged from the crucible the most profitable of the nation's ten largest banks as measured by return on equity. (Management improved a lot in the process, too.) In a moment of pique a few years ago, Walter Wriston of Citicorp threatened to abandon his banking license to gain access to the business ventures the law and the Fed forbade him. It was not entirely an idle threat: only 20% of Citicorp's assets are funded by deposits in domestic branches, which is all he would have to give up.

"The commercial banks went into the consumer business for the cheap money," John Heimann said while Comptroller of the Currency. "Now the cheap money is gone, they will go into other businesses." Many large banks have already begun the process of withdrawing their services from smaller depositors, usually by imposing high minimum-balance requirements. "We looked at the data," said chairman Charles Zwick of Southeast Banking Corp. in Miami. "Seventy-five percent of our profits came from ten percent of the customers. So we drove out the low-balance loss-leader accounts." Citibank, which has calluses where its bump of public relations ought to be, decided to accomplish this result by denying smaller depositors access to tellers in the branches: they could continue to keep their money at Citibank, if they were very good, but they would have to use the machines. Newspapers, consumer groups, politicians, and the like, landed on the bank with hobnailed boots, and the unwashed were again allowed access to tellers. But there are three separate lines for teller windows at Citibank branches:— *very* long for ordinary people, moderate for CitiExpress customers with more than $5,000 on deposit, short for Priority Service Customers with more than $25,000 in the bank—and that should do the trick in short order.

This may not be the right way to go. "It shouldn't be assumed you can't make money off the mass market," Stephen LaTour of Northwestern University told Julie Salamon of *The Wall Street Journal*. "McDonald's makes a whole lot of money selling cheap food to lots of people." In an age of electronic banking—the only way banks can cut their costs—universality yields benefits beyond the profitability of individual accounts. The corporate customer cannot arrange automatic depositing of payrolls (and thus the bank cannot avoid hiring tellers to cash paychecks written by the corporate customers, who are certainly not going to undertake the expense and danger of returning to the old days of pay envelopes) unless the employees have bank accounts. Not everyone agrees that the marginal customer imposes heavy burdens on the bank. "We run a fixed-cost system," says Robert Thaler of Security Pacific in Los Angeles. "If I get rid of your account, what do I save? The postage in sending you the statement. It's better to bring down the costs, eliminate the paper."

It is better still to get people to pay for things they now get for free. Zwick noted that his rival, Barnett Banks of Florida, "kept all the low-balance customers, and they are service-charging the hell out of them, and getting away with it." Thaler envisions a future for Security Pacific: "I get a package to the consumer. For ten dollars a month, you get ten checks, unlimited electronic transfers—including telephone bill-paying services, credit card, debit card, point-of-sale terminals, cash machines. You get a printout every month—you don't get check return, that's extra. But you're happy, you stay with the bank. It costs me six bucks, I'm happy." Thaler envisions a future in which Security Pacific continues to maintain a network of hundreds of branches, but much smaller than most of those it operates today. "You plan the branch for the customer: transaction account, savings account, overdraft account, brokerage service. You want to be convenient to the customer. You do your business lending out of other offices." Thaler hailed the decisions by Wells Fargo and Bank of America to cut back on their branches (in Bank of America's case, by no less than 200 offices). "They're going to make me rich," he said. "Where do they think they're going to get the high-quality assets they'll need without a presence in the community?"

There is a hole in this argument, well-concealed because the bankers really don't know it's there. What if the credit unions, or Sears or Penney, Merrill Lynch or Shearson/ American Express or Prudential–Bache, National Data, National Cash Register, American Bell, or General Electric can offer similar services for less than $10 a month? What is the importance of the convenience of a branch if there are shared ATMs in the supermarkets? Security Pacific offers me a bundle of services, but suppose I don't need the full bundle? ADP` dominates payroll processing and telephone bill-paying, runs shared ATM networks for banks, and is one of the organizers of a homebanking/information service collaborative. Suppose ADP comes along and offers the customer complete bill-paying and cash services for $5 a month (no checks, which are the expensive part of the bundle; but you don't need checks if you've got a complete bill-paying service).

Suppose I want *more* than Thaler's bundle—a Merrill Lynch Cash Management Account, plus the chance to write checks against the security of a second mortgage on my house, with interest charges on the loan at a rate only two percentage points above broker's call rates? Suppose I don't like machines—lots of people don't—and I find out I can do banking business evenings and weekends at the First Nationwide Savings offices already in being at Penney's, or quasi-banking business at the financial services centers at Sears? Very cheaply, too, because they have other reasons to pull me into the building.

Can the banks compete? "Sears and AT&T," said William Bolleran of Houston's First City, "are very narrow-margin businesses. They understand retailing; banks don't." Until they gingerly dipped their toes into the overdraft pool in the 1970s, banks found it hard to win business from finance companies (which borrowed their money mostly from banks until the mid-1960s: it should have been easy to whomp them). Though the merchants and consumers involved were their customers, the banks abdicated to Visa and MasterCard the safe-and-sure part of the income from retail credit. (They even, George Mitchell comments sadly, "gave away the name of the bank.") With a few notable exceptions, banks have been unable to sell data-processing services at a profit, unless the prices were negotiated privately on a correspondent basis as a trade-off for deposits. Citi gave Automatic Data Processing its payroll business to get rid of a loser. In electronic funds transfer, the banks have spent their money on equipping themselves to move high-value items through FedWire and CHIPS, on the controlled disbursement services that yield float or fees in large packages from a few customers—and on the ATMs, for which they made no charge.

"Bankers are inherently cheap," said a man who is a major supplier to hundreds of them and would not appreciate having his name on the quote. "They'll do anything they can to operate on other people's money—they understand that. I can name five companies that have lost $500 million each doing things they were encouraged to do by the banks, and then the banks didn't buy anything. These are the bluebloods of American industry—IBM, Burroughs, National Cash—so now they move only if they can see a nonbank market." Paul Henderson of the New York Fed feels the problem is systemic and temporary: "I haven't seen a bank yet that has a handle on its own 'on-us' [internal] telecommunications. They can't coordinate their own functions, and they're just not ready to deal electronically with the outside world." Eventually the banks, too, will learn to walk and chew gum at the same time, and then they'll be ready to take on the world.

Maybe. "It is possible," David Hopton of the Bank of England notes dryly in his cross-cultural 1983 study of *Payments Systems* for the Bank for International Settlements, "that banks may begin to turn their competitive energies from non-price competition in the infrastructure used to deliver payments services and toward competition in the business of financial intermediation." Banks have been able to get away with being slow and insensitive to their markets because anyone who wished to compete with them had to duplicate their infrastructure, which gave the government plenty of time to ride to their rescue. Now technology permits competitors to short-circuit banking systems and supply services from outside. To the extent that these competitors need access to the big switch at the Federal Reserve, they can get it from any pliant bank (and with 19,000 "end points" for Fed services, any of which can be made electronic for about $200 a month, there are sure to be pliant banks), even if Paul Volcker wins his war to clamp a permanent moratorium on the acquisition of banks by companies that are not banks.

The most obvious example of the banks' failure is the Automated Clearing House, which seems to have been deliberately structured to minimize its competition with the checking system in which the Fed and the banks have invested so heavily. As a result, the shared ATM networks that will play so important a role in the future of banking for consumers will be run by outsiders, from data processors to supermarket chains. Visa, expert at low-cost clearing, can run a nationwide point-of-sale system. Penney can win the contract to process Gulf Oil's credit-card business. The banks have been unable to seize the opportunity to carry electronic banking services on the chassis of the information nets created to serve law firms, accountants, small broker/dealers, and other professionals. These were the natural customers for "home banking," but they could not be served efficiently unless the banks did the marketing work of "prenotification" so they could pay their bills and receive payments electronically.

Competitors from Merrill Lynch to General Electric to AT&T will be well placed to fight the banks for the new electronically based correspondent business that will arise between the financial markets and the small institutions—the thrifts, credit unions, stockbrokers, and mortgage bankers. The question is whether the banks will be able to gear the services they offer to customer needs rather than to their own internal requirements—and then produce them at a profit when their customers can turn to alternate sources of supply. Experience to date argues that they will remain high-cost, inflexible providers, with a diminishing share of the financial services market, not only to individuals and companies (where they have always faced competition) but to other financial institutions (where they have long been unchallenged, except by each other and the Feds).

The banks' "ability to provide payment services," David Hopton writes, "has been an important factor distinguishing them from their competitors and enabling them to put together, in-house, the most convenient package of financial services available on the market. . . .[But] payment services can be operated on a basis other than that of demand deposits. . . . their operation is essentially an information process capable of computerization. . . . Non-banks are beginning to use the provision of payment services in much the same way as banks have done; they, too, now seem to regard the provision of payment services as an instrument of competition. . . . The configuration of some payment systems could be a residual outcome of competition for the financial assets of the personal sector. . . . History tends to show that more efficient practices and institutions have emerged after periods of more intense competition, but it also shows that the transition has seldom been orderly. . . ." In other words, it isn't only the banks that have to worry.

2

Though dealings with individuals have created an increasing share of the assets of the larger banks (46% of Citibank's total domestic loans in 1982, and—astonishingly—more than a sixth of its foreign loans), the basic business of the banks continues to be lending to businesses. And for the big banks, inescapably, the business has been one of lending to big businesses. That was what happened on the fortieth floor, where lending officers perched in handsomely furnished rooms with splendid views and with secretaries to handle the phone calls and begin the process—the endless process—of moving the paper. The perches were brief: "line" officers spent their time on the road, traveling first-class because they represented their bank, staying at the best hotels, renting much more than minimal cars, visiting the customers, wining and dining and golfing, establishing the "relationships" that involved so much of deposits, so much of fees, collection services, disbursement services, foreign services, loans. Presumably these officers also kept an eye on how the customer's business was going, how much credit they could handle, at what rates.

Each officer had a "calling" schedule, kept in touch, tried to monitor his customers' contacts with other banks. If the customer seemed to be doing well, it was a plus for the line officer, inside the bank. He was a salesman for the bank's money at the customer company, a salesman for the company at the bank. And he was the liaison for the company at the bank: if they needed forward pounds, they would call the line officer who handled the account, and he would check the trading floor and call back, then handle the order if the company liked the price. The line officer was a "generalist," on temporary assignment, usually very personable and WASP: Jews and Italians and East Europeans didn't mind dealing with Protestant bankers, but corporate executives might be annoyed, it was thought, by kikes or dagos from the bank.

Some of this has changed: women and ethnic minorities (though rarely blacks) have been assigned as calling officers, mostly because businessmen have grown less bigoted. In some industries, the banks have hired or trained specialists who will remain in this area of expertise for years. But the name of the game remains "relationships." The more services a bank provides to a customer, the more willing it is to lend him money when money is tight, the better his position in negotiating rates, the smaller the unit charge for any specific service. Chase as much as Len Weil of Manufacturers in Los Angeles would love to have borrowers do all their banking (personal banking, too) at Chase.

But Weil's customers have only checking accounts: they

make deposits and payments, borrow money, pay interest, maybe buy some Treasury bills, maybe make the bank the trustee of their estate. It's not terribly complicated in a well-run middle-sized bank for management to sit down and look at the accounts every so often and come to a view of whether this customer relationship is profitable or not. If not, somebody goes off and tells the customer that the number of transactions in the account is too big for the average balance maintained, and a fee will have to be paid—or the interest rate on the loan will have to go up. Changing banks is a nuisance for the small business, and the bank will have to push the small businessman pretty hard before he starts from scratch with somebody else, even assuming that his cash position is such that he can pay off his former banker and go out with a clean slate.* One of the more ominous developments in recent months, from the banks' point of view, is the effort by Dean Witter to win the accounts of small businesses and professional offices. "Ordinarily," says the Dean Witter ad, "as a small business, you cannot earn interest on balances in checking accounts. Now, your balances can be earning income with Dean Witter's new Active Assets Account for Businesses, Non-Profit Organizations and Institutions . . . Need extra cash? Simply write a check or charge purchases on your VISA card—and a loan is automatically made against the marginable securities in your brokerage account. There's no application—no red tape. And *you* decide when and how much to repay. . . . Your Dean Witter Account Executive can help you keep abreast of a wide range of

---

*Sometimes it can be done: George Brockway, chairman of the publishing house of W. W. Norton, reports that Chase gave him a sticky time during the money crunch of 1979, though his firm had been a steady customer for forty years, with up to $10 million outstanding. At first the bank delayed his financing requests, then finally consented to lend him money at three percentage points over an already outrageous prime. Norton recast its way of doing business, paid down all its loans from Chase, and now relates to the bank solely as a purchaser of their CDs, if they have the day's best rate. It was a particularly admirable accomplishment if one reflects that Norton was at this period publishing a book of mine, which bombed.

financial services. . . ." Most small business and professional borrowers from banks have positive asset positions (they'd have a lot of trouble borrowing if they didn't). Dean Witter's service enables them to continue to be financial intermediaries, as they wish to be (that is, they wish to be in debt with their assets as security, rather than net out their positions) in a more convenient and comfortable process than anything presently offered by their bank.

The work done by a big bank for a big customer is so extensive that it's difficult for the bank to get a handle on whether or not the account is profitable. The key fact about the development of banking in the 1970s was that the corporate treasurer often came to know more about what he was paying his bank(s) and what he was getting for his money, than the bank(s) knew about what they were charging and what they were giving. "We all developed these cash-management systems for corporate customers," said chairman John LaWare of Boston's Shawmut Bank. "They've become very sophisticated; they overmanage." George Mitchell commented that if you really wanted to know how big banks ran in the 1980s, you had to become a fly on the wall in the meetings between the treasurers of the big corporations and the senior officers of the banks: "So much for each payment in, so much for each payment out, so much credit for balances . . ."

Morgan's James Byrne denies that the banks are necessarily at a disadvantage in these negotiations. "People have been talking since I came to the bank in the early sixties that banks don't know about pricing, and it's not true. I know more about my cost structure and prices than General Motors. Where bankers are bad is at collecting the bills—you hear all these arguments about the value of balances."

In the past, an undeterminable share of bank earnings came from this sector's monopoly rents on the payments system. When loans to big companies are unbundled from the bank's package of services, the market can handle them more cheaply than the banks: commercial paper rates are usually a percentage point or so below the bank's announced prime. (The gap looks larger, but the prime is a "simple" rate and commercial paper sells on a discount basis.) Starting with Aetna and Prudential and Travelers in the mid-1970s, the insurance companies have opened intermediate-term credit operations that underbid the banks for middle-market business. General Electric Credit, Westinghouse Credit, and financing companies like C.I.T. and Commercial Credit (which own banks), Walter Heller (now absorbed by Fuji Bank of Japan), and The Associates (a Gulf + Western subsidiary, and thus sister company to a bank) have grown in the industrial lending market more rapidly than the banks.

Banks benefited for years from the demand-deposit base on which interest was not paid (by law) and from the time-deposit base on which interest payments were limited by government order. While nobody was watching, they became, in the absence of insurance, no more creditworthy than other enterprise: uninsured negotiable bank CDs of more than $100,000 often trade on the market to yield roughly the same rates as prime commercial paper. And the perceived value of government insurance seems to have diminished very substantially in an era when the public believes that the government really won't let anybody fail: when the banks were freed of interest-rate restraints in December 1982, they had to pay more than the money-market funds to garner money in the new accounts. Initially, this imbalance between rates paid on the uncontrolled bank deposits and rates paid on the funds could be explained by the need to overcome inertia—but six months after the introduction of the new accounts, the banks still seemed to find it necessary to outbid (or at least match) the finds. There was no special menace in this differential in spring 1983, when the yield slope was strongly positive: even the most liquid bank has an asset structure considerably longer than the law permits a money-market fund, and can afford to pay more. But if 1981 returns—and it may—the need to keep the money in these accounts will clobber the profitability of the industry.

Indeed, a relatively trivial rise in interest rates put bank profits under pressure in the second half of 1983. Money-market mutuals in upstairs offices, using the telephone and the mails, are inherently cheaper funds-gatherers than banking offices can ever be.

Comparative advantage in the cost of funds was what made it possible for banks to offer attractive packages both to borrowers and service purchasers. Take that advantage away, and it is hard to see how the banks can carry the burden of their bureaucracy, redundant offices, sometimes antiquated equipment, often inappropriate software.

3

In the next decade, the strength in banking will be in the regional banks, which will grow substantially, partly at the expense of the money-center institutions. The failure of the international banks to compel the regionals to continue their Fed Funds sales to Brazilian banks marked a watershed in the relations of these institutions. This development was unexpected— when I asked Comptroller C. T. Conover whether he, like the Fed, was leaning on the regionals to provide funds for Brazil, he said, "We have been asked to apply pressure, but we won't. The big private bankers have plenty of clout. They can say, 'Remember that correspondent relationship we *used* to have.'"

But by 1983 the value of that correspondent relationship was greater for the international bank: the regional had the access to deposits, the relations with the nation's growing industries, and for international purposes, its own offices in London and/or the Bahamas. They even had some advantages in approaching foreign money: "International customers," says the head of one of the regionals, "like the idea of having some money in Cincinnati. They say, 'If the world is coming to an end, I want to be in Cincinnati, because the news will take six months to get there.'" (One banker reports that the Polish central bank has money squirreled away in the form of Fed Funds sold to U.S. regional banks.) And, of course, they have their own, regional boards of directors, who look at the international banks' agonies in Mexico, Brazil, and Argentina and tell any bank president who suggests increasing their exposure in such places that throwing good money after bad is unsound practice in banking, as in any other business.

Charles Zwick of Miami's Southeast Banking Corp., a brisk, bald Yankee who was the first in Florida to grab the holding-company ball and run with it, sees the driving force of recent years as "the migration of economic activity away from the Northeast. The New York banks saw that, and in the 1960s they went overseas. They played that hand out, so now you get the upper tier banks looking south. 'Just trying to serve our customers,' they say. When we had to put together the credit for our new headquarters building," Zwick said, looking affectionately across the street to where his own skyscraper was rising, "and we didn't want to be the lead bank ourselves, we didn't even consider going to New York; we went to Texas Commerce."

Having proceeded from the Comptroller's office to the job of chairman of the executive committee at the investment banking house of Becker–Paribas, John Heimann saw a future in which "twenty-five to fifty financial institutions, not all of them banks, will dominate the financial services industry worldwide." Maybe so. With four giants each to contribute, the Europeans have a stake in such an outcome. Certainly there is something awesome about the size of the giant American banks and their rate of growth since World War II. John LaWare of Boston's Shawmut is an alumnus of New York's Chemical: "When I joined in 1953, the total footings were $1.8 billion." In 1983 Chemical was a $50 billion bank; the thirty years had produced a growth rate of 11.7%, compounded. And the great banks have the resources to acquire some of the regionals, if McFadden and Douglas restrictions are lifted. But nobody has answered the question of how the money-center banks can expand profitably at a time when their stocks sell at a discount of 30% from book value.

Of the ten bank holding companies that showed the greatest total return to investors in 1972–82 in *Fortune*'s 1983 compilation of the hundred largest banks, the only two that were among the thirty largest were Texas Commerce (the 19th) and Edmond Safra's maverick Republic New York (the 29th), with only 27% of its assets in the form of loans. Of the others, one was in Pittsburgh, one in Seattle, one in Dallas, three in Boston, and two in Philadelphia. Before the stockholders in these banks will sell, the giants will have to pay multiples of earnings much greater than the market gives their own stocks. Moreover, it is far from certain that the international banks could operate such subsidiaries profitably. In 1975, when New York State released its international banks from the restrictions that had confined their deposit-taking offices to the city, all of them, with the possible exception of Chemical and Bank of New York, lost money on their upstate expansion. By 1979 (before such activity came to be fashionable) they were closing more branches than they were opening.

When Citicorp began wholesale distribution of its Visa cards in North Carolina, Wachovia's John Medlin reacted scornfully with the comment that "We can collect bills in Winston–Salem a lot better than they can." To the extent that banking profitability in the next decade will be a function of credit judgment—and the view here is that this will be the largest single factor—the international bank, forever seduced by the big deal, trying to economize on the costs of keeping in touch, staffed with lending officers looking to move on to managerships in Paris and Hong Kong, is likely to be in hot water much more often than the market likes. There is no need to go abroad to find examples of careless behavior. Just look at Penn Square or Drysdale, Nucorp (run by a man who had already gone bust once in questionable circumstances) or Baldwin–United (with its easily discoverable Mickey Mouse bookkeeping through its insurance subsidiaries: how wise the Fed was to force Baldwin's divestiture of its banking subsidiaries before the empire collapsed)—or United American Bank of Knoxville, an essentially crooked operation with which Chemical Bank had got buddy-buddy to a greater extent than has yet been revealed.

In any event, the international banks will be hobbled by their unwise foreign lending of 1979–81. There are stigmata all over the 1982 annual reports, if one cares to look. The largest percentage category of asset growth at most of the big banks was "banker's acceptances." At Citibank, net loans rose by $3 billion, or just under 5%, in 1982; customers' acceptance liability rose by $3.3 billion, or just under 51%. At Bank of America, loans rose by $2.7 billion, or 3.8%; customers' acceptance liability by $1.4 billion, or 26%. Banker's acceptances are used almost exclusively in normal times to finance world trade, and world trade shrank in 1982. What is happening here is an abuse of the acceptance instrument as a means of making term loans both the bank and the borrower do not wish to categorize in this way. ("We are all being induced to close our eyes to loose banking practices," growled Paul Volcker.) And the banks are leaning on the accountants to exclude acceptances from assets (and liabilities) to make the return on assets look bigger. At Citibank, loans from domestic offices to financial institutions more than doubled in 1982, and a footnote mentions that in this context "financial institutions" includes loans to governments and official institutions (i.e., the nationalized Mexican banks); loans to financial institutions from overseas offices were up $700 million. Between the two categories, they accounted for half the loan growth in the Citibank portfolio—and this is the very risky stuff the regional banks wouldn't touch.

In his annual report for 1982 Anthony Solomon, president of the Federal Reserve Bank of New York, noted almost plaintively that reported loan loss experience was much worse at the regional banks than it was at the New York multinationals. "But the greatest asset quality imponderable for these banks,"

374

he then admitted, "—some of their loans to developing countries—are not included in nonperforming assets." If half your loans are abroad, and your auditors and regulators allow you to continue accruing interest from those loans though it isn't being earned, your credit judgment looks pretty good. The fact is that the regionals were dealing with their problems, helping troubled debtors survive by reducing or even eliminating their interest liabilities, at a penalty to their reported profits. With a few honorable exceptions, the international banks were being permitted—even encouraged—to fake it.

The IMF has said, soothing people, that "most" of the loans to developing countries were for investment purposes (in other words, if the investments were chosen decently, they will earn out the loans) rather than for consumption purposes (where they form an uncompensated burden on the future earnings of a poor economy). Let us say that only 25% of such lending was comsumption-oriented "balance of payments" lending, that only 25% of that will cease to generate revenues, and that the international banks, on the average, get 15% of their total interest receipts from loans to developing countries. The reduction in revenues would then be 0.94%, which would knock down pretax profits by anywhere from one-fifth to one-third. If the banks prudently wrote off, say, half the nonaccruing loans at a rate of 10% a year, profits would drop another 7% or so. Even if these realities are denied, and the regulators permit the international banks to continue accruing interest on this junk in their financial statements, the drain of constant borrowing to substitute the bank's credit for that of countries no longer creditworthy will suck strength from these giants, year after year. Interestingly, the stock market appears to be applying a discount of roughly these dimensions in valuing the shares of the giant banks, which at this writing sell for five or six times reputed earnings, while the stocks of the regional banks trade at seven to eight times earnings.

Where the law permits, the regionals have been merging with each other—especially in Pennsylvania, New England,

and Florida—and acquiring smaller banks around their territories, especially in Texas and, again, Florida, and Missouri. Most significant regionals are already too big for the international banks to acquire by any means other than a stock swap, which can be done only to the disadvantage of the stockholders in the international bank. As they grow, the regional banks tend to displace the New York, Chicago, and San Francisco banks as the leading financial agent for even the largest enterprises in their territory. And because all politics reduces to local politics, their influence in Washington far exceeds that of the giants.

In the intermediate term, then, the prospects are for a relative shrinkage of the money-center banks, an accelerating growth at the regional banks. They will become much more active in the money markets, where they will form a preferred tier for investors and purchasers of CDs. They will absorb—or perhaps franchise, which may be the best arrangement for all concerned—much of the army of community banks now scattered about the country, which will find it hard to operate alone in an environment where stockholders and retailers and money-market funds are competing for the deposits that have given them the money they lend. There will continue to be a banking presence in small towns and suburbs because only locally based offices can do the profitable small-business lending that supports community banks, and it will be cheaper to handle customers' telecommunications with financial services providers over short lines. But the presence of both local and regional banks will diminish on the streets simply because the ordinary banking office or banking branch has become a high-cost way of agglomerating funds, supplying cash, and making loans.

Even someone who sympathizes strongly with Paul Volcker's insistence that there is something unique about a bank must concede that nothing but history justifies a system that denies consumers the chance to deposit as well as cash their checks at the supermarket, that forces poor people either to pay high fees at banks or use expensive storefront check-chasing services, that seeks to deny to the quarter of the population that owns common stocks or the three-fifths that owns a house the right to pledge their assets as security for loans at institutions, brokerage houses, or the like, that do not call themselves banks.

Ultimately, the banks qua banks will recede from public view. Mortgages will be arranged by mortgage bankers operating through real estate brokers, with funds supplied in the bond market; personal loans will be overwhelmingly on the credit-card chassis; small businesses will borrow mostly from finance companies. Consumer banking transactions will be accomplished through telecommunications, at stores that are not exclusively money shops, at unimposing low-cost offices, some of them called banks, some called credit unions or S&Ls or loan companies.

This does not mean the banks are goners. Internationally, they will continue to intermediate between the generators of trade surpluses and the nations incurring deficits, so that the capital needs of the latter can be met—though this activity will never again occur on the scale of the 1970s. They will participate in a wider spectrum of financial activities and earn increasing fees. Domestically, to a large extent, they will own the finance companies and the mortgage bankers, and their credit facilities will back the credit cards. Their success or failure in these roles will be determined by their ability to run such operations more cheaply than the retailing chains, the stockbrokers, and insurance companies, the finance subsidiaries of the great industrial corporations that will all be in competition for this business. The real battle the banks must fight in the years ahead is the struggle to maintain primacy—even with government help, they can no longer hope for exclusivity—in the management of the switching system that all these nonbank providers of financial services will require. On the evidence available today, the banks will maintain their leading role in servicing wholesale transactions, the cash flows of the money markets and the great corporations, and the rest will gravitate to other data processors.

"The importance of the payments system, the risks involved, the compensation for them—that hasn't yet penetrated the armies of the CEOs at the banks," said James Boisi of Morgan Guaranty, who chaired the Reserve City Bankers study of payments systems in 1982. "I've put on dog-and-pony shows for the Senate and House Banking committees, the Federal Reserve Board, the Treasury, the Comptroller, the FDIC, *and* the banking community; but it hasn't penetrated." The bankers look on distributed data processing, packet switching, digital communications as a world they never made. But that is the real world of the future of banking, and the people who are making that world happen will gradually, inevitably—quietly, if we are lucky—come to control it.

4

In the larger view, banks, as we have known them, should be seen as creatures of a time when information was expensive. When computers first became important in the delivery of financial services, it appeared that they would be a factor for concentration, because the economies of scale from the use of giant mainframes with giant memories would sweep aside the benefits of decentralized decision-making. But with the exponential growth in telecommunications resources and the astonishing decline in the cost of units of processing, the most efficient systems are those that process and store remotely, communicating with the central processing unit only as necessary. Access to the sort of information once laboriously entered on bank ledgers is now cheap and widespread and will be even cheaper and less exclusive with the passage of time. Society was willing to pay high prices for banking services because only banks could do what the economy needed. Now, technologically, any number can play; and the old games with their rigid rules and limited participation are gone forever, whether or not the Federal Reserve gives its approval.

Anything that diminishes the costs of financial services is to be welcomed, for these costs are, in the end, a burden that must be carried by the producers of goods and services that more directly satisfy human needs and wants. But as we move to an era when cheap information permits financial intermediation through flexible, low-cost markets rather than ponderous, bureaucratic banks, we should be calculating the social and political costs of the change and seeking ways to minimize them.

The growth of the banks since World War II has been a blessing—one of few such—for the downtown areas of the nation's cities. Banks have built the ornaments of the skyline, rented and furbished the best storefront locations. The need to visit the bank has been a significant source of street life, without which the other storefronts perish. Because speed in moving pieces of paper to recipients has been crucial, banking operations have mostly been housed downtown, so the check that arrives at 9:30 can be got over to the clearinghouse by 10:00. As electronic operations take over, processing centers disperse to the periphery, where rents are cheaper. The competitors who will fight for what have been banking functions will not be downtown, and in any event will not employ as many people for these purposes as the banks did. The banks themselves, largely because of the competition, are ardently committed to reducing payroll. The impact on our already shaky urban downtowns—*all* of them—is likely to be considerable. The degree to which the cities are unprepared for this crisis can be measured by New York's recent masochistic increases in its already high real estate taxes on downtown commercial property. Out in the neighborhoods, community activists are beginning to concern themselves about what will happen to the shopping streets when the banks move out; typically, they are looking for ways to force the banks to stay (which can't be done), rather than organizing more modest credit union and S&L substitutes that might be able to survive on the locally available deposits and lending opportunities.

Rationalization imposes costs as well as offering benefits. As we move from our government-protected banking system to a competitive financial-services industry, the costs of operations will be transferred from the larger depositors to the smaller ones. At a guess, the breakpoint of a system where interest is paid on all deposits and service fees are charged for all withdrawals (plus a maintenance fee for the account) will come at about $2,000 for accounts in banks, perhaps $750 for accounts at S&Ls and credit unions. All those with accounts larger than that size will be better off than they were in the era of free checking; all those with accounts smaller than that size will be worse off. Much of this was unavoidable: just as the microwave and the satellite made it possible for lightly capitalized competitors to undercut long-distance telephone rates and force AT&T to eliminate the old subsidy from long distance to local telephony, the arrival of computer-based transaction-processing systems meant that banks to remain competitive would have to pay interest on deposits. In eliminating Reg Q, the government merely recognized that it gets cold in the winter.

In effect, the old order had done good by stealth, providing unintended subsidies to the less wealthy. Even in the area where social benefit as well as economic logic was claimed for the new order—home mortgages, long subsidized by inadequate interest payments on the savings of people less well off than the average home buyer—the initial results of deregulation were discouraging. The poor—by definition, poor in information as well as money—have kept their funds in fixed-rate savings accounts and have not benefited by the floating rates on certificates and money-market accounts, and the lower reaches of the home-buying market have been priced out of the chance to buy a house by higher rates. If the reduction in the costs of financial services through the introduction of competition implies an increase in the relative share of the GNP taken by the rentier class, deregulation will create costs in the form of a society perceived as less just while it generates benefits in the form of economic efficiency. Managing trade-offs of this kind is not something the political process has handled well, and the demand that government do something about them tends to produce irrational actions in legislatures.

The most serious and difficult of the problems created by the movement from banking to financial services is the damage to monetary policy as a tool for regulating economic activity. As late as fall 1980, an article in the *Harvard Business Review* could claim that the Federal Reserve was a "major proponent of deregulation." The Fed has learned better since. Its inability to find an acceptable definition of the money supply results in part from the development of interest-bearing checking accounts, which are neither all M–1 (transaction balances) or all M–2 (M–1 plus savings instruments). And the Fed must some-day consider the impact on the money supply of schemes that permit people to write checks against their stock-market holdings and the equity in their homes. The Fed's operations rest on the premise that the money supply can be controlled through requiring reserves against transaction accounts. If some un-known part of the value of a house can be used for transaction purposes at the owner's initiative, what does it mean to make a depository system keep reserves? What would be an adequate reserve against the equity in a home, and who would have to put it aside?

One of the oddities of the early 1980s was the rise of con-cern—in Congress, the White House, the press—over an al-leged unlimited power wielded by the unelected board mem-bers of the Federal Reserve. The real difficulty is the severe erosion of the Fed's powers. There was a time when the Fed could regulate "by lifted eyebrow," when a minor change in reserve requirements or the discount rate, a barely palpable push in the open market, would send bankers scurrying to do whatever it was the Fed wanted them to do. "Today," Volcker complained toward the end of 1982, "they're *proud* of the fact they're fighting us." To work its will, then, the Fed must get out front and tell the world what behavior it wants from the banks and the borrowers—and then push aggressively on all the markets until everyone falls in line or the economic situation changes enough (partly because of the Fed's actions) that the policies can be, must be, changed.

Attentive readers will have noted that I am no monetarist. The theory that a central bank can control the course of the economy through controlling the supply of money seems to me hopelessly out of touch with a real world in which people respond to such governmental restrictions by finding other ways to get their business done, monetizing credit instruments not previously used as money. Charles Goodhart of the Bank of England, after studying dramatic changes in the velocity of sterling M_3 (the Bank's tool) during the mid-1970s, proposed Goodhart's Law, which I have phrased as "Any monetary aggregate controlled by a central bank loses significance." (Geoffrey E. J. Dennis of the Bank for International Settlements states Goodhart's Law somewhat differently in his recent pamphlet on *Monetary Aggregates and Economic Activity:* "Growth of the target aggregates is distorted and that of broader concepts of money is artificially raised as a result of the adherence to a restrictive target path for narrow money." Thus do the journalist and the economist diverge in their perceptions of the world.)

But there can be no question that changes in the price level are *primarily* monetary phenomena, and that such changes have profound effects, varying over time, on the levels and the quality of economic activity. These effects are created, in large part, by the interest rates that derive from the plenitude or scarcity of the cheapest money to generate, which is the central bank's money. As the Fed can control the quantity of such money, it can control short-term interest rates; indeed, the moving floor from which all other rates now rise, formerly the rate on Treasury bills, has become the Fed Funds rate, which the Fed can pretty much manipulate at will through its open market operations.

When regulation by lifted eyebrow worked, the relationship between short-term rates and long-term rates was relatively predictable. Rising short-term rates drew money from longer-term investments, forcing up the interest rate on bonds; falling short-term rates made long-term lending more attractive and made money more easily available for capital formation. Today the yield slope changes shape too easily: not only the size, but the direction of the gaps between short-term and long-term rates has become unpredictable. Because it is the long-term rates that most seriously affect economic activity, the Fed's power over short-term rates has become less and less useful as a tool of governance.

We are dealing here with the erosion of the crucial middle ground between centrally planned and market economies. I have argued elsewhere, in a book called *Today and Tomorrow in America,* for government action in the economy that puts a thumb in the scale of market measurements, avoiding both the arrogance and impotence of office, both blind denial and supine acceptance of the often distasteful information generated by the most accurate and timely information system in any society. There must be some way for the markets to let the governments know that their policies are wrong without setting off the loose cannons of political process; there must be some way for the governments to tell the markets that they should seek a greater good for a greater number without imposing results that impoverish the society. The type example of the thumb-on-the-scale has always been the operation of the Federal Reserve System in controlling the creation of bank liabilities. If the central banks cannot influence efficiently what happens in the markets for the one commodity created by government itself, the theory of liberal democracy is in some trouble.

There was a genie in this bottle, and it got out: no way can Paul Volcker or Walter Wriston or Milton Friedman or James Tobin put it back. Fractional rather than full insurance of bank deposits is a good idea, and its time may have come; reallocating bank supervision to a smaller and more coherent body of regulators is a consummation devoutly to be wished; both the welfare state and the garrison state must get their deficits under control if we are to have any hope for honest money and economic growth over time; government economic policies must be related to the foreign-exchange markets in ways that keep relative currency values within hailing distance of purchasing-power parity. But none of this will matter much if we cannot structure sturdy domestic financial markets in which both euphoria and panic are rebuked, so that money can be made the servant rather than the master of economic activity.

Our previous system of financial intermediation was none too effective for these purposes, and its destruction by technological change would be an occasion for pleasure rather than fear if we could only work up some confidence that the amorphous nonsystem now in the making can be controlled. That we have not yet mastered our new world is not troublesome: we still don't know enough about where our technology is taking us. But we do need some ideas about where we hope to wind up, and why, and how we can get there. Right now, we don't have them.

5

Still, on the level of the daily lives of ordinary people, the flashy electronic world of financial services will indeed be a better place than the cold marble world of just plain banks. Future generations of getters and spenders will look back at today's *sarariman* (to use the Japanese) as today's jet travelers look at the pilgrims who walked to Canterbury. They will wonder how anybody ever got anything done if he had to stand on line to cash a paycheck, and bring in a passbook to withdraw from savings, and wait for checks to clear before drawing against them, and pay bills by writing in a checkbook and sealing envelopes and licking stamps. How did he keep his money anxieties under control without being able to call up his bank account on his television screen and see what he's got on account, which checks he has written have not yet been presented, what purchases of recent vintage have yet to be paid for, how much his stockholdings are worth at this hour and what he can borrow against them? Wasn't he offended by the need to stand, hat in hand, before some pipsqueak of a bank platform officer when he wanted a loan? And wasn't he scared to carry around all that cash in the days before everybody had a Smart Card to use at the checkout counter? With just the minor revolution of the ATM, it already seems peculiar that people used to have to rush "to get to the bank before three" because they needed money for the weekend.

A generation of bankers has tried to present banks and savings associations as cheerful, friendly places to visit, on your side in the vicissitudes of life. But of course it was never true: except for the con men borrowing money they shouldn't get and the widows who have to visit with the handsome young men in the trust department, no sane person ever enjoyed visiting a bank, or felt his time at a bank was well spent. Worse yet, the system was expensive: people earned less on their money and paid more for their loans because this cumbersome behemoth of financial intermediation stood in the way. Banks were important to the economy because they stored and judged information not easily available to others— but today information is cheap, and the quality of judgment at the banks, always suspect, has been found wanting by a newly sophisticated market.

The gold has not yet gone back to the Rhinemaidens, and the gods still walk the earth, but a practiced ear can hear distant drumbeats. This is the twilight of the banks. It would be a more cheerful spectacle if we could envision the dawn of the institutions that will replace them.

INDEX

Index

Index

Index

money-center banks, 103, 232–33, 371, 372, 373; future of, 376
money instruments, new, 103, 265–66, 283–84, 342, 344–45, 346, 381
money-market accounts, 47, 55–56, 63, 69, 296
money-market funds (MMF), 5, 27, 28, 39–40, 192, 204, 267–69, 270, 283, 289, 299, 370–71
money-market savings certificate, 269–70, 272
money markets, 222–32, 259–60, 376
money supply, 17, 237, 322–23, 381–82; control of by Fed, 19–22, 23, 161, 164, 224–25, 340–47, 381–83; daylight overdrafts and, 108–9
Money Trust, 39, 42, 44, 47, 53
Moreno, Roland C., 146–47, 148, 150
Morgan, J. P., 17, 290
Morgan Guaranty, 201, 249, 250–51, 327, 360
Morris, Frank, 321, 327, 341–42, 346–47, 357, 358
mortgage bankers, 278, 365, 377
mortgage instruments, 279–81, 282
mortgage lenders, lending, 31, 41, 282; Sears, 49, 52
mortgage portfolios, 263, 265, 272, 284
mortgages, 15, 190, 275–76, 277–79, 295, 329, 377. *See also* fixed-rate mortgages
mutual funds, 5, 10, 54, 108–9, 289, 291–92
mutual savings banks, 263–76

National Automated Clearing House Association, 119, 121, 124, 127, 128, 140
National Bank Act of 1863, 13–14, 322
National Cash Register, 291, 362–63, 364
National Credit Union Administrator, 20, 348–49
National Data, 133, 362
national debt(s), 161, 239, 240–41
National Steel, 66, 279, 338
nationally chartered banks, 13–15, 17, 71, 330–31, 335
New Deal, 6, 18, 194, 265
New York banks, 109, 112, 122, 247, 372, 376
New York City, 102, 213, 217, 379
New York Clearing House, 122, 128, 167
New York Stock Exchange, 17, 53, 152, 155, 288, 293, 303
niche banking, 218, 222–52, 285, 301
NOW accounts, 8–9, 164, 269, 296

Office of the Comptroller of the Currency (OCC), 57, 65, 198, 330, 331, 332, 335, 348–49, 350–52, 354
oil prices, 238–41, 244

overnight exposure problem, 110–13
overnight investments, 80–81, 82–83, 91–92, 103, 246, 345

Paine Webber, 49, 289
passbook accounts, 265, 266, 269–70, 353
Patrikis, Ernest, 109, 111–12
payments system, 100–01, 112, 157, 183, 187, 196, 237, 357, 366, 369–70, 378; Federal Reserve as competitor in, 158–84
Penn Central, 25, 257, 293–94
Penn Square, 204, 208, 232, 339, 373
Penn Square Bank (Oklahoma City), 24
Penn Square National Bank, 198–201
Penney, J. C. (co.), 65, 66, 142, 144, 151, 309, 314, 362
petrodollar recycling, 239–42
Philadelphia National Bank, 168, 173, 181
Phillips, Howard, 129–30, 132
Pinola, Joseph, 58–59, 336
point-of-sale (POS) terminals, 10, 137–39, 142, 145, 154, 291, 360; nationwide system of, 365
politics, 10, 381; of banking, 321–57, 376
Pratt, Richard, 21, 68, 275, 339–40, 346, 353
presentment, 88, 89, 179–82, 183
price level, 323, 382–83
prime rate, 26, 27, 213, 258–59, 370
Private Sector Adjustment Facor (PSAF), 165, 172, 173
profitability, 24, 78, 87, 188, 189, 257, 324, 370–71, 373; ATM service, 134–35; effect of inflation on, 255–56; S&Ls, 284; Sears, 51
profits (bank), 116, 188, 232–33, 242, 258, 293; reduction of, 250, 252. *See also* fees
Pronto, 305–8, 316, 317
Provident National Bank (Philadelphia), 171, 287, 292–93
Prudential-Bache, 52, 62, 63, 362
PTT (Post-Telegraph-Telephone) (France), 147–48, 153–54
public interest, 11–19
public policy, 330–39
public utilities, 123, 132–39
Publix chain, 135–36, 137

Reagan, Ronald, 37, 208, 276, 348
Reagan administration, 53, 198, 295, 342
real estate brokerage, 52, 377
Real Estate Settlement Procedures Act (RESPA), 222, 278, 347
Regan, Donald, 35–37, 205, 243, 352
regional banks, 243, 252, 300, 371–78
Regional Check Processing Centers (RCPCs), 42, 82, 174, 179–80, 181
regulators, 62, 63, 196, 203, 252, 296, 328, 350, 356–57; in Latin American